Set a study plan and a goal!

______________________________'s study plan for Grammar Gateway Intermediate

Write your goal and what you hope to accomplish.

I'll finish this book by ________ / ________ / ________.

My goal is to ____.

Choose a study plan.

- ☐ within a month : 4 lessons a day
- ☐ within two months : 2 lessons a day
- ☐ within ____________ : ____ lessons a day

Cross out lessons when you finish them. Review lessons that were difficult for you.

1 2	3 4	5 6	7 8	9 10	11 12	13 14	15 16	17 18	19 20
21 22	23 24	25 26	27 28	29 30	31 32	33 34	35 36	37 38	39 40
41 42	43 44	45 46	47 48	49 50	51 52	53 54	55 56	57 58	59 60
61 62	63 64	65 66	67 68	69 70	71 72	73 74	75 76	77 78	79 80
81 82	83 84	85 86	87 88	89 90	91 92	93 94	95 96	97 98	99 100
101 102	103 104	105 106	107 108	109 110					

HACKERS

Grammar Gateway

Intermediate

GRAMMAR GATEWAY INTERMEDIATE

PREFACE

Grammar Gateway Intermediate is...

an English grammar book for those who have already strengthened basic grammar and seek a more in-depth learning experience.

The book has 110 lessons covering essential grammar points. The lessons are based on observation and analysis of the way native English speakers write and speak. Each lesson is made up of two pages. On the left is a grammar lesson, and on the right are activities to practice the grammar points you just learned. The book provides easy explanations and a variety of illustrations to make learning more fun. Most important of all, the examples and various practice questions contain sentences that are used in real life. This allows you to not only learn grammar but to also improve your speaking and writing skills.

Grammar Gateway Intermediate will make English less difficult and get you closer to mastering English grammar than ever before. We hope that this book will put you on the path that leads to your success.

CONTENTS

C O N T E N T S

THE FEATURES OF THE BOOK

1

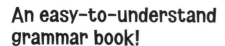

An easy-to-understand grammar book!

- Simple terms and clear explanations
- Charts and graphs that explain grammar points

2

A fun way to learn grammar!

- Lively illustrations that make learning more enjoyable and more effective
- A variety of practice questions to keep you interested

An effective tool for self-study!

- 110 lessons with the most important grammar points for intermediate learners
- One lesson comprised of two pages to help you absorb and complete each lesson easily
- A study schedule that allows you to check your progress and finish the book on your own

A grammar book to improve speaking and writing!

- Examples from real life that you can apply in everyday conversation and writing
- Practice activities where you complete sentences and conversations to help you develop your speaking and writing skills

THE STRUCTURE OF THE BOOK

Illustrations

The fun and lively illustrations help you learn each lesson more effectively.

Grammar lessons + Charts/Graphs

The grammar lessons are explained with easy terms, and the charts/graphs help you understand the lessons at a glance.

Example sentences

The example sentences help you understand how grammar points are used.

* You can listen to and follow along the example sentences and practical passage questions with the MP3 files provided at HackersIngang.com.

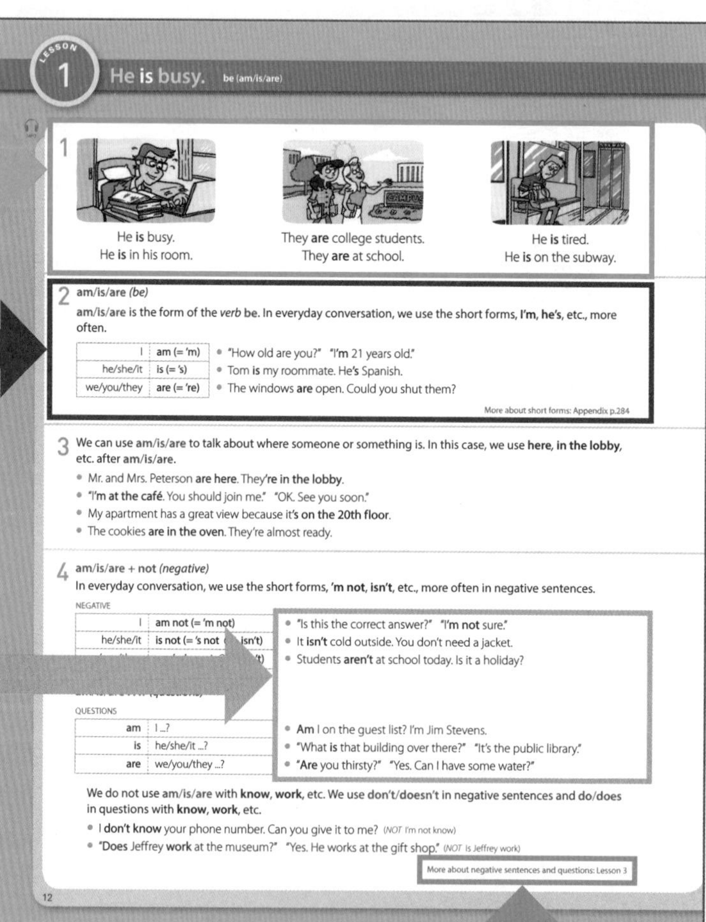

LESSON 1 **He is busy.** be (am/is/are)

1

He **is** busy.
He **is** in his room.

They **are** college students.
They **are** at school.

He **is** tired.
He **is** on the subway.

2 **am/is/are** *(be)*

am/is/are is the form of the *verb* **be**. In everyday conversation, we use the short forms, **I'm, he's**, etc., more often.

I	am (= 'm)
he/she/it	is (= 's)
we/you/they	are (= 're)

- "How old are you?" "**I'm** 21 years old."
- Tom **is** my roommate. **He's** Spanish.
- The windows **are** open. Could you shut them?

More about short forms: Appendix p.284

3 We can use **am/is/are** to talk about where someone or something is. In this case, we use **here, in the lobby**, etc. after **am/is/are**.

- Mr. and Mrs. Peterson **are here**. **They're in the lobby**.
- "**I'm at the café**. You should join me." "OK. See you soon."
- My apartment has a great view because **it's on the 20th floor**.
- The cookies **are in the oven**. They're almost ready.

4 **am/is/are + not** *(negative)*

In everyday conversation, we use the short forms, **'m not, isn't**, etc., more often in negative sentences.

NEGATIVE

I	am not (= 'm not)
he/she/it	is not (= 's not / isn't)

- "Is this the correct answer?" "**I'm not** sure."
- It **isn't** cold outside. You don't need a jacket.
- Students **aren't** at school today. Is it a holiday?

QUESTIONS

am	I ...?
is	he/she/it ...?
are	we/you/they ...?

- **Am** I on the guest list? I'm Jim Stevens.
- "What **is** that building over there?" "It's the public library."
- "**Are** you thirsty?" "Yes. Can I have some water?"

We do not use **am/is/are** with **know, work**, etc. We use **don't/doesn't** in negative sentences and **do/does** in questions with **know, work**, etc.

- I **don't know** your phone number. Can you give it to me? (NOT I'm not know)
- "**Does** Jeffrey **work** at the museum?" "Yes. He works at the gift shop." (NOT Is Jeffrey work)

More about negative sentences and questions: Lesson 3

12

Reference notes

The notes guide you to the pages that give you further understanding of what you learned.

PRACTICE

A. Look at the pictures and write sentences with the words from each box.

~~a painter~~	a reporter	a soldier	baseball players	nurses

\+

at the airport	in a cafeteria	in a helicopter	on a bench	~~on a hill~~

DANIEL / SARAH and JULIA / BETTY / MARVIN / JIM and ALAN

1. *Daniel is a painter. He's* OR *He is on a hill*.
2. ______________.
3. ______________.
4. ______________.
5. ______________.

B. Complete the sentences with **am/is/are** and the words in the box. Write negative sentences if necessary.

at the theater	Chinese	happy	in my bag	~~on 2nd Avenue~~	twins

1. "The post office *is on 2nd Avenue*." "OK. Thanks."
2. I can't find my keys. They ______________.
3. "What's wrong?" "I ______________ with my exam results."
4. Jane ______________. She is watching a movie with her friends.
5. Ella and Emma ______________, but they don't look the same.
6. David ______________. He's from Korea.

C. Put **am/is/are** and the words in *italics* in the correct order.

1. *(17 years / old / he)* My brother is in high school. *He's 17 years old* OR *He is 17 years old*.
2. *(in Seattle / Johnny and Robert)* ______________ right now.
3. *(the bathroom)* "Where ______________?" "It's around that corner."
4. *(not / I / familiar)* ______________ with this neighborhood.
5. *(a photographer / you)* "______________?" "Yes, I am."
6. *(expensive / not / this necklace)* ______________. I should buy it.

D. Complete the conversation with **am/is/are** and the words in *italics*. Write negative sentences if necessary.

LINDA: 1. Dinner *is ready*. Where are the kids? *(ready)*
2. ______ Chris ______? *(in his room)*
JAMES: Yes. I think he has a lot of work. 3. He ______________. *(busy)*
LINDA: How about Justin and Amy?
JAMES: They're not home yet.
4. Amy ______________ with Kate, and Justin ______________. *(at school, back from the library)*
LINDA: Well, it's 7 o'clock. 5. ______ you ______? *(hungry)*
JAMES: Not really. 6. I ______________ for now. *(OK)*
LINDA: Then let's wait for the kids.

LINDA JAMES

Answers p.304 Review Test 1 p.234

Present Simple and Present Progressive

LESSON 1

Practice questions

Various questions help you practice what you learned.

Practical passage questions

The forms of these practical passage questions include conversations, e-mails, essays, advertisements, and other forms of speech and writing we use in daily life.

Review Test notes

The notes guide you to the Review Test that allows you to review the lessons comprehensively.

LESSON 1

He **is** busy. be (am/is/are)

1

He **is** busy.
He **is** in his room.

They **are** college students.
They **are** at school.

He **is** tired.
He **is** on the subway.

2 am/is/are *(be)*

am/is/are is the form of the *verb* **be**. In everyday conversation, we use the short forms, **I'm**, **he's**, etc., more often.

I	am (= 'm)
he/she/it	is (= 's)
we/you/they	are (= 're)

- "How old are you?" "I**'m** 21 years old."
- Tom **is** my roommate. He**'s** Spanish.
- The windows **are** open. Could you shut them?

More about short forms: Appendix p.284

3

We can use **am/is/are** to talk about where someone or something is. In this case, we use **here**, **in the lobby**, etc. after **am/is/are**.

- Mr. and Mrs. Peterson **are here**. They**'re in the lobby**.
- "I**'m at the café**. You should join me." "OK. See you soon."
- My apartment has a great view because it**'s on the 20th floor**.
- The cookies **are in the oven**. They're almost ready.

4 am/is/are + not *(negative)*

In everyday conversation, we use the short forms, **'m not**, **isn't**, etc., more often in negative sentences.

NEGATIVE

I	am not (= 'm not)
he/she/it	is not (= 's not *OR* isn't)
we/you/they	are not (= 're not *OR* aren't)

- "Is this the correct answer?" "I**'m not** sure."
- It **isn't** cold outside. You don't need a jacket.
- Students **aren't** at school today. Is it a holiday?

am/is/are . . .? *(questions)*

QUESTIONS

am	I ...?
is	he/she/it ...?
are	we/you/they ...?

- **Am** I on the guest list? I'm Jim Stevens.
- "What **is** that building over there?" "It's the public library."
- "**Are** you thirsty?" "Yes. Can I have some water?"

We do not use **am/is/are** with **know**, **work**, etc. We use **don't/doesn't** in negative sentences and **do/does** in questions with **know**, **work**, etc.

- I **don't know** your phone number. Can you give it to me? (*NOT* I'm not know)
- "**Does** Jeffrey **work** at the museum?" "Yes. He works at the gift shop." (*NOT* Is Jeffrey work)

More about negative sentences and questions: Lesson 3

PRACTICE

A. Look at the pictures and write sentences with the words from each box.

~~a painter~~	a reporter	a soldier
baseball players	nurses	

\+

at the airport	in a cafeteria	in a helicopter
on a bench	~~on a hill~~	

1. *Daniel is a painter. He's* OR *He is on a hill* ______.
2. ______.
3. ______.
4. ______.
5. ______.

B. Complete the sentences with **am/is/are** and the words in the box. Write negative sentences if necessary.

at the theater	Chinese	happy	in my bag	~~on 2nd Avenue~~	twins

1. "The post office *is on 2nd Avenue* ______." "OK. Thanks."
2. I can't find my keys. They ______.
3. "What's wrong?" "I ______ with my exam results."
4. Jane ______. She is watching a movie with her friends.
5. Ella and Emma ______, but they don't look the same.
6. David ______. He's from Korea.

C. Put **am/is/are** and the words in *italics* in the correct order.

1. *(17 years / old / he)* My brother is in high school. *He's 17 years old* OR *He is 17 years old* ______.
2. *(in Seattle / Johnny and Robert)* ______ right now.
3. *(the bathroom)* "Where ______?" "It's around that corner."
4. *(not / I / familiar)* ______ with this neighborhood.
5. *(a photographer / you)* "______?" "Yes, I am."
6. *(expensive / not / this necklace)* ______. I should buy it.

D. Complete the conversation with **am/is/are** and the words in *italics*. Write negative sentences if necessary.

MP3

LINDA

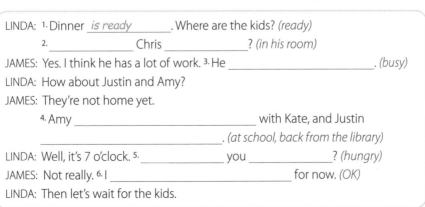

LINDA: 1. Dinner *is ready* ______. Where are the kids? *(ready)*
2. ______ Chris ______? *(in his room)*
JAMES: Yes. I think he has a lot of work. 3. He ______. *(busy)*
LINDA: How about Justin and Amy?
JAMES: They're not home yet.
4. Amy ______ with Kate, and Justin ______. *(at school, back from the library)*
LINDA: Well, it's 7 o'clock. 5. ______ you ______? *(hungry)*
JAMES: Not really. 6. I ______ for now. *(OK)*
LINDA: Then let's wait for the kids.

JAMES

Answers p.304 / Review Test 1 p.234

LESSON 2

She is selling books. *Present progressive*

1

She **is selling** books.

Now

She is at a garage sale. She is sitting at a table and talking to a customer now.
"is selling" is in progress now and it is the *present progressive.*

2 **am/is/are + -ing** *(present progressive)*

We use the *present progressive* to talk about actions in progress now.

I	am		washing
he/she/it	is	(not)	playing
we/you/they	are		watching

am	I	washing ...?
is	he/she/it	playing ...?
are	we/you/they	watching ...?

More about spelling rules: Appendix p.278

I'**m washing** the dishes.

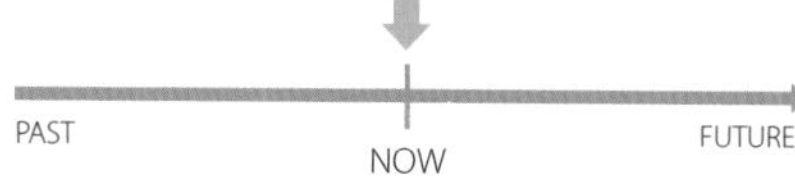

- Sophia, can you answer the phone? I'**m washing** the dishes.
- Mike **isn't playing** video games anymore. He'**s watching** TV.
- "**Are** you **using** that pen? May I borrow it?" "Sure. Here you go."
- It'**s not snowing** a lot outside. Just a little.

3 We can also use the *present progressive* to talk about actions in progress around now but not exactly at the moment of speaking.

We'**re planning** a Christmas party.

- "We'**re planning** a Christmas party. Do you want to come?" "Sure."
  (= The planning of a party is not in progress at the moment, but it's in progress around now.)
- I'm very busy this week. I'**m writing** a report for my English class.
  (= The writing of a report is not in progress at the moment, but it's in progress around now.)
- Ann **isn't living** in the dorm this semester. She'**s staying** at her aunt's house.
- What **are** you **doing** these days? **Are** you **practicing** for the soccer match?

4 We often use the *present progressive* with the following words:

(right) now	at the moment
these days	this week/month/year

- I can't go out with you. I'**m studying right now**.
- Our website **isn't working at the moment**. We need to find the problem.
- "Michelle! You look great!" "Thanks. I'**m exercising** more **these days**."
- "**Are** the stores **having** big sales **this week**?" "Yes. Let's go shopping tomorrow!"

P R A C T I C E

A. Look at the pictures and complete the sentences with the words in the box.

hold a cup	read a book	ride bikes	~~run~~

NICK and HARRY
FRANK
OLIVIA

1. Dogs *are running* ______________ by the lake.
2. Frank ______________.
3. Olivia ______________.
4. Nick and Harry ______________.

clean the desk	fix a photocopier	move a plant	stand at the door

ANNA and JOSEPH
MARY
KEVIN
BRIAN and DONALD

5. Brian and Donald ______________.
6. Mary ______________.
7. Kevin ______________.
8. Anna and Joseph ______________.

B. The actor, Johnny, is giving an interview on a talk show. Complete the conversation with the words in *italics*. Write negative sentences if necessary.

Host: 1. *Are you working* these days? *(you, work)*
JOHNNY: 2. No, ______________ at the moment. *(I, act)*
3. ______________ a break. *(I, take)*
Host: I see. 4. And what ______________ with your time? *(you, do)*
JOHNNY: 5. Well, ______________ my son about acting. *(I, teach)*
He wants to become an actor.
Host: Oh, that sounds nice. 6. ______________ acting in college? *(he, study)*
JOHNNY: 7. Yes, but ______________ classes this year. *(he, attend)*
He's taking a year off.
Host: Well, your son is lucky! 8. ______________ from the best! *(he, learn)*

C. Complete the sentences with the given words. Write negative sentences if necessary.

bake	change	date	hire	listen	sleep	spend	~~wear~~

1. *(he)* "Which person is John?" "*He's wearing* OR *He is wearing* ______________ a blue sweater."
2. *(I)* Can you be quiet, please? ______________ to the radio.
3. *(they)* "Bella and David are always together. ______________?" "I think so."
4. *(She)* "Nicole looks so tired."
"______________ much these days because she's busy at work."
5. *(we)* "Are there any jobs at your company?" "No, ______________ right now."
6. *(Mom)* "______________ cupcakes?" "No. Muffins."
7. *(I)* ______________ a lot of money this month. I'm saving for a new car.
8. *(the leaves)* ______________ colors. The weather will be cold soon.

Answers **p.304** / Review Test 1 **p.234**

He **works** at a bank. *Present simple* (1)

MP3

1

He **works** at a bank.

It's nice to meet you.
FIRST BANK

He is a banker. He goes to the bank and meets new clients every day. **"works"** happens regularly for him and it is the *present simple*.

2 We use the *present simple* to talk about things that happen regularly. We also use the *present simple* to talk about things that are true for a long time or scientific facts.

I/we/you/they	live	clean	cover	brush
he/she/it	lives	cleans	covers	brushes

I **live** in Los Angeles.

PAST NOW FUTURE

- I **live** in Los Angeles.
- We **clean** our house on Saturdays.
- Water **covers** 72 percent of the Earth.
- Susan **brushes** her teeth after every meal.

We add -(e)s to the *verbs* after he/she/it. But we use has after he/she/it and have after I/we/you/they.

- Claire **enjoys** cooking. She also **has** many cookbooks. (*NOT* Claire enjoy, *NOT* She also have)
- I have a history lecture on Thursdays. It **finishes** at 5 o'clock. (*NOT* It finish)

More about spelling rules: Appendix p.278

3 We use the *present simple* in negative sentences and questions in the following ways:

NEGATIVE

I/we/you/they	don't	go
he/she/it	doesn't	take

QUESTIONS

do	I/we/you/they	go ...?
does	he/she/it	take ...?

- I **don't go** out much on weekdays.
- "**Does** that store **take** credit cards?" "No, it **doesn't accept** them."
- "What **do** you **wear** to work?" "Suits."

We do not add -(e)s to the *verbs* after doesn't.

- Mr. Warren lived in Japan, but he **doesn't speak** Japanese. (*NOT* he doesn't speaks)
- "That movie looks good. **Does** it **seem** OK to you?" "Sure." (*NOT* Does it seems)

4 We often use the *present simple* with **always**, **sometimes**, **never**, etc. We use these words before **walk**, **drive**, etc. to say how often the action happens.

- "Do you **always walk** to school?" "No, I **sometimes drive**."
- My friends **never forget** my birthday. They send me gifts every year.
- Betty **often goes** to parties on weekends.
- Mark doesn't **usually read** newspapers in the morning.

More about adverbs of frequency: Lesson 71

P R A C T I C E

A. Complete the sentences with the verbs in the box. Use the *present simple*.

cost	eat	fix	~~play~~	see	teach	travel	wake

1. On Sundays, Nick _plays_ basketball with Ronald.
2. My brother lives in San Diego, so we only ________ each other twice a year.
3. "Do you always get up early?" "Yes. I ________ up at 6 every day."
4. John is often out of town. He ________ almost every month.
5. "How much are tickets to the amusement park?" "They ________ $40."
6. My sister ________ English at my school. All of the students like her.
7. My computer breaks down sometimes, and Chloe ________ it. She's very helpful.
8. I ________ a lot of vegetables because they are good for my health.

B. Connect the two parts and complete the sentences.

fall in the rainforest •	• 1. The sun _sets in the west_.
fly south in the winter •	• 2. Pine trees ________.
not have flowers •	• 3. Oil ________.
not mix with water •	• 4. A lot of rain ________.
~~set in the west~~ •	• 5. Many birds ________.

C. Complete the conversations with the words in *italics*.

1. A: *(you, take)* _Do you take_ a lot of pictures?
   B: *(I, bring)* Yes. ________ my camera with me everywhere.
2. A: *(you and your friends, go)* How often ________ to the mall?
   B: A few times each month.
3. A: *(this bus, stop)* ________ at Rose Park?
   B: *(it, turn)* No. ________ before Rose Park.
4. A: *(Jennifer, enjoy)* ________ swimming?
   B: No. She's scared of water.
5. A: *(you, spell)* How ________ your last name?
   B: C-H-O.
6. A: *(Peter, send)* ________ you e-mails often?
   B: *(he, call)* No, but ________ me every week.

D. Complete the conversation with the words in *italics*. Write negative sentences if necessary.

JUSTIN: Mom, I have a few questions about Dad's job.
1. Dad works at a bank, but what _does_ he actually _do_? *(do)*

LINDA: 2. He ________ people with their money. *(usually, help)*
3. And he ________ questions about finance. *(often, answer)*

JUSTIN: 4. ________ he ________ his job? *(like)*

LINDA: I don't know.
5. He ________ about it much, but I think he enjoys it. *(talk)*
6. He says he ________ interesting people. *(always, meet)*

Answers **p.304** / Review Test 1 **p.234**

LESSON 4 He knows her. *Present simple (2) Non-progressive verbs*

1 He is waving at her.

He **knows** her.

We use the *present progressive* to talk about actions in progress now. But we use the *present simple* rather than the *present progressive* with the following *verbs* that describe states or thoughts:

know	remember	understand	believe	agree
want	need	love	like	hate
own	possess	belong	contain	

- I **remember** you! You're Helen, right? (*NOT* I'm remembering)
- Max **doesn't want** a watch for Christmas. He **wants** a new computer. (*NOT* Max isn't wanting, *NOT* He's wanting)
- "**Do** Mr. and Mrs. Jackson **own** a house in Hawaii?" "Yes. It's very close to the sea."
- "I **don't understand** this menu. Can you read Italian?" "A little."

2 When **have** means "to own," we use the *present simple*.

- Diane **has** a cute dog. His name is Rocky. (*NOT* Diane is having)
- I can't think of anything good. **Do** you **have** any idea? (*NOT* Are you having)

But we can use both the *present progressive* and *present simple* when **have/has** is used in the following expressions:

have salad/a hamburger	have breakfast/lunch/dinner
have a meeting/party	have a good time/nice day

- Julie often **has salad** for lunch, but she**'s having a hamburger** today.
- "**Is** Mr. Walker **having a meeting**?" "Yes. He **has a meeting** every Monday at 2 o'clock."
- I usually **have a good time** at parties. At this one, I**'m not having a good time**.

3 We usually use the *present simple* with the following *verbs* that describe senses:

look	sound	taste	smell	feel

- Tim isn't wearing his glasses today. He **looks** different.
- "Do you know this song?" "No. It **doesn't sound** familiar."
- These strawberries **taste** so fresh. Let's buy some.

But we can use the *present progressive* with **taste** and **smell** when they describe actions.

- Charles **is tasting** the pasta.
- The children **are smelling** the flowers.

We can also use the *present progressive* with **look** and **feel**. In this case, the meaning is the same as in the *present simple*.

- You**'re looking** lovely tonight. *OR* You **look** lovely tonight.
- "I**'m feeling** sick." *OR* "I **feel** sick." "Maybe you should go home early, then."

PRACTICE

A. Complete the sentences with the verbs in the box using the *present simple* or *present progressive*. Write negative sentences if necessary.

agree	belong	go	have	have	lie	~~need~~	plant

1. Can I talk to you? I *need* ____________ your advice.
2. I respect your opinion. However, I ____________ with you.
3. Greg is in the garden with his dad. He ____________ a tree with him.
4. "________ Sarah ________ a car?" "No. She uses public transportation."
5. "Where ________ you ________ now?" "To the dentist. I have an appointment."
6. This pen ____________ to me. Is it yours?
7. Jessica ____________ on the beach right now. She's swimming.
8. My parents ____________ dinner at a nice restaurant. Today is their wedding anniversary.

B. Complete the sentences with the verbs in *italics* using the *present simple* or *present progressive*. Write negative sentences if necessary.

1. *(smell)* "What are you doing?" "I *'m smelling* ____________ this perfume. It has lovely scent."
2. *(sound)* My computer is making a strange noise. It ____________ terrible.
3. *(feel)* "________ you ________ nervous?" "Yes. I'm really worried about my speech."
4. *(taste)* This cherry pie looks tasty, but it ____________ very good.
5. *(smell)* These socks seem dirty, but they ____________ bad.
6. *(taste)* "Is the soup ready?" "Almost. The chef ____________ it right now."

C. Find and change any mistakes in each sentence. Put ✓ if the sentence is correct.

1. Each box is containing 20 pieces of chocolate. *is containing → contains*
2. The neighbors have a party. Can you hear the music? ____________
3. The hotel room doesn't look clean. Let's ask for a different room. ____________
4. Ms. Brown tastes some new wines right now. ____________
5. "What's your favorite kind of movie?" "Well, I really like action films." ____________
6. I'm not believing Jerry. He often tells lies. ____________
7. Derek is a great golf player. He is possessing a lot of talent. ____________
8. "Are you having a nice day?" "Yes. Thank you!" ____________

D. Complete the conversation with the verbs in *italics*. Use the *present simple* or *present progressive*.

MP3

CHRIS

CHRIS: Hi, Rachel. 1. *Do* ________ you *remember* ________ me? *(remember)*
We went to high school together.

RACHEL: Of course! Don't tell me . . . 2. I ____________ your name! *(know)*
You're Chris, right?

CHRIS: Yes. It's nice to see you again. 3. You ____________ great! *(look)*

RACHEL: Thanks! You too!
4. What ________ you ________ these days? *(do)*

CHRIS: 5. I ____________ for a job. *(search)*

RACHEL: I see. How about getting some coffee together? Do you have time?

CHRIS: 6. Sure, that ____________ great! *(sound)*

RACHEL

Answers p.304 / Review Test 1 p.234

LESSON 5

I'm doing vs. I do *Present progressive vs. Present simple*

MP3

1 She **is watching** TV now.

She **studies** art.

She **is watching** TV now.

She studies art in school every day. But now she is watching TV at home.
"studies" is an action that happens regularly and **"is watching"** is an action in progress now.

2 ***Present progressive***

We use the *present progressive* to talk about actions in progress now.

- Please be quiet. The babies **are sleeping**.
- Can I call you later? I**'m driving** right now.
- The wind **is blowing** hard tonight.
- "Is Professor Jones in her office?"
  "No. She**'s teaching** a class downstairs."

Present simple

We use the *present simple* to talk about things that happen regularly or are true for a long time.

- Babies **sleep** about 13 hours a day.
- I **drive** an hour to my office every morning.
- The wind **blows** hard during a thunderstorm.
- Professor Jones **teaches** politics at my university.
  Her lectures are a little boring.

3 We use the *present progressive* to talk about temporary situations, and we use the *present simple* to talk about permanent situations.

- I**'m living** in Paris at the moment. I really enjoy it. (Living in Paris is a temporary situation.)
  I **live** in France. I'm French. (Living in France is a permanent situation.)
- Kathy **is working** as a volunteer at a hospital this summer.
  "What does Kathy do?" "She **works** in a hospital. She's a doctor."

4 We use the *present progressive* of **be** to talk about a person's temporary actions. But we use the *present simple* of **be** to talk about a person's permanent characteristics, such as personality.

- "Why **are** you **being** so kind today?" "What do you mean? I'm always nice."
  (You're being kind only today. You're usually not kind.)
  Dorothy always helps other people. She**'s** very kind.
  (She's always kind. It's her personality.)
- I usually clean my room every day, but I**'m being** lazy right now.
  My brother never cleans his room. He**'s** so lazy.

PRACTICE

A. Complete the sentences with the verbs in the box. Use the *present progressive* or *present simple*.

bring	freeze	look	run	shop	sing	smoke	~~wait~~

1. "Can I help you with anything?" "I *'m waiting* to see Dr. Bowman."
2. ______ you usually ______ your lunch to work?
3. "______ Jenny ______ at the mall?" "Yes. She wants new curtains."
4. Kent ______ in a marathon every year.
5. Listen! Rosa and Cindy ______. They sound beautiful together.
6. "______ Mr. Johnson ______ cigarettes?" "No. Not anymore."
7. Water ______ at zero degrees Celsius.
8. I'm really hungry. ______ you still ______ at the menu?

B. Complete the conversations with the verbs in *italics*. Use the *present progressive* or *present simple*.

1. John is still not home. — *(come)* Really? He usually *comes* early.
2. When is your concert? — *(practice)* Next week. I ______ hard for it.
3. Is Ted your best friend? — *(see)* Yes. We ______ each other every day.
4. How is your business? — *(grow)* Good. It ______ a lot.
5. Where is your hotel room? — *(stay)* We ______ at the Plaza Hotel.
6. Is Carol a guitarist? — *(play)* No. She ______ the drums.

C. Complete the sentences with the correct form of **be**. Use the *present progressive* or *present simple*.

1. Melissa doesn't like meeting new people because she *'s* shy.
2. Our neighbors ______ very polite. They always say hello to us.
3. Patricia ______ silly at the moment. She's not usually so childish.
4. "What is Julie's boyfriend like?" "He ______ very intelligent."
5. Don't eat all the cake! You ______ really selfish right now.
6. "Walk slowly. The floor is very slippery." "I know. I ______ careful."

D. Amy and Kate are on the phone. Complete the conversation with the verbs in the box. Use the *present progressive* or *present simple*.

be	~~do~~	meet	take	want	watch

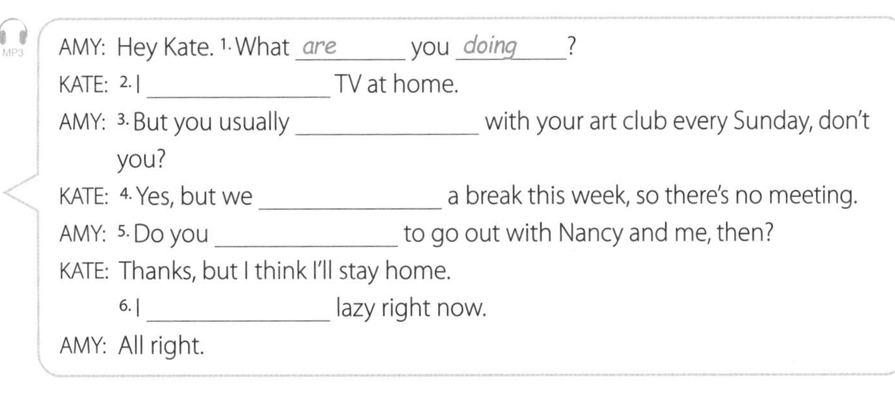

MP3

AMY: Hey Kate. 1. What *are* you *doing*?

KATE: 2. I ______ TV at home.

AMY: 3. But you usually ______ with your art club every Sunday, don't you?

KATE: 4. Yes, but we ______ a break this week, so there's no meeting.

AMY: 5. Do you ______ to go out with Nancy and me, then?

KATE: Thanks, but I think I'll stay home.
6. I ______ lazy right now.

AMY: All right.

Answers p.304 / Review Test 1 p.234

LESSON 6

Her parents first **met** 30 years ago. *Past simple*

1

Her parents first **met** 30 years ago.

They **had** a wedding in Paris in 1989.

"met" and **"had"** happened in the past and they are the *past simple*.

2 boil/receive/etc. + -(e)d *(past simple)*

We use the *past simple* to talk about things that happened and finished in the past. We usually add -(e)d to the *verb*, but there are some *irregular verbs*.

	boil	receive	end	begin	buy	eat
Past simple	boiled	received	ended	began	bought	ate

More about spelling rules: Appendix p.278
More about irregular verbs: Appendix p.281

- I **boiled** water to make tea.
- "Christina **received** a letter from Jeff." "Really? When?"
- World War I **began** in 1914 and **ended** in 1918.
- "Is that a new hat?" "Yes. I **bought** it a week ago."
- We **ate** at that Chinese restaurant last time. Let's try somewhere different.

3 did not + see/play/etc. *(negative)*

I/we/you/they he/she/it	did not (= didn't)	see play

- "I **didn't see** you at the meeting yesterday." "I had a lunch appointment."
- We **didn't play** golf last weekend because of the rain.
- Ten years ago, our town **didn't have** any tall buildings.

did + *subject* + **get/go**/etc. . . .? *(questions)*

did	I/we/you/they he/she/it	get ...? go ...?

- "**Did** you **get** my message?" "Yes, I did."
- "When **did** the children **go** to sleep?" "Around 11 o'clock."
- "**Did** Matt **tell** you about his accident?" "Yes. He already told me about it."

4 was/were (past of am/is/are)

I/he/she/it	was	(not)
we/you/they	were	

was	I/he/she/it	...?
were	we/you/they	

- The sky **was** beautiful this morning. Did you see it?
- We **were** at the library with Tim. We had a group project.
- "**Was** the musical good?" "No, it **wasn't**."
- Where **were** you earlier? You **weren't** in your office.

PRACTICE

A. Look at the pictures about the things Brad did last Sunday. Complete the sentences with the words in the box.

exercise at a gym	get a haircut	go to a restaurant	~~have a sandwich~~	watch a movie

1 BRAD → 2 → 3 → 4 → 5

1. In the morning, Brad *had a sandwich* ________ for breakfast.
2. After that, he ________________.
3. In the afternoon, he ________________.
4. In the evening, he ________________.
5. Later that night, he ________________.

B. Complete the sentences with the verbs in the box using the *past simple*. Write negative sentences if necessary.

~~be~~	be	be	hear	join	swim	write

1. "Did you talk to your parents?" "No. I called them, but they *weren't* OR *were not* home."
2. I ________________ the book club two months ago. It's a lot of fun.
3. I don't think the doorbell rang. I ________________ anything.
4. Sandra brought two friends to the party on Saturday. Their names ________________ Bill and Helen.
5. Josh ________________ at the beach last weekend. He said the water was too cold.
6. William Shakespeare ________________ *Romeo and Juliet* in the late 16th century.
7. "I'm sorry about the delay." "It's OK. It ________________ your fault."

C. Complete the conversations with the words in *italics*.

1. A: *(we, have)* *We had* ________ a family picnic yesterday.
   B: *(it, be)* ________________ fun?
2. A: *(you, be)* ________________ on time for your meeting?
   B: *(I, arrive)* No. ________________ after it started.
3. A: *(Roy, play)* ________________ tennis in college?
   B: *(he, be)* Yes. In fact, ________________ the university champion in 2012.
4. A: *(I, work)* ________________ late last night.
   B: *(you, leave)* Really? What time ________________ the office?

D. Complete the sentences with the verbs in *italics* using the *past simple* or *present simple*. Write negative sentences if necessary.

Love at the Eiffel Tower

By Amy Wilson

1. *(grow up)* My father was born in the US, but he *grew up* ________ in France.
2. *(be)* He ________________ just a baby when his parents moved to Paris.
3. *(meet, fall)* Thirty years ago, he ________________ my mother near the Eiffel Tower and ________________ in love at first sight.
4. *(give up)* My mother didn't like him much at the time, but my father ________________.
5. *(get)* Eventually, they became a couple, and they ________________ married a year later.
6. *(live, visit)* Now they ________________ in the US, but they ________________ Paris every year.

Answers **p.305** / Review Test 2 **p.236**

LESSON 7

He was reading a book. *Past progressive*

MP3

1 He **was reading** a book at 2 p.m. yesterday.

At 2 p.m. yesterday

Yesterday, Chris started reading a book at 1 p.m. and finished it at 3 p.m. **"was reading"** was in progress at 2 p.m. yesterday and it is the *past progressive*.

2 **was/were + -ing** *(past progressive)*

We use the *past progressive* to talk about actions in progress at a certain time in the past.

I/he/she/it	was	(not)	talking
we/you/they	were		doing

was	I/he/she/it	talking ...?
were	we/you/they	doing ...?

I **was talking** on the phone.

- At 6 o'clock last night, I **was talking** on the phone with my boyfriend.
- My roommate **wasn't doing** anything when I got home. He **was** just **lying** on the sofa.
- "Who **were** you **waiting** for this morning?" "My friend Jack."
- Paula **was printing** something when the power went out.

3 ***Past simple***

We use the *past simple* to talk about things that happened and finished in the past.

- "What did you do last summer?"
  "I **traveled** around Europe."
  (= The trip around Europe happened and finished last summer.)
- Jerry and Cindy **had** pizza for lunch.
  (= Eating pizza happened and finished at lunch.)
- Tim **rode** his bike to the park. He needed some fresh air.
- We **climbed** the mountain yesterday. Luckily, it didn't rain.

Past progressive

We use the *past progressive* to talk about actions in progress at a certain time in the past.

- "Where were you on New Year's Day?"
  "I **was traveling** in Europe."
  (= The trip to Europe was in progress on New Year's Day.)
- I saw Jerry and Cindy at the restaurant at noon. They **were having** pizza.
  (= Eating pizza was in progress at noon.)
- Tim **was riding** his bike in the park at 8:30 yesterday.
- We **were climbing** the mountain when the rain started.

Note that we do not use the *past progressive* with **know**, **believe**, etc. that describe states or thoughts. We usually use the *past simple* with these *verbs*.

- I **knew** everyone at the party, so I felt comfortable. (*NOT* I was knowing)
- "**Did** you **believe** in ghosts when you were young?" "No, I didn't." (*NOT* Were you believing)

More about non-progressive verbs: Lesson 4

P R A C T I C E

A. Look at the pictures and complete the sentences with the verbs in *italics*. Write negative sentences if necessary.

At 3:00 p.m. yesterday,

1. *(work)* Jason *wasn't working* OR *was not working* on the computer.
2. *(attend)* He __________________ a meeting.
3. *(hold)* He __________________ a pen.
4. *(give)* He __________________ a presentation.

When Lucy arrived at the restaurant,

5. *(sit)* Mary and Eve __________________ at a table.
6. *(talk)* Mary __________________ to a waiter.
7. *(look)* Eve __________________ at a menu.
8. *(eat)* They __________________ anything.

B. Complete the sentences with the verbs in the box using the *past progressive*. Write negative sentences if necessary.

argue	carry	~~change~~	hide	pay	wear

1. Rick *was changing* his clothes when his mom walked in his room. He was embarrassed.
2. The police officer gave us tickets because we __________________ seatbelts.
3. Sorry , I __________________ attention. What did you say?
4. I saw you in the lobby earlier. Why __________________ you __________________ a huge suitcase?
5. Perry __________________ with the taxi driver. They both looked very upset.
6. Where did you find the cat? __________________ it __________________ under the sofa again?

C. Complete the conversations with the words in *italics*. Use the *past progressive* or *past simple*.

1. A: *(Mr. Kent, leave)* *Did Mr. Kent leave* the office?
   B: *(he, meet)* I don't think so. __________________ with a client a minute ago.
2. A: *(you, drive)* __________________ when I called?
   B: *(I, go)* Yes. __________________ to the mall.
3. A: *(you, not exercise)* __________________ at the gym when I got there at 8.
   B: *(I, walk)* Oh, __________________ my dog.
4. A: *(you, know)* __________________ Christy in college?
   B: *(we, be)* Yes. __________________ classmates.
5. A: *(you, turn)* Why __________________ off the TV?
   B: *(you, watch)* Oh, sorry. __________________ it?
6. A: *(you, show)* __________________ everyone the picture?
   B: *(they, like)* I did. __________________ it.

D. Complete the conversation with the verbs in *italics* using the *past progressive* or *past simple*. Write negative sentences if necessary.

PAUL

MP3

PAUL: 1. What *were* you *doing* yesterday at 2 p.m.? *(do)*
CHRIS: 2. I __________________ a book in my room. Why? *(read)*
PAUL: 3. I __________________ over to meet Amy and I __________________ to say hi to you. *(come, want)* I knocked on your door but you didn't answer.
CHRIS: I'm sorry. 4. I __________________ you. *(hear)* 5. I __________________ to music. *(listen)*
PAUL: Oh. 6. I thought maybe you __________________. *(sleep)*

CHRIS

Answers p.305 / Review Test 2 p.236

LESSON 8

I did, I was doing *Past simple* and *Past progressive*

MP3

1 We can use the *past simple* and *past progressive* together.

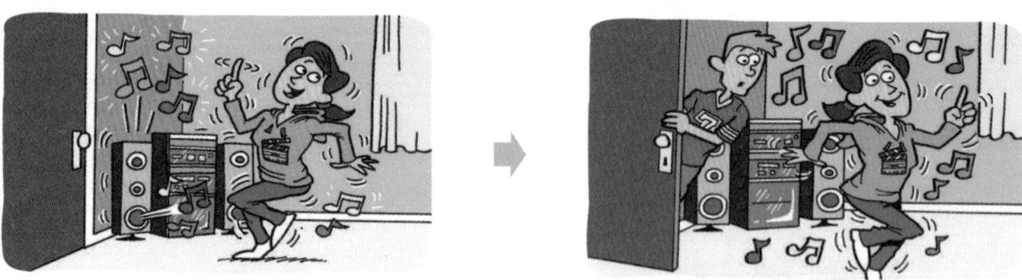

While she **was dancing**, he **entered** her room.
(= He entered her room during the time she was dancing.)

"was dancing" is the action that was already in progress for a while. **"entered"** is the action that happened during that time.

- When we **met** Jenny in China, we **were traveling**.
  (= Traveling was already in progress and meeting Jenny happened during that time.)
- I **was driving**, so I **didn't answer** my phone.
  (= Driving was already in progress and not answering my phone happened during that time.)
- Julie **was** still **working** in the office when somebody **turned** off the lights.
- Max **spilled** some of his coffee. He **was walking** too fast with it.

When we use the *past simple* and *past progressive* together, we usually use **while** with the *past progressive*.

- **While** we **were going** home, the fireworks **began**.
- "How did you hurt your arm?" "I **fell while** I **was getting** off the bus."
- **While** Ms. Johnson **was cleaning** her house, she **found** some old photos.

2 We only use the *past simple* when one action happened after another action.

When he **entered** her room, she **turned** off the music.
(= He entered her room and then she turned off the music.)

- Last night we **wrapped** all the presents and **put** them under the Christmas tree.
  (= We wrapped the presents and then put them under the Christmas tree.)
- When Andy and Robert **finished** dinner, they **went** to get ice cream.
  (= Andy and Robert finished dinner and then went to get ice cream.)
- After I **moved** to Chicago, I **got** a job as a news reporter.
- The crowd **cheered** when the singer **stepped** onto the stage.

P R A C T I C E

A. Look at the pictures and complete the sentences with the verbs in *italics*. Use the *past simple* or *past progressive*.

1. *(call, shave)* Somebody called ______ while he was shaving ______.
2. *(jump, swim)* He ______ in the water while she ______.
3. *(pay, leave)* She ______ the bill and ______ the restaurant.
4. *(lose, jog)* He ______ his keys while he ______.
5. *(land, get)* When the plane ______, the passengers ______ off.
6. *(snow, go)* It ______ when they ______ outside.

B. Complete the sentences with the verbs in *italics*. Use the *past simple* or *past progressive*.

1. *(invite)* Last Friday, my wife Carla and I invited ______ our friends to dinner.
2. *(get, cook)* When I ______ home from work, Carla ______ in the kitchen. I decided to help her.
3. *(prepare, put)* While she ______ the salad, I ______ the chicken in the oven. Then, I fell asleep on the sofa.
4. *(sleep, go)* While I ______, Carla ______ out to buy drinks. When she returned, she was shocked.
5. *(ring)* The smoke alarm ______!
6. *(have)* The chicken was badly burned, so we ______ dinner at a restaurant nearby.

C. Put the words in *italics* in the correct order. Use the *past simple* or *past progressive*.

1. *(Samantha / while / hike)* While Samantha was hiking ______ in the woods, she saw a deer.
2. *(give / I / my presentation / while)* I made some errors ______.
3. *(the rain / when / stop)* The rainbow appeared ______.
4. *(I / park / while)* ______, I hit my neighbor's car.
5. *(watch / we / while / TV)* The deliveryman arrived ______.
6. *(wake up / Maria / when)* ______, she made some coffee and toast.
7. *(when / shut down / his computer)*
   Steve was writing a report ______.
8. *(the glass / when / drop / the child)* ______, it broke.

Answers p.305 / Review Test 2 p.236

LESSON 9

She **used to** take the bus every day. used to

1 She drives a car now.

She **used to take** the bus every day.

Past

Now

She bought a car a month ago. She took the bus regularly in the past but not now. **"used to take"** is the thing that happened regularly in the past but not now.

2 We use **used to** + **study**/**call**/etc. to talk about things that happened regularly in the past but not now.

I/we/you/they he/she/it	used to	study call

- I **used to study** German, but I don't study it anymore. (= I studied German, but now I don't.)
- Nora **used to call** me once a week. She doesn't call me often anymore. (= Nora called me once a week, but now she doesn't.)

didn't use to . . . *OR* **never used to . . .** *(negative)*

- I **didn't use to listen** to classical music. I started liking it only a few months ago.
- My mother **never used to work** on weekends. Now she often works on Saturdays.

did + *subject* + **use to . . .?** *(questions)*

- "**Did** you **use to eat** at Jimmy's Burgers in college?" "Yes! I miss that place."

3 We also use **used to** to talk about situations that existed in the past but not now.

- This bookstore just moved here. It **used to be** on Carson Street. (= This bookstore was on Carson Street, but now it isn't.)
- I bought this laptop recently. I **didn't use to have** one. (= I didn't have a laptop, but now I do.)
- Wild lions **used to live** in Europe too. They are only in Africa and Asia nowadays.
- Eddie and I **didn't use to like** each other. Lately, we've become good friends.

4 There are differences in meaning between **used to**, the *past simple*, and the *present simple*.

used to
- I **used to work** out at the gym every weekend. I'm too busy these days. (= I worked out at the gym every weekend, but I don't work out these days.)

Past simple
- I **worked** out at the gym on weekends last year. (= I worked out at the gym on weekends last year, but I might or might not work out this year.)

Present simple
- I **work** out at the gym every weekend. (= I work out at the gym every weekend now.)

5 Note that we use **used to . . .** and **be used to + -ing** in different ways. **be used to + -ing** means that someone is familiar with doing something.

- I **used to wake** up early, but these days I usually sleep until noon. (= I woke up early in the past, but now I don't.)
  I have class at 7 o'clock every morning, so I'**m used to waking** up early. (= I'm familiar with waking up early.)
- I **used to share** clothes with my sister when we were the same size.
  My sister and I **are used to sharing** clothes. We often wear each other's shirts and pants.

PRACTICE

A. Look at the pictures and complete the sentences with **used to**. Write negative sentences if necessary.

1-2: I live in London. / I never wear skirts. — 10 years ago → I live in Beijing. / I enjoy wearing skirts. — now

3-4: I'm a college student. / I never grow a beard. — 30 years ago → I'm a professor. / I love my beard. — now

1. She *used to live* ________ in London.
2. She ________________ skirts.
3. He ________________ a college student.
4. He ________________ a beard.

B. Complete the sentences with **used to** and the verbs in the box. Write negative sentences if necessary.

bake	be	belong	check	drink	have	~~visit~~

1. I *used to visit* ________ my parents every weekend. These days, I see them only once a month.
2. " ________ you ________ a lot of soda?" "Yes, I usually had five cans every day."
3. Mary ________________ much free time. She was always so busy.
4. We ________________ bread when we had an oven at home. It was so delicious.
5. Your dad is in a sailor's uniform in the photo. ________ he ________ a sailor?
6. I ________________ my e-mail very often. I do it at least three times a day now.
7. This desk ________________ to my grandfather. He gave it to me last year as a gift.

C. Complete the sentences with the verbs in *italics*. Use **used to** or **be used to + -ing**.

1. *(fly)* Alison travels a lot for her job, so she *'s used to flying* ________ in airplanes.
2. *(run)* I ________________ long distances because I often compete in marathons.
3. *(be)* Alaska ________________ part of Russia. Then, the US bought it in 1867.
4. *(take)* I ________________ care of children. I have two younger sisters.
5. *(ski)* When Jim and Ray lived in Switzerland, they ________________ a lot. They don't ski much anymore.

D. Complete the conversation with the verbs in *italics*. Use **used to** or the *present simple*.

AMY

MP3

AMY: Kate, I got a new car!
KATE: Wow! I'm so jealous! 1. I *used to have a car* ________ but I sold it. *(have)*
AMY: Why did you sell it?
KATE: 2. I ________________ too much money on gas. *(spend)*
I drove everywhere.
AMY: 3. Yeah, gas ________________ a lot. *(cost)*
4. But I'm happy that I ________________ a car. *(have)*
5. I ________________ the bus every day, and it was very tiring. *(take)*
KATE: I know. 6. I ________________ driving sometimes. *(miss)*
AMY: Why don't you buy another car?
KATE: 7. I ________________ to save money. *(need)*

KATE

Answers p.305 / Review Test 2 p.236

LESSON
10

It has snowed for three days. *Present perfect* (1) Continuous actions

1 It started snowing two days ago. It's still snowing.

It **has snowed** for three days.

3
4
5

Two days ago | Yesterday | Now

The snow started in the past and continues until now.
"has snowed" is the *present perfect*.

2 **have/has + lived/seen**/etc. *(present perfect)*

We use the *present perfect* to talk about actions that started in the past and continue until now. We often use the *present perfect* with **for** or **since**.

I/we/you/they	have	(not)	lived
he/she/it	has		seen

have	I/we/you/they	lived ...?
has	he/she/it	seen ...?

More about irregular verbs: Appendix p.281
More about short forms: Appendix p.284

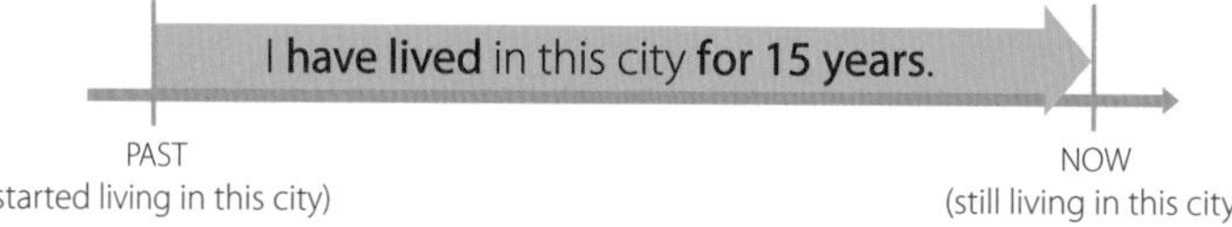
I have lived in this city for 15 years.

PAST (started living in this city) — NOW (still living in this city)

- I **have lived** in this city **for 15 years**. (= I moved to this city 15 years ago, and I still live here.)
- Jim is studying abroad. He **hasn't seen** his family **since last year**. (= Jim didn't see his family, and he's still not seeing them.)
- "This tree is huge! How long **has** it **been** here?" "For a century."

3 There is the following difference between **for** and **since**:

for + *period of time* (four years, a few days, etc.)

- **I've owned** this camera **for four years**.
- Luke **hasn't watched** TV **for a few days**. He's been busy with final exams.
- Cindy **has studied** cancer **for decades**.

since + *starting point* (2010, Tuesday, etc.)

- **I've owned** this camera **since 2010**.
- Mary is on vacation. She **hasn't attended** classes **since Tuesday**.
- Bob **has felt** sick **since lunchtime**.

4 We can also use **since** + *subject* + *verb*. In this case, we use the *past simple*.

- Robert **has wanted** to be a lawyer **since he was** a little boy.
- **Since we had** our baby, we **haven't slept** very well. She cries a lot at night.
- I always take my bike to work. I**'ve ridden** it to the office every day **since I bought** it.

5 Note that we do not use the *past simple* to talk about actions that started in the past and continue until now.

- Ken and I first met at a tennis club. I**'ve known** him for over seven years. (*NOT* I knew)
- We don't have many customers these days. We **haven't been** busy since January. (*NOT* We weren't)

PRACTICE

A. Complete the sentences with the verbs in the box. Write negative sentences if necessary.

check	have	make	~~play~~	visit	work

1. Mike *has played* football for three hours. He's really tired now.
2. "__________ Ms. Ross __________ here for a long time?" "Yes. She's the manager now."
3. I __________ our hometown since 2007. I miss it.
4. Since our marriage, my husband and I __________ all of our decisions together.
5. Penny __________ her e-mail for a few months and now she's forgotten the password.
6. How long __________ you __________ this MP3 player? It looks quite old.

B. Look at the pictures and complete the sentences with **for/since** and the given words. Write negative sentences if necessary.

~~be in Hawaii~~	brush my hair	come	do the laundry	drive that car	teach here

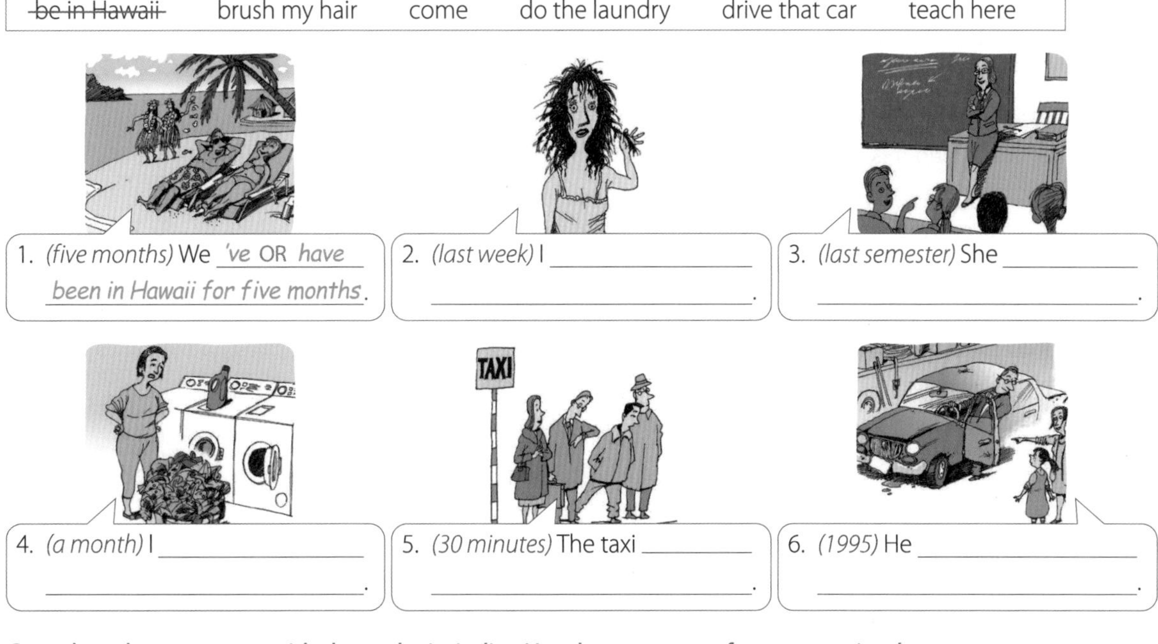

1. *(five months)* We *'ve OR have been in Hawaii for five months*.
2. *(last week)* I __________.
3. *(last semester)* She __________.
4. *(a month)* I __________.
5. *(30 minutes)* The taxi __________.
6. *(1995)* He __________.

C. Complete the sentences with the verbs in *italics*. Use the *present perfect* or *past simple*.

1. *(open, become)* Since the restaurant *opened*, it __________ very popular.
2. *(not go)* We __________ to the gym for weeks. We should go more often.
3. *(be, be)* Donna and I __________ best friends since I __________ eight.
4. *(sell)* Brian works at a furniture store. He __________ furniture for 12 years.
5. *(not listen, break)* I __________ to the radio since my brother __________ it on Friday.

D. Look at the charts and complete the sentences with **since**.

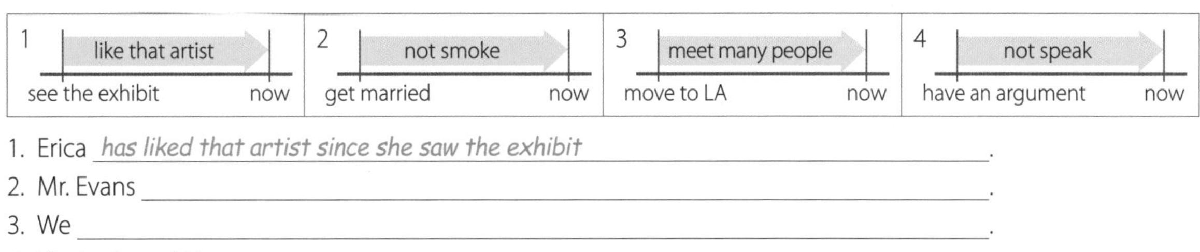

1. Erica *has liked that artist since she saw the exhibit*.
2. Mr. Evans __________.
3. We __________.
4. Kimberly and Lisa __________.

Answers p.305 / Review Test 3 p.238

11 She has worked at a library before. *Present perfect* (2) Experiences

MP3

1 We use the *present perfect* to talk about someone's experiences until now.

- She **has worked** at a library before.
- "Excuse me. **Have** we **met**?" "Yes, I think we have."
- Is the new mall nice? I **haven't visited** it yet.
- We **have eaten** sushi a few times. We didn't like it.

Past

2 We often use the *present perfect* with **ever/never**.

We usually use **ever** to ask if someone has experienced something in life until now.

- "**Have** you **ever read** Romeo and Juliet?" "Yes. Have you?"
- "Tina has lived alone for years." "**Has** she **ever wanted** a roommate?"
- "**Have** you **ever baked** muffins?" "No, I haven't."

We use **never** to say that someone has not experienced something in life until now.

- I'**ve never climbed** this mountain. It's beautiful.
- Our children are excited about going to the zoo. They'**ve never seen** a panda.
- Jane **has never watched** an opera, but she has attended many musicals.

3 We can use **have/has been (to)** to talk about visiting experiences.

- "I want to go to Paris one day." "I'**ve been** there. It's amazing."
- Tony **has been to** the new stadium. Let's ask him for directions.
- I **haven't been to** campus for a while because I'm taking a year off.

We do not use **have/has gone (to)** to talk about visiting experiences. We use **have/has gone (to)** to say that someone went somewhere and is there now.

- Terry'**s gone to** Denmark. He's not here anymore. (= Terry went to Denmark, and he's there now.)
- "Is Betty in her office?" "She'**s gone**. She'll be back tomorrow." (= Betty left her office, and she's somewhere else now.)
- Luke and Barbara **have gone to** the park. They like to take walks there.

4 We often use the following expressions with the *present perfect*:

once	twice	three/four/ . . . /many times

- I'**ve worn** a tuxedo **once**. It was at my sister's wedding.
- Dan **has skied** only **twice**, but he's quite good at it.
- We'**ve made** this same mistake **many times**. Let's focus.

5 We use **the best . . . I've ever . . .** to talk about our favorite experiences until now.

- Thanks so much for the new watch. It's **the best present I've ever received**!
- **The best pizza I've ever tasted** was at Gusto Pizzeria.
- Rick, that's **the best story I've ever heard**. You should write a book about it!

PRACTICE

A. Complete the sentences with the verbs in the box using the *present perfect*. Write negative sentences if necessary.

give	listen	live	receive	~~ride~~	use

1. We *'ve ridden* ______ on a camel once. It was a wonderful experience.
2. Kevin ______ in a foreign country, but he wants to try it one day.
3. "______ you ______ to Alisha Rose's new song yet?" "No. Is it good?"
4. "Do you need some help with the photocopier?" "Yes. I ______ it before."
5. Eddie is the best runner at this school. He ______ many trophies.
6. "______ Richard ever ______ you flowers?" "No, never."

B. Write about your experiences with the words in the box. Add never if necessary.

1. study Chinese
2. break a bone
3. try scuba diving
4. make bread at home

1. *I've (never) studied Chinese* ______.
2. ______.
3. ______.
4. ______.

YOU

Ask Pam questions about the experiences above with ever.

5. ______?
6. ______?
7. ______?
8. ______?

YOU

No, I haven't.
Yes, twice.
No, have you?
Yes, but only once.

PAM

C. Write have been / have gone.

1. I *'ve been* ______ to the dentist twice this year.
2. "Where's Susan?" "She ______ out with her friends."
3. ______ we ______ to that restaurant? It looks familiar.
4. "______ the children ______ to school?" "Yes. They left a few minutes ago."
5. Karen is interested in art. She ______ to many art exhibitions.

D. Complete the conversation with the words in *italics*. Use the *present perfect*.

MP3

KATE: Vacation is almost here. Do you have any plans, Amy?
AMY: Not yet. 1. But I want to do something *I've never done* ______. *(I, never, do)*
KATE: 2. ______ any volunteer work? *(you, ever, do)*
AMY: 3. ______ at a library before. *(I, volunteer)*
How about you?
KATE: 4. ______ to help children. *(I, be, to Africa once)*
5. It was the best experience ______. *(I, ever, have)*
Why don't you try it?
AMY: 6. ______ about going to Africa. *(I, never, think)*
But maybe I should consider it. Thanks!

KATE

AMY

Answers p.306 / Review Test 3 p.238

LESSON 12

I have done vs. I did

Present perfect vs. Past simple

1 We use the *present perfect* to talk about past actions that have a connection with the present.

- The train **has arrived** at the station.
  (= The train arrived in the past and is at the station now.)
- We **have moved** the bookshelf upstairs.
  (= We moved the bookshelf in the past and it's upstairs now.)
- I **have deleted** the file from my computer.

We use the *past simple* to talk about finished actions in the past.

- The train **arrived** at the station two minutes ago.
  (= The train arrived in the past.)
- We **moved** the bookshelf upstairs yesterday.
  (= We moved the bookshelf in the past.)
- I **deleted** the file after I printed it.

2 We only use the *present perfect* to talk about actions that started in the past and continue until now.

- Anna **has used** the same cell phone for six years. It's so old. (*NOT* Anna used)
- My wife and I are vegetarians. We **haven't eaten** meat since 2003. (*NOT* We didn't eat)

We only use the *past simple* to talk about finished actions that have no connection with the present or are not continuing now.

- I don't have a pet now, but I **raised** a cat when I was young. (*NOT* I have raised)
- Mr. Parker **was** one of my employees a year ago. Now he owns a business. (*NOT* Mr. Parker has been)

3 We only use the *past simple* with the following expressions that refer to finished time periods:

yesterday	last night/week/month
... ago	in + (past time)

- **Did** you **check** the mail **yesterday**? (*NOT* Have you checked the mail yesterday)
- I'm tired because I **didn't sleep** well **last night**. (*NOT* I haven't slept well last night)
- We're late. The movie **began five minutes ago**.
- Columbus **discovered** America **in 1492**.

We only use the *present perfect* with the expressions that refer to unfinished time periods, such as **today**, **this morning/week**/etc.:

- "**Have** you **checked** the mail **today**?" "Not yet." (**today** hasn't yet ended.)
- I'm so upset. My car **has broken** down twice **this week**. (**this week** hasn't yet ended.)

4 We can use **just**, **already**, and **yet** with both the *present perfect* and *past simple*. There is no difference in meaning.

- Our team **has just won** the game! *OR* Our team **just won** the game!
- Steve **has already opened** his birthday presents. *OR* Steve **already opened** his birthday presents.
- **Have** you **met** your new boss **yet**? *OR* **Did** you **meet** your new boss **yet**?

We usually use **yet** in negative sentences and questions.

- I **haven't made** my vacation plans **yet**. ~~*OR* I~~ **didn't make** my vacation plans **yet**.
- **Have** you **finished** cleaning your room **yet**? *OR* **Did** you **finish** cleaning your room **yet**?

PRACTICE

A. Complete the sentences with the verbs in the box. Use the *present perfect* or *past simple*.

go	lose	paint	play	~~publish~~	visit	wake	want

1. Ben and Frank *have published* a magazine for 12 years. It's very popular.
2. Josh looks thinner. ______________ he ______________ weight since we last saw him?
3. The storm last night was so loud. I ____________________ up in the middle of the night.
4. We ____________________ Vietnam when we were traveling in Asia.
5. "______________ Monet ______________ *Sunflowers*?" "No. The artist was Van Gogh."
6. Sharon ____________________ that hat since she saw it in the store.
7. "Sara and Tim are our guitarists." "How long ______________ they ______________ in your band?"
8. "Why ______________ you ______________ home early yesterday?" "My son was sick."

B. Complete the conversation with the words in *italics*. Use the *present perfect* or *past simple*.

SUE: Hi Jane! 1. *I received* your wedding invitation yesterday. *(I, receive)*
2. ____?
(you, choose a wedding dress, yet)

JANE: 3. Yes. ____________________ a beautiful one two days ago. *(I, buy)*

SUE: That's great! How about the honeymoon?
4. ____ to go?
(you, already, find a place)

JANE: Yes. 5. ____.
(we, just, make reservations)

SUE: I'm so happy for you. I can't wait to see you in your dress!

C. Find and change any mistakes in each sentence. Put ✓ if the sentence is correct.

1. Mr. Jenkins has started taking guitar lessons last month. *has started → started*
2. I exercised at that gym for a week now. I like it a lot. ______________
3. "Is dinner ready?" "No. We haven't cooked it yet." ______________
4. "Patrick didn't smoke a cigarette since January." "Good for him!" ______________
5. "Did you already wash the dishes?" "Yes. There weren't very many." ______________
6. "Have you gone to the concert yesterday?" "No. I had to work." ______________

D. Complete the conversation with the verbs in *italics*. Use the *present perfect* or *past simple*.

MP3

CHRIS

CHRIS: 1. I *called* you earlier, but you didn't answer. *(call)*
2. Where ______________ you? *(be)*

JUSTIN: I was at work. I got a job at a fast-food restaurant.

CHRIS: Really? 3. How long ______________ you ______________ there? *(work)*

JUSTIN: 4. I ______________ yesterday. *(start)* Please don't tell Mom, though.
5. I ______________ her yet. *(not tell)*

CHRIS: Why?

JUSTIN: I want to surprise her with a gift when I get my first pay.

JUSTIN

Answers p.306 / Review Test 3 p.238

She has been waiting for an hour. *Present perfect progressive*

MP3

1 She arrived an hour ago.

She **has been waiting** for an hour.

1 hour ago

Now

She arrived at the amusement park an hour ago and began to wait.
"has been waiting" started in the past and is still continuing now.
It is the *present perfect progressive*.

2 **have/has been + -ing** *(present perfect progressive)*

We use the *present perfect progressive* to talk about actions that started in the past and are still continuing now.

I/we/you/they	**have**	(not)	been	talking
he/she/it	**has**			saving

have	I/we/you/they	been	talking ...?
has	he/she/it		saving ...?

More about spelling rules: Appendix p.278

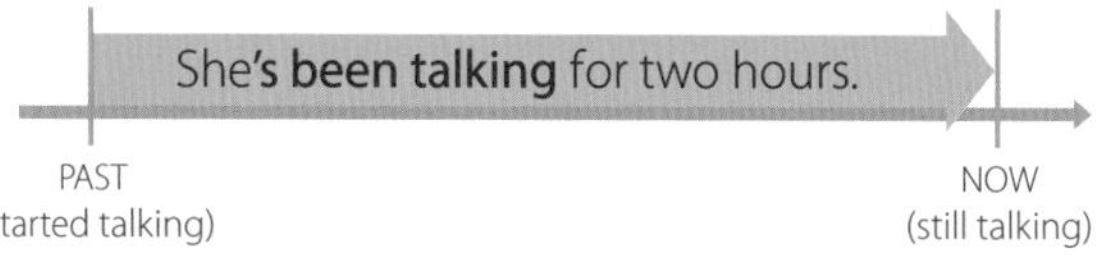

- Nancy is still on the phone. She**'s been talking** for two hours.
  (= She started talking two hours ago and is still talking now.)
- We **have been saving** a lot of money since last year. We want to buy a new house.
  (= We started saving money last year and are still saving money now.)
- I **haven't been working** for the past few days. I caught a bad cold.
- "What **has** Kevin **been doing** lately?" "I don't know. I haven't seen him for six months."

3 We often use **for**, **since**, and **how long** with the *present perfect progressive* to talk about the duration of a continuing action that started in the past.

- Let's go to the mall. I **haven't been shopping for four weeks**.
- My neighbor's dog **has been barking since 6 a.m**. It's so annoying!
- "**How long have** you **been attending** the art school?" "For about three years."

4 We can also use the *present perfect progressive* to talk about actions that just ended. In this case, the *present perfect progressive* describes a just ended action that has effects now.

- "Your eyes are red. **Have** you **been crying**?" "Yes. I failed my exam again."
  (The crying just ended, so the eyes are red now.)
- The children **have been playing** in the mud. Their shoes are dirty.
  (The playing in the mud just ended, so the shoes are dirty now.)
- "Why is Scott upset?" "He **has been arguing** with his roommate."

5 We do not use the *present perfect progressive* with **know**, **believe**, etc. that describe states or thoughts. We usually use the *present perfect* with these *verbs*.

- Patricia and I **have known** each other since high school. (*NOT* Patricia and I have been knowing)
- My mother **has** always **believed** in me. She always supports my decisions. (*NOT* My mother has always been believing)

More about non-progressive verbs: Lesson 4

P R A C T I C E

A. Look at the pictures and complete the sentences with the words in the box. Use the *present perfect progressive*.

clean the windows	listen to	paint a picture	run	sit	~~speak~~

1-3   10 minutes ago → now

4-6   one hour ago → now

1. A woman *has been speaking* at a meeting.
2. Three people ______ a presentation.
3. A man ______.
4. A man ______.
5. A woman ______ on a blanket.
6. Two people ______.

B. Rewrite the two sentences as one with for/since. Use the *present perfect progressive*.

1. Nate is camping by the river. He went there on Friday.
   → *He's been camping by the river since Friday* OR *He has been camping by the river since Friday*.
2. Eve is cooking dinner. She began cooking at 5 o'clock.
   → ______.
3. The workers are building a bridge. The project began six months ago.
   → ______.
4. Tina and Kim are playing tennis. They started at noon.
   → ______.
5. Jack is using his laptop. He turned it on an hour ago.
   → ______.

C. Look at the pictures and complete the sentences with the verbs in the box. Use the *present perfect progressive*.

climb	~~eat~~	pack	sleep	swim

We're ready to move now.
1
I'm full.
2
3
4
5

1. She *'s been eating* OR *has been eating*.
2. They ______.
3. He ______.
4. She ______.
5. They ______.

D. Complete the questions with the words in *italics*. Use the *present perfect progressive*.

1. *(Liz and Ron, date)* *Have Liz and Ron been dating* for a long time?
2. *(how long, you, watch)* ______ TV?
3. *(where, John, stay)* ______ this week?
4. *(you, enjoy)* ______ the book club?
5. *(how long, Lucy, plan)* ______ her trip?

Yes. For several years.
About two hours.
At his friend's house.
Yes. I love it.
For a month.

Answers **p.306** / Review Test 3 **p.238**

LESSON 14

I have done vs. I have been doing

Present perfect vs. Present perfect progressive

MP3

1 He started fixing his computer at 2 p.m. It is now 4 p.m.

He **has fixed** his computer.
It works now.

He **has been fixing** his computer.
He is tired.

"has fixed" emphasizes that the computer now works as a result of the fixing that started in the past. But **"has been fixing"** emphasizes the fixing that started 2 hours ago and is still continuing.

2 ***Present perfect***

We use the *present perfect* to emphasize the present result of the action that started in the past.

- Finally I'**ve done** my homework. Now I can help you with the laundry.
- Elizabeth **has made** some delicious tomato soup. Would you like to try some?
- The workers **have completed** the construction. We can use that road now.

Present perfect progressive

We use the *present perfect progressive* to emphasize the action itself that started in the past and is still continuing.

- I'**ve been doing** my homework since 3 o'clock. I need a break.
- Maria **has been cleaning** the house all morning and she's still not finished.
- "Why are you and Jane laughing?"
  "Oh. We'**ve been watching** a comedy show."

3 We can use **live**, **study**, etc. with both the *present perfect* and *present perfect progressive*. In this case, there is no difference in meaning.

- I **have lived** in this house for a long time. *OR* I **have been living** in this house for a long time.
- **Have** you **studied** Russian for many years? *OR* **Have** you **been studying** Russian for many years?

4 We use the *present perfect* to talk about how many times someone did something until now. In this case, we do not use the *present perfect progressive*.

- "Do you want some more wine?" "No. I'**ve had three glasses** already." (*NOT* I've been having three glasses)
- "**How many times has** Peter **run** a marathon?" "Just twice so far." (*NOT* How many times has Peter been running)

We can use both the *present perfect* and *present perfect progressive* to talk about how long an action has continued until now. In this case, we use the *present perfect progressive* more often.

- I'**ve taken** this medicine **for several days**. *OR* I'**ve been taking** this medicine **for several days**.
- **How long has** Gina **practiced** ballet? *OR* **How long has** Gina **been practicing** ballet?

P R A C T I C E

A. Look at the pictures and complete the sentences with the words in the box. Use the *present perfect*.

bake eight muffins	drive 90 miles	have three cups of coffee
~~miss five calls~~	pick a basket of oranges	

1. She *'s missed five calls*________.
2. He ________ so far.
3. They ________.
4. He ________.
5. She ________.

B. Read what Judy says and complete the sentences with **for/since**. Use the *present perfect progressive*.

JUDY

1. I'm working now. I began at 9 a.m.
2. I keep a diary. I started it when I was 10.
3. My dogs are sleeping. They fell asleep an hour ago.
4. I wear glasses. I got them five years ago.
5. My parents are renovating the house. They started in May.

1. She *'s been working since 9 a.m.*________.
2. She ________.
3. Her dogs ________.
4. She ________.
5. Her parents ________.

C. Complete the sentences with the words in *italics*. Use the *present perfect* or *present perfect progressive*.

1. *(we, live)* My husband and I love our house. *We've lived* OR *We've been living* ________ in it since we got married.
2. *(I, call, her)* Can you call Julie? ________ twice already but she didn't answer.
3. *(I, read, this book)* ________ three times. It's really good.
4. *(it, sell)* That shoe store is old. ________ shoes in this town for many years.
5. *(Sandra, spend)* Tom is moving soon, so ________ a lot of time with him recently.
6. *(Sue, visit)* ________ the museum five times. She's interested in history.
7. *(Ken and Mark, not work)* ________ at our company long, so they still have much to learn.
8. *(they, have)* This isn't Jill and Ian's first date. ________ dinner a few times before.
9. *(you, go out for drinks)* "How many times ________ this week?"
   "Only once."
10. *(you, design, clothes)* "How long ________?"
    "I started when I was in college."

Answers p.306 / Review Test 3 p.238

LESSON

15 When he got to the bus stop, the bus **had** already **left**. *Past perfect*

MP3

1

When he got to the bus stop, the bus **had** already **left**.

Both actions happened in the past, but the bus leaving happened first. The bus **"had left"** before he arrived at the bus stop. **"had left"** is the *past perfect*.

2 **had** + **ended**/**fixed**/etc. *(past perfect)*

We use the *past perfect* to talk about actions that happened before another past action.

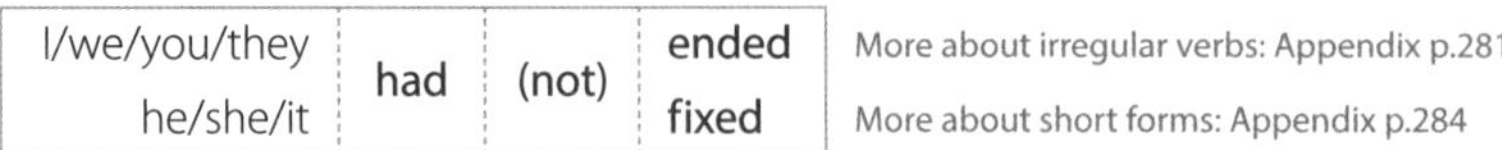

I/we/you/they he/she/it	had	(not)	ended fixed

More about irregular verbs: Appendix p.281

More about short forms: Appendix p.284

The show **had ended**.

- When we turned on the TV, the show **had** already **ended**.
  (The show ended before we turned on the TV.)
- The mechanics still **hadn't fixed** my car when I returned to the repair shop.
  (The mechanics didn't fix the car before I returned to the repair shop.)
- Jack found his hat, but he **had** already **bought** a new one.
- My parents went to India last year. They **hadn't been** there before.
- According to the news, the thief **had robbed** six banks when the police finally caught him.

3

We use the *past perfect* to talk about actions that happened before another past action. But we use the *past simple* to talk about actions that happened after that past action.

The rain **had stopped**. I **saw** a rainbow.

PAST
(went outside)
NOW

- When I **went** outside, the rain **had** already **stopped**. (= The rain stopped before I went outside.)
  When I **went** outside, I **saw** a rainbow. (= I saw a rainbow after I went outside.)
- We **had** already **been** married for a year when we **graduated** from college.
  We **graduated** from college and then we **got** jobs.

4

When we use **before**, **after**, etc., the order of actions is clear. In this case, we can also use the *past simple* instead of the *past perfect*.

- I **had called** Dave **before** I went to his house.
  OR I **called** Dave **before** I went to his house.
- **After** the guests **had finished** their steak, the waiters served dessert.
  OR **After** the guests **finished** their steak, the waiters served dessert.

P R A C T I C E

A. Look at the pictures and complete the sentences with the words in the box.

break the lamp	~~deliver a package~~	eat all the cookies	go to bed	leave a note

When Stacy got home yesterday,

1. Someone *had delivered a package* __________.
2. Her dog ____________________.
3. Her parents ____________________.
4. Her mom ____________________.
5. Her brother ____________________.

B. Complete the sentences with the verbs in *italics* using the *past perfect*. Write negative sentences if necessary.

1. *(melt)* I wanted to go skiing last month, but the snow *had melted* __________.
2. *(see)* Carol realized that she ____________________ her cousin for three years. She decided to call him.
3. *(order)* When I arrived, everybody ____________________ and some people were already eating.
4. *(expect)* The actor was surprised about the award. He ____________________ to win it.
5. *(open)* The bank ____________________ when I got there, so I had to wait.
6. *(practice)* We ____________________ enough for the match. We didn't need to be worried.

C. Complete the sentences with the verbs in the box. Use the *past perfect* or *past simple*.

answer	~~buy~~	go	reach	save	watch

1. I needed a new dress, so I *bought* __________ one.
2. Paula ____________________ only half of her exam questions when the bell rang.
3. Scott's computer stopped working suddenly, but luckily he ____________________ his files already.
4. I met Karen and we ____________________ a scary movie.
5. When we ____________________ the beach, the sun had already gone down.
6. "Was Ben at the party when you got there?" "No. He ____________________ home."

D. Complete the conversation with the verbs in *italics*. Use the *past perfect* or *past simple*.

MP3

Teacher

Teacher: Why are you late, Justin?
JUSTIN: I'm sorry. 1. I *woke* __________ up late this morning. *(wake)*
2. When I ____________________ at the bus stop, the bus ____________________. *(arrive, already leave)*
I thought my brother could drive me.
3. But when I ____________________ back home, he ____________________ to work. *(get, already go)*
Teacher: 4. Why ____________________ you ____________________ up so late? *(get)*
JUSTIN: I didn't sleep much last night.
5. I ____________________ coffee before I went to bed. *(drink)*
Teacher: I see. Well, please be more careful next time.

JUSTIN

Answers p.307 / Review Test 3 p.238

LESSON 16 She will become a famous painter one day. will

MP3

1

THE TIMES
You'll become famous.

I'll take this.
Study Art In Italy

She **will become** a famous painter one day. She **will take** art classes in Italy.

"will happen" and **"will take"** are future events that have not happened yet.

2 We use **will** + **have**/**see**/etc. to talk about future events that we expect to happen.

I/we/you/they he/she/it	will (= 'll) will not (= won't)	have see

will	I/we/you/they he/she/it	have ...? see ...?

More about short forms: Appendix p.284

- I'm excited about camping this weekend. We'**ll have** so much fun.
- Julie is moving abroad. I **won't see** her very often now.
- "**Will** the new city hall **be** open next weekend?" "I don't think so."
- Tom **will love** this chocolate cake. He really likes chocolate.

3 We also use **will** to talk about something that we decide to do in the future.

- "You need to return these DVDs." "OK. I'**ll return** them today."
- This milk smells bad. I **won't drink** it.
- "I miss you and Tom." "We miss you too. We'**ll visit** you soon."

We can also use **will** to suggest things or make promises.

- "I need to get to the train station." "I'**ll give** you a ride."
- I **won't forget** your birthday again. I'm so sorry.
- "Can someone set the table, please?" "I'**ll do** it."

4 We often use the following expressions with **will**:

I think / I don't think . . . will
I guess . . . will
I'm sure . . . will
I'm afraid . . . will

- **I think** you'**ll** enjoy that book. It's great.
- **I guess** I **won't** find my lost wallet.
- "I can't go to Mike's graduation." "**I'm sure** he'**ll** understand."
- **I'm afraid** I **won't** be on time for the meeting.

We usually use **I don't think . . . will** rather than **I think . . . won't**.

- "Can Emily help us with our homework?" "**I don't think** she'**ll** have time."
- **I don't think** we'**ll** stay at that hotel again. It wasn't very nice.

PRACTICE

A. Complete the sentences with **will** and the verbs in the box. Write negative sentences if necessary.

arrive	be	buy	call	have	help	hurt	~~lend~~

1. "My laptop isn't working, but I need to write a report." "I *'ll lend* OR *will lend* you mine."
2. I'm sure Jack ________________ you soon. Stop looking at your phone.
3. I want to wear my new miniskirt. ____________ the weather ____________ warm tomorrow?
4. "Mom, I don't want to go to the dentist." "Don't worry. It ________________ much."
5. "May I take your order?" "Yes. I want the shrimp and my wife ________________ the fish."
6. When ____________ the pizza ____________? I ordered it an hour ago.
7. "I can't open this jar." "Let me see it. I ________________ you."
8. The clock seems cheaper at that store across the street. I ________________ it here.

B. Look at the pictures and complete the sentences with **will** and the verbs in the box. Write negative sentences if necessary.

~~cook~~	eat	explain	play

1. I *'ll cook* OR *will cook* something for you.
2. We ________________ too long. Don't worry.
3. All right. I ________________ it.
4. I ________________ it to you.

C. Write sentences about yourself with **I think . . . will** or **I don't think . . . will** and the words in the box.

1. wake up early tomorrow
2. get a haircut next week
3. see a movie next weekend
4. travel abroad next year
5. go to the beach next summer

1. *I (don't) think I'll wake up early tomorrow*.
2. ________________________________.
3. ________________________________.
4. ________________________________.
5. ________________________________.

YOU

D. Complete the conversation with **will** and the words in *italics*. Write negative sentences if necessary.

MP3

Professor: Your paintings are amazing!

KATE: Thank you! But I hope to get better. 1. *I'll practice* OR *I will practice* more. *(I, practice)*

Professor: 2. ________________ a famous painter. *(I'm sure, you, become)* 3. ________________ more classes here next year? *(you, take)*

KATE: No. 4. ________________ abroad. *(I guess, I, study)* Maybe in Europe.

Professor: Then how about Italy? There are great art schools there. 5. ________________ disappointed. *(you, be)*

KATE: Thanks for the advice. 6. ________________ about it. *(I, think)*

Professor

KATE

Answers **p.307** / Review Test 4 **p.240**

LESSON 17

I'm going to look beautiful in this dress. am/is/are going to

MP3

1 We can use **am/is/are going to** + **look/let**/etc. to talk about future events that we expect to happen.

I	am	(not)	going to	look
he/she/it	is			let
we/you/they	are			stop

am	I	going to	look ...?
is	he/she/it		let ...?
are	we/you/they		stop ...?

- **I'm going to look** beautiful in this dress. It's lovely!
- "My parents **aren't going to let** me travel abroad alone." "They might. You should ask them."
- "**Is** it **going to stop** raining soon?" "Maybe."

We can also use **will . . .** to talk about future events that we expect to happen.

- Jeff **won't come** for dinner this evening. (= Jeff isn't going to come.)

But we do not use **will** to talk about things that we expect to happen based on the present situation. In this case, we use **am/is/are going to.**

- Look at the baby! He **is going to cry**. (*NOT* He'll cry)
- The traffic is really bad. **I'm going to be** late for work. (*NOT* I'll be)

2 We also use **am/is/are going to** to talk about things that we have decided to do in the future. There is the following difference with **will**:

We usually use **am/is/are going to** to talk about decisions that we made before the moment of speaking.

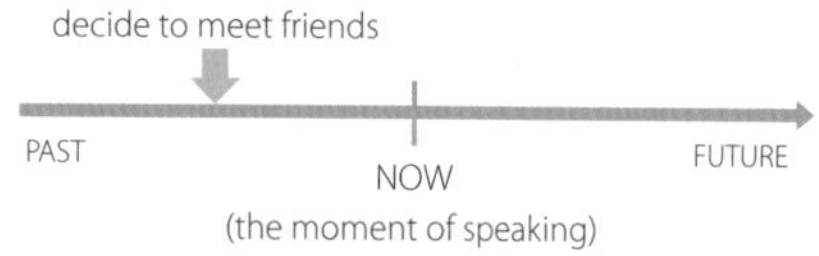

- "Do you have plans tonight?"
  "Yes. **I'm going to meet** some friends at a party."
  (= I decided to meet friends before the moment of speaking.)
- Brandon **is going to buy** a bike. He has saved $200 already.

We usually use **will** to talk about decisions that we are making at the moment of speaking.

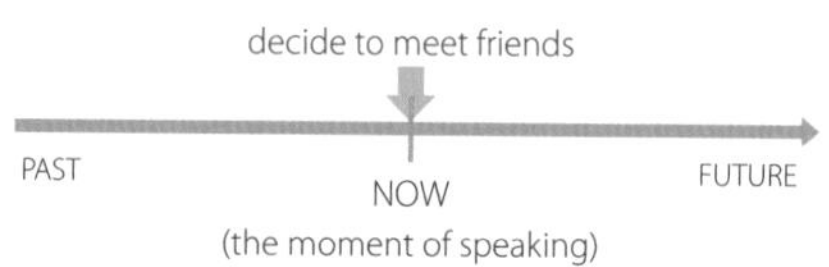

- "Do you want to go to the party with us tonight?"
  "Sure. **I'll meet** you there after work."
  (= I'm deciding to meet friends at the moment of speaking.)
- "This bike costs only $250."
  "Really? **I'll buy** it, then."

3 We use **was/were going to** to talk about the past. We often use **was/were going to** to talk about things that we decided to do in the past but did not do.

- Bob **was going to stay** at a hotel last night, but there were no rooms available.
  (= Bob decided to stay at a hotel last night, but he didn't.)
- We **were going to study** at the library yesterday, but it was closed.
  (= We decided to study at the library yesterday, but we didn't.)

We also use **was/were going to** to talk about things that we expected to happen in the past.

- Jane was confident. She was sure she **was going to get** the scholarship.
- "I thought the exhibits **were going to start** on June 21." "Yes, but the schedule changed."

PRACTICE

A. Look at the pictures and complete the sentences with **am/is/are going to** and the words in the box.

~~blow out the candles~~	fall into the box	melt	sleep on the sofa	wash the dog

Good night.

1. He *'s going to blow out the candles* __________.
2. The oranges __________.
3. She __________.
4. They __________.
5. The ice __________.

B. Complete the sentences with **am/is/are going to** or **will** and the verbs in *italics*.

1. *(be)* I broke the window again. I *'m going to be* __________ in big trouble!
2. *(help)* "What do you think of the new website?"
   "I like it. I think it __________ our business."
3. *(have)* My sister is at the hospital. She __________ her baby very soon.
4. *(find)* "I lost my dog. I'm so sad." "Don't worry. You __________ him."
5. *(learn)* I __________ a lot at the workshop. I'm excited about it.
6. *(complete)* Bob and Joe are near the finish line! They __________ the marathon!

C. Read each situation and complete the sentences with **am/is/are going to** or **will** and the words in *italics*. Write negative sentences if necessary.

1. Sarah asks you to help her move this weekend, and you are free.
   YOU: *(I, help)* Sure. *I'll help* __________ you this weekend. What time should I be there?
2. Kyle asks you why Peter is taking Chinese lessons lately. It is because his New Year's plan was to visit China.
   YOU: *(He, visit)* __________ China this year, so he needs to study a lot.
3. You are in the restroom washing your hands. Somebody knocks on the door.
   YOU: *(I, be)* Wait a second. __________ out soon.
4. Jessie and you just arrived at an Italian restaurant. She tells you that she doesn't like mushrooms.
   YOU: *(I, order)* OK. __________ mushroom pizza then. Do you like pepperoni?
5. Mr. Brown wants to have a lunch meeting with your boss, but she already has a doctor's appointment.
   YOU: *(She, be)* __________ in the office at lunch. She'll be back around 3 o'clock.

D. Complete the sentences with **was/were going to** and the verbs in the box.

attend	give	~~make~~	wait

1. Hi kids,
   I *was going to make* __________ spaghetti for dinner, but there was no pasta! I'll be home from the supermarket soon.

2. Dear Kelly,
   Happy Birthday!
   We __________ you a scarf, but we bought something else. I hope you like it.

3. Marcia,
   I'm sorry I wasn't at your wedding.
   I __________, but unfortunately I had to work that weekend.

4. Jason,
   We've gone to the mall.
   We __________ for you, but the mall closes at 8 o'clock. Sorry!

Answers p.307 / Review Test 4 p.240

They are watching a soccer game tonight.

Present progressive and *Present simple* for the future

MP3

1 They **are watching** a soccer game tonight.

The game **starts** at 7 p.m.

It is 6:30 p.m. now. The game starts at 7 p.m. **"are watching"** is the *present progressive* and **"starts"** is the *present simple*, but they are both future events.

2 We can use the *present progressive* to talk about future plans with a specific time or place (appointments, reservations, etc.).

- "Are you doing anything this weekend?" "Yes. I**'m meeting** Josh."
- We **aren't returning** from Mexico until next Wednesday.
- Why are we hiring a new secretary? **Is** Ms. Rogers **retiring**?
- I**'m seeing** the doctor today. I made an appointment for 6 o'clock.
- "When **are** you **moving** out?" "In three months."

We can also use **am/is/are going to** instead of the *present progressive*.

- We**'re having** a company picnic on Monday.
  OR We**'re going to have** a company picnic on Monday.
- **Is** Andy **spending** his summer vacation with his family?
  OR **Is** Andy **going to spend** his summer vacation with his family?

3 We can use the *present simple* to talk about future events with fixed schedules (public transportation, movies, class schedules, etc.).

- The train to Rome **departs** at 9 p.m. tonight.
- "The movie **finishes** at midnight." "It will be late when we get home."
- Anna's yoga class **starts** on September 5th.
- We don't have time to go to the bank. It **closes** soon.
- Each interview **lasts** for 20 minutes, and you will have a short break after each one.

Note that we do not use the *present simple* to talk about personal plans. In this case, we use the *present progressive*.

- I**'m speaking** at a meeting next Saturday.
- My daughter **is taking** her driving test next week. She's excited about getting her license.

4 We can use **am/is/are about to** + **begin/come**/etc. to talk about things happening in the very near future.

- The presentation **is about to begin**. Please take your seats.
- We have been awake all night. The sun **is about to come** up!
- Stop! You**'re about to hit** that car!
- "Do you want to have some coffee?" "No, thanks. I**'m about to go** to bed."
- Jake, put on your coat. We**'re about to leave**.

P R A C T I C E

A. Look at the pictures and complete the sentences with the words in the box. Use the *present progressive*.

~~attend a seminar~~	get married	meet	open a bakery	run in a marathon

1. *She's attending a seminar* at 3 p.m. tomorrow.
2. ______________________ tonight.
3. ______________________ on July 15.
4. ______________________ on Sunday.
5. ______________________ next month.

B. Complete the sentences with the words in the box. Use the *present simple*.

arrive at	depart on	~~open on~~	play on	start at

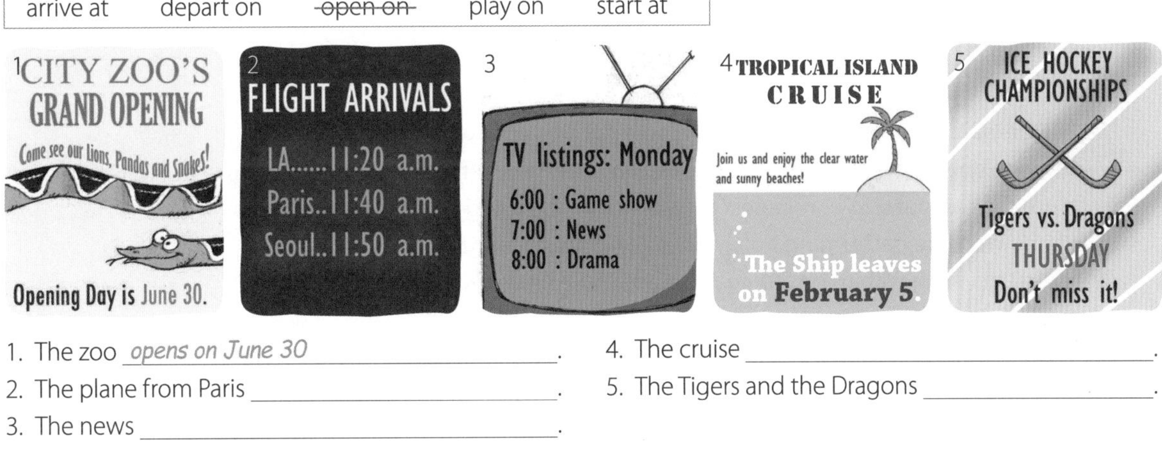

1. The zoo *opens on June 30*.
2. The plane from Paris ______________________.
3. The news ______________________.
4. The cruise ______________________.
5. The Tigers and the Dragons ______________________.

C. Complete the sentences with the words in *italics*. Use the *present progressive* or *present simple*.

1. *(I, travel)* *I'm traveling* to India next week. I'm really excited!
2. *(the class, begin)* ______________________ at 3 o'clock today, so we need to leave by 2:30.
3. *(she, not join)* Mary will be out of town tomorrow, so ______________________ us for lunch.
4. *(the musical, end)* "What time ______________________?" "I don't know. Let's check the tickets."
5. *(Alex and I, go)* ______________________ fishing on Sunday. I think it'll be fun.
6. *(the bus, not leave)* We don't need to run. ______________________ until 9:30.

D. Complete the sentences with **am/is/are about to** and the verbs in the box.

announce	break	check	close	~~sing~~

1. Ellen and Susan are on the stage. They *'re about to sing* a song.
2. Let's hurry. The elevator door ______________________.
3. "Is it going to be hot today?" "Maybe. I ______________________ today's weather."
4. That chair ______________________. We need to repair it.
5. Attention, please. Mr. and Mrs. Robbins ______________________ the winner of the art contest.

Answers **p.307** / Review Test 4 **p.240**

LESSON 19 They **will be studying** at 8 p.m. tomorrow. *Future progressive*

MP3

1 There is a Spanish class from 7 p.m. to 9 p.m. every day.

They **will be studying** at 8 p.m. tomorrow.

The students will come to the Spanish class at 7 p.m. tomorrow and studying Spanish will be in progress at 8 p.m. **"will be studying"** is the *future progressive*.

2 **will be + -ing** *(future progressive)*

We use the *future progressive* to talk about actions in progress at a certain time in the future.

I/we/you/they	will (= 'll)	be	waiting
he/she/it	will not (= won't)		taking

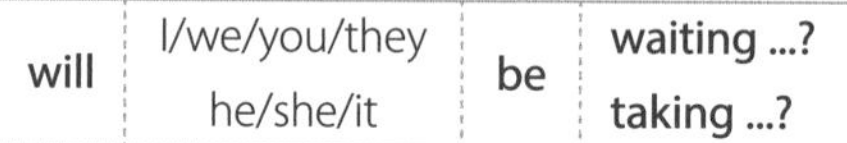

will	I/we/you/they	be	waiting ...?
	he/she/it		taking ...?

We **will be waiting** for Janet at the station.

- We **will be waiting** for Janet at the station at 5 o'clock tomorrow.
- Mandy **won't be taking** exams next week. Her last exam is this Thursday.
- Can I use the computer in 10 minutes? Or **will** you still **be using** it then?
- That band **won't be performing** in July. They're taking a break from June to August.
- Peter can't go skiing with us on Saturday because he**'ll be working** then.

3 There is the following difference in meaning between the *future progressive* and **will** or **am/is/are going to**:

- "I'll be home at 7." "OK. I**'ll be making** dinner when you arrive." (= Making dinner will be in progress when you arrive.)
  "I'll be home at 5." "OK. We**'ll make** dinner together when you arrive." (= We'll start making dinner when you arrive.)
- The girls **will be singing** when the bride enters.
  The girls **will sing** after the bride enters.

We do not use the *future progressive* with **know**, **believe**, etc. that describe states or thoughts. We use **will** or **am/is/are going to** with these *verbs*.

- "Doctor, will Melissa be all right?" "We**'ll know** more when we get the test results." (*NOT* We'll be knowing)
- "I broke John's camera, but it was an accident." "Tell him that. I'm sure he**'ll believe** you." (*NOT* he'll be believing)

More about non-progressive verbs: Lesson 4

4 We also use the *future progressive* to talk about future actions that are fixed or certain to happen. Note that it is not necessary for the actions to be in progress at that moment.

- I**'ll be leaving** for Hawaii on April 7. I'm so excited!
- "**Will** the guests **be arriving** soon?" "No, they **won't be arriving** until 1 o'clock."

In this case, we can also use **am/is/are going to** instead of the *future progressive*.

- **I'm going to leave** for Hawaii on April 7. I'm so excited! (= I'll be leaving)

PRACTICE

A. Claire is going to move next Friday. Look at her plans for the next week and complete the sentences using the *future progressive*.

MON	TUE	WED	THU	FRI
6:00-8:00 clean the new house	12:00-2:00 buy some furniture	10:00-2:00 paint the new house	10:00-4:00 pack	2:00-6:00 move into the new house

1. Claire *will be cleaning the new house* at 7 on Monday.
2. She ______________ at 1 on Thursday.
3. She ______________ on Wednesday at 11.
4. She ______________ at 1:30 on Tuesday.
5. She ______________ at 5 on Friday.

B. Complete the sentences with the verbs in *italics* using the *future progressive* or **will**. Write negative sentences if necessary.

1. *(drive)* "Do you want to go for a walk at 7 tonight?"
   "I can't. I *'ll be driving* OR *will be driving* to my grandmother's house then."
2. *(remember)* Jennifer ______________ my birthday. She always forgets it.
3. *(sleep)* "I'll be home around midnight. ______________ you ______________?"
   "I don't think so. I'll probably be reading my book."
4. *(go)* I need some cash. Let's stop by the bank first, and then we ______________ shopping.
5. *(prepare)* "Are you doing something after lunch?" "Yes. I ______________ for a presentation."
6. *(attend)* Ray ______________ the workshop at 3. He has an appointment at the same time.
7. *(show)* "I can't open this lock. ______________ you ______________ me how it works?"
   "Sure. Let me see it."
8. *(play)* "Can we have dinner at 6?"
   "No. The children ______________ soccer. Their game doesn't finish until 6:30 today."

C. Complete the conversations with the verbs in the box using the *future progressive*. Write negative sentences if necessary.

come	~~receive~~	stay	volunteer

1. A: *Will* I *be receiving* the delivery soon?
   B: Yes. You'll get them this Friday.
2. A: Are your parents visiting you this week?
   B: No, they ______________. Maybe I'll see them next week.
3. A: We ______________ at the children's hospital this weekend.
   B: That's a very kind thing to do.
4. A: I'm going on a business trip next month.
   B: Where ______________ you ______________? At a hotel?

D. Complete the conversation with the words in *italics* using the *future progressive*. Write negative sentences if necessary.

MP3

SARA

SARA: 1. Linda, *will you be taking* your Spanish class tonight? *(you, take)*
LINDA: 2. No, ______________ to class this evening. *(I, go)*
SARA: 3. What ______________? *(you, do)*
LINDA: 4. ______________ dinner with James. *(I, have)*
SARA: I see. I was going to have dinner with you. Maybe next time.
LINDA: 5. ______________ anything after work tomorrow. *(I, do)*
How about tomorrow night?
SARA: Great! 6. ______________ for you at the gate at 6. *(I, wait)*

LINDA

Answers p.307 / Review Test 4 p.240

LESSON 20 She will have graduated by this time next year. *Future perfect*

MP3

1 She is in her last year of high school.

She **will have graduated** by next June.

It is June, and she has not graduated yet. She will be finished with high school by next June. **"will have graduated"** is the *future perfect*.

This year

Next year

2 **will have + climbed/left**/etc. *(future perfect)*

We use the *future perfect* to talk about actions that will be finished by a certain time in the future.

I/we/you/they	will (= 'll)	have	climbed
he/she/it	will not (= won't)		left

will	I/we/you/they	have	climbed ...?
	he/she/it		left ...?

More about irregular verbs: Appendix p.281

- We **will have climbed** to top of the mountain by noon.
- "Will you be home at 6 p.m.?" "No. I **won't have left** campus by then. I have evening classes."
- "**Will** Flight BK702 **have landed** at 11 o'clock?" "Yes. There's no delay."
- On January 15, Mr. Jones **will have worked** at the company for a year.
- "By the end of your trip, how many countries **will** you **have visited**?" "Six."

We often use the *future perfect* with **by** + *certain time in the future.*

- The leaves **will have changed** color **by the end of October**.
- "**Will** you **have fixed** the printer **by lunchtime**?" "Maybe."

3 We also often use the *future perfect* with **by the time**. In this case, we use *subject + verb* after **by the time**.

- **I'll have learned** a lot **by the time I complete** this course.
- **By the time the meeting starts**, we **won't have prepared** the sales report. Let's put off the meeting.
- **By the time I see** Mila again, she **will have had** her baby.
- Steve **will have retired by the time he turns** 65.

Note that we use the *present simple* after **by the time**. We do not use **will** or **am/is/are going to**.

- **I'll have made** coffee for you **by the time** you **wake** up tomorrow morning.
  (*NOT* by the time you'll wake)
- **By the time** my children **are** in college, tuition fees **will have increased** a lot.
  (*NOT* By the time my children are going to be)

4 There is the following difference in meaning between the *future perfect* and **will** or **am/is/are going to**:

- By January, I **will have moved** to Florida. (The move will be finished before the end of January.)
  In January, I**'m going to move** to Florida. (The move will take place in January.)
- Tom will be very late. By the time he checks in at the hotel, we **will have toured** the city.
  When Tom checks in at the hotel, we**'ll tour** the city. Let's wait for him in the room.

PRACTICE

A. Look at the graphs that predict the future and complete the sentences with the verbs in the box.

drop	~~increase~~	lose	produce	save

1 Gold Price Forecast
($) 2,000 / 1,800 / 1,600
Apr. Aug. Dec.

2 Greg's Savings
($) 1,500 / 1,000 / 500
Sept. 1 Sept. 15 Sept. 30

3 Total Weekly Production
50 100 150 200 250
MON TUE WED THU FRI

4 Country's Population
million 55 / 50 / 45
2030 2040 2050

5 Leo's weight
kg 90 88 85
June 1 June 15 June 30

1. The price of gold *will have increased* ________ $400 by December.
2. Greg ________________ $1,500 by September 30.
3. The company ________________ 250 cars by the end of the week.
4. The population of the country ________________ to 45 million by 2050.
5. Leo ________________ 5 kilograms by the end of this month.

B. Complete the sentences with the words in *italics*. Use the *future perfect* or *present simple*.

1. *(get, find)* It *will have gotten* ________ dark by the time Kyle ________________ the station.
2. *(not finish)* Can we change our date to 8:30? I ________________ work by 8.
3. *(melt, get)* Let's eat the ice cream here. It ________________ by the time we ________________ home.
4. *(reach, walk)* By the time we ________________ the park, we ________________ 5 kilometers.
5. *(not read, return)* I ________________ the entire book by the time I ________________ it to the library.
6. *(wait)* If the package doesn't come by tomorrow, I ________________ for three weeks.

C. Complete the sentences with the verbs in the box. Use the *future perfect* or **will**.

call	clean	live	pass	pay	~~receive~~

1. I sent you a postcard. By next weekend, you *will have received* ________ it.
2. "________________ Mr. Riley ________________ the driving test this time?" "I hope so."
3. "Here's my phone number." "OK. I ________________ you tonight."
4. The kitchen is a mess now, but we ________________ it by the time the guests arrive.
5. Our family ________________ in this house for 10 years next month.
6. I have no money right now. But when I get my paycheck, I ________________ my electricity bill.

D. Look at Sandy's future plans and complete the sentences about them.

SANDY'S FUTURE PLANS
- By this time next year... graduate from high school
- By 2017... complete college
- By 2020... direct several movies
- By the time I'm 45... win a big award

1. By this time next year, *I'll have graduated from high school* .
2. By 2017, ________________ with a degree in film.
3. If I'm lucky, by 2020 ________________.
4. Hopefully, ________________ by the time I'm 45.

SANDY

Answers p.308 / Review Test 4 p.240

LESSON 21 He will call her **when he leaves** the house. **when, if,** etc. for future events

1 They are going on a picnic tomorrow.

He will call her **when he leaves** the house.

"leaves" is the *present simple*, but after **"when,"** it refers to a future event.

I'll call you **when I leave.**

2 We use *subject + present simple* after expressions of time (when, before, etc.) to talk about future events. In this case, we do not use **will** or **am/is/are going to.**

		subject + present simple	
• We will go fishing	**when**	**the weather gets**	nicer. (*NOT* when the weather will get)
• Let's get some popcorn	**before**	**the movie starts.**	(*NOT* before the movie is going to start)
• Will you check my e-mail	**after**	**you come**	back from lunch?
• Please do not stand up	**until**	**the bus stops.**	

	subject + present simple	
• **While**	**we're**	in Germany next month, we are going to visit Berlin.
• **Before**	**you exercise,**	you should stretch.
• **After**	**we eat**	dinner, can you clean the table?
• **Until**	**she feels**	better, Sally will not be attending class.

Note that we add -**(e)s** to the *verbs* when the *subject* is **he/she/it** after **when**, **before**, etc.

- **When Rob saves** enough money, he'll open a restaurant.
- Kara will stop at the bank **before she goes** to the supermarket.

3 We can also use *subject + present simple* after **if** to talk about future events. In this case, we also do not use **will** or **am/is/are going to.**

- **If Bill wins** the contest, we're going to celebrate. (*NOT* If Bill will win)
- I'm having trouble with my homework. Will you help me **if you have** time later? (*NOT* if you're going to have)
- **If I don't find** my car key, Shannon is going to give me a ride home.
- Can you buy some stamps on your way home **if the post office is** still open?

4 We do not use the *future progressive* or *future perfect* after **while, if,** etc. We use the *present progressive* and *present perfect* instead.

- We're going to discuss our vacation plan **while** we**'re having** coffee. (*NOT* while we'll be having)
- **If** Danny **hasn't prepared** the report by 1 o'clock, we'll cancel the meeting. (*NOT* If Danny won't have prepared)

P R A C T I C E

A. **Read the sentences and complete the new ones with when.**

1. Tammy will choose a wedding date. She will send us an invitation.
   → *When Tammy chooses a wedding date* ______, she will send us an invitation.
2. I'm going to move to New York City. I'm going to rent an apartment.
   → ______, I'm going to rent an apartment.
3. Brian will buy a present for his wife. He will get a bonus next month.
   → Brian will buy a present for his wife ______.
4. I'll order pizza. Lisa and Jake will feel hungry.
   → I'll order pizza ______.
5. Mr. Harris is going to retire next year. He's going to write a book.
   → ______, he's going to write a book.

B. **Complete the sentences with the words in *italics*. Use the *present simple* or will.**

1. *(cook, make)* Steve *will cook* ______ the steak while I ______ the salad.
2. *(not pay, charge)* If we ______ our bill on time, the credit card company ______ a fee.
3. *(travel, study)* Before I ______ to China, I ______ Chinese.
4. *(be, not come)* I ______ sad if Natalie ______ to my party.
5. *(buy, give)* If my brother ______ a new laptop, he ______ me his old one.
6. *(not start, arrive)* We ______ the seminar until you ______.
7. *(become, receive)* ______ Tara ______ a professor after she ______ her degree?

C. **Find and change any mistakes in each sentence. Put ✓ if the sentence is correct.**

1. I'll set the alarm before I will sleep. I have to wake up early. *will sleep → sleep*
2. Will you excuse me while I go to the restroom? ______
3. Tom will lend me his camera next week if he won't be using it. ______
4. If you haven't found a good hairdresser, I'll take you to mine. ______
5. Gina will watch the kids until their mother will return home. ______
6. When you will have completed the application, give it to me. ______

D. **Complete the conversation with the words in *italics*. Use the *present simple* or will.**

MP3

RACHEL: I'm so excited about our trip tomorrow.
1. *Will* ______ you *call* ______ me when you ______ the house? *(call, leave)*

CHRIS: Sure! But I'll have to go to the mechanic first.
2. After he ______ my car, I ______ you up. *(fix, pick)*

RACHEL: Great. By the way, we'll need some snacks for our trip.
3. ______ you ______ at the grocery store before you ______ to the repair shop? *(stop, go)*

CHRIS: I don't think I'll have enough time to do that.
4. If you ______ time today, ______ you ______ the shopping? *(have, do)*

RACHEL: OK. But I'll need to borrow my mom's car.
5. I ______ her when she ______ home. *(ask, come)*

RACHEL

CHRIS

Future, Future Progressive, and Future Perfect

LESSON 21

Answers p.308 / Review Test 4 p.240

LESSON

22 Lisa can walk. **can** (ability, possibility)

MP3

1 Justin has two cousins.

Lisa **can walk**.

Denny **can't walk**.

"can walk" expresses that Lisa has the ability to walk.
"can't walk" expresses that Denny doesn't have the ability to walk.

2 We use **can** to say that someone has the ability to do something or that something is possible.

I/we/you/they	can	ride
he/she/it	cannot (= can't)	move

can	I/we/you/they	ride ...?
	he/she/it	move ...?

- My son **can ride** a bicycle now. He really enjoys it.
- Carla broke her arm. She **can't move** it at the moment.
- "**Can** penguins **fly**?" "No, but they **can swim** very well."

We can also use **am/is/are able to** instead of **can**. In everyday conversation, we use **can** more often.

- **I'm able to visit** my grandparents often because I live near them. (= can visit)
- Many Americans **aren't able to use** chopsticks, but some can. (= can't use)

3 We use **could** to talk about the past. We can also use **was/were able to** instead of **could**.

- I **could read** some words when I was two years old.
  OR I **was able to read** some words when I was two years old.
- In Miami, we **could jog** on the beach every day.
  OR In Miami, we **were able to jog** on the beach every day.

But we cannot use **could** to talk about what someone actually did in a particular situation. In this case, we use **was/were able to**.

- There were lots of cars on the road, but Matt **was able to get** to the movies on time. (*NOT* could get)
- We **were able to clean** our messy house before the guests arrived. (*NOT* could clean)

There is no difference in meaning between **couldn't** and **wasn't/weren't able to**.

- We **couldn't go** to the party. *OR* We **weren't able to go** to the party.
- Brent **couldn't dance** well in the past. *OR* Brent **wasn't able to dance** well in the past.

4 We do not use **can** after **will**/**have**/etc. We use **be able to** instead as in the following ways:

will/**might**/**should**/etc. + **be able to**

- I **won't be able to meet** you this Saturday. I have an appointment. (*NOT* won't can meet)
- Laura **might be able to join** our book club. She'll let us know soon.

have/**has been able to**

- Peter **has been able to work** faster since he got a new laptop. (*NOT* has can work)
- My friend is in town this week, so we'**ve been able to spend** some time together.

PRACTICE

A. Complete the conversations with **can** and the verbs in the box. Write negative sentences if necessary.

do	~~drive~~	eat	pay	play	reach

1. A: I need to go to the supermarket.
   B: I *can drive* ______ you there. I'll get my key.
2. A: I ______ that book. It's too high.
   B: Here, let me try.
3. A: ______ your dog ______ any tricks?
   B: Yes. I'll show you.
4. A: Steve ______ the violin very well.
   B: I know. He's really good at it.
5. A: ______ we ______ with a credit card?
   B: I'm sorry, but we only accept cash.
6. A: Do you want some more pasta?
   B: No. I ______ anymore. I'm full.

B. Complete the sentences with **can/could** and the words in *italics*. Write negative sentences if necessary.

1. *(we, buy)* There's a café across the street. *We can buy* ______ some coffee there.
2. *(I, type)* In college, ______ 80 words in one minute, but I can't now.
3. *(they, get)* Mike and Ann bought the tickets too late, so ______ good seats.
4. *(I, run)* "Can we stop for a break? ______ anymore." "Sure. Let's sit here."
5. *(he, throw)* That pitcher has been training hard. Now ______ a baseball much faster.
6. *(Josh, afford)* ______ a house at the moment. He doesn't have enough money.
7. *(you, read)* "I have to wear my glasses when I read now."
   "I know. ______ without them in the old days."
8. *(Kelly, ski)* ______ well before she took the lessons last year. But now she's quite good.

C. Write **could/couldn't** or **was/wasn't able to**.

1. Lucas *could* OR *was able to* ______ make bread at home after he took a baking class.
2. Although no one helped her, Mia ______ finish the project without any problem.
3. We ______ complete the puzzle because some pieces were missing.
4. Our best player didn't play, but we ______ win the game anyway.
5. I ______ remove the lid from the jar. It was too tight.
6. Jeff was very strong when he was young. He ______ lift 150 kilos.

D. Complete the sentences with **can / be able to** and the verbs in *italics*. Write negative sentences if necessary.

Clara's Diary

August 01, 2019

I enjoy learning new languages. Right now, I'm taking a French class.

1. *(speak)* At first, I *couldn't* OR *wasn't able to speak* ______ French very well.
2. *(speak)* But now I ______ it much better.
3. *(learn)* The teacher always explains everything clearly, so I have ______ it quickly.

This summer, I'm going to take a Japanese class.

Judy recently introduced me to Japanese music.

4. *(understand)* Although I ______ the words, the music was beautiful.
5. *(sing)* Maybe I'll ______ these songs in Japanese after taking the class.

Modal Verbs

LESSON 22

Grammar Gateway Intermediate

Answers **p.308** / Review Test 5 **p.242**

LESSON 23

It could belong to James. could (possibility)

MP3

1 She found a cell phone.

It **could belong** to him.

It **couldn't belong** to him.

"could belong" expresses that it is possible that the phone belongs to him. **"couldn't belong"** expresses that it is certainly not possible that the phone belongs to him.

2 **could** + **stop**/**be**/etc.

We use **could** to say that something is possible now or in the future. In this case, **could** does not talk about the past.

- I think the rain **could stop** soon. The sky looks brighter.
- "Where's Emma?" "She **could be** in her room."
- I probably won't win the lottery, but it **could happen**!

3 **couldn't** + **be**/**jump**/etc.

We use **couldn't** to say that something is certainly not possible.

- "Is that Pete over there?" "It **couldn't be** Pete. He went to Tokyo this morning."
- My dog **couldn't** possibly **jump** over the fence. It is 3 meters tall.
- People **couldn't live** on Mars because there's no oxygen.

In this case, we can also use **can't** instead of **couldn't**.

- "Is that a real diamond ring?" "It **can't be**. It's only $25." (= couldn't be)
- It's only 4 o'clock. The store **can't close** so early. (= couldn't close)

4 **could have** + **gone**/**stayed**/etc. *(past participle)*

We use **could have** to say that something was possible in the past.

- "Mr. Rogers wasn't in his office." "He **could have gone** out to meet a customer."

We can also use **could have** to say that something was possible but did not happen.

- We **could have stayed** at the beach longer, but we came back. (It was possible that we stayed longer, but we didn't.)
- "Sorry I'm late." "You **could have called**. We were waiting for you." (It was possible that you called, but you didn't.)

5 **couldn't have** + **moved**/**known**/etc. *(past participle)*

We use **couldn't have** to say that something was certainly not possible in the past.

- Jenny **couldn't have moved** this desk by herself. It's too heavy.
- Nobody told my brother about the surprise party. He **couldn't have known** about it.

In this case, we can also use **can't have** instead of **couldn't have**.

- Greg and Jay **can't have drunk** all of the wine. There were four bottles! (= couldn't have drunk)

P R A C T I C E

A. Complete the sentences with **could/couldn't** and the verbs in the box.

~~be~~	be	have	join	see	tell

1. We should check the chicken in the oven. It *could be* ready.
2. You ______________ all of Rome in two days. There are so many places to visit.
3. "That store doesn't sell cranberry juice." "The one across the street ______________ some."
4. "How do we get to the bank?" "Let's ask that man. He ______________ us."
5. Charles ______________ the ski club. He hates going outside in the winter.
6. "Why isn't Angela in class today?" "I'm not sure. She ______________ sick."

B. Complete the sentences with **couldn't / couldn't have** and the verbs in *italics*.

1. *(be)* That *couldn't be* Nate's glove. His is black, but that one is brown.
2. *(fly)* The storm is too strong right now. Planes ______________ in this weather.
3. *(do)* Katie finished all of her work in just one day. She ______________ it alone.
4. *(know)* Your wife ______________ me. We've never met before.
5. *(write)* Mike ______________ this letter. His handwriting is completely different.
6. *(get)* Jack ______________ his new shoes there. That store was closed yesterday.
7. *(eat)* Let's order a medium pizza. We ______________ a large one by ourselves.
8. *(arrive)* My parents ______________ home already. They left here 10 minutes ago.

C. Rewrite the sentences with **could have + past participle**.

1. I didn't take a train to Geneva even though there was one.
   → *I could have taken a train to Geneva*.
2. We didn't visit the Great Wall even though we were in China.
   → ______________.
3. Bill and Helen didn't sell their old car even though a few people wanted to buy it.
   → ______________.
4. You didn't go shopping with me although you had free time.
   → ______________.

D. Complete the conversation with **could /could have** and the verbs in *italics*. Write negative sentences if necessary.

MP3

LINDA

LINDA: I found your phone in the garage, honey.
JAMES: 1. It *couldn't be* mine. *(be)* Mine is here.
LINDA: Then whose is it?
JAMES: Isn't it Chris's?
2. He ______________ it in the garage yesterday. *(drop)*
LINDA: 3. He ______________ that. *(do)*
He went camping yesterday and called us when he got there.
JAMES: Oh, that's right.
LINDA: 4. It ______________ to Amy. *(belong)*
She always loses her things.
JAMES: I think you're right.

JAMES

Answers p.308 / Review Test 5 p.242

LESSON 24 He might eat at the restaurant. might, may (possibility)

1 He **might eat** at the restaurant.

He **might not eat** at the restaurant.

"might eat" expresses that it is possible that he will eat at the restaurant.
"might not eat" expresses that it is possible that he will not eat at the restaurant.

2 We use **might** or **may** to say that something is possible now or in the future. In everyday conversation, we use **might** more often.

I/we/you/they	might	(not)	be
he/she/it	may		sell

- The seminar **might be** interesting. *OR* The seminar **may be** interesting.
- I **might not sell** my motorcycle. *OR* I **may not sell** my motorcycle. I'm still thinking about it.

3 **might/may** and **could** have similar meaning.

- "There's someone at the door." "It **might/may be** Ben." *OR* "It **could be** Ben."

But there is the following difference in meaning between **might/may not** and **couldn't**:

might/may not (It is not likely, but it is still possible.)	• Matthew doesn't have much experience, so he **might not get** that job. (It's not likely that Matthew gets the job, but it's still possible that he'll.)
couldn't (It is certainly not possible.)	• Matthew has no experience at all. He **couldn't** possibly **get** that job. (It's certainly not possible that Matthew gets the job.)

4 We use **might/may have** to say that something was possible in the past.

might/may have + **done**/**gone**/etc. *(past participle)*

- "Who turned off the heater?" "It wasn't me. Alex **might/may have done** it."
- I haven't seen my neighbors for a few days. They **might/may have gone** on a vacation.

might/may not have + **locked**/**been**/etc.

- I **might/may not have locked** the door. I'll go back and check.
- Jason **might/may not have been** to the exhibit yet. Let's ask him to go with us.

5 We can also use **could have** instead of **might/may have.** In everyday conversation, we use **might/may have** more often.

- The exam wasn't hard, but I **could have made** a few mistakes. (= might/may have made)

But there is the following difference in meaning between **couldn't have** and **might/may not have.**

- The man **couldn't have stolen** the car. He was in another city.
(It was certainly not possible that he stole it.)
The man **might/may not have stolen** the car. We don't really know.
(It was not likely that the man stole the car, but it's still possible that he did.)

P R A C T I C E

A. Read the conversations and write sentences with **might**. Write negative sentences if necessary.

1 Are you going to stay home tonight? / Possibly.	4 Will the package arrive today? / Perhaps.
2 Will you help Jo with her presentation? / I don't know if I can.	5 Will you go to the festival next week? / Maybe not.
3 Are you going to buy that shirt? / I'm not sure.	6 Are we going to have dinner with Tom? / Possibly. I'll ask him.

1. *He might stay home tonight*.
2. ______.
3. ______.
4. ______.
5. ______.
6. ______.

B. Complete the conversations with **might / might have** and the verbs in the box. Write negative sentences if necessary.

attend	~~be~~	hear	know	leave	miss	order	wear

1. A: I don't want to go bowling.
   B: Why not? It *might be* fun.
2. A: Where do we keep the files?
   B: Ask Ross. He ______ where they are.
3. A: I ______ a coat tonight.
   B: But you should. It's going to get cold later.
4. A: I called Mary's name, but she ignored me.
   B: Well, she ______ you.
5. A: Where did Edward get his new hat?
   B: I'm not sure. He ______ it online.
6. A: I ______ the meeting. I have a lot of work.
   B: Oh. John and I probably aren't going either.
7. A: We ______ the bus.
   B: I guess so. We got here too late.
8. A: I wanted to say goodbye to Tom, but I couldn't.
   B: He ______ yet. Let's call him.

C. Complete the sentences with **might not / couldn't** and the verbs in *italics*. Use **have + past participle** if necessary.

1. *(rain)* The ground is so dry. It *couldn't have rained* last night.
2. *(feel)* "Why did Sara leave the concert early?" "She didn't tell me. She ______ well."
3. *(be)* "That man looks like Jim." "Yes, but it ______ him. Jim is much taller."
4. *(have)* "Tom ______ a pet. He is scared of animals." "Then, whose cat is that in his yard?"
5. *(provide)* Maybe we should take some shampoo for our trip. The hotel ______ it.
6. *(begin)* The show ______ already. It starts at 7:30, but it's only 7:15 now.
7. *(work)* You can use the printer, but it ______. I haven't used it in months.
8. *(wake)* Jessie ______ up yet. She sometimes sleeps late on Sunday mornings.

Answers **p.308** / Review Test 5 **p.242**

LESSON 25 He must be scared. must (certainty)

1 He **must be** scared.

He **must not want** to enter.

"must be" expresses that it is certainly true that he is scared.
"must not want" expresses that it is certainly true that he doesn't want to enter.

2 We use **must** to say that something is certainly true.

I/we/you/they he/she/it	must	(not)	listen use

- Terry **must listen** to a lot of music. His apartment is full of CDs.
- Your laptop still looks new. You **must not use** it much.
- The children **must be** excited about their trip. They've been talking about it all morning.

3 We use **must have** to say that something was certainly true in the past.

must have + **slipped/gotten**/etc. *(past participle)*

- Mark is covered in mud! He **must have slipped**.
- "Wendy is still not here." "She **must have gotten** lost. She doesn't know this area very well."

must not have + **washed/paid**/etc.

- This shirt is dirty. I **must not have washed** it.
- My roommate **must not have paid** the electricity bill. The lights won't turn on.

4 There are the following differences in meaning between **must** and **might/could**:

must (It is certainly true.)	• Steve **must be** very busy. He has worked late a lot this week. (It's certainly true that Steve is busy.)
might, could (It is likely, but it is not certain.)	• "Steve isn't answering his phone." "Well, he **might be** busy." *OR* "Well, he **could be** busy." (It's likely that Steve is busy, but it's not certain that he's.)

There are the following differences in meaning between **must not, might not**, and **couldn't**:

must not (It is certainly not true.)	• Andrea always drives her dad's car. She **must not own** one. (It's certainly not true that Andrea owns a car.)
might not (It is not likely, but it is still possible.)	• Andrea **might not own** a car now. She said she wanted to sell it. (It's not likely that Andrea owns a car, but it's still possible that she owns one.)
couldn't (It is certainly not possible.)	• Andrea **couldn't own** a car. She can't drive. (It's certainly not possible that Andrea owns a car.)

P R A C T I C E

A. Complete the conversations with **must** and the verbs in the box. Write negative sentences if necessary.

~~be~~	be	cook	have	know	play

1. It's midnight, but I think I'll keep reading. — You *must not be* __________ sleepy.
2. Peter's fridge is usually empty. — He __________ at home often.
3. Tom said hello to Jane. — They __________ each other.
4. I have won several piano competitions. — You __________ the piano well.
5. Only a few people are watching that movie. — It __________ very good.
6. Julia is coughing a lot. — She __________ a cold.

B. Complete the sentences with **must / must have** and the verbs in *italics*.

1. *(be)* Ben seems very nervous today. He *must be* __________ worried about something.
2. *(get)* Joanna __________ a haircut. Her hair looks shorter today.
3. *(enjoy)* "I've worked for the same company for 20 years." "You __________ your job."
4. *(exercise)* Karen __________ a lot these days. She's in great shape.
5. *(come)* "There's a package at the door." "Oh, it __________ while we were out."
6. *(drink)* Somebody __________ all of the beer. There's none in the kitchen.

C. Write sentences with **must / must have** and the words in the box. Write negative sentences if necessary.

be married	~~be twins~~	learn Italian there	like chicken	ride it to school	sleep enough

1. Don and Dan look exactly alike. *They must be twins* __________.
2. Andrea hasn't eaten any of her food. __________.
3. Eric seems tired. __________.
4. Nancy and Robert went to college in Rome. __________.
5. Tina doesn't wear a wedding ring. __________.
6. Jim's bicycle isn't in the garage. __________.

D. Jenny and Lucas are watching a movie. Write **must/might** or **must not / might not**.

JENNY: Who stole Mrs. Parker's necklace?
LUCAS: I'm not sure. 1. It *might* __________ have been Ms. Johnson. I think she wanted the necklace.
JENNY: True. 2. But she was out of town, so it __________ have been her.
LUCAS: You're right. So who's left?
JENNY: 3. Well, Jack __________ have stolen it. What do you think?
LUCAS: Hmm. Maybe you're right, but I'm not sure... 4. Jack __________ have stolen it because he didn't seem very interested.
JENNY: Wait a minute. The cook was home alone! 5. He __________ have taken it!
LUCAS: You're right! Nobody knew he was home. 6. Mr. and Mrs. Parker __________ have thought it was him!

Modal Verbs

LESSON 25

Grammar Gateway Intermediate

Answers p.309 / Review Test 5 p.242

LESSON 26

She **must** follow the rules. **must** and **have to** (necessity)

1 She **must follow** the rules.

She **must not feed** the animals.

ZOO RULES
YOU MUST NOT FEED THE ANIMALS.
ZOO
ZOO STAFF
You must follow the rules.

"must follow" expresses that it is necessary to follow the rules.
"must not feed" expresses that it is wrong to feed the animals.

2 **must** + **stop**/**pay**/etc.

We use **must** to say that something is necessary. We often use **must** to talk about rules and regulations.

- Cars **must stop** at the red traffic light.
- I **must pay** rent at the end of every month.

must not + **make**/**be**/etc.

We use **must not** to say that it is wrong to do something.

- Please be quiet. You **must not make** noise in the library.
- Students **must not be** late to the exam. They cannot come in after 10 a.m.

3 We can also use **have/has to** to say that something is necessary. In everyday conversation, we use **have/has to** more often than **must**.

I/we/you/they	**have to**
he/she/it	**has to**

I/we/you/they	**don't**	have to
he/she/it	**doesn't**	

do	I/we/you/they	have to ...?
does	he/she/it	

- I don't have any clean clothes. I **have to do** my laundry soon.
- Your dog **doesn't have to wait** outside. Dogs are welcome in this store.
- "**Do** I **have to apply** for the scholarship by tomorrow?" "No. The deadline is next Friday."

But there is the following difference in meaning between **don't/doesn't have to** and **must not**. We use **don't/doesn't have to** to say that something is not necessary.

- You **don't have to call** Mr. Watson again. I already did. (Calling Mr. Watson is not necessary.)
  You **must not call** Mr. Watson. He's in an important meeting right now. (It's wrong to call Mr. Watson.)

4 Note that we use **had to** to talk about the past. We do not use **must**.

- I **had to finish** my homework first, so I arrived at the party late yesterday.
- Ms. Morgan isn't in her office. She **had to leave** for a doctor's appointment.

didn't have to . . . *(negative)*

- I **didn't have to worry** about the test. It was easy.

did + *subject* + **have to . . .?** *(questions)*

- "We went to the Chinese restaurant last week." "**Did** you **have to make** a reservation?"

5 We do not use **must** after **will**/**might**/etc. We use **have to** instead.

- The bank isn't open yet. We'**ll have to come** back later. (*NOT* will must come)
- I **might have to borrow** your tent to go camping. I don't own one. (*NOT* might must borrow)

PRACTICE

A. Look at the pictures and complete the sentences with **must** and the verbs in the box. Write negative sentences if necessary.

~~bring~~	drive	show	take	touch	wear

Rules for Museum Visitors

1. You *must not bring* ______ in food or beverages.
2. You ______ the artwork.

Construction Site Rules

3. You ______ a safety helmet.

Rules for Airline Passengers

4. You ______ your passport.

ROAD SIGNS

SPEED LIMIT 50

5. You ______ over 50 miles per hour.
6. You ______ a different route.

B. Complete the sentences with **have/has to** and the words in *italics*. Write negative sentences if necessary.

1. *(we, be)* "Our plane leaves at 8:30." " *We have to be* ______ at the airport by 7 o'clock, then."
2. *(She, take)* Megan is better now. ______ her medicine anymore.
3. *(we, work)* " ______ late again tonight?" "I'm afraid so."
4. *(the mayor, give)* " ______ a speech at the ceremony?" "Yes. It's a tradition."
5. *(you, walk)* ______ to the grocery store. I'll give you a ride.
6. *(he, pass)* Tim is studying hard. ______ his science exam to graduate.

C. Complete the sentences with **must not / don't have to** and the verbs in *italics*.

***Hadley Park** - General Information*

1. *(smoke)* You *must not smoke* ______ within the park. It's a no-smoking area.
2. *(bring)* You can rent tennis rackets. You ______ yours.
3. *(fish)* You ______ in the pond. It is not allowed.
4. *(carry)* There's a locker room. You ______ heavy bags around.
5. *(pay)* You ______ a parking fee. Parking is free.
6. *(feed)* You ______ bread to the ducks. It's bad for them.

D. Complete the sentences with **must / have to** and the verbs in the box. Write negative sentences if necessary.

apologize	hire	move	revise	sleep	~~stay~~	teach	tell

1. Stacey *had to stay* ______ home last night because her baby was sick.
2. Professor Franklin is absent. Professor Taylor might ______ our class today.
3. I ______ to Roy after the fight. He said he was sorry first.
4. "Tara left her car keys here." "You ______ her. She could be looking for them."
5. Jeff ______ his seat closer to the front. He couldn't see very well.
6. " ______ you ______ your article?" "Yes. It still had some errors."
7. Sara and Eric had an extra bedroom, so I ______ on the sofa.
8. One of our employees suddenly quit, so now we ______ a new one.

Answers **p.309** / Review Test 5 **p.242**

LESSON 27

He should exercise. should (advice, suggestions)

MP3

1

He **should exercise**.

He **shouldn't eat** so much.

"should exercise" expresses that it is a good idea to exercise.
"shouldn't eat" expresses that it is not a good idea to eat so much.

2

We use **should** to give advice or to suggest that something is a good idea.

I/we/you/they he/she/it	should	(not)	sleep drive

- "I sleep only three hours every night." "You **should sleep** more!"
- It's snowing hard. I **shouldn't drive** tonight.
- You **should say** "thank you" when people help you.
- "I don't think Kim **should drink** so much coffee." "I agree."
- Tommy, you **should be** nice to your brother. You **shouldn't fight** with him.

We can also use **ought to** instead of **should**. In everyday conversation, we use **should** more often.

- You **ought to stop** smoking. It's bad for you. (= should stop)

3

should I/we . . .?

We use **should I/we . . .?** to ask for advice or suggestions.

- "**Should I bring** anything to the party?" "Maybe some wine."
- We've been practicing our dance for two hours. **Should we take** a break?
- "Where **should I put** the Christmas tree?" "In front of the window."

4

We use **should have** to show regrets about past actions.

should have + **been/taken**/etc. *(past participle)*

- I told Julia's secret to Tina by accident. I **should have been** more careful. (= I wasn't careful, and I regret it.)
- We **should have taken** the subway. The traffic is horrible today.

shouldn't have + **lent/moved**/etc.

- Jim lost my camera. I **shouldn't have lent** it to him. (= I lent my camera to him, and I regret it.)
- "Do you like your new apartment?" "Not really. I **shouldn't have moved**."

5

There is the following difference in meaning between **must** / **have to** and **should**:

- All employees **must attend** the seminar. It's required. (Attending the seminar is necessary.)
  We **should attend** the seminar. It'll be interesting. (Attending the seminar is a good idea, but it's not necessary.)
- You **have to wear** a uniform to school. It's a rule.
  You **should wear** that blue tie. It looks nice on you.

PRACTICE

A. Complete the conversations with **should** and the verbs in the box. Write negative sentences if necessary.

give	leave	listen	open	~~visit~~	worry

1. I haven't seen Derek for so long. — I think you *should visit* ________ him.
2. I'm nervous about my interview. — You ________. You'll do fine.
3. Let's get Ellen some roses! — We ________ her flowers. She's allergic.
4. Jason is always giving me advice. — He's smart. I think you ________ to him.
5. Mr. Brown isn't answering his phone. — We ________ him a message.
6. What's in this box? Can I see? — It's Tom's. You ________ it.

B. Complete the sentences with **should I . . .?** and the verbs in the box.

~~cut~~	hang	meet	order	plan	throw

1. "*Should I cut* ________ my hair?" "Yes. I think you will look great with short hair."
2. "When ________ you at the café?" "How about in an hour?"
3. I bought a new painting to put on our wall. Where ________ it?
4. "I'm hungry." "Oh, ________ some food?"
5. "________ away these old receipts?" "Sure. You don't need them."
6. Don and Lisa are coming to see me. What activities ________ for their visit?

Modal Verbs

LESSON 27

C. Complete the sentences with **should have** and the words in *italics*. Write negative sentences if necessary.

1. *(I, prepare more)* I did badly on my presentation. *I should have prepared more* ________.
2. *(Jack, play)* ________ the music so loudly. The neighbors complained.
3. *(I, ask you first)* "Did you use my bike this morning?" "Yes. Sorry. ________."
4. *(we, help her)* We didn't help Jill clean the house, so she's mad at us. ________.
5. *(she, sell it)* "Tracy sold her guitar. She regrets it." "That's too bad. ________."
6. *(you, scare your little sister)* Tony, ________. She was crying for hours.
7. *(you, come with us)* ________. The tour was a lot of fun.

D. Complete the conversation with **should / should have** and the verbs in *italics*. Write negative sentences if necessary.

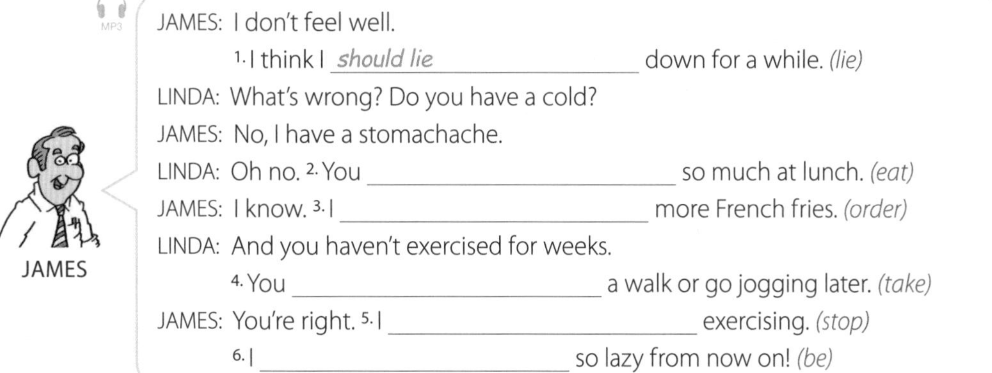

MP3

JAMES: I don't feel well.
1. I think I *should lie* ________ down for a while. *(lie)*
LINDA: What's wrong? Do you have a cold?
JAMES: No, I have a stomachache.
LINDA: Oh no. 2. You ________ so much at lunch. *(eat)*
JAMES: I know. 3. I ________ more French fries. *(order)*
LINDA: And you haven't exercised for weeks.
4. You ________ a walk or go jogging later. *(take)*
JAMES: You're right. 5. I ________ exercising. *(stop)*
6. I ________ so lazy from now on! *(be)*

JAMES

LINDA

Grammar Gateway Intermediate

Answers p.309 / Review Test 5 p.242

LESSON 28 He had better be careful. had better (strong advice)

1 Chris might fall off the ladder.

He **had better be** careful.

"had better be" expresses a strong advice that Chris needs to be careful.

2 We use **had better** to give strong advice or to strongly suggest that someone needs to do something. In everyday conversation, we use the short forms, **we'd better**, **you'd better**, more often.

I/we/you/they he/she/it	had better (= 'd better)	hurry start

- "The train will arrive soon." "We**'d better hurry**."
- You**'d better start** on that report now. You only have a few days before the deadline.
- I**'d better change** my shirt. I dropped ketchup on it.
- "Smoke is coming out of the photocopier." "You**'d better call** the technician."

3 We use **had better not** to give strong advice or to strongly suggest that it is wrong to do something.

I/we/you/they he/she/it	had better (= 'd better)	not	stay touch

- I have to wake up early tomorrow, so I**'d better not stay** up late.
- The wall has just been painted. You**'d better not touch** it.
- We**'d better not park** here. That sign says "No Parking."
- Frank **had better not jump** on the bed. He might damage it.

Note that **had not better** is incorrect.

- You**'d better not sit** there. That's Carla's seat. (*NOT* You'd not better sit)
- I promised Dave that I will write to him. I**'d better not forget**. (*NOT* I'd not better forget)

4 We can also use **should** to give advice. But there is the following difference in meaning between **had better** and **should**:

We use **had better** to warn that there will be bad results if someone does not do something.

- Tickets will be sold out soon. You**'d better buy** some today.
  (There'll be no tickets if you don't buy some today.)
- "We**'d better take** the pie out of the oven now."
  "You're right! It might burn."
  (The pie will burn if we don't take it out now.)
- I**'d better follow** you, or I might get lost.

We use **should** to suggest that it is a good idea to do something, but it is not necessary.

- You **should buy** those tickets. The seats are closer to the stage.
  (Buying those tickets is a good idea, but it's not necessary.)
- "We **should take** a pie to the party tonight."
  "Good idea."
  (Taking a pie to the party is a good idea, but it's not necessary.)
- Mr. Park **should join** our golf club. He enjoys golf.

PRACTICE

A. Look at the pictures and complete the sentences with **'d better** and the words in the box.

close the window	keep quiet here	slow down
stay away	wash your hands	~~wear a helmet~~

1. You *'d better wear a helmet* OR *had better wear a helmet*.

2. You ______________________ .

3. We ______________________ .

4. I ______________________ .

5. We ______________________ .

6. You ______________________ .

B. Complete the sentences with **'d better** and the verbs in the box. Write negative sentences if necessary.

arrive	forget	play	quit	register	~~rest~~	sweep	turn

1. "My feet hurt. We've been hiking all morning." "We *'d better rest* OR *had better rest* under this tree."
2. "The floor in your room is very dirty." "Oh, you're right. I ______________________ it."
3. You ______________________ with that knife, Sally. It's not a toy and you could get hurt.
4. Ms. Miller's class is almost full. If students want to take her class, they ______________________ now.
5. "Max got a warning about coming to work late." "Well, he ______________________ late anymore."
6. I ______________________ to pay the credit card bill or I'll get another late fee.
7. You ______________________ off the music. I'm taking an important phone call.
8. "I heard Patrick may stop playing volleyball." "He ______________________ the team! We need him!"

C. Give advice with **'d better** for each situation.

1. John is crossing a busy intersection. You think he should watch out.
   YOU: *You'd better watch out* OR *You had better watch out*.
2. There is a bad storm and you and Amanda are going outside. You think you and Amanda shouldn't.
   YOU: ____ .
3. The children might break the vase. You think you and your wife should put the vase on the top shelf.
   YOU: ____ .
4. Your employees are working very slowly. You think they shouldn't miss the deadline.
   YOU: ____ .
5. Joe wants to take a vacation next month. You think he shouldn't spend a lot of money this month.
   YOU: ____ .

Answers p.309 / Review Test 5 p.242

LESSON 29

Is it raining outside? *Questions (1)*

MP3

1 We use **be/have/can/do**/etc. in questions in the following ways:

what/how/etc.	*be/have/can/etc.*	*subject*	
	Is	it	raining outside?
"What	has	Tim	been doing lately?" "Mostly looking for a new job."
	Can	you	call me later? I'm busy at the moment.
"How	did	Jen	get home?" "She took a taxi."

2 We can use *nouns* and *adjectives/adverbs* after the following *question words* (what, how, etc.):

what/which/whose + *noun* (time, tie, etc.)

what/which/whose	*noun*	
"What	time	is it right now?" "It's 10:45."
"Which	tie	should I wear?" "That red one."
"Whose	laptop	did you borrow?" "Martin's."
"What	year	was your sister born?" "1995."

how + *adjective/adverb* (tall, fast, etc.)

how	*adjective/adverb*	
"How	tall	is Tokyo Tower?" "It's over 2,000 feet."
"How	fast	can you type?" "Around 40 words a minute."
"How	long	have you been teaching art?" "For five years."

3 We can use **about/with**/etc. *(prepositions)* at the end of questions with *question words*.

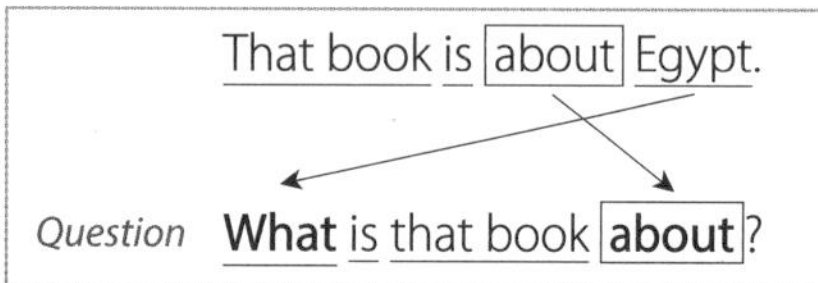

That book is about Egypt.
Question What is that book about?

- "**Who** did you go to the beach **with**?" "I went alone."
- "**Where** are you walking **to**?" "The grocery store."
- "Ann has been standing there for a while. **Who** is she waiting **for**?" "Her boyfriend."
- "I need a hobby." "Well, **what** kinds of things are you interested **in**?"

4 What . . . for?

We use **What . . . for?** to ask about the purpose of someone's action or the purpose of something.

- "Ouch! **What** did you hit me **for**?" "Sorry. It was an accident!"
- "**What**'s this button **for**?" "It turns on the printer."

What . . . like?

We use **What . . . like?** to ask for a description of someone or something.

- "**What** are your bosses **like**?" "They are usually friendly."
- "I went to the new restaurant last night." "Really? **What** is it **like**?"

PRACTICE

A. Put the words in *italics* in the correct order.

1. *(David / how / preparing / is)* How is David preparing ______ for his interview?
2. *(you / will / when / return home)* ______?
3. *(has / sent / Jenny / the documents)* ______ yet?
4. *(have / your neighbor / does)* ______ a garden?
5. *(your friends / are / graduating)* ______ tomorrow?
6. *(have / traveled / where / you)* ______ in Canada?
7. *(visit / Sarah / who / did)* ______ last weekend?

B. Complete the questions with **what/whose/how** and the words in the box.

car	idea	~~instrument~~	languages	much	often

1. "What instrument ______ do you play?" "I play the piano."
2. This is a brilliant suggestion! ______ was it?
3. "______ can you speak?" "English and Korean."
4. "______ do you see your parents?" "A few times a year."
5. We have a lot of luggage. ______ has the biggest trunk?
6. "An economy ticket is $300." "Then ______ is a business class ticket?"

C. Look at the pictures and complete the questions with **what** and the words in the box. Use the *present progressive*.

apologize for	argue about	hide from	laugh at	reach for	~~think about~~

1. What are you thinking about ?
2. ______ ?
3. ______ ?
I'm sorry.
4. ______ ?
5. ______ ?
6. ______ ?

D. Complete the questions with **What . . . for/like?** and the words in *italics*. Use the *present simple* or *past simple*.

1. *(these balloons, be)* What are these balloons for ______? — They're for my nephew's visit.
2. *(your roommate, be)* ______? — He's very nice. And he's funny.
3. *(your first date, be)* ______? — It was really boring.
4. *(the cake, be)* ______? — It was my mom's birthday.
5. *(this big bowl, be)* ______? — It's for fruit.

Answers p.309 / Review Test 6 p.244

LESSON 30 Who did Rachel invite? *Questions (2) Question words* **who/what/which**

MP3

1 Rachel invited someone.
object

Who did Rachel invite?

"Who" is the *object* in the question.

Someone invited Chris.
subject

Who invited Chris?

"Who" is the *subject* in the question.

2 We can use **who/what/which** as the *object* in questions.

- "**Who is Lucas helping**?" "An old lady."
  (**Who** is the object of **is helping**.)
- "**What did you buy** at the mall?" "A wallet."
  (**What** is the object of **buy**.)
- "**Which does Jim prefer**, steak or pasta?"
  "He prefers steak."
- "**Who can we ask** about gardening?"
  "Let's ask Nina. She knows a lot."
- "**What did Emily bring** to class?"
  "It's a violin. She's going to play it for us."

In this case, we use **do/does/did** in questions.

- "**Who did you call** last night?" "I called Mike."
- "**What do you want** for breakfast?"
  "How about an omelet?"

We can use **who/what/which** as the *subject* in questions.

- "**Who is helping** the old lady?" "Lucas."
  (**Who** is the subject of **is helping**.)
- "**What's** in that box?" "It's a new wallet."
  (**What** is the subject of **is**.)
- "I've eaten the steak and the pasta here."
  "**Which is** better?"
- "**Who has taught** you to dance?"
  "My sister has. She's a dance teacher."
- "**What caused** the accident?"
  "A deer jumped in front of the car."

In this case, we do not use **do/does/did** in questions.

- "**Who called** you last night?" "Richard did."
- "**Which travels** faster? Sound or light?"
  "Light."

3 We can also use **whom** instead of **who** as the *object* in questions. In everyday conversation, we use **who** more often.

- **Who** did you meet yesterday? *OR* **Whom** did you meet yesterday?
- "**Who** is Tony marrying?" *OR* "**Whom** is Tony marrying?" "I don't know."

4 We can also use *question word + noun* as the *object* or *subject* in questions.

- **What sports do you play**?
  (**What sports** is the object of **play**.)
- **Which camera should I buy**? I can't decide.
  (**Which camera** is the object of **buy**.)
- "**Whose classes are you taking** next semester?"
  "Mr. Peterson's."
- "**How many people have you hired** this month?"
  "We've hired ten so far."

- **What sports are** popular in Brazil?
  (**What sports** is the subject of **are**.)
- **Which camera costs** less? I want the cheaper one.
  (**Which camera** is the subject of **costs**.)
- "**Whose classes are** the most interesting?"
  "Professor Kent's. His classes are always full."
- "**How many people have visited** the Grand Canyon this year?" "A few million."

PRACTICE

A. Look at the pictures and complete the questions with **who** and the words in *italics*.

1. *(Craig)* A: *Who told Craig the secret* ?
   B: Anna told him the secret.
2. *(Craig)* A: ______________________ to?
   B: He told Bill the secret.
3. *(the Bears)* A: ______________________?
   B: The Lions beat them.
4. *(the Owls)* A: ______________________?
   B: They beat the Dragons.

B. Write questions with **who/what** about the information that you cannot see.

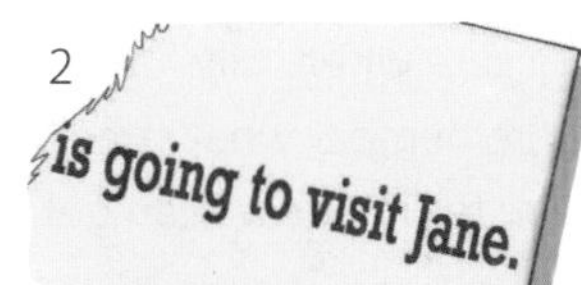

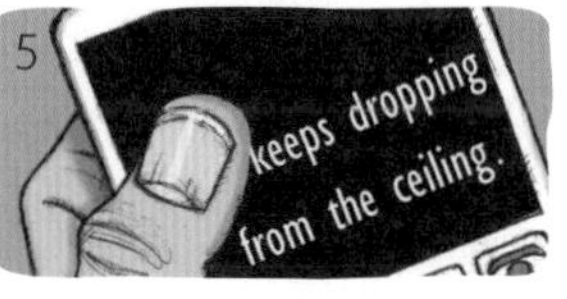

8 memo called this morning.

1. *Who did Samantha meet at the park* ?
2. ______________________?
3. ______________________?
4. ______________________?
5. ______________________?
6. ______________________?
7. ______________________?
8. ______________________?

C. Put the words in *italics* in the correct order.

CHRIS

CHRIS: Hey Paul. I'm going to a party tonight.
1. *Which shirt looks better* on me? *(looks / shirt / which / better)*

PAUL: A party? 2. ______________________ to a party? *(you / who / invited)*

CHRIS: Rachel. It's her birthday.

PAUL: Oh, that will be fun. 3. ______________________? *(people / are coming / how many)*

CHRIS: Around 10, I think. 4. ______________________ for a gift? *(give / should / I / what / her)*

PAUL: Maybe flowers or a cake. 5. ______________________ more? *(she / will / like / which)*

CHRIS: I don't know. I'll just get both.

PAUL

Answers p.310 / Review Test 6 p.244

LESSON 31 Do you know where the dog is? *Indirect questions*

MP3

1 Where is the dog?

Do you know where the dog is?
indirect question

The question **"Where is the dog?"** is inside the sentence **"Do you know . . .?"** In this case, **"where the dog is"** is an *indirect question.*

Do you know **where the dog is**?

2 We use *indirect questions* to include questions inside other sentences. We use *indirect questions* in the following ways:

question word + subject + verb

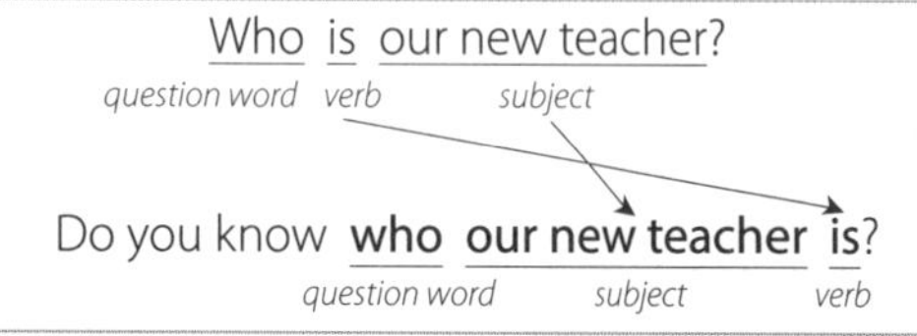

- Do you know **who our new teacher is**?
- I'm not sure **where Lily has gone**.
- I don't remember **what street Frank lives** on.
- Can you tell me **how I can get** to Herald Square?

When we use **who/what/which** as the *subject*, we use **who/what/which** + *verb*.

- I wonder **who is going to sing** at Cindy's wedding.
- This story is a mystery. I don't know **what will happen** next.
- Can you tell me **which store sells** baby clothes?

if/whether + *subject + verb*

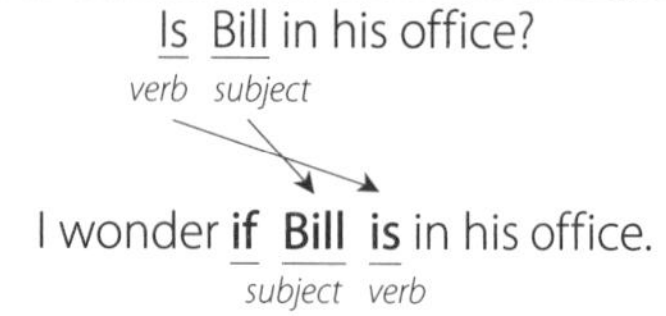

Is Bill in his office?
verb subject
I wonder if Bill is in his office.
subject verb

- I wonder **if Bill is** in his office.
- I don't remember **whether I saw** that movie.
- I'm not sure **if I'll have** time to meet you tonight.
- Do you know **whether Julie has finished** the assignment?

3 Note that we do not use **do/does/did** in *indirect questions.*

When did Sue go to lunch? → • I don't know **when Sue went to lunch.** (*NOT* When Sue did go)

Do students receive a discount? → • Can you tell me **if students receive a discount**? (*NOT* if students do receive)

What time does Jim's flight arrive? → • I wonder **what time Jim's flight arrives**.

4 We often use *indirect questions* with the following expressions:

I don't know . . .
Do you know . . .?
I wonder . . .
I'm not sure . . .
I don't remember . . .
Can you tell me . . .?

- **I don't know** if I've studied enough for the exam.
- **Do you know** how many lakes are in this city?
- **I wonder** who will become class president this year.
- **I'm not sure** which way the post office is. Do you know?
- **I don't remember** whether I turned off the stove.
- "**Can you tell me** what your phone number is?" "Of course. It's 555-6400."

P R A C T I C E

A. Look at the pictures and write indirect questions about what each person is wondering.

When will Joseph come home?
Where can I buy that laptop?

1. Do you know *when Joseph will come home* ?

Why does she look worried?

2. I wonder ______________________.

3. Can you tell me ______________________?

Who is that singer?

4. Do you know ______________________?

B. Put the words in *italics* in the correct order. Use the *past simple*.

1. *(what time / go to school / Mandy)* I don't remember *what time Mandy went to school* yesterday.
2. *(in Lucy's backpack / what / be)* I wonder ______________________. It seemed heavy.
3. *(get into / how / the thief)* I don't know ______________________ our house.
4. *(who / this file / leave)* Do you know ______________________ in the meeting room?
5. *(stay in LA / where / you)* Can you tell me ______________________? I'm going there soon.
6. *(which sandwich / want / Laura)* I wasn't sure ______________________, so I just ordered.

C. Complete the conversations with **if/whether** and the questions in the box.

Are these shoes on sale?	Did I tell you about the art exhibit?	Does the bus to Oak Park stop here?
~~Has Henry read my e-mail?~~	Is someone sitting here	

1. I wonder *if/whether Henry has read my e-mail*.
2. I'm not sure ______________________.
3. I don't know ______________________.
4. Do you know ______________________?
5. Can you tell me ______________________?

He said he'll check.
Let's ask the salesman.
You did. Let's go see it.
No. The seat is empty.
Yes. It will arrive in a bit.

D. Complete the sentences with the words in *italics* and the questions in the box. Add **if/whether** if necessary.

~~Has Todd had lunch yet?~~	Should I believe her?	Was it a dog or a cat?
What is it called?	When will my suit be ready?	Who did Christine call?

1. *(I'm not sure)* *I'm not sure if/whether Todd has had lunch yet*. I want to eat with him.
2. *(do you know)* I can't remember the name of this plant. ______________________?
3. *(I don't know)* Kayla lies sometimes. ______________________.
4. *(can you tell me)* ______________________? I need it before Sunday.
5. *(I don't remember)* Karen had a pet, but ______________________.
6. *(I wonder)* ______________________. She was on the phone for a long time.

Answers **p.310** / Review Test 6 **p.244**

Rita's birthday is tomorrow, **isn't it?** *Tag questions* and *Negative questions*

MP3

1 We use *tag questions* at the end of statements to ask for agreement or to make sure something is correct. We always use **it**/**we**/etc. *(pronouns)* as the *subject* in the *tag question*.

positive statement + negative tag question

- Rita's birthday is tomorrow, **isn't it**?
- "We have been to that restaurant before, **haven't we**?" "We might have."
- "You can help me move tomorrow, **can't you**?" "Sorry, I can't. I'll be busy."

negative statement + positive tag question

- "Nick isn't quitting his job, **is he**?" "I don't think so."
- "You haven't done the laundry yet, **have you**?" "No, but I'll do it soon."
- "Your dog won't bite, **will he**?" "No. He's friendly."

When we use *verbs* such as **play**/**enjoy**/etc. in the previous statement, we use **do**/**does**/**did** in the *tag question*.

- You play golf, **don't you**? (**don't** is used because of the verb **play**.)
- Jessica didn't enjoy the movie, **did she**? (**did** is used because of the verb **enjoy**.)

2 When we ask for agreement, our tone should go down at the end of the *tag question*.

- "Jonathan's house is beautiful, **isn't it**?" "Yes, it is."
  (I want others to agree that Jonathan's house is beautiful.)
- "This assignment doesn't look easy, **does it**?" "No, it looks quite difficult."
  (I want others to agree that the assignment doesn't look easy.)

When we want to make sure something is correct, our tone should go up at the end of the *tag question*.

- "These are your gloves, **aren't they**?" "Oh, yes. Thanks."
  (I want to make sure that the gloves are yours.)
- "We don't have to work on Christmas Day, **do we**?" "Of course not."
  (I want to make sure that we don't have to work on Christmas Day.)

3 We use *negative questions* to ask for agreement or to express surprise about something. We use *negative questions* in the following ways:

Isn't/Aren't/Wasn't/Weren't . . .?	Haven't/Hasn't . . .?
Don't/Doesn't/Didn't . . .?	Won't/Wouldn't/Can't/Couldn't . . .?

- **Wasn't that** a great performance? (Asks for agreement that the performance was great)
- "Is Santana Park nice?" "It's great! **Haven't you** been there before?" (Expresses surprise about not having been there before)
- **Don't you** remember my phone number? We have been friends for three years!
- "I think I'll buy this shirt for Jessica. **Won't she** love it?" "I think so."

4 When we answer *tag* or *negative questions*, we say **Yes** for positive answers and **No** for negative answers.

- "That soup tastes salty, **doesn't it**?" "**Yes**, it does." (= Yes, it tastes salty.)
- "**Aren't you** excited about your vacation?" "**Yes**, I am."
- "Gina hasn't left yet, **has she**?" "**No**, she hasn't." (= No, she hasn't left yet.)
- "**Can't Mike** drive?" "**No**, he can't."

PRACTICE

A. **Jennifer and Sam are talking about going swimming. Complete the conversation with tag questions.**

JENNIFER: 1. The weather is great today, *isn't it*?
SAM: It's perfect! 2. We should do something outside, __________?
JENNIFER: How about swimming?
Oh, wait. 3. You can't swim, __________?
SAM: No, but you can teach me.
4. You've taken swimming lessons before, __________?
JENNIFER: Yes, I have.
SAM: Great. But I don't have a swimsuit.
5. You don't mind if we stop by the store, __________?
JENNIFER: Not at all. Let's go!

B. **Put the words in *italics* in the correct order. Write tag questions at the end of each statement.**

1. *(you / will / me / call / later)* *You will call me later, won't you*?
2. *(take / me / can't / to the concert / you)* __________?
3. *(rides / her bike / Melissa / to work)* __________?
4. *(on a business trip / is going / Chad)* __________?
5. *(haven't / we / hiking / gone / together)* __________?

C. **Ask negative questions for each situation.**

1. You think the pie is delicious. You want your friend to agree with you.
   YOU: *Isn't the pie delicious*?
2. You're surprised that Lucas wasn't waiting for his sister at the airport.
   YOU: __________?
3. You think you look good in blue jeans. You want your friend to agree with you.
   YOU: __________?
4. You're surprised that Melanie didn't leave for work yet.
   YOU: __________?
5. You think you and your friend will have fun at the beach. You want your friend to agree with you.
   YOU: __________?
6. You're surprised that Roger hasn't had a girlfriend before.
   YOU: __________?

D. **Write Yes or No.**

1. Eric isn't coming over for dinner, is he? — *Yes*, he is. And he's bringing his wife.
2. Don't you have an interview this morning? — __________. It was yesterday.
3. Graham doesn't have a brother, does he? — __________. He's an only child.
4. Didn't Shelley look pretty at her wedding? — __________. She was very beautiful.
5. Can't you play the guitar? — __________. I've never learned how to play.
6. Jenny will graduate from university next week, won't she? — __________. Her graduation is next Saturday.

Answers p.310 / Review Test 6 p.244

LESSON 33 The fence was painted. *Passive (1)*

1

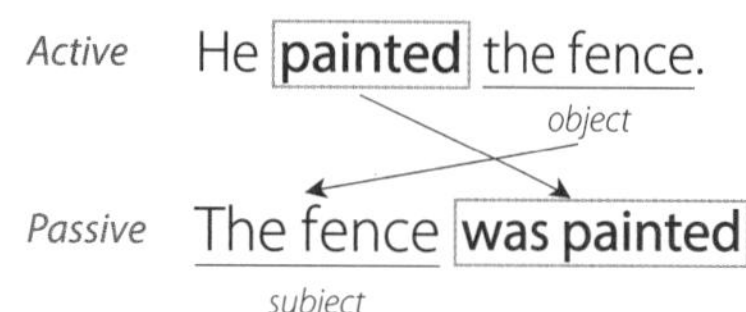
Active He painted the fence.
object
Passive The fence was painted.
subject

"was painted" is the *passive*. In this case, **"the fence"** is the target of painting.

2 We use the *passive* when the *subject* is the target of an action. The *passive* is **be + past participle.**

(Present simple)	**am/is/are + past participle**	• Salt **is used** in almost every dish. • Cameras **are not allowed** inside the museum.
(Past simple)	**was/were + past participle**	• Donna **was taken** to the hospital. She had a bad stomachache. • "Where **were** these grapes **grown**?" "Chile."

We use the *active* when the *subject* does the action. There is the following difference between the *active* and *passive*:

Active • **We planned** the party a month ago. (The subject **We** did the action of planning.)

Passive • **The party was planned** a month ago. (The subject **The party** is the target of the action of planning.)

3 We can use the *passive* in many different ways.

be + being + past participle

	Active		*Passive*
(Present progressive)	A bird **is building** a nest.	→	A nest **is being built**.
(Past progressive)	Workers **were making** shoes at the factory.	→	Shoes **were being made** at the factory.

- "Did you buy all the presents?" "Yes. They**'re being wrapped** right now."
- "The elevators **were being repaired**." "Did you take the stairs, then?"
- I turned off the TV because it **wasn't being watched**.

have/has/had been + past participle

	Active		*Passive*
(Present perfect)	Mr. Smith **has changed** the meeting time.	→	The meeting time **has been changed**.
(Past perfect)	They **had delivered** the groceries when we got home.	→	The groceries **had been delivered** when we got home.

- The prices of all products **have been reduced**. The store is having a sale.
- The piano in my room **hasn't been played** for years.
- When I came back from my vacation, the office building **had been renovated**.

will/can/must/etc. **+ be + past participle**

Active		*Passive*
They **will serve** dinner soon.	→	Dinner **will be served** soon.
You **can purchase** tickets online.	→	Tickets **can be purchased** online.

- All refunds **must be requested** within 90 days.
- We're working on a huge project. It **won't be completed** until next year.

PRACTICE

A. Look at the pictures and complete the sentences with the words from each box. Use the *past simple*.

the juice	the letters	the onion
~~the statue~~	the windows	

\+

cut	~~make~~	send
spill	wash	

1. *The statue was made* ______ in 1892.
2. ______ over the keyboard.
3. ______ into four pieces.
4. ______.
5. ______ to Michael.

B. Complete the sentences with the verbs in the box. Use the active or passive.

cancel	carry	cook	include	join	know	~~speak~~	wear

1. In Canada, both English and French *are spoken* ______. They are the national languages.
2. Mark ______ a book club last month. He's enjoying it very much.
3. Tomorrow's baseball game might ______ because of the storm.
4. "These boxes are so heavy." "Give them to me. I'll ______ them for you."
5. That singer is famous. She ______ around the world.
6. These noodles should ______ for at least 10 minutes in boiling water.
7. Samantha always ______ pants. I've never seen her in a skirt.
8. Meals ______ in the travel package. We didn't have to pay extra for them.

C. Complete the sentences with the verbs in *italics*. Use the *present progressive* or *past progressive*.

1. *(fix)* "Why is it so cold in here?" "Our heater *is being fixed* ______ at the moment."
2. *(plant)* When I went to the farm last spring, potatoes ______.
3. *(not use)* Those chairs ______ right now. We can sit there.
4. *(not clean)* The pool ______ this morning, so we went swimming.
5. *(develop)* New cancer drugs ______ at the moment. This gives hope to patients.
6. *(perform)* We got to the theater late. The play ______ when we arrived.
7. *(not help)* That old lady ______ right now. Let's go and help her get on the bus.
8. *(print)* While our wedding invitations ______, we waited at a coffee shop.

D. Complete the sentences with the words in *italics*. Use the *present perfect* or *past perfect*.

1. *(the deadline, move)* I have to work all night tonight. *The deadline has been moved* ______ to tomorrow.
2. *(North America, not discover)* ______ before Columbus found it in 1492.
3. *(my purse, take)* When I returned to the café, ______ already.
4. *(it, update)* My computer was slow for months, but ______ recently. Now it's very fast.
5. *(we, introduce)* "Have you met Ms. Paulson?" "Yes, ______."
6. *(the ring, sell)* ______ when I visited the store the next day.
7. *(it, close)* There was a big fire at the museum last Friday. ______ since then.
8. *(all of the things, pack)* ______. Finally, we can leave now!

Answers **p.310** / Review Test 7 **p.246**

The new city hall **will be designed by** a French architect. *Passive* (2)

MP3

1 We use **by** in passive sentences to show who or what does the action.

- The new city hall **will be designed by a French architect**.
- *A Christmas Carol* **was written by Charles Dickens**.
- The security system in this building **is controlled by computers**.

We do not use **by** when it is obvious or not important who or what does the action.

- Rice **is eaten** in many countries around the world. (It's obvious who eats rice.)
- The winners of the contest **were announced** yesterday. (It's not important who announced the winners.)
- "I like your sweater. **Is** it **made** of wool?" "Yes, it is."

2 We do not use the *passive* with the following *verbs*:

seem/appear	happen/occur	belong	consist

- I met John's girlfriend yesterday. She **seems** nice. (*NOT* She's seemed)
- What **happened**? The window is broken. (*NOT* What was happened)
- "Whose car is that?" "It **belongs** to Mr. Bradley."
- This survey **consists** of 12 questions. Please answer all of them.

3 We use the *passive* in the following expressions:

be married	be born	be done/finished	be lost

- "Is Charlie single?" "No. He**'s married**."
- "I **was born** in Toronto." "Really? Me too!"
- "**Are** you **finished** with your homework?" "Yes, I**'m done**."
- "Where are we?" "I'm not sure. I think we**'re lost**."

4 **get + past participle**

We can use **get + past participle** instead of **be + past participle** for some *verbs*. We often use the following expressions:

get married	get invited	get dressed	get caught
get paid	get promoted	get hired	get fired
get hit	get hurt	get burned	get broken

- My wife and I **got married** in 2012.
- We usually go out for a beer when we **get paid**.
- Tony **got hit** by the baseball during practice yesterday.
- "Do you want to see a movie?" "Sounds great. I'll **get dressed**."

We use **don't/doesn't/didn't get + past participle** *(negative)* and **do/does/did . . . get + past participle . . .?** *(questions)*.

- These wine glasses **don't get broken** easily. They're quite strong.
- "I **didn't get promoted**. I heard the news this morning." "That's too bad."
- "**Did** you **get invited** to Amanda's birthday party?" "Yes, but I can't go."
- "How **did** Maria **get burned**?" "She spilled hot coffee on her arm."

P R A C T I C E

A. **Complete the sentences with the first words in *italics*. Write the second words with by only if necessary. Use the *present simple* or *past simple*.**

1. *(invent) (Chester Carlson)* The photocopier *was invented by Chester Carlson* .
2. *(bake) (a baker)* The bread at that bakery ______________ every day, so it's always fresh.
3. *(cause) (a tornado)* The damage to the house ______________.
4. *(deliver) (a postman)* These packages are for Sara. They ______________ this morning.
5. *(prepare) (Antonio Bruno)* Now our meals ______________. He's our new chef.
6. *(arrest) (the police)* Frank ______________ because he was driving without a license.

B. **Find and change any mistakes in each sentence. Put ✓ if the sentence is correct.**

1. The cereal is consisted of natural ingredients. *is consisted → consists*
2. The actress is surrounded photographers. ______________
3. A cat suddenly was appeared in the doorway. ______________
4. "Was this book published last year?" "Yes, it was." ______________
5. Olivia got burned while she was cooking, but she's OK now. ______________
6. That jacket isn't belonged to me. ______________
7. We were lost in a strange place and didn't have a map. ______________
8. Some trains delayed by an accident yesterday. ______________

C. **The following is an article about Michelle O'Neal. Complete the sentences with the appropriate passive expressions.**

1. Michelle O'Neal, a romance novelist, *was born* in Canada in 1976.
2. She ______________ to a Japanese man and has two kids.
Michelle met her husband when she was visiting Japan.
3. She ______________ and he helped her to find her hotel.
Michelle is currently writing a book about their love story.
4. By next month, she will ______________ with it.
There's more good news. Michelle is expecting her third child.
5. The baby will ______________ in November.

D. **Complete the conversations with the verbs in the box using get + past participle. Use the *past simple* and write negative sentences if necessary.**

break	catch	dress	fire	hurt	~~invite~~

1. A: Taylor *got invited* to the White House.
B: Wow! That's amazing!

2. A: These dishes ______________ during delivery.
B: Oh, no. Those were really expensive.

3. A: Some men robbed a bank downtown today.
B: ______________ they ______________ yet?

4. A: The bus crashed, but the passengers ______________.
B: They were very lucky.

5. A: ______________ you ______________? We need to go.
B: OK. I'm putting on my coat now.

6. A: Dave was worried about losing his job.
B: Fortunately, he ______________.

Passive

LESSON 34

Answers p.310 / Review Test 7 p.246

LESSON 35 Justin was given a skateboard. *Passive (3)*

MP3

1

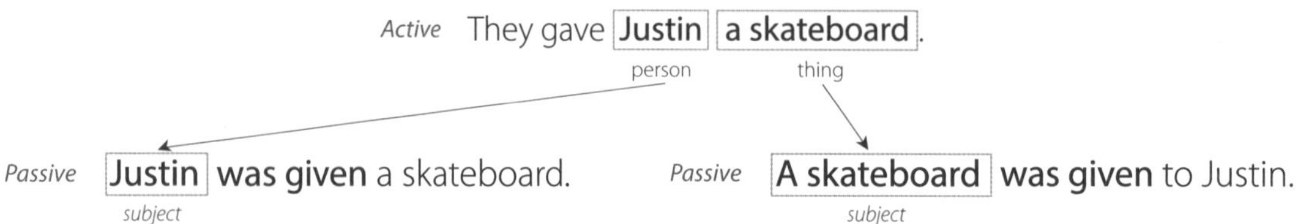

Active They gave Justin a skateboard.
person
thing
Passive Justin was given a skateboard.
subject
Passive A skateboard was given to Justin.
subject

In the active sentence, **"Justin"** (person) and **"a skateboard"** (thing) are both the *objects* of **"gave."**
We can make two passive sentences by using each of them as the *subject*.

2 When there are two *objects* (person and thing) after the following *verbs*, we can make two passive sentences:

give	offer	send	lend	tell	show	teach	ask	pay

Active
Ms. Williams offered the guests (person) tea (thing). → (person) • **The guests were offered** tea by Ms. Williams.
(thing) • **Tea was offered** to the guests by Ms. Williams.

Readers send the editor (person) letters (thing) every day. → (person) • **The editor is sent** letters by readers every day.
(thing) • **Letters are sent** to the editor by readers every day.

Passive (column heading for the sentences on the right)

3 When a *person* is the *subject* of a passive sentence, we say a *thing* after **be + past participle**.

person	*be + past participle*	*thing*	
• I	**was asked**	**some questions**	by the police officer.
• The children	**are shown**	**a video**	once a week.
• Jane	**will be paid**	**$50**	for babysitting.

When a *thing* is the *subject* of a passive sentence, we say **to +** *person* after **be + past participle**.

thing	*be + past participle*	*to + person*	
• Headphones	**were lent**	**to passengers**	during the flight.
• Art history	**is taught**	**to all students**	at our school.

We use a *person* as the *subject* more often.

- **Ms. Ross was given** earrings on Valentine's Day.
- **We were told** the news about Gary's accident today.

P R A C T I C E

A. Look at the pictures and complete the sentences with **give** and the words in the box. Use the *past simple*.

a gold medal	a good grade	a package	balloons
cards	some cookies	some medicine	~~some money~~

1. He *was given some money* ________.
2. He ________.
3. They ________.
4. She ________.
5. They ________.
6. She ________.
7. They ________.
8. He ________.

B. Read the sentences and complete the new ones using the underlined words as the subject. Add **to** if necessary.

1. The store sends customers calendars every year. → *Customers are sent calendars* by the store every year.
2. Bob paid me $50 for my old bike. → ________ for my old bike.
3. That bank lends foreign residents money. → ________ by that bank.
4. Ms. Sanders will show visitors the gardens. → ________.
5. Mr. Harrison told his grandchildren the story. → ________ by Mr. Harrison.
6. The clerk offered us a discount. → ________ by the clerk.
7. Ashley teaches students yoga twice a week. → ________ by Ashley twice a week.
8. The reporter will ask the movie star some questions. → ________.

C. Read the sentences and complete the new ones with the given subjects.

1. A joke was told to the audience by the comedian.
   → The audience *was told a joke by the comedian*.
2. The driver will be paid a delivery fee.
   → A delivery fee ________.
3. Passports must be shown to the security guard.
   → The security guard ________.
4. Manners are taught to children by their parents.
   → Children ________.
5. The girl was sent a box of chocolate by Ned.
   → A box of chocolate ________.

Answers p.311 / Review Test 7 p.246

LESSON 36

Playing chess is difficult. -ing / It . . . to . . . as *subjects*

MP3

1

Chess is difficult.

Playing chess is difficult.

"Playing chess" is the *subject* of the *verb* **"is."**

Playing chess is difficult.

2 We can use **-ing** as the *subject* in a sentence.

- **Skiing** is exciting. It's my favorite sport!
- Let's take a plane to Dallas. **Flying** will save time.
- **Writing letters** has become less common these days.
- "You have a lot of old coins!" "**Collecting coins** used to be my hobby."

More about spelling rules: Appendix p.278

In this case, we can use various words after **-ing** as in the following sentences:

- **Wearing a seatbelt** can protect you from injury.
- **Going for a walk** sounds nice. Let's go.
- **Dancing at the party last night** was great. I hadn't danced in a long time.

3 We use a *singular verb* when we use **-ing** as the *subject* in a sentence.

	singular verb	
Working from home	**is**	very convenient.
Driving a car during rush hour	**wasn't**	a good idea.
Reducing the use of paper cups	**has helped**	to decrease waste.
Renting an apartment in this city	**doesn't cost**	much. It's quite cheap.

4 We can also use **to . . .** as the *subject* in a sentence. We also use a *singular verb* after **to . . .**

- **To understand Mr. Bentley's lectures is** easy.
- **To become a good musician takes** time.

But we use **It . . . to . . .** more often than **to . . .**

It		*to . . .*
It	is easy	**to understand Mr. Bentley's lectures.**
It	was important	**to finish the project on time.**
It	takes a lot of effort	**to achieve success in life.**
It	will be fun	**to go camping this weekend.**

In **It . . . to . . .** sentences, **It** replaces **to . . .** as the *subject*.

- **It** is impossible **to predict the future.** (= **To predict the future** is impossible.)
- **It** seems hard **to find a quiet café around here.** (= **To find a quiet café around here** seems hard.)

P R A C T I C E

A. Complete the sentences with the words from each box using **-ing** as the subjects.

cook	find	park	+	a job	a meal at home	a room
see	share	~~tell~~		on this road	the singer on stage	~~the truth~~

1. *Telling the truth* ________ isn't always easy, but I always try to be honest.
2. I'm glad I don't live in a dorm now. ________________ with someone else gave me stress.
3. ________________ often costs less than going to a restaurant.
4. ________________ might take time. Not many companies are hiring these days.
5. You must move your car. ________________ is not allowed.
6. "Are you excited about the concert tonight?" "Yes. ________________ will be great."

B. Put the words in *italics* in the correct order using **-ing** as the subjects.

Dr. Smith Discusses Health Myths

1. *(prevents / vitamin C / take)* *Taking vitamin C prevents* ________ colds.
2. *(coffee / drink / is)* ________________ not good for your health.
3. *(close to the TV / leads / sit)* ________________ to bad eyesight.
4. *(fruits / eat / affect / doesn't)* ________________ your weight.
5. *(wear / causes / a hat)* ________________ hair loss.

These ideas are either wrong or not proven yet.
DR. SMITH

C. Complete the sentences with the given words using **-ing** as the subjects. Use the *present simple*.

become a famous actress	~~learn about other cultures~~	review the article again
ride an elephant	speak in front of people	take care of children

1. *(help)* *Learning about other cultures* ____ *helps* ____ you to understand people from different countries.
2. *(require)* It's hard to be a parent. ________________ ________ patience.
3. *(not seem)* ________________ ________ necessary. I've read it twice already.
4. *(be)* Carrie is performing in a musical. ________________ ________ her dream.
5. *(not sound)* ________________ ________ fun to me. I'm afraid of animals.
6. *(not make)* I like giving speeches. ________________ ________ me nervous.

D. Choose the one you agree with and write sentences using **It . . . to . . .**

1. swim in the ocean	☑ exciting	☐ scary
2. sleep on a sofa	☐ comfortable	☐ uncomfortable
3. have a cell phone	☐ necessary	☐ unnecessary
4. take the bus	☐ convenient	☐ inconvenient
5. watch movies alone	☐ fun	☐ boring

1. *It's exciting to swim in the ocean* ________.
2. ________________________.
3. ________________________.
4. ________________________.
5. ________________________.

Answers **p.311** / Review Test 8 **p.248**

They enjoyed watching the game. -ing as *objects*

MP3

1

They enjoyed the game.

They **enjoyed watching** the game.

"watching" is the *object* of the *verb* **"enjoyed."**

2 We use **-ing** as the *object* of the following *verbs*:

enjoy	finish	miss	keep	practice	
quit	mind	avoid	deny	risk	-ing
suggest	recommend	consider	imagine	admit	(reading, using, going, etc.)
give up	put off				

- I **finished reading** this book. The ending is so sad.
- That store **quit using** plastic bags last week. It only provides paper bags now.
- "My friends **suggested going** to Bali for our honeymoon." "Sounds good to me."
- I **gave up looking** for my sunglasses. I guess I lost them.
- "Do you **mind paying** for lunch? I forgot my wallet." "No problem."
- We're going to **put off buying** a house. We can't afford it right now.

3 **not + -ing** *(negative)*

- I **recommend not wearing** that tie. It doesn't match your suit.
- Brad has a lot of work these days. He **misses not working** so much.
- Matt hasn't slept for three days. Can you **imagine not sleeping** for that long?

There is the following difference in meaning between **not + -ing** and negative sentences in general:

- Sara **considered not attending** the seminar because she had a headache.
(She considered a choice, and the choice was not attending the seminar.)

Sara **didn't consider attending** the seminar at all. She just wasn't interested.
(She never considered the choice.)

4 **being + past participle** *(passive)*

- I spilled hot tea, but fortunately, I **avoided being burned**.
- We expected the delivery last week, but it **kept being delayed**.
- Let's take the train. I can't **risk being caught** in traffic.

5 We use **having + past participle** after a *verb* to talk about an event that happened before the time of the *verb's* action.

- The suspect **admitted having committed** the crime. (The crime was committed before the time the suspect admitted it.)

We can also use **-ing** instead of **having + past participle**.

- Bill **denied having eaten** my sandwich. *OR* Bill **denied eating** my sandwich.
- Jake **admitted having cheated** on the test. *OR* Jake **admitted cheating** on the test.

P R A C T I C E

A. Put the words in *italics* in the correct order using -ing as the objects.

1. *(lie / miss)* I *miss lying* ____________ on the beach every weekend. It's too cold now.
2. *(lose / risk)* Don't take your phone on the rollercoaster. You'll ____________ it.
3. *(deny / meet)* Peter didn't ____________ Nancy last night. They went on a date!
4. *(walk / keep)* If you ____________ in that direction, you'll see the bank on the right.
5. *(finish / eat)* My friends eat so fast. They always ____________ before me.
6. *(take / suggest)* "What airline do you recommend?" "I'd ____________ Swift Air."
7. *(give up / skate)* The skater is going to ____________ after the Olympics.

B. Read what Alex says and complete the sentences using -ing as the objects. Add not if necessary.

ALEX

1. I'm tired. I'll clean the house tomorrow.
2. I don't put sugar in my coffee.
3. I didn't lock the door. I'm sorry.
4. I used to study Spanish, but I changed my major.
5. I might not go to Susie's party. I'm busy.

1. Alex put off *cleaning the house* ____________.
2. He avoids ____________.
3. He admitted ____________.
4. He quit ____________.
5. He's considering ____________.

C. Complete the sentences with the verbs in the box using -ing or being + past participle.

injure	live	photograph	spend	teach	~~wash~~

1. "I finished *washing* ____________ the dishes." "OK. I'll dry them now."
2. Simon has been in a small town all his life. He can't imagine ____________ in a big city.
3. The actress doesn't mind ____________. She likes being in front of the cameras.
4. "Why do the students enjoy ____________ by Mr. Miller?" "Because he's fun."
5. My best friend moved to Miami. I miss ____________ time with her.
6. Fortunately, everyone avoided ____________ in the accident.

D. Find and change any mistakes in each sentence. Put ✓ if the sentence is correct.

World Tour Magazine's Travel Tips!

1. Don't put off being made hotel reservations. Early reservations are cheaper. *being made → making*
2. We suggest read a guidebook before you take a trip. ____________
3. Practice speaking the local language before you visit a foreign country. ____________
4. Consider having rented a car. You can visit more sites with it. ____________
5. When on a group tour, don't risk being left alone. It can be dangerous. ____________
6. We recommend carrying not your passport when sightseeing. It might get stolen. ____________

Answers **p.311** / Review Test 8 **p.248**

LESSON 38

She wants to drink some coffee. to . . . as *objects*

MP3

1 She wants some coffee.

She **wants to drink** some coffee.

"to drink" is the *object* of the *verb* **"wants."**

2 We use **to . . .** rather than **-ing** as the *object* of the following *verbs*:

want	hope	expect	agree	prepare	
plan	decide	choose	offer	promise	to . . .
learn	refuse	fail	manage	intend	(to meet, to invite, to speak, etc.)
seem	appear	claim	pretend		

- "I **hope to meet** Ken at the party." "I think he's coming." (*NOT* hope meeting)
- I didn't forget Bob's birthday. I'm **planning to invite** him to dinner. (*NOT* planning inviting)
- "Where did you **learn to speak** Chinese?" "In Shanghai."
- "Did you give the present to Sam?" "Yes. He **seemed to like** it."

3 **not to . . .** *(negative)*

- My husband and I **agreed not to sell** our car. We're keeping it.
- Jake **decided not to join** the football club. He's joining the tennis club instead.
- "I'll tell you what happened if you **promise not to be** angry." "OK, I won't."

There is the following difference in meaning between **not to . . .** and negative sentences in general:

- I thought about taking the writing class, but **chose not to register**.
  (I made a choice, and the choice was not registering.)
- I **didn't choose to register** for the writing class. It was required.
  (I never made the choice.)

4 **to be + past participle** *(passive)*

- When I retire from this company, I **want to be remembered** as a good manager.
- The band **refused to be interviewed** and left quickly after the concert.
- I was surprised when I was given the award. I didn't **expect to be chosen**!

5 We use **to be + -ing** after a *verb* to talk about an event that is happening at the time of the *verb's* action.

- "How is Diane's project going?" "It **appears to be going** OK."
- I didn't want to talk to Beth, so I **pretended to be sleeping**.
- "The kids **seem to be having** fun." "Yes, they like this playground."

We use **to have + past participle** after a *verb* to talk about an event that happened before the time of the *verb's* action.

- John **claims to have met** the president. (John met the president before the time he claimed it.)
- We **seem to have passed** the park. We should have turned at the traffic light.
- Doris isn't answering the door. She **appears to have gone** out.

P R A C T I C E

A. Complete the sentences with the verbs in the box using **to . . .** or **-ing**.

allow	catch	finish	live	move	shop	~~visit~~

1. "Why is Greg going to Chicago during the holidays?" "He wants *to visit* ______ his friends."
2. John failed ______ the last bus. He had to walk home.
3. I miss ______ in my old house. I loved it.
4. Your luggage is blocking the way. Would you mind ______ it?
5. We had a lot of work to do, but we managed ______ all of it.
6. The prices at that supermarket are high. I'd suggest ______ at a different store.
7. We can't eat there. That restaurant refuses ______ pets inside.

B. Complete the sentences with the given words using **to . . .** or **not to . . .** Use the *past simple*.

arrive	call	hide	~~play~~	ride	share	watch

1. *(learn)* Shawn is an excellent violinist. He *learned to play* ______ the violin at a young age.
2. *(expect)* We ______ early, but we were just on time.
3. *(promise)* Jimmy, you ______ TV after ten o'clock. Please turn it off.
4. *(offer)* Donald didn't bring his umbrella, so Holly ______ hers with him.
5. *(decide)* I ______ my bicycle to the office today because it was too cold.
6. *(agree)* Sally and Brian ______ anything. Now, they tell each other everything.
7. *(intend)* Ron ______ Mr. Watson, but he dialed someone else's number.

C. The following is an advertisement for Pizza Palace. Complete the sentences with the verbs in *italics* using **to . . .** or **to be + past participle**.

PIZZA PALACE GRAND OPENING!

1. *(open)* Pizza Palace plans *to open* ______ a restaurant in Jonesville!
2. *(build)* Our brand new restaurant is expected ______ by the end of May.
3. *(provide)* Pizza Palace promises ______ good quality food.
4. *(use)* We choose ______ only the freshest ingredients.
5. *(recognize)* We hope ______ as the best pizza restaurant in town.
6. *(amaze)* Prepare ______ by our delicious pizzas!

D. Complete the conversations with the verbs in *italics* using **to be + -ing** or **to have + past participle**.

1. A: How are Ryan and Melissa these days?
   B: *(do)* Well, they appear *to be doing* ______ OK. Why?
2. A: The photocopier doesn't work.
   B: *(fix)* Are you sure? The repairman claimed ______.
3. A: *(grow)* Our new tree in the backyard seems ______ fast.
   B: Yes. It's getting taller every week.
4. A: It's still snowing.
   B: *(stop)* Still? It appeared ______ earlier.
5. A: *(change)* Wow! You seem ______ your hairstyle.
   B: Yes, I got my hair cut yesterday.
6. A: I thought the lecture was really boring.
   B: *(listen)* I totally agree with you. I only pretended ______.

Answers p.311 / Review Test 8 p.248

LESSON 39

Hannah **likes working** in the garden. *Verb* + -ing/to . . .

MP3

1 We can use -ing or to . . . after the following *verbs*, and there is no difference in meaning:

like	love	prefer	hate	bother	-ing (working, talking, etc.)
start	begin	continue	propose		to . . . (to work, to talk, etc.)

- Hannah **likes working** in the garden.
  OR Hannah **likes to work** in the garden.
- My little brother **started talking** when he was 18 months old.
  OR My little brother **started to talk** when he was 18 months old.
- Our friends said the movie was terrible, so we didn't **bother seeing** it.
  OR Our friends said the movie was terrible, so we didn't **bother to see** it.

2 We can also use -ing or to . . . after the following *verbs*, but there are differences in meaning:

remember/forget	-ing	remember/forget something that happened before
	to . . .	remember/forget something that has not happened yet

- I can't find my passport, but I **remember bringing** it.
  Please **remember to bring** your passport tomorrow.
- I'll never **forget meeting** my favorite singer. It was so exciting.
  "Don't **forget to meet** Jane after school." "I won't."

regret	-ing	feel sorry about something that happened before
	to . . .	feel sorry about something that is going to happen

- I **regret telling** Max my secret. He told everyone.
  I **regret to tell** you that no more tickets are available.

try	-ing	do something to see what happens
	to . . .	do something with effort

- "I need to lose some weight." "**Try swimming**. It really helps."
  I **tried to swim** along the coast, but the waves were too big.

stop	-ing	not do something anymore
	to . . .	not do something to do something else

- Joe finally **stopped eating** after he had finished a whole pizza.
  The pizza arrived when we were cleaning the house. We **stopped to eat**.

need	-ing	need an action done to someone or something
	to . . .	need someone to perform an action

- The sheets on the bed **need changing**. I spilled juice on them.
  I **need to change** the sheets on the bed. They're dirty.

We can also use **need to be + past participle** instead of **need + -ing**.

- My camera **needs fixing**. *OR* My camera **needs to be fixed**.
- We hired some new staff. They **need training**. *OR* They **need to be trained**.

PRACTICE

A. Complete the sentences with the verbs in the box using **-ing** or **to . . .**

keep	make	quit	~~read~~	rise	work

1. When the teacher began *reading* OR *to read* ________ the book, the children became quiet.
2. "You should stop smoking." "Actually, I plan ________________ on January 1."
3. Jane likes group projects. She hates ________________ alone.
4. I'd recommend ________________ a reservation. That restaurant is always busy.
5. Peter was going to throw away his old computer, but decided ________________ it.
6. The temperature will continue ________________ all afternoon.

B. Put the words in *italics* in the correct order using **-ing** or **to . . .**

1. *(invite / forget)* "Don't *forget to invite* ________ Mr. Anderson for lunch." "Don't worry. I won't."
2. *(go / remember)* "I ________________ to the circus when I was young." "Me too. It was always fun."
3. *(remember / pick)* ________________ up my blouse from the dry cleaner's. I need it tomorrow.
4. *(regret / buy)* I don't like my new hat. I ________________ it.
5. *(visit / forget)* Venice was a wonderful place. I'll never ________________ that city.
6. *(regret / announce)* We ________________ that the flight to Sydney has been canceled.
7. *(pack / forget)* You shouldn't ________________ the sunscreen. The sun is really strong at the beach.

C. Complete what Keith says with the words in Box A using **tried to . . .** (1-3).
Then, give him solutions with the words in Box B using **try -ing** (4-6).

A

call Sarah	~~learn Arabic~~	make an omelet

1. I *tried to learn Arabic* ________________, but it's a difficult language.
2. Cooking is so hard. I ________________, but I couldn't.
3. I ________________, but she didn't answer.

KEITH

B

follow the recipe	send her a text message	study with a partner

4. Why don't you ________________?
5. ________________ more carefully.
6. You could ________________.

YOU

D. Complete the sentences with **stop/need** and the verbs in *italics* using **-ing** or **to . . .**

1. *(go)* "Can you stay a little longer?" "No. Unfortunately, I *need to go* ________ now."
2. *(check)* Let's ________________ the tire. I think there's something wrong with it.
3. *(spend)* Ted always wastes money. He should ________________ so much.
4. *(sign)* These forms ________________. I'll put them on your desk.
5. *(change)* I'm watching that show. ________________ the TV channel, please.
6. *(take)* We ________________ out the garbage. It's starting to smell.
7. *(update)* Those websites ________________. The information on them is old.

Answers p.311 / Review Test 8 p.248

LESSON 40 He wants the clerk to find the book. *Verb + object + -ing/to . . .*

MP3

1 He wants to buy a book.

He **wants the clerk to find** the book.

"the clerk" is the *object* of the *verb* **"wants"** and who performs the action **"find."**

Could you find a book for me?

2 We can use *object* + **to . . .** after the following *verbs*:

want	cause	expect	require	force
allow	enable	teach	advise	encourage
tell	invite	ask		

- The storm last night **caused a lot of trees to fall**.
- The Internet **allows us to share** information very quickly.
- "What did the doctor **tell Nick to do**?" "He **advised him to drink** less coffee."
- Mike's job **requires him to work** on weekends.
- I got in trouble. My teacher **forced me to remain** after class.

3 We can use *object* + **-ing** after the following *verbs*:

dislike	remember	imagine	mind	keep	leave

- My parents **dislike me going** out late at night.
- "Did Jeff find a roommate?" "I think so. I **remember someone telling** me that."
- "Can you **imagine Monica saying** bad things about people?" "No. She's always so nice."
- "Do you **mind us sitting** here?" "Not at all."
- I'm so tired. Our football coach **kept us running** for hours.

We usually use *object* + **from** + **-ing** after **stop** and **prevent**.

- Give the baby some milk. It will **stop her from crying**.
- The fog **prevented the driver from seeing** the road clearly.

4 **I want to get** and **I want you to get**

- **I want to get** a haircut.
  (= I think I should get a haircut.)
- **Do you remember dancing** with Sam?
  (= Do you remember that you danced with Sam?)
- **Jerry expects to win** the competition.
- **We don't mind staying** in a small room.
- **I can't imagine wearing** that skirt. It's not my style.

- **I want you to get** a haircut.
  (= I think you should get a haircut.)
- **Do you remember me dancing** with Sam?
  (= Do you remember that I danced with Sam?)
- **Jerry expects Alice to win** the competition.
- **We don't mind you staying** at our house.
- **I can't imagine Liz wearing** that skirt. It's not her style.

P R A C T I C E

A. Complete the sentences with **want** and the words in the box. Use the *present simple*.

~~go with them~~	meet her	move back	sell it to him	take him

LENA

1. My friends are going to a concert tonight. They *want me to go with them*.
2. Robert asked about my old grill. He ________________.
3. My dog ________________ to the park. He is bored.
4. I live alone. My parents ________________ home.
5. My aunt ________________ at the airport. She is coming tomorrow.

B. Mr. Ross is speaking to his employees. Complete the sentences with the verbs in *italics* and the appropriate objects. Use the *past simple*.

Mr. ROSS

1. Bill, can you bring the reports?
2. Prepare for the presentation, Cori.
3. Kevin, do you want to go out for drinks tonight?
4. If you're sick, you can go home early, Denise.
5. You should call the customer soon, Jane.
6. Steve, you should attend the seminar.

1. *(ask)* He *asked Bill to bring the reports*.
2. *(tell)* He ________________.
3. *(invite)* He ________________.
4. *(allow)* He ________________.
5. *(advise)* He ________________.
6. *(encourage)* He ________________.

C. Complete the sentences with the verbs in the box and the appropriate objects. Add **from** if necessary.

join	laugh	say	~~spend~~	spread	take	wait

1. My husband dislikes *me spending* too much money on clothes, so I try not to.
2. "Can Josh come with us to the basketball game?" "Sure. I don't mind ________________ us."
3. There was a fire at a hotel, but the firemen prevented ________________ to other buildings.
4. "Did Cathy tell you the meeting was canceled?" "No, I don't remember ________________ that."
5. Eric and Ann were upset with Sarah. She left ________________ at the station for an hour!
6. We took the camera to the museum, but the guards stopped ________________ pictures.
7. Fred often tells me funny jokes. He keeps ________________ all the time.

D. Complete the sentences with the verbs in *italics* using **-ing** or **to . . .** Add the appropriate objects if necessary.

1. *(fish)* My grandfather taught *me to fish* when I was five years old.
2. *(live)* "Is Bob moving to Seattle or Portland?" "He decided ________________ in Portland."
3. *(go)* Olivia and Harry hate winter sports. I can't imagine ________________ skiing.
4. *(study)* Greg wants ________________ engineering in college. He enjoys the subject very much.
5. *(take)* "Did Lisa take her medicine?" "Yes. I remember ________________ it after breakfast."
6. *(apologize)* Whenever our son says something rude, my wife forces ________________.
7. *(play)* My neighbors kept ________________ loud music all night. I called them to complain.
8. *(do)* We started using a new program at work. It enables ________________ our work faster.

Answers **p.312** / Review Test 8 **p.248**

LESSON 41 He made her laugh. make/help/see/etc. + *object* + base form

1 make/have/let + *object* + base form

	make/have/let	object	base form	
• He	**made**	**her**	**laugh.**	
• I	**have**	**a mechanic**	**check**	my car regularly.
•	**Let**	**me**	**pay**	for the coffee today.

We can also use **get** + *object* + **to . . .** instead of **make/have/let** + *object* + **base form.**

- Ms. Hill always **gets her secretary to reserve** her flights for business trips. (= makes her secretary reserve)
- I **got Nick to change** his schedule, so now he can go to the concert with us. (= had Nick change)

2 have/get + *object* + past participle

	have/get	object	past participle	
• We	**have**	**our office**	**cleaned**	every Sunday.
• Ron	**will get**	**the invitations**	**printed**	next week.
• I	**had**	**my hair**	**cut.**	How do I look?

3 help + *object* + base form

	help	object	base form	
• I	**will help**	**you**	**do**	the laundry.
• Mistakes	**help**	**people**	**learn.**	

We can also use **to . . .** instead of **base form.**

- Will you **help me (to) choose** a birthday present for my mother?

4 see / hear / listen to / feel / etc. + *object* + base form

	see/hear/etc.	object	base form	
• She	**saw**	**him**	**fall**	into the water.
• I	**heard**	**the dog**	**bark.**	Is someone outside?
• Ted	**felt**	**something**	**hit**	him on the head. It was an apple.

We can also use **see** / **hear** / **listen to** / **feel** / etc. + *object* + **-ing**, but there is the following difference in meaning.

- I **saw Carrie come out** of the house and **get** into a car. (I saw Carrie's action from the beginning to the end.)
- I **saw Carrie talking** on her phone when I was on the bus. (I saw Carrie, and she was in the middle of talking on her phone.)

PRACTICE

A. Look at the pictures and complete the sentences with the verbs in *italics*. Use the *past simple*.

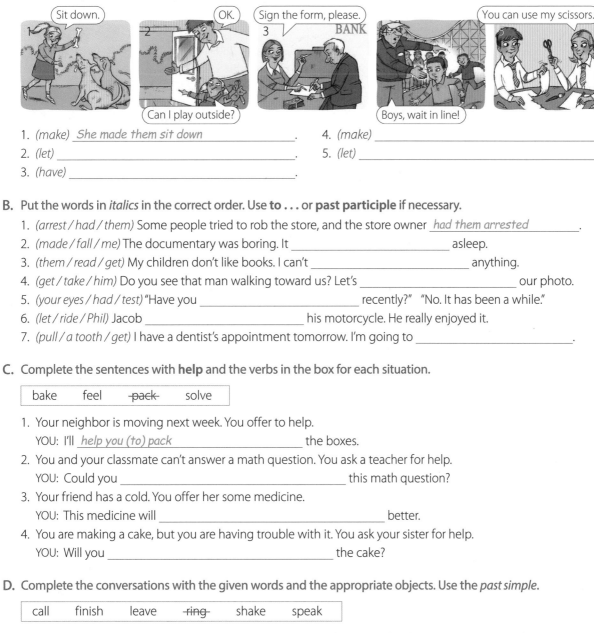

Can I play outside?
Sign the form, please.
BANK
Boys, wait in line!
You can use my scissors.

1. *(make)* She made them sit down.
2. *(let)* ______.
3. *(have)* ______.
4. *(make)* ______.
5. *(let)* ______.

B. Put the words in *italics* in the correct order. Use **to . . .** or **past participle** if necessary.

1. *(arrest / had / them)* Some people tried to rob the store, and the store owner had them arrested.
2. *(made / fall / me)* The documentary was boring. It ______ asleep.
3. *(them / read / get)* My children don't like books. I can't ______ anything.
4. *(get / take / him)* Do you see that man walking toward us? Let's ______ our photo.
5. *(your eyes / had / test)* "Have you ______ recently?" "No. It has been a while."
6. *(let / ride / Phil)* Jacob ______ his motorcycle. He really enjoyed it.
7. *(pull / a tooth / get)* I have a dentist's appointment tomorrow. I'm going to ______.

C. Complete the sentences with **help** and the verbs in the box for each situation.

bake	feel	~~pack~~	solve

1. Your neighbor is moving next week. You offer to help.
   YOU: I'll help you (to) pack the boxes.
2. You and your classmate can't answer a math question. You ask a teacher for help.
   YOU: Could you ______ this math question?
3. Your friend has a cold. You offer her some medicine.
   YOU: This medicine will ______ better.
4. You are making a cake, but you are having trouble with it. You ask your sister for help.
   YOU: Will you ______ the cake?

D. Complete the conversations with the given words and the appropriate objects. Use the *past simple*.

call	finish	leave	~~ring~~	shake	speak

1. Was that the bell for class?
2. Did Dr. Wall give a speech at the seminar?
3. Where's Mary? Has she gone out?
4. Are Mom and Dad looking for me?
5. Did John complete the marathon?
6. The ground was moving. Did you feel it?

(hear) Yes. I heard it ring.
(listen to) Yes, he did. I ______.
(see) Yes. I ______ a minute ago.
(hear) I think so. I ______ you.
(see) Yes. I ______ it.
(feel) I ______ too. I think it was an earthquake!

-ing and to . . .

LESSON 41

Grammar Gateway Intermediate

Answers p.312 / Review Test 8 p.248

LESSON 42

He boiled some water **to make** spaghetti. to . . . of purpose

MP3

1 He boiled some water.

He boiled some water **to make** spaghetti.

"to make" describes the purpose of boiling some water.

2 We can use **to . . .** to talk about the purpose of an action.

- I went to the gym **to exercise**, but it was closed.
- "Why did Helen quit her job?" "**To look** after her grandmother."
- We should put this milk in the fridge **to keep** it cool.

We can also use **in order to . . .** instead of **to . . .** In everyday conversation, we use **to . . .** more often.

- Plants need water **(in order) to survive**.
- I called the doctor's office **(in order) to cancel** my appointment.

We use **in order not to . . .** *(negative)*. Note that we do not use **not to . . .**

- I ran to the gate **in order not to miss** my flight. (*NOT* not to miss)
- **In order not to waste** electricity, please turn off the printer when you're not using it. (*NOT* Not to waste)

3 We can also use **so that** to talk about the purpose of an action. We use *subject + verb* after **so that**.

- I need to start on the report fast **so that I can meet** the deadline.
- We came home early **so that we could watch** our favorite TV show.
- Jane hired a tutor **so that she would do** better in her physics class.

We can use **so that . . . not** *(negative)* instead of **in order not to**. In everyday conversation, we use **so that . . . not** more often.

- Be careful on the ladder **so that you don't fall.** (= in order not to fall)
- We spoke quietly **so that we wouldn't wake** the baby. (= in order not to wake)
- Dry your hair before you go outside **so that you won't catch** a cold.

More about **so that**: Lesson 93

4 We can also use **for** + *noun* to talk about the purpose of an action.

- "I'm bored. Let's go **for a drive**." "Sounds good." (= to drive)
- After jogging for an hour, we sat down on a bench **for some rest**. (= to rest)
- Melissa invited us **for dinner** tomorrow. Would you like to go?

5 We can use *noun* + **to . . .** to talk about the purpose of something.

- Many parents don't get much **time to spend** with their children these days.
- "This is a perfect **place to have** a picnic." "I agree."
- The charity is raising **money to help** poor people. It has raised over $10,000 this week.

PRACTICE

A. Look at the pictures and complete the sentences with **went** and the words in the box.

deliver groceries	fly kites	get some cash	listen to the speech	~~pick up Jessica~~

Please put them here.

1. He *went to the airport to pick up Jessica* ________.
2. They ________________.
3. She ________________.
4. They ________________.
5. He ________________.

B. Complete the sentences with **so that** and the words in the box. Write negative sentences if necessary.

an old lady could sit there	I can look at the stars at night	I would forget
~~we can hear you better~~	we will get hungry later	you injure yourself

1. Could you speak louder *so that we can hear you better* ________?
2. Let's eat something now ________________.
3. "I bought a telescope ________________." "Really? Can I see it?"
4. Mr. Brown reminded me about the meeting ________________.
5. You should stretch before soccer practice ________________.
6. Jenny gave up her seat ________________.

C. Complete the sentences with the words in *italics* using **to . . . / for**.

1. *(attend his graduation)* We visited our son's school *to attend his graduation* ________.
2. *(a conference)* Kevin had to travel to Texas ________________.
3. *(enter the National Museum)* A fee is not required in order ________________.
4. *(wish her good luck)* I called Sally ________________ on her interview.
5. *(a hammer)* My neighbor came by my apartment ________________.
6. *(help the environment)* Some people drive electric cars ________________.
7. *(my cousin's wedding)* I took the day off from work ________________.
8. *(a drink)* Tom and I usually meet on Friday night ________________.

D. Complete the sentences with the words from each box using **to . . .**

chance	decision	dress
letter	movies	~~place~~

\+

~~eat~~	listen	make
send	watch	wear

1. Let's find a *place to eat* ________. How about the café over there?
2. Could you get me a stamp from that drawer? I have a ________________.
3. Emily bought a nice ________________ to the party. She looks so pretty in it.
4. "Have you chosen a college yet?" "No. It's a difficult ________________."
5. "Do you know this song?" "No. I haven't had the ________________ to it."
6. Would you like to go to the theater tonight? There are some good ________________ these days.

Answers p.312 / Review Test 8 p.248

LESSON 43

I'm happy to be back. *Adjective* + **to . . .**

MP3

1

We can use **to . . .** after the following *adjectives* to talk about the reasons for feelings:

happy	glad	pleased	proud	to . . .
afraid	relieved	sorry	surprised	(to be, to receive, etc.)

- "How was Paris?" "It was good, but I'm **happy to be** back."
- "Were you **surprised to receive** the news?" "A little."
- We are **proud to announce** the winners of this year's contest.
- Ray is **afraid to go** to the hospital tomorrow.

2

We can also use **to . . .** after the following *adjectives* to talk about opinions about an action:

easy	cheap	expensive	impossible	to . . .
hard	difficult	safe	dangerous	(to cook, to solve, etc.)

- Pasta is **easy to cook**. I'll teach you.
- "This puzzle is **hard to solve**." "Let me try."
- Houses weren't **cheap to buy**, so we decided to rent one.
- Our beauty products are **safe to use** on any skin type.

In this case, we can also use **It is/was** + *adjective* + **to . . .**

It is/was	*adjective*	*to . . .*	
It's	easy	to cook	pasta. I'll teach you.
"It's	hard	to solve	this puzzle." "Let me try."
It was	impossible	to read	John's handwriting. It was so messy.
It wasn't	expensive	to stay	at the hotel. It was only $20 per night.

We can use **for** + *person* before **to . . .**

	for + person	*to . . .*	
This book is difficult	for me	to understand.	
It's dangerous	for women	to travel	alone.
It was impossible	for the scientists	to do	the experiment due to the weather.
This medicine is safe	for children	to take.	

3

We use **of** + *person* before **to . . .** for the following *adjectives* that describe people's character:

kind	nice	brave	generous	careless	selfish

It is/was	*adjective*	*of + person*	*to . . .*	
It was	kind	of Lynn	to bring	us flowers.
It isn't	brave	of Jed	to lie	about his mistakes.
It's	generous	of Cindy	to forgive	you for forgetting the appointment.
"It was	careless	of you	to leave	the door unlocked." "I'm sorry."

PRACTICE

A. Rewrite the two sentences as one using **to . . .**

1. Steve met Stacy. He was pleased. → *Steve was pleased to meet Stacy* .
2. Maria missed the phone call. She was sorry. → ______ .
3. I found my credit card! I was relieved. → ______ .
4. I got so many presents for my birthday. I was surprised. → ______ .
5. Don helped his wife with the housework. He was glad. → ______ .

B. Write your opinions with the words in *italics* using **to . . .** Write negative sentences if necessary.

1. *(safe, drive)* Race cars *are safe to drive* OR *aren't safe to drive* .
2. *(difficult, learn)* Languages ______ .
3. *(expensive, own)* A car ______ .
4. *(hard, get)* A good job ______ .
5. *(easy, grow)* Plants ______ .

Rewrite the sentences in 1-5 using **It is . . . to . . .**

6. *It is safe to drive race cars* OR *It isn't safe to drive race cars* .
7. ______ .
8. ______ .
9. ______ .
10. ______ .

C. Complete the sentences with the words in the box using **to . . .** Add **for/of.**

(cheap, me, get)	(dangerous, beginners, try)	(generous, him, lend)
(impossible, us, carry)	~~(nice, you, say)~~	(selfish, Evan, eat)

1. "You look lovely in that dress!" "It is *nice of you to say* so."
2. I work for an airline, so it's ______ plane tickets. I get a 50 percent discount!
3. Could you help us? This heavy luggage is ______ .
4. "Mr. Franklin is going to let us borrow $1,000!" "Really? It is ______ us money."
5. Rock climbing is ______ without enough training. They could hurt themselves.
6. It was ______ all of the cookies last night. He didn't share them.

D. Complete the conversation with **to . . .** and the words in *italics*. Add **for/of** if necessary.

DAN

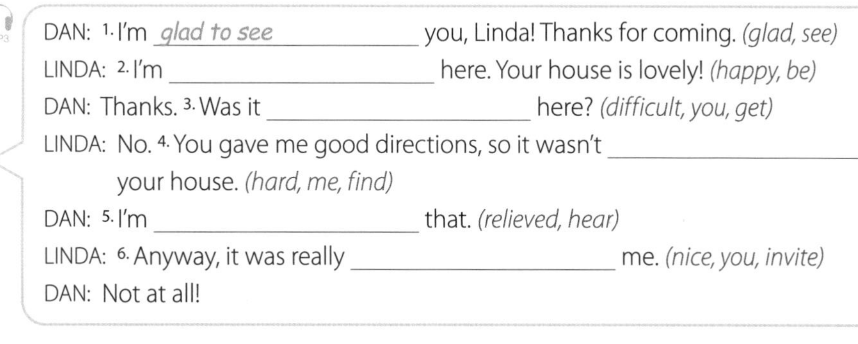

MP3

DAN: 1. I'm *glad to see* you, Linda! Thanks for coming. *(glad, see)*
LINDA: 2. I'm ______ here. Your house is lovely! *(happy, be)*
DAN: Thanks. 3. Was it ______ here? *(difficult, you, get)*
LINDA: No. 4. You gave me good directions, so it wasn't ______ your house. *(hard, me, find)*
DAN: 5. I'm ______ that. *(relieved, hear)*
LINDA: 6. Anyway, it was really ______ me. *(nice, you, invite)*
DAN: Not at all!

LINDA

-ing and to . . .
LESSON 43
Grammar Gateway Intermediate

Answers p.312 / Review Test 8 p.248

I don't know **what to do** during my vacation. *Question word* + **to ...**

1 We can use **to . . .** after **what/who/where**/etc. *(question words)*.

what + to . . .

- I don't know **what to do** during my vacation.
- There are so many good movies. I can't decide **what to watch**.

who + to . . .

- I'm not sure **who to take** to the dance party.
- Would you let me know **who to contact** for more information?

where + to . . .

- "Have you asked Nancy **where to meet**?" "Not yet."
- "Could you tell me **where to find** a cheap hotel?" "Try Main Street."

when + to . . .

- We haven't decided **when to move**. Maybe in August or September.
- Jane and David are still discussing **when to send** their wedding invitations.

how + to . . .

- I used to take piano lessons, but I've forgotten **how to play**.
- My mother taught me **how to make** delicious chicken soup. She is a good cook.

But we do not use **to . . .** after **why**. We use *subject* + *verb* after **why**.

- Sam didn't tell me **why he was** upset this morning. Did he tell you? (*NOT* why to be)
- "Do you have any idea **why Liz left** early?" "She had to meet a client." (*NOT* why to leave)

2 We can also use **to . . .** after **what/which/whose** + *noun*.

what/which + noun + to . . .

- I've finally decided **what major to choose**. I'm going to study biology.
- Derrick has looked at three cars so far, but he isn't certain **which car to buy**.
- Jamie and I have picked **which city to visit** on our trip to Europe.

whose + noun + to . . .

- Rick couldn't choose **whose gift to open** first.
- Two of my best friends were arguing and I wasn't sure **whose side to take**.
- My favorite bands are performing on the same night. I can't decide **whose concert to attend**.

3 We can also use **to . . .** after **whether**.

whether + to . . .

- I don't know **whether to help** Jim with his homework. Maybe he should do it himself.
- Neil is going to be late. I'm not sure **whether to wait** for him.
- The company is considering **whether to build** a new factory.

PRACTICE

A. Look at the pictures and complete the sentences using **to . . .**

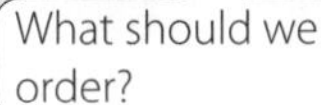

1. They aren't sure *what to order*.
2. She doesn't know __________.
3. He's wondering __________ his shirt.
4. They're deciding __________ again.
5. She's asking __________ the light bulb.

B. Complete the sentences with the words from each box.

how	when	where
~~whether~~	whether	who

\+

come	hire	join
play	put	~~shave~~

1. "I'm still thinking about *whether to shave* my beard." "I think you look better with it."
2. "Could you tell me __________ these boxes?" "Just leave them on that table."
3. Can you teach me the rules again? I don't remember __________ this game.
4. "Did Tara say __________ to her house?" "No, but let's go around 8 o'clock."
5. We interviewed several people, but we still aren't sure __________.
6. I'm considering __________ the tennis club next month. I might not have time.

C. Read what Eddie says and complete the sentences using **to . . .**

1. What gift should I buy for Grace?
2. Whose story should I believe?
3. Which book am I going to read first?

EDDIE

4. What color should I paint the wall?
5. Which way should I go?
6. Whose advice should I follow?

1. He doesn't know *what gift to buy for Grace*.
2. He's confused about __________.
3. He hasn't decided __________ first.
4. He isn't sure __________.
5. He has no idea __________.
6. He's uncertain __________.

D. Complete the conversation with **what/who/whether**/etc. and the verbs in *italics*.

MP3

JUSTIN

JUSTIN: 1. I want to throw a party, but I don't know *what to do*! *(do)*
CHRIS: That's easy. 2. First, pick __________ the party. *(have)*
The place is the most important thing.
3. Then, choose __________. *(invite)*
4. Oh, and decide __________ the food or make it. *(buy)*
JUSTIN: 5. Well, I don't know __________. *(cook)*
I've never tried. I guess I'll buy something.
CHRIS: OK. 6. And think about __________ at the party. *(do)*
Let me know if you need any help.

CHRIS

LESSON 45 I'm thinking **about moving** to a bigger apartment. *Preposition + -ing*

MP3

1 We use **-ing** after **about/in/on/without**/etc. ***(prepositions)***. Note that we do not use **base form** or **to . . .**

- I'm thinking **about moving** to a bigger apartment. (*NOT* about move)
- I lent Mark a book, but he wasn't interested **in reading** it. (*NOT* in to read)
- "When are you planning **on traveling** to Africa?" "In October."
- Don't swim in the lake **without wearing** a life jacket. It's dangerous.

2 We also use **-ing** rather than **base form** or **to . . .** after the following expressions:

in favor of	in spite of	instead of
as a result of	in addition to	

- Most people are **in favor of building** a new mall in town.
- I was late for work yesterday **in spite of leaving** home early.
- It's a nice day. Let's go outside **instead of staying** inside.
- **As a result of losing** his passport, Robert could not board the plane.
- **In addition to buying** jeans and a shirt, Lucy also got a new hat.
- Rick usually uses cash **instead of paying** with his credit card.

3 We also use **-ing** in the following expressions that end with **to**:

be used to + -ing

- **I'm used to having** my camera with me all the time.
- Cathy recently got her license, so she**'s not used to driving** yet.

look forward to + -ing

- I **look forward to hearing** from you soon.
- "Are you **looking forward to meeting** Julie's family?" "Yes, but I'm a little nervous."

object to + -ing

- I **object to having** the meeting on the weekend.
- My wife didn't **object to getting** a new TV, so I bought one.

when it comes to + -ing

- **When it comes to studying**, I prefer going to the library.
- Jim is the best **when it comes to fixing** things.

Note that **to** is used as a *preposition* in these expressions, so we use **-ing** rather than **base form.**

- **I'm used to living** alone. I rarely feel lonely. (*NOT* I'm used to live)
- It was nice doing business with you. We **look forward to working** with you again. (*NOT* look forward to work)

P R A C T I C E

A. Complete the advertisements with the given words.

call	clean	cook	leave	make	~~write~~

1 **Essay Help**
(about) Are you worried *about writing* your next essay? Come to the Learning Center for help.

2 ***MAKE YOUR SINKS SHINE!***
(for) Shine Bright products are perfect ____________ ____________ kitchens and bathrooms.

3 ***Home-Shop.com***
(without) Shop any time ____________ your home! Visit our website.

4 ***Become a master chef!***
(at) If you are bad ____________ ____________, try our online programs. You'll become an expert chef in two months!

5 **Watkins Institute**
(by) Get more information about our great art classes ____________ 555-9867.

6 **J&T Financial Group**
(on) Do you want to be rich? We offer seminars ____________ money.

B. Complete the sentences with the words from each box.

as a result of	in addition to	in favor of
in spite of	~~instead of~~	instead of

\+

celebrate	change	have
offer	train	~~use~~

1. I want to lose weight, so I usually walk up the stairs *instead of using* an elevator.
2. ____________ every day, Sam won the race.
3. The employees are ____________ the business hours during the holidays.
4. ____________ discounts, the store also gives free gifts.
5. Carla still went to school ____________ a cold.
6. "Why did you stay home ____________ Kim's birthday with us?" "I was sick."

C. Complete the sentences with the given words.

be used to	look forward to	object to	~~when it comes to~~	when it comes to

1. *(give)* Ben is great *when it comes to giving* advice. His opinion is always helpful.
2. *(speak)* Ms. Clark gives lectures every week. She ____________ in front of people.
3. *(stay)* I ____________ at that hotel again. The room was so dirty last time.
4. *(build)* Turner Construction has the most experience ____________ bridges.
5. *(take)* "Are you ____________ Mr. Wallace's class?" "Yes. It will be interesting."

D. Find and change any mistakes in each sentence. Put ✓ if the sentence is correct.

1. I never go to bed without brush my teeth. *brush → brushing*
2. In addition to have a big lunch, I ate a huge dinner too. ____________
3. When the dog saw the mailman, it began to bark loudly. ____________
4. I'd like to begin the interview by ask you a personal question. ____________
5. I look forward to start a new project. It'll be exciting! ____________
6. I go to the gym every day, so I'm used to exercising regularly. ____________

Answers p.313 / Review Test 8 p.248

LESSON 46 She spent two hours getting ready. Expressions with -ing and to . . .

MP3

1 We use **-ing** in the following expressions:

spend/waste . . . + -ing

- She **spent two hours getting** ready.
- We **waste too much money eating** out. We should cook more.

feel like + -ing

- This song is so good! I **feel like dancing**!
- "I don't **feel like driving**. Can we take a taxi?" "Sure."

be busy + -ing

- I haven't seen you much lately. Have you **been busy working**?
- Joan and Jackie **are busy making** plans for the holidays.

have trouble/difficulty + -ing

- I'm **having trouble using** this photocopier. Can you help me?
- "Do you **have difficulty sleeping** at night?" "Yes, sometimes."

can't help + -ing

- Jane is in love with Pete. She **can't help thinking** about him.
- I **couldn't help buying** this jacket. It looked so good on me.

be (not) worth + -ing

- "I didn't get the job." "Well, it **was worth trying**."
- "The problems aren't serious. They**'re not worth arguing** about." "I guess you're right."

Would/Do you mind + -ing . . .?

- "I'm a bit cold. **Would you mind turning** off the fan?" "Of course not."
- "**Do you mind getting** some orange juice from the store?" "Not at all."

2 We use **to . . .** in the following expressions:

It takes/costs . . . + to . . .

- **It took 30 minutes to get** to work.
- I like that hotel, but **it costs too much to stay** there.

We can use a *person* after **takes/costs**.

- **It didn't cost Marie** much money **to renovate** her kitchen.

can/can't afford + to . . .

- I **can't afford to buy** that laptop. It's too expensive.
- After saving up for three years, I **could afford to rent** a small apartment downtown.

can't wait + to . . .

- I **can't wait to play** this video game. I heard it's really good!
- Peter got promoted. He **can't wait to tell** everybody.

PRACTICE

A. Put the words in *italics* in the correct order using **-ing.**

1. *(you / mind / would / change)* "*Would you mind changing* ______ the channel?" "No. Which channel?"
2. *(have / like / felt)* Jason ______ a beer, so he went out for a drink.
3. *(push / do / mind / you)* I'm going to the ninth floor. ______ the button for me?
4. *(was / clean / busy)* Sorry I missed your call. I ______ the house.
5. *(difficulty / understand / have)* Troy and I ______ each other sometimes.
6. *(worth / was / read)* The novel ______. I enjoyed it.

B. Read the sentences and complete the new ones using the expressions with **-ing** (feel like + -ing, be busy + -ing, etc.).

1. Danny wants to go to the beach this weekend.
   → Danny *feels like going to the beach this weekend* ______.
2. I fixed my car. It cost a lot of money.
   → I ______.
3. Ms. Carson is busy because she is preparing for her presentation.
   → Ms. Carson ______.
4. Parents worry about their children all the time. They can't stop.
   → Parents ______.
5. Melissa can't see very well without her glasses.
   → Melissa ______.

C. Look at the pictures and complete the sentences with the verbs in *italics* using **It took/cost + person.**

1. *(wash)* *It took him 30 minutes to wash* the dishes.
2. *(make)* ______ the sweater.
3. *(buy)* ______ a new phone.
4. *(watch)* ______ the movie.
5. *(see)* ______ the concert.
6. *(get)* ______ to the hotel.

D. Complete the sentences with **can't help / can(can't) afford / can't wait** and the verbs in the box.

feel	laugh	leave	meet	~~pay~~	stay

1. Jack *can't afford to pay* ______ tuition this year, so he's taking a year off.
2. "Are you excited about your trip to Russia?" "Yes! I ______!"
3. I ______ bad for Sarah. She is sick right now.
4. I'm sorry, but I ______. You look so funny in that costume.
5. "Do you have to go home now?" "No. I think we ______ a little longer."
6. "I want to introduce you to my friends." "I ______ them!"

Answers **p.313** / Review Test 8 **p.248**

There's a cup on the table. There's water in the cup. *Countable and uncountable nouns (1)*

MP3

1 *Nouns* can be countable or uncountable.

The following are *countable nouns*:

cup	chair	store	dog	ant
singer	teacher	orange	apple	flower

- There's **a cup** on the table.
- Two **singers** are on stage.
- I bought **an orange** and three **apples**.
- Smell these **flowers**, Mary! They're so nice.

The following are *uncountable nouns*:

water	oil	rice	salt	rain
love	air	weather	music	traffic

- There's **water** in the cup.
- **Love** is the greatest gift.
- Many people around the world eat **rice**.
- **Traffic** is terrible on the weekends.

2 *Countable nouns* can be singular or plural. We use a *singular noun* for one person/thing and a *plural noun* for two or more people/things.

Singular	a brother	the room	my bag	the child
Plural	two brothers	the rooms	my bags	children

More about spelling rules: Appendix p.279

- Ryan has **a brother**. His name is Nick.
- **The rooms** at that hotel aren't very clean. Don't go there.
- Can you hold **my bag** please? I need to tie my shoes.
- **Children** are chasing **butterflies**. They are trying to catch them.

We always use **a**/**an**/**the**/**my**/etc. before *singular nouns*.

- "Can I borrow **a pencil**?" "Sure. Look in **the drawer**." (*NOT* Can I borrow pencil?, *NOT* Look in drawer)
- Rita isn't going to sell **her car** until next year. (*NOT* Rita isn't going to sell car)

We can use **the**/**my**/etc. or **two**/**three**/etc. before *plural nouns*. We can also use *plural nouns* alone, but we do not use **a**/**an** with *plural nouns*.

- "Where can we hang **our coats**?" "Over there." (*NOT* a coats)
- Matt gave me **flowers** and **two tickets** to the ballet for my birthday. (*NOT* a flowers, *NOT* a tickets)
- **The artists** are going to open a gallery together.

3 *Uncountable nouns* cannot be singular or plural. Therefore, we do not use **a**/**an** or **two**/**three**/etc. before *uncountable nouns*.

- Some people believe that true **happiness** comes from helping others. (*NOT* a happiness)
- I usually use **oil** to fry eggs, but sometimes I use **butter**. (*NOT* an oil, *NOT* two butters)

But we can use **the**/**my**/etc. before *uncountable nouns*. We can also use *uncountable nouns* alone.

- I hope **the weather** doesn't get worse this week.
- **My coffee** needs **sugar**. It's not sweet at all.

4 We use *singular verbs* for *singular/uncountable nouns* and *plural verbs* for *plural nouns*.

- This **sofa costs** too much. I don't think I can buy it.
- **Honesty is** important between friends.
- Those **gloves aren't** big enough for my hands.

More about subject-verb agreement: Appendix p.276

PRACTICE

A. Look at the pictures and complete the sentences with the nouns in the box. Add **a/an** or **two/three**/etc.

bicycle	bird	book	calendar	~~girl~~	umbrella

1-3 / 4-6

1. *There are two girls* ______ on the bench.
2. ______ under the tree.
3. ______ in the sky.
4. ______ on the desk.
5. ______ by the door.
6. ______ on the wall.

B. Complete the sentences with the nouns in the box. Add **a/an** or use the plural form if necessary.

air	apartment	athlete	~~knowledge~~	novel	rain	table	tourist

1. Your *knowledge* ____ of computers will be useful for this job.
2. "Do many ______ come here?" "Yes. The streets are full of visitors in spring."
3. I'd like to reserve ______ for tonight. Could I get one by the window?
4. My tire is almost flat. It needs ______.
5. Many ______ from around the world compete in the Olympics.
6. We got so much ______ last night. The roads are still wet.
7. Jackie moved to ______ close to her university. Now, she can walk to campus.
8. "What ______ did you borrow from the library?" "*Moby-Dick* and *Little Women*."

C. Complete the sentences with the words in *italics*. Use the *present simple*.

1. *(climate, be)* In the Sahara desert, the *climate is* ____ very dry.
2. *(movie, look)* "These three ______ interesting." "Then let's watch one of them."
3. *(juice, contain)* This ______ a lot of vitamin C.
4. *(museum, display)* The ______ a lot of paintings. It has various statues, too.
5. *(cookie, have)* You aren't allergic to nuts, are you? These ______ nuts in them.
6. *(delivery truck, bring)* A ______ fresh ingredients to our bakery each day.

D. Find and change any mistakes in each sentence. Put ✓ if the sentence is correct.

1. I think a salt makes food taste better. I put it on everything. *a salt → salt*
2. "Music aren't very creative these days." "Yes. I agree." ______
3. My sister had baby yesterday. It's a girl. ______
4. A people are using public transportation more because it is convenient. ______
5. The trees in my yard aren't oaks. They're maples. ______
6. Some dishes at this restaurant are served with rices. ______
7. The key to success is hard work. ______
8. "I got two new video game." "Really? Can we play them?" ______
9. This street have no space for more buildings. It's full. ______

Answers **p.313** / Review Test 9 **p.250**

LESSON 48

This bread has cheese in it. *Countable and uncountable nouns (2)*

1 The following *nouns* are usually used as *uncountable nouns*:

bread	cheese	chocolate	meat	food	ice
paper	wood	information	advice	news	

- This **bread** has **cheese** in it.
- **Paper** is usually made from **wood**.
- There's so much **information** on the Internet.
- My cousin just told me great **news**. She's getting married!

bread

cheese

The following names of academic fields that end with s are also *uncountable nouns*:

mathematics	economics	politics	physics

- **Mathematics** is important in most fields of science.
- I don't understand **economics**. It's too hard for me.

2 We can use a cup of, two slices of, etc. before *uncountable nouns* to talk about quantity.

- I had **a cup of coffee** and **two slices of toast** for breakfast today.
- "May I offer you **a piece of advice**?" "Sure."
- There is going to be 50 guests, so we need about **five kilos of rice**.
- "A **bottle of water** costs $5 at this resort." "That seems expensive."

3 The following *nouns* can be both *countable* and *uncountable nouns*, but their meanings change:

light	(Uncountable)	We get a lot of **light** in the hallway.
	(Countable)	The **lights** in the hallway are on. (= "an object making light")
paper	(Uncountable)	That shop sells **paper** and office supplies.
	(Countable)	I read **a paper** on the plane this morning. (= "a newspaper")
exercise	(Uncountable)	It's important to eat well and get plenty of **exercise**.
	(Countable)	I need help doing these math **exercises**." "Let me see." (= "a task")
time	(Uncountable)	Kenny didn't have **time** to do his homework yesterday.
	(Countable)	"Have you been to Japan?" "Yes. Four **times**." (= "one of a series of repeated actions")
glass	(Uncountable)	This bowl is made of **glass**.
	(Countable)	"Could you get some **glasses** from the cabinet?" "Sure." (= "a cup made from glass")
work	(Uncountable)	"Let's meet this weekend." "Sorry, I have too much **work**."
	(Countable)	*Oliver Twist* is one of Dickens's greatest **works**. (= "a result of creative effort")

4 Hair is an *uncountable noun* when it means all of someone's hair, but it is a *countable noun* when it means one strand of hair.

- Everyone in Jenny's family has blond **hair**.
  (= all of Jenny's family's hair)
- The restaurant gave me a free meal because I found **a hair** in my soup.
  (= one strand of hair)

hair　　a hair

P R A C T I C E

A. **Complete the sentences with the nouns in the box. Add a/an if necessary.**

engineer	~~food~~	ice	news	tie

1. You can't eat here, sir. *Food* ____________ isn't allowed in the museum.
2. Evan was always interested in machines. When he grew up, he became ____________.
3. In Sweden, there is a hotel made of ____________. It's only open during the winter.
4. Bill couldn't find ____________ to match his shirt.
5. Did you hear the ____________ about John? He's moving to LA.

envelope	information	meat	picture	politics

6. Do you have ____________? I need something to put this document in.
7. If you major in ____________, you can learn a lot about social issues and policies.
8. "This is ____________ of me a few years ago." "You look very young."
9. "What kind of ____________ is this?" "I think it's beef."
10. This magazine contains a lot of ____________ about cars.

B. **Look at the pictures and complete the sentences with the words in the box.**

(bar, soap)	(bottle, beer)	(jar, jam)	(kilo, cheese)	~~(sheet, paper)~~

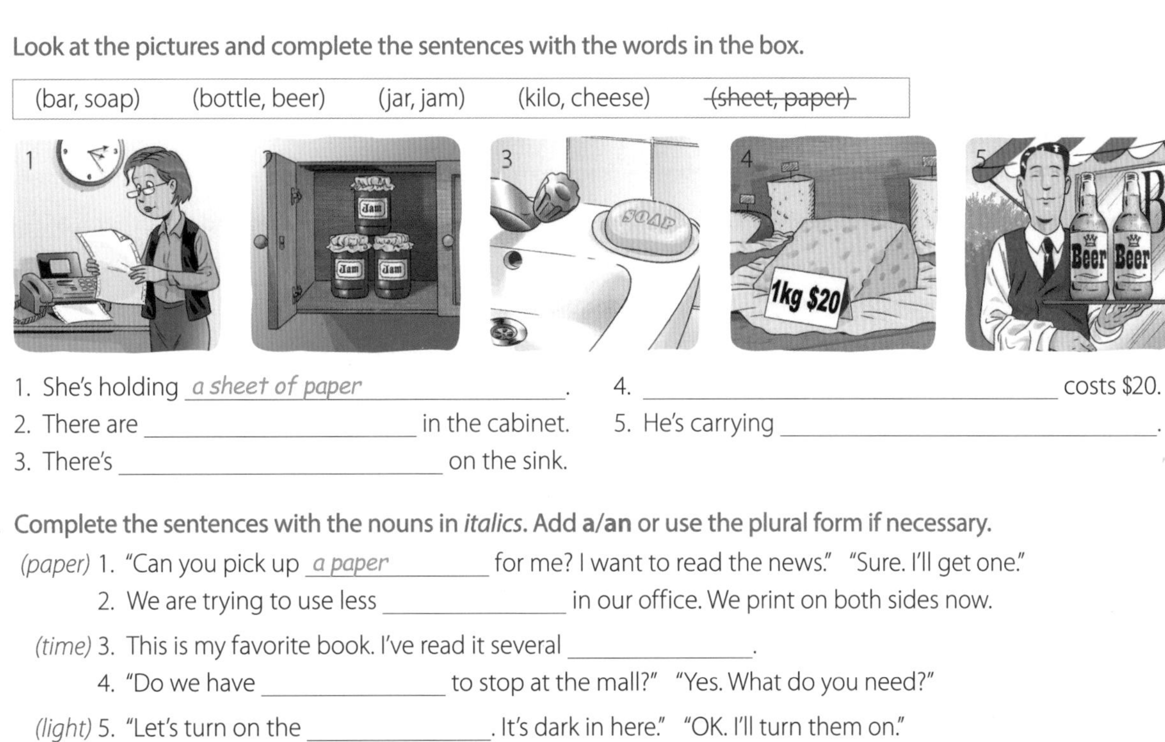

1. She's holding *a sheet of paper* ____________.
2. There are ____________ in the cabinet.
3. There's ____________ on the sink.
4. ____________ costs $20.
5. He's carrying ____________.

C. **Complete the sentences with the nouns in *italics*. Add a/an or use the plural form if necessary.**

(paper) 1. "Can you pick up *a paper* ____________ for me? I want to read the news." "Sure. I'll get one."
2. We are trying to use less ____________ in our office. We print on both sides now.

(time) 3. This is my favorite book. I've read it several ____________.
4. "Do we have ____________ to stop at the mall?" "Yes. What do you need?"

(light) 5. "Let's turn on the ____________. It's dark in here." "OK. I'll turn them on."
6. Bright ____________ came in through my window this morning. It woke me up.

(glass) 7. Most tall buildings today are made of steel and ____________.
8. The ____________ in the sink need to be washed. They're dirty.

(room) 9. I reserved ____________ with an ocean view. You'll like it.
10. There isn't enough ____________ to put the sofa here. It's too big.

(hair) 11. You have ____________ on your sweater. I'll remove it for you.
12. The hairdresser cut off too much ____________. Now it's too short.

Answers **p.313** / Review Test 9 **p.250**

49 We bought some new **furniture.**

Countable and *uncountable nouns* (3)

1 Some *nouns* (furniture, jewelry, etc.) that represent a category are *uncountable nouns*, but *nouns* (chair, earring, etc.) that represent specific items in the category are *countable nouns*.

Uncountable nouns (category)	*Countable nouns (item in a category)*			
furniture	a chair	a desk	a bed	a table
jewelry	an earring	a necklace	a ring	a bracelet
baggage/luggage	a bag	a backpack	a suitcase	a handbag
money	a dollar	a coin	a penny	a bill
mail	a letter	a card	a postcard	an e-mail

- We bought some new **furniture**. It's for our living room.
  I need **a chair** and **a desk** for my bedroom.
- "Do you usually wear **jewelry**?" "No."
  There's **an earring** under the table. Is it yours?
- "Could you lend me some **money**?" "How much do you need?"
  I found a couple of **dollars** and a few **coins** in my pocket.

2 **Work** and **job** are similar in meaning, but **work** is an *uncountable noun* and **job** is a *countable noun*.

- "How's **work** these days?" "Good, but busy."
  "Have you found **a job** yet?" "Yes! Just yesterday."

The following word pairs are also similar in meaning, but one is an *uncountable noun* and the other is a *countable noun*:

vocabulary	(Uncountable)	• I need to study **vocabulary** for my Italian test.
a word	(Countable)	• Shakespeare created more than a thousand **words**.
travel	(Uncountable)	• "Where can I find books on **travel**?" "On the second floor."
a trip	(Countable)	• Dana's family took **a trip** to India last year.
homework	(Uncountable)	• Mr. Larson gives his students a lot of **homework**.
an assignment	(Countable)	• These two **assignments** must be finished by Friday.
advice	(Uncountable)	• Tim always gives me **advice**, but it's not helpful.
a suggestion	(Countable)	• Kim made some **suggestions** for my wedding.
news	(Uncountable)	• "I heard you got promoted!" "Wow, **news** travels fast!"
an article	(Countable)	• There were many interesting **articles** in today's newspaper.
scenery	(Uncountable)	• The **scenery** in Switzerland was amazing.
a view	(Countable)	• Look outside! There's **a** lovely **view** of the sunset.
food	(Uncountable)	• I ordered Chinese **food**. Do you want some?
a meal	(Countable)	• We're having **a meal** with Phillip next week.

PRACTICE

A. Complete the sentences with the nouns in *italics* in the given order. Use the plural form if necessary.

1 ***AA Jewelry Store***

(necklace, earring, bracelet, jewelry)

You can get 50% off on all our *necklaces*, ______________, and ______________. Come see our fine ______________!

2 **Looking for Collectors**

(money, coin, penny)

I would like to sell some old ______________. I have many rare ______________. In fact, two of the ______________ are from the early 1900s!

3 ***For Sale***

(table, chair, furniture)

I'm moving, and I have a ______________, and four ______________ for sale. If you are interested in buying my ______________, give me a call.

4 ***Postage Rates Increase***

(mail, regular letter, postcard)

Postage rates for ______________ have increased. All ______________ and ______________ are now 48 cents.

5 *Found*

(luggage, brown suitcase, backpack)

I found some ______________ near my apartment. There's a ______________ and two ______________. I'm in apartment 102.

B. Complete the sentences with the nouns in the box. Add **a/an** or use the plural form if necessary.

big meal	~~homework~~	news	suggestion	travel	word

1. I forgot to do my *homework* again. The teacher is going to be angry.
2. You can learn a lot of new ______________ while watching foreign films.
3. Can I make ______________? I have an idea about how we can improve sales.
4. ______________ costs money, but sometimes you can find cheap flights online.
5. We rarely hear any ______________ from Timothy. He hasn't called any of us in years.
6. I had ______________ at lunch, but I'm already hungry again.

C. Complete the conversation with the nouns in the box. Use the plural form if necessary.

article	job	~~postcard~~	scenery	trip	work

MP3

JUSTIN

JUSTIN: What are you reading, Dad?
JAMES: 1. It's a *postcard* from your uncle Nick.
2. You know, his company sent him to Belgium for ______________.
JUSTIN: What does he do?
JAMES: 3. He writes ______________ for a travel magazine.
You can read them online.
JUSTIN: Is he a reporter? 4. That sounds like a fun ______________!
JAMES: Yeah. 5. He takes many ______________ and experiences many cultures.
6. He also sees a lot of beautiful ______________.
JUSTIN: Wow. He's so lucky!

JAMES

Answers p.313 / Review Test 9 p.250

Can you pass me those **scissors?** Singular and Plural

MP3

1 The following *nouns* that refer to things with two parts are always plural:

scissors	jeans	pants	shorts	pajamas	glasses	binoculars

- "Can you pass me the **scissors**?" "Sure."
- These **pants** feel really comfortable. You should buy these too.
- "I didn't know you wore **glasses**." "Only for reading."
- I have had my blue **jeans** since I was in high school.

We always use *plural verbs* rather than *singular verbs* after these *nouns*.

- "Your **shorts look** nice. Where did you get them?" "At the department store." (*NOT* Your shorts looks)
- **Pajamas were** on sale at L-Mart. They only cost $20. (*NOT* Pajamas was)

We do not use **a/an** or **two/three**/etc. to count these *nouns*. We use **a pair of**, **two pairs of**, etc. before these *nouns*.

- He brought **two pairs of binoculars** to the football game. (*NOT* two binoculars)
- Doris gave her sister **a pair of jeans** because they didn't fit her anymore. (*NOT* a jeans)

two pairs of binoculars

2 The following *nouns* are always plural:

belongings	clothes	congratulations	goods	surroundings

- Make sure to take all your **belongings** with you when you exit the train.
- Your room is a mess. Please put away your **clothes**.
- "Jim and Lisa are having a baby." "Give them my **congratulations**."
- This lake is beautiful. The **surroundings** seem perfect for hiking.

We always use *plural verbs* rather than *singular verbs* after these *nouns*.

- The **goods were** imported from China. They are sold for 5 dollars. (*NOT* The goods was)
- Phil's apartment is great, but the **surroundings are** noisy. It's by a highway. (*NOT* the surroundings is)

3 We use *singular verbs* after the following *nouns* that refer to groups of many people:

family	class	team	staff	audience	crowd	committee

- My **family is** going to Greece next summer.
- Jerry's **class has** only 12 students in it. He goes to a very small school.
- The city's baseball **team hasn't** improved much over the past two years.
- You should stay at Hotel Valencia. The **staff** there **provides** excellent service.

4 The word **police** is a *plural noun*, so we always use a *plural verb* after **police**.

- The **police have** been looking for a man in a red jacket. (*NOT* The police has been looking)
- "Why **are** the **police** standing outside?" "There was a robbery." (*NOT* Why is the police standing)

We use **a police officer** to talk about one person who is in the police force.

- Maria didn't want her son to become **a police officer**. She thought the job was too dangerous.

P R A C T I C E

A. Look at the customers' order list for Jamie's Closet. Complete the sentences with **one/two**/etc. or **a pair of** / **two pairs of** / etc. and the items on the list.

Jamie's Closet ORDER LIST		ANDY	JENNY	DAVID	TINA
	SHIRT	/		////	
	PANTS	//		/	
	CAP				///
	SUNGLASSES		/		
	SKIRT		//		/
	SHORTS				///

1. Andy ordered *one shirt* ______ and ______.
2. Jenny wants ______ and ______.
3. David is getting ______ and ______.
4. Tina will buy ______, ______, and ______.

B. Complete the sentences with the given words. Use the *present simple*.

a museum ticket	binoculars	my vocabulary	~~the post office~~	the surroundings	these pants

1. *(be)* You can't send mail today. *The post office is* ______ closed because of the holiday.
2. *(help)* ______ you see things from far away.
3. *(improve)* ______ every day. I'm always learning new words.
4. *(be)* The temple is in the mountains. ______ very peaceful.
5. *(seem)* "______ too big for me?" "No, I think they're OK."
6. *(cost)* ______ $6. It includes a free coffee from our cafeteria.

my son	pajamas	personal belongings	these shoes	time	your steak

7. *(feel)* ______ soft because they are for sleeping.
8. *(be)* ______ precious. We should spend every minute wisely.
9. *(play)* ______ the drums quite well. He wants to join a band.
10. *(make)* "______ my feet hurt." "Maybe they're too small for you."
11. *(need)* The gym is not responsible for stolen items. ______ to be watched carefully.
12. *(smell)* "______ delicious." "It's tasty. Here, try some!"

C. Find and change any mistakes in each sentence. Put ✓ if the sentence is correct.

1. Your jeans is in the washing machine. ______ *is → are*
2. "I won the art competition!" "Congratulation!" ______
3. "Whose scissors are these?" "They're mine." ______
4. These shoes is new. They were a gift from my boyfriend. ______
5. "How often does your committee meet?" "Once a week." ______
6. "The police still hasn't arrived." "But you called hours ago!" ______
7. There is a pair of glass on the desk. Are they yours? ______
8. It's too hot to wear pants today. I should have worn a shorts. ______
9. "What good do you sell at your store?" "We sell phones." ______
10. The crowd was excited to see the rock star. ______

Answers **p.314** / Review Test 9 **p.250**

They want to watch **a movie.** a/an and the (1)

1

They want to watch **a movie**.

"a movie" describes one movie that is not specific.

They want to watch **the movie**.

"the movie" describes one specific movie.

2 We use **a/an** before one person/thing that is not specific.

- I need **a lawyer**. Do you know one?
  (= one lawyer that is not specific)
- Can I borrow **a pencil**? I forgot to bring one.
  (= one pencil that is not specific)
- "I'd like to buy **an alarm clock**."
  "How about this one?"

We use **the** before specific people/things.

- I know **the lawyer** that Jim hired. I went to law school with him. (= one specific lawyer)
- Here is **the pencil** I borrowed. Thanks for letting me use it. (= one specific pencil)
- **The alarm clock** I just bought is very loud.
  It will wake my whole family up.

We use **a/an** to talk about someone or something for the first time. We use **the** to talk about them again.

- Mike sent me **a rose** and **a cake**. **The rose** was beautiful, and **the cake** was delicious.
- "I have to write **an essay**." "Oh, what's the topic of **the essay**? Maybe I can help."
- If you see **a man** with **a boy**, please contact the police. **The man** is wearing a brown hat, and **the boy** is wearing blue shorts.

3 We use **the** when it is clear which person/thing the speaker refers to.

- "Where are **the children**?" "They're playing outside."
  (It's clear which children they refer to.)
- "I think I just heard **the bell** ring." "Me too. I'll go and check **the door**."
  (It's clear which bell and which door they refer to.)
- We should fix **the dishwasher**. We haven't been able to use it for weeks.

4 We use **a/an** before *singular nouns*. We do not use **a/an** before *plural/uncountable nouns*.

- I took **a picture** of my **friends** on the beach. The sun was setting behind them. (*NOT* a friends)
- "How is the salmon?" "It needs **salt**." (*NOT* a salt)

We can use **the** before both *singular* and *plural nouns* and also before *uncountable nouns*.

- "Where did you get your jewelry? I really like it."
  "Thanks. **The necklace** was a gift, but I bought **the earrings**."
- Fred got a bonus at work. He spent **the money** on a new stereo.

PRACTICE

A. Complete the sentences with **a/an/the** and the words in *italics*.

1. *(score)* "What's *the score* ________ of the baseball game?" "It's 6 to 3."
2. *(newspaper)* "Could I get ________ for the flight?" "Sure. Which one?"
3. *(dream)* "I had a bad dream." "Really? What was ________ about?"
4. *(bike)* ________ with a flat tire belongs to Adam.
5. *(umbrella)* "Can you lend me ________?" "Sorry. I don't have an extra."
6. *(vase)* "I broke a vase today." "Was it ________ you got from your mom?"
7. *(old man)* There's ________ trying to carry boxes. Let's help him.
8. *(store)* "Is there ________ nearby? I want a snack." "There's one around the corner."

B. Write **a/an/the**.

1. A: Can I borrow *a* ____ hammer?
   B: Sure. We keep one in ____ garage.
2. A: They're building ____ café across ____ street.
   B: Really? When will ____ café open?
3. A: We saw ____ accident on the road this morning.
   B: Oh no. Was anyone hurt in ____ accident?
4. A: I had ____ question but the speaker's gone.
   B: You could send him ____ question by e-mail.
5. A: I didn't see you at ____ dorm. Where were you?
   B: I went to ____ library to study.
6. A: I need ____ bowl for ____ grapes we bought.
   B: OK. I'll bring you one.

C. Find and change any mistakes in each sentence. Put ✓ if the sentence is correct.

1. "Do you see the taxi anywhere?" "Yes, there's one over there!" *the taxi → a taxi*
2. How many a bathrooms does the apartment have? ________
3. A mayor of our city is traveling to Asia. ________
4. Jessica couldn't move the furniture by herself. ________
5. "Did you put a sugar on the grocery list?" "Yes." ________
6. I sent you a postcard. Did you get it? ________
7. "I'm bored." "I have the idea. Let's go to the amusement park!" ________

D. The following is Sandy's movie review. Complete the sentences with **a/an/the** and the words in the box.

~~action movie~~	city	city	enemy	enemy	motorcycle	superhero

Clone Man – A Great Movie!

By Sandy Smith

1. If you are in the mood for *an action movie* ________, I recommend *Clone Man*.
2. It is a movie about ________.
3. Clone Man is his name, and he lives in ________ with a lot of criminals.
4. Every night, he drives ________ around the city to fight crime.
5. He also has ________ who is trying to destroy the city.
6. But in the end, Clone Man saves ________ and everybody is happy.
7. My favorite part was when Clone Man defeated ________.

It was amazing! Go watch *Clone Man* today!

Answers **p.314** / Review Test 10 **p.252**

A baby needs more sleep than an adult. a/an and the (2)

1 We use **a/an** to talk about people/things in general.

- **A baby** needs more sleep than **an adult**.
- **A bicycle** is a convenient way to get around this town.
- "How many legs does **a spider** have?" "Eight."
- **An egg** consists of an egg white and a yolk.

But we do not use **a/an** before *uncountable nouns*, even when they refer to things in general.

- **Honesty** is the most important thing in a relationship. (*NOT* An honesty)
- Some students love doing **homework**. Other students don't like it. (*NOT* a homework)

2 We can also use *plural nouns* to talk about people/things in general. We usually use *plural nouns* more often than **a/an** + *singular noun*.

- **Children** can learn **foreign languages** easily.
- How do **bees** make honey?
- "Do you enjoy watching **operas**?" "No. I prefer **plays**."
- **Oranges** are rich in **vitamins**.

3 Note that we do not use **the** to talk about people/things in general. We use **the** for specific people/things.

- **An architect** designs buildings.
  "Who is **the architect** for this building?" "Mr. Duval."
- **Backpacks** are useful for hiking and camping.
  The backpacks designed by Jimmy King are on sale.
- "What is **cheese** made from?" "Milk."
  "When did you buy **the cheese** in the refrigerator?" "I just got it yesterday."

4 When we talk about animals, machines, and instruments, we can also use **the** to talk about them in general. In this case, we use *singular nouns* after **the**.

- **The lion** is commonly known as the king of the jungle. (= A lion *OR* Lions)
- **The sunflower** turns toward the sun. (= A sunflower *OR* Sunflowers)
- "When was **the telescope** invented?" "In the early 1600s."
- In jazz music, you can often hear **the saxophone**.

5 We also usually use **a/an** to talk about someone's job or the type of something.

- Craig is **an editor** for a fashion magazine. He's great at his job.
- Monaco is **a country**. It's near France.
- The woman standing over there is **an illustrator**. She's very talented.
- "What is your hometown like?" "Well, it isn't **a** large **town**. It's very quiet."

P R A C T I C E

A. Write sentences explaining the nouns in *italics* with the words in the box. Use the plural form of the nouns in *italics*.

be great for breakfast or as a snack	be words for people, places, or things
~~create paintings and sculptures~~	help you keep in touch with friends
provide space to park cars	travel on ships

1. *(artist)* *Artists create paintings and sculptures* ______.
2. *(muffin)* ______.
3. *(garage)* ______.
4. *(cell phone)* ______.
5. *(noun)* ______.
6. *(sailor)* ______.

B. Read the blogs of twins Fred and Peter. Write **a/an/the** or put – if nothing is necessary.

http:// Fred.foodblog.com
Fred .blog
1. I'm a good cook and I love __–__ food!
2. I especially like ______ sandwiches.
3. ______ good sandwich needs good bread.
4. ______ bread in my sandwiches is delicious, and it's homemade. I have a great recipe.
5. If you want my recipe, send me ______ e-mail.
http:// Peter.myblog.com
Peter .blog
6. I think cooking is a waste of ______ time.
7. My brother Fred cooks all the time, but I prefer going out to eat at ______ restaurants.
8. Near my house, there's ______ Thai restaurant.
9. ______ food there is really good!
10. I especially like ______ spicy soup on their menu.

C. Complete the sentences with the words in the box using the singular or plural form. Add **the** if necessary.

~~bed~~	blue whale	bone	judge	microscope	tile

1. I like *the bed* ______ in this hotel room. It's very comfortable.
2. ______ can be 30 meters long. That's longer than all other animals.
3. It was not possible to see very small things before ______.
4. ______ break more easily as you get older because they become weaker.
5. I like ______ in this catalog. They seem perfect for our bathroom.
6. Being fair is an important quality for ______. They must not be affected by their own opinions.

D. Put **a/an** and the words in *italics* in the correct order.

1. *(Bill's wife / newspaper reporter / is)* *Bill's wife is a newspaper reporter* ______.
2. *(the tomato / vegetable / is)* ______ that is often used in pasta.
3. *(is / excellent singer / Todd)* ______. I love his voice.
4. *(is / Judy / lawyer in Florida)* ______.
5. *(old desk / this / is)* ______. It was my grandmother's.
6. *(the cactus / tough plant / is)*
______. It grows in deserts and requires little water.

Answers **p.314** / Review Test 10 **p.252**

The sun is at the center of our solar system. the (1)

MP3

1 We usually use **the** with the following *nouns*:

Only one in the world	the sun	the moon	the earth	the world	the universe
Nature	the sea	the ocean	the sky	the ground	
	the rain	the wind	the environment		

- **The sun** is at the center of our solar system.
- **The sky** became cloudy and **the rain** began to fall.
- Mr. Watson owns one of the biggest computer manufacturers in **the world**.

Theater	the theater	the cinema	the movies
Media	the Internet	the radio	

- **The theater** offers discount tickets on Tuesdays.
- "Where did you buy those gloves?" "On **the Internet**."

We do not use **the** when **TV** means a broadcast, but we use **the** when **TV** means a piece of equipment.

- I don't watch **TV**. I prefer reading books. (= a broadcast)
  Sitting close to **the TV** is bad for your eyes. (= an equipment)

We do not use **the** when **movies** means movies in general, but we use **the** when **movies** means a theater.

- I like **movies**. I watch them often. (= movies in general)
  I haven't been to **the movies** in months. I've been very busy. (= a theater)

Government agency	the police	the government	the army

- We called **the police** right after we saw the traffic accident.
- My brother works for **the government**. He's in **the army**.

2 We also usually use **the** in the following expressions:

the only + *noun*

- Kelly is **the only woman** in our department.
- "Do you play tennis, too?" "No. Badminton is **the only sport** I play."

the same + *noun*

- "Are we wearing **the same dress**?" "Yes. We look like twins!"
- Karen and I have been in love with **the same man** since college.

the first/second/third/etc. + *noun*

- "Who was **the first president** of the United States?" "George Washington."
- Our seats for the concert are in **the fifth row**.

the best/worst/fastest/etc. + *noun*

- "I had **the worst day** of my life today!" "Why? What happened?"
- "How do I get to Wentworth Tower?" "**The fastest way** is by subway."

P R A C T I C E

A. Write **the** in the correct places.

1. Look! ^The^ Moon is full tonight!
2. TV uses a lot of electricity.
3. In 2010, China had largest population in world.
4. Sky is beautiful. There are so many stars.
5. We go to movies a lot. We enjoy it.
6. I use Internet every day for research.
7. Do you prefer listening to radio or watching TV?
8. "I hope rain stops soon." "I do too."
9. Government passed a new child protection law.
10. Ronald and I went fishing in ocean yesterday.

B. Complete the sentences with the nouns in *italics*. Add **the** if necessary.

1. *(TV)* Michael moved <u>the TV</u>. It's in the living room now.
2. *(cinema)* "Are there any good movies at ________?" "I don't know. Let's check."
3. *(books)* Paula likes reading ________ in her free time.
4. *(flour)* ________ is an important ingredient for baking.
5. *(wind)* ________ is perfect for flying kites today.
6. *(universe)* Scientists are searching for life on other planets in ________.
7. *(TV)* There are so many advertisements on ________ these days. I get tired of watching them.
8. *(songs)* I need to choose music for my wedding. Can you recommend ________ about love?

C. Put **the** and the words in *italics* in the correct order.

1. *(is / museum / The Central Gallery / only)* <u>The Central Gallery is the only museum</u> in this city.
2. *(fourth / April / month / is)* ________ of the year.
3. *(oldest / child / is / who)* ________ in your family?
4. *(best / serves / Brad's Café / coffee)* ________ in town.
5. *(person / my class / in / I'm / only)* ________ without a cell phone.
6. *(Matthew / same / in / house / has lived)* ________ all his life.

D. The following is Justin's report. Write **the** in the correct places.

1. **Protect ^the^ Earth!**

By Justin Wilson 

2. It is very important to save environment.

The earth gives us food and water, so we must protect it.

3. Plants and animals living on the land and in ocean need a clean environment, too.

So what is the solution?

4. Recycling is first thing we can do. And it's easy!

5. Second thing is reducing pollution.

6. There are many ways to help, but best way is to do something right now before it's too late.

Answers **p.314** / Review Test 10 **p.252**

LESSON 54

Is he at home? the (2)

MP3

1 We do not use **the** with the following expressions that include **home**, **work**, **bed**, etc.:

at home	go/come home	leave home
at work	go to work	leave work
in bed	go to bed	

- "I'm here to see Mr. Smith. Is he **at home**?" "No. He's at work."
- "Why is Pete still **in bed**?" "He didn't **go to bed** until midnight last night."
- "When are you **coming home**?" "In about an hour. I'll be **leaving work** soon."
- I **left home** early but I was still late to the movie.

2 We can use **school**, **church**, **prison**, and **jail** without or with **the**. In this case, there is the following difference in meaning:

We do not use **the** when the place is used for its general purpose.

- John is at **school**. His class hasn't finished yet.
  (**school** = a place for learning)
- My family attends **church** every Sunday.
  (**church** = a place for worship)
- The police caught the thief and now he is in **prison**.

We use **the** when the place is used as a location for a specific event.

- We went to **the school** to see Jack's graduation.
  (**the school** = a location for Jack's graduation)
- Lucy attended a wedding at **the church** last Friday.
  (**the church** = a location for a wedding)
- The journalist visited **the prison** to interview prisoners about their lives.

3 We usually do not use **the** with the following expressions:

Day, Month, Year	Sunday	Monday	March	November	1987	2020
Holiday	Thanksgiving	Easter	Christmas	New Year's Day		
Meal	breakfast	lunch	dinner			

- "Do you have plans on **Sunday**?" "No, not yet."
- In the US, **Thanksgiving** is in **November**. In Canada, it's in **October**.
- "What's in that bag?" "Just some food I brought for **lunch**."
- In **1987**, we started our business. Thankfully, it has been a success.

We can use or leave out **the** with seasons. In this case, there is no difference in meaning.

- We don't travel in **the summer**. We always take a vacation in **the winter**.
  OR We don't travel in **summer**. We always take a vacation in **winter**.

4 We do not use **the** before a person's name or their title.

- "Who wrote this story?" "I think it was **Marsha Cole**." (*NOT* the Marsha Cole)
- "Have you met **Dr. Sanders** before?" "Yes, I have."

But we can use **the** before a last name to talk about a whole family. In this case, we use the plural form for the last name.

- "I'm looking for Jack Dawson. I have a package for him." "Oh, **the Dawsons** live next door."
- "How do you know **the Parkers**?" "Their son and my son go to the same school."

P R A C T I C E

A. Complete the sentences with the nouns in the box. Add **the** if necessary.

bed	bed	earth	home	home
sea	theater	universe	~~work~~	work

1. I don't have to go to *work* __________ today. I took the day off.
2. Most dolphins live in __________, but some are found in rivers.
3. Before you leave __________ today, please clean your bedroom.
4. "There's a new play at __________. I want to see it." "What's it called?"
5. Michelle brushed her teeth, put on her pajamas, and went to __________.
6. There are so many stars in __________. There are too many to count.
7. Elise is still at __________. She has a lot to do at the office today.
8. "How long does it take __________ to go around the sun?" "About 365 days."
9. Jason had to turn back and go __________. He forgot to lock his front door.
10. Your father is in __________. Keep the noise down so you don't wake him.

B. Look at the pictures and write sentences with **at school / at church / in jail**. Add **the** if necessary.

1. *Julia is at school* __________.
2. __________.
3. __________.
4. __________.
5. __________.

C. The following is an e-mail from Linda. Complete the sentences with the words in *italics*. Add **the** if necessary.

Subject	Christmas Party
To	georgesusan@fastmail.com
From	lindawilson@fastmail.com

Dear Susan and George,

1. We are having a party to celebrate *Christmas* __________ this year! *(Christmas)*
2. It will be on __________ night at 7 o'clock. *(Saturday)*
3. We will have __________ and drinks. *(dinner)*
4. Please call me at __________ and let me know if you can come. *(home)*
5. I know you don't like leaving your house in __________. *(winter)*
6. But you should come out! It'll be __________ of the year! *(best party)*

7. P.S. I've already invited __________. *(Jacksons)*
8. And I want to invite __________ too. *(Mrs. Carson)* Do you have her phone number?

Linda

Articles

LESSON 54

Grammar Gateway Intermediate

Answers **p.315** / Review Test 10 **p.252**

LESSON 55

She met him at the party. *Pronouns*

MP3

1 We can use **I/me/you/they/them**/etc. *(pronouns)* to refer to a person/thing.

Subjective	I	we	you	he	she	it	they
Objective	**me**	**us**	**you**	**him**	**her**	**it**	**them**

- "How does Janet know Sean?" "**She** met **him** at the party."
- "What do **you** think of these earrings?" "**They**'re beautiful. Where did **you** get **them**?"

We can use **me/us**/etc. after **for/of**/etc. *(prepositions)*, but we do not use **I/we**/etc.

- I might be late to dinner, so don't wait **for me**. (*NOT* for I)
- "Look at this old picture **of us**!" "Wow! We were so young." (*NOT* of we)

2 We use **my/your/their**/etc. to talk about possession. We always use *nouns* after these *pronouns*.

Subjective	I	we	you	he	she	it	they
Possessive	**my**	**our**	**your**	**his**	**her**	**its**	**their**

- "I can't find **my wallet**." "Have you checked in **your bag**?"
- "This is **our** new **office**." "It's nice! I like **its** big **windows**."

We can use **own** after **my/your/their**/etc. to emphasize possession.

- For **your own safety**, you should always wear your seatbelt.
- "Does Tanya live in the dorm?" "No. She has **her own apartment**."

3 We use **mine/yours/theirs**/etc. *(possessive pronouns)* to talk about something that belongs to someone.

Possessive	my	our	your	his	her	its	their
Possessive pronoun	**mine**	**ours**	**yours**	**his**	**hers**	-	**theirs**

- "Somebody's phone is ringing." "Oh, it's **mine**. I'll answer it."
- "Does that scarf belong to Sarah?" "It might be **hers**. I think she left it here."

We always use *nouns* after **my/your/their**/etc., but we do not use *nouns* after **mine/yours/theirs**/etc.

- "I put **your ice cream** in the freezer." "Oh, OK. Thanks."
  "Did you buy ice cream?" "Yes. I put **yours** in the freezer." (*NOT* yours ice cream)

When **mine/yours/theirs**/etc. is used as the *subject*, the *verb* form depends on what it refers to.

- Your room is so clean. **Mine is** always messy. (**Mine** refers to the singular noun, my room.)
- "Are those your children?" "No. **Ours are** at home." (**Ours** refers to the plural noun, our children.)
- I think the chef put too much salt in my soup. How **does yours taste**?

4 We do not use **a/an/the** before **my/your/mine/yours**/etc.

- **Your computer** is so fast! **Mine** is really slow. (*NOT* A your computer, *NOT* The mine)
- Our company is celebrating **its anniversary** this year. (*NOT* an its anniversary)

PRACTICE

A. Write **I/we**/etc. or **me/us**/etc.

1. This shirt fits me and *it* ________ is on sale. Should I buy ________?
2. Jim has my old bicycle. ________ told him to keep it.
3. "Do ________ know John and his brothers?" "No, I've never met ________."
4. "Can you return my dictionary?" "Of course. I'll bring it to ________ tonight."
5. Our teacher didn't give ________ any homework on Friday. Everyone was happy.
6. "Marie, these letters came for you." "Oh, are ________ for ________?"
7. "Does Tony like swimming?" "Yes. ________ really enjoys it."
8. I haven't spoken to Helen in weeks. Have you heard from ________ recently?

B. Write **my/your**/etc. or **mine/yours**/etc.

1. A: Are those Tommy's sunglasses?
   B: They aren't *his* ________. They belong to Ian.
2. A: Why isn't Sandra at work this morning?
   B: ________ son had to go to the hospital.
3. A: I have my ticket. Where's ________?
   B: I thought you had mine!
4. A: Rick and Tina sold ________ house.
   B: Why? Are they moving?
5. A: I'm so tired of riding the bus.
   B: Me too. We need ________ own car.
6. A: Is this your sweater?
   B: Yes, it's ________. I made it.

C. Find and change any mistakes in each sentence. Put ✓ if the sentence is correct.

1. "Is Ms. Morrison here today?" "Yes. She's at hers desk." *hers → her*
2. The Millers built their own garage last year. ________
3. "Are Debbie and Rob staying at that hotel?" "No. Their is the one next to it." ________
4. "My parents are going on a trip this weekend." "Really? Mine is, too." ________
5. "Someone left this briefcase in the meeting room." "Oh, that's mine briefcase." ________
6. "How was a your date?" "I had a great time!" ________
7. "Kevin gave a great presentation, didn't he?" "Yes. His were very interesting." ________
8. We need a new soccer ball. The ours has a hole in it. ________

D. The following is a letter from Chris. Write **I/me**/etc. or **your/theirs**/etc.

Dear Alberto,

1. I'm going to Mexico City with *my* ________ sister for summer vacation.
2. ________ will arrive next Thursday and will be taking a tour together on Friday.
3. My sister is really excited because it will be ________ first time in Mexico.
4. Since your parents haven't met ________, we'd like to have dinner with ________ family on Friday.
5. Can you ask them if ________ are interested?

By the way, I think I lost your phone number.

6. ________ is (810) 555-6477. 7. What's ________? Let me know.
8. I hope to talk to ________ soon!

AIR MAIL

From Chris

Pronouns and Possessives

LESSON 55

Grammar Gateway Intermediate

LESSON 56 What is Mr. Elliott's address? -'s and of

MP3

1 We can use **-'s** with a person or an animal to talk about possession. We use *nouns* after **-'s**.

- "What is **Mr. Elliott's address**?" "I'm not sure." (= The address possessed by Mr. Elliott)
- **Sheep's wool** is often used in clothing. (= The wool possessed by sheep)
- "I like your car!" "Oh, this is **my brother's car**. I just borrowed it."

More about spelling rules: Appendix p.279

We can also use **-'s** after the following time expressions:

today	yesterday	tomorrow	this/next/last + week/month/year/etc.

- "Have you read **today's newspaper**?" "Not yet."
- **Tomorrow's weather** is going to be cold.
- Professor Nash will not speak at **this year's forum**. We'll have a different speaker.

2 We can use **-'s** without a *noun* when it is clear what the speaker refers to.

- "Is this your watch?" "No, it's **Colin's**." (It's clear that **Colin's** refers to the watch possessed by Colin.)
- "Whose magazine is this?" "It's **Emily's**. She bought it earlier." (It's clear that **Emily's** refers to the magazine possessed by Emily.)

We can also use **-'s** without a *noun* to talk about someone's house.

- We went to **Alison's** last night to study. We have a test today. (= Alison's house)
- "What are you doing tonight?" "I'm going to a party at **Jimmy's**." (= Jimmy's house)

We can also use **-'s** without a *noun* in the following expressions:

the dentist's/doctor's (office) the hairdresser's (shop)

- I went to **the dentist's** because I had a toothache.
- Sue has an appointment **at the hairdresser's** later today.

3 We can also use **of** to talk about possession. We usually use **of** for things rather than people or animals.

- Look at **the color of the sky**. It's beautiful.
- I don't remember **the title of this song**.
- "Who's **the author of that book**?" "Dale Addams."

4 We can use either **-'s** or **of** for countries, cities, agencies, etc.

- **Egypt's pyramids** are famous. *OR* **The pyramids of Egypt** are famous.
- **The UN's main office** is in New York City. *OR* **The main office of the UN** is in New York City.

5 We can use the following expressions to talk about a part of a larger group:

a/an	noun	of	mine/yours/theirs/etc.
some			Laura's / my father's / etc.

OR

one	of	my/your/their/etc.	noun
some		Laura's / my father's / etc.	

- **A friend of mine** went to the same high school as Brad.
  OR **One of my friends** went to the same high school as Brad.
- These are **some paintings of Laura's**.
  OR These are **some of Laura's paintings**. They will be sold at the auction.
- We are preparing a nice meal because **a client of my father's** is coming to dinner.
  OR We are preparing a nice meal because **one of my father's clients** is coming to dinner.

P R A C T I C E

A. Put **-'s/of** and the words in *italics* in the correct order.

1. *(sister / Jack)* Jack's sister ________ is a waitress at a steakhouse nearby.
2. *(the owner / this truck)* Who is ________? It's blocking the street.
3. *(that movie / the director)* "I met ________." "Really? What is he like?"
4. *(concert / last night)* We had a great time at ________. It was amazing.
5. *(the food / the ingredients)* My friend always asks about ________ when she eats out.
6. *(a turtle / shell)* ________ protects it from other animals.
7. *(election / next month)* "Who will win ________?"
   "I'm not sure. Maybe Nate Lewis."
8. *(the building / the roof)* When the tree fell, it damaged ________.

B. Complete the sentences with **-'s** and the words in *italics*. Use only one word in *italics* if possible.

1. *(the doctor, office)* "Is Max coming with us?" "No. He's at the doctor's ________ right now."
2. *(Angela, suitcase)* "Whose suitcase is this?" "I think it's ________."
3. *(yesterday, picnic)* We met a lot of people at ________. It was fun.
4. *(Brazil, president)* "Who is ________?" "I don't know."
5. *(Ron, house)* "Where are we going to watch the football game?" "How about at ________?"
6. *(the hairdresser, shop)* I saw Michelle at ________ last week. She was getting a haircut.
7. *(rabbit, hair)* This paintbrush is made from ________.
8. *(my neighbor, flowers)* "I like the flowers beside your house!" "They're actually ________."

C. Put **of** and the words in *italics* in the correct order.

1. *(coworker / a / his)* Mr. Lim went out for lunch with a coworker of his ________.
2. *(his / one / coworkers)* Mr. Lim went out for lunch with ________.
3. *(some / my brother's / toys)* ________ are missing. He's upset.
4. *(goals / my / one)* Losing weight is ________ for this year.
5. *(some / classmates / Rita's)* Those people in the photo are ________.
6. *(a / ours / tradition)* Sam and I cook together every Christmas. It's ________.
7. *(drinks / their / some)* My friends just opened a café. ________ are great.
8. *(hobby / Melinda's / a)* ________ is playing cards. She always wins.

D. Put **-'s/of** and the words in *italics* in the correct order.

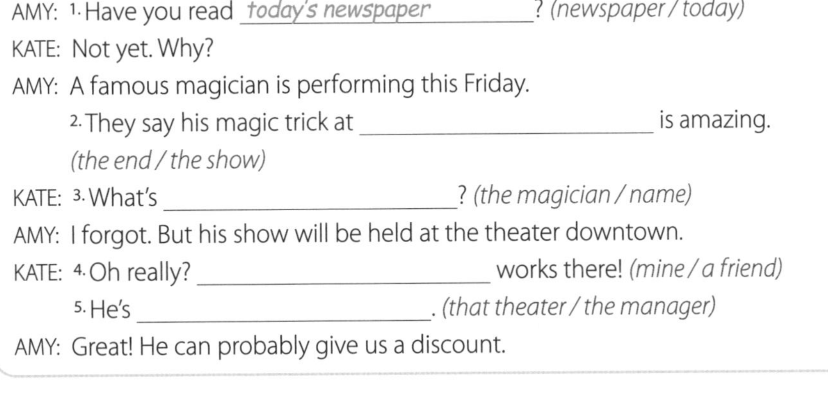

AMY: 1. Have you read today's newspaper ________? *(newspaper / today)*
KATE: Not yet. Why?
AMY: A famous magician is performing this Friday.
2. They say his magic trick at ________ is amazing. *(the end / the show)*
KATE: 3. What's ________? *(the magician / name)*
AMY: I forgot. But his show will be held at the theater downtown.
KATE: 4. Oh really? ________ works there! *(mine / a friend)*
5. He's ________. *(that theater / the manager)*
AMY: Great! He can probably give us a discount.

LESSON 57

Let me introduce **myself.** myself/yourself/etc.

MP3

1 We use **myself/yourself**/etc. *(reflexive pronouns)* as the *object* when the *subject* and *object* refer to the same person/thing.

Subjective	I	you (singular)	he	she	it	we	you (plural)	they
Reflexive pronoun	**myself**	**yourself**	**himself**	**herself**	**itself**	**ourselves**	**yourselves**	**themselves**

- Let me introduce **myself**. My name is Chris Wilson.
- Just try your best. You might surprise **yourself**.
- Chameleons hide **themselves** by changing their skin color.
- Todd is going to quit smoking. He promised **himself**.

We use **me/you**/etc. rather than **myself/yourself**/etc. when the *subject* and *object* do not refer to the same person/thing.

- "Who taught Henry how to ride a bike?" "He taught **himself**." (He = himself)
  "Who taught Henry how to ride a bike?" "His cousin taught **him**." (His cousin ≠ him)

2 We can also use **myself/yourself**/etc. for emphasis. In this case, we use it at the end of a sentence or after the person/thing we want to emphasize.

- "I took those pictures **myself**." "They're great. You're like a photographer!"
- The resort **itself** is small, but the location is perfect.
- I went to a job interview yesterday. I met the CEO **himself**.

We can leave out **myself/yourself**/etc. when we use it for emphasis. But we use it when it is the *object*.

- When her parents aren't home, Joanne takes care of her sister **(herself)**.
  Joanne is old enough to take care of **herself**. (*NOT* Joanne is old enough to take care of.)

3 We use **by myself/yourself**/etc. to mean "alone" or "without any help."

- "Who went shopping with you?" "No one. I went **by myself**."
- I heard Jill went on a trip to Vietnam **by herself.** That's pretty brave.

We can use **all** before **by myself/yourself**/etc. to emphasize the meaning.

- "Did you clean up the whole house **all by yourself**?" "Yes, I did."

We can also use **on my own** / **on your own** / etc. instead of **by myself/yourself**/etc.

- "Did Ed's mom make him apply to medical school?" "No. He decided **on his own**." (= by himself)
- Nobody helped us with the project. We finished it **on our own**. (= by ourselves)

4 We use **-self** in the following expressions:

enjoy -self (= "have great time")
behave -self (= "act politely")
help -self (to) (= "take something freely")
make -self at home (= "relax like someone is at their home")

- The guests **enjoyed themselves** at the party.
- My daughter didn't **behave herself** today.
- There are some drinks on the table. Please **help yourselves**.
- "Come in and **make yourself at home**." "Thanks!"

PRACTICE

A. Write **me/you**/etc. or **myself/yourself**/etc.

1. I wasn't careful with the scissors, so I cut *myself*__________.
2. Amanda's husband surprised __________ with a lovely dinner for her birthday.
3. "We failed our group project because of me." "Don't blame __________. We picked a hard topic."
4. Kim and I visited Kevin last night. He showed __________ his new apartment.
5. In some countries, women have to cover __________ when they're outside.
6. Can you please pay attention to __________? I'm trying to tell you a story.
7. My son is only a year old. He can't feed __________ yet.
8. You and Molly did a great job. You should be proud of __________.

B. Complete the sentences with **myself/yourself/themselves**/etc. and the words in the box. Use the *past simple*.

book all of the tickets	fix the sink	make them	not bake this pie	pack everything	~~see it~~

1. "How does Bill know about the car crash?" "He *saw it himself*__________."
2. "__________ the Smiths __________?" "No. I helped them get ready to move."
3. We __________. We got it at the bakery.
4. "Where did you buy these baby clothes?" "Actually, I __________."
5. Karen didn't use a travel agency. She __________ on the Internet.
6. "__________ you __________?" "No. Bob repaired it for me."

C. Complete the sentences with **myself/yourself/themselves**/etc. and the verbs in the box.

behave	~~enjoy~~	help	make	see	trust	turn

1. I always *enjoy myself*__________ in Tahiti. It is such a beautiful island.
2. "Was Jim excited to __________ on TV?" "Yes. It was his first TV interview."
3. "Welcome, Sue! Please __________ at home." "Thank you! Your home is very nice."
4. We are a good team and we can win this game! We just have to __________!
5. Boys, don't run in the hallway. __________, please.
6. Hotel guests may __________ to breakfast from 6 a.m. to 9 a.m.
7. That lamp is automatic. It will __________ off.

D. The following are guidelines for new Bio-Tech employees. Write **yourself / by yourself**.

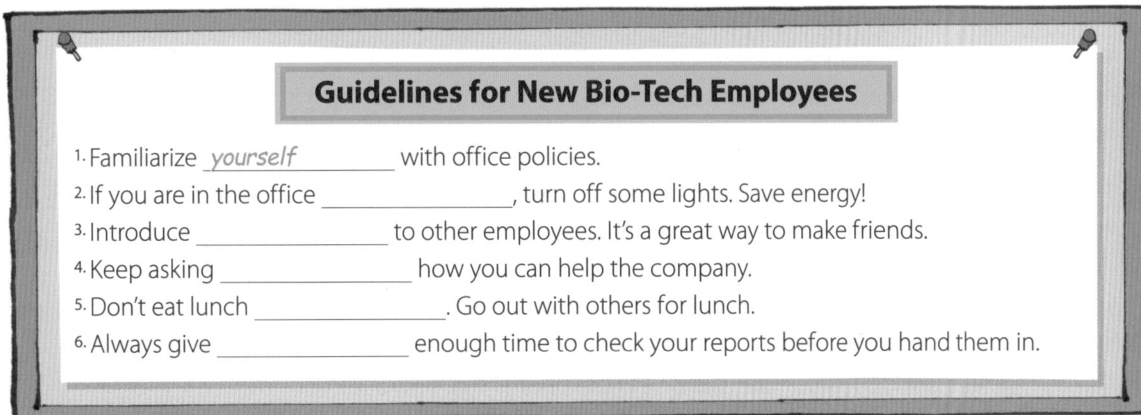

Guidelines for New Bio-Tech Employees

1. Familiarize *yourself*__________ with office policies.
2. If you are in the office __________, turn off some lights. Save energy!
3. Introduce __________ to other employees. It's a great way to make friends.
4. Keep asking __________ how you can help the company.
5. Don't eat lunch __________. Go out with others for lunch.
6. Always give __________ enough time to check your reports before you hand them in.

Answers **p.315** / Review Test 11 **p.254**

My brother has a car, but I don't have **one**. one, ones

MP3

1 We use **one/ones** to avoid repeating a *noun* that has already been mentioned. We use **one** for *singular nouns* and **ones** for *plural nouns*.

- My brother has a car, but I don't have **one**. (one = a car)
- "Which types of flowers do you like best?" "Roses and tulips are the **ones** I like." (ones = flowers)

We do not use **one/ones** for *uncountable nouns*. In this case, we use **some/any**.

- "I forgot to bring money." "I can lend you **some**." (*NOT* I can lend you one)
- "Was there more salad in the kitchen?" "I didn't see **any**, so maybe not." (*NOT* I didn't see ones)

2 There is the following difference between **one/ones** and **it/they/them**:

- My printer stopped working, so I bought a new **one**. (My printer ≠ one)
- These keys aren't mine. The **ones** on the table are mine. (These keys ≠ ones)

- My printer stopped working, so I took **it** to a repair shop. (My printer = it)
- "Are these keys yours?" "Yes. **They** are mine." (these keys = They)

3 We can use **one/ones** in the following ways:

a/an/the/my/etc. + *adjective* + **one**

- "Did you answer the last question on the test?" "No. That was **a hard one**."
- "Which desk is yours?" "**The tidy one**, of course. I never make a mess."
- I enjoy Mark Twain's books. **My favorite one** is *The Adventures of Tom Sawyer*.

some/the/my/two/etc. + *adjective* + **ones**

- The movie had some exciting moments and **some boring ones**.
- "Which forks do you need?" "Pass me **the silver ones**."
- "How many milkshakes would you like? And what flavor?" "**Two chocolate ones**, please."

4 We can also use **one/ones** with **this/that** and **these/those**.

this/that (+ *adjective*) + **one**

- Which report should be done first, **this one** or **that one**?
- "Can I open my Christmas present?" "Sure! **That big one** is for you."

these/those + *adjective* + **ones**

- "My drawer is full of socks." "Why don't you throw away **these old ones**?"
- Let's put these red candles in the living room, and **those yellow ones** in the kitchen.

But we usually use **these/those** alone rather than with **one/ones**.

- "These chopsticks are broken." "Here, use **these**."
- "The show's about to start. Do you see any seats?" "**Those** over there are empty."

5 We often use **in/on**/etc. *(prepositions)* after **the** (+ *adjective*) + **one/ones**.

- "Who's that woman?" "Do you mean **the one in the photo**? That's my aunt."
- I already washed my dishes. **The dirty ones on the table** are Susan's.

P R A C T I C E

A. Write **one/ones** or **it/they/them**.

1. "Do you want a hot drink?" "No. I want a cold *one* ________. Maybe I'll have an iced tea."
2. "Are Mike and Julie in the office today?" "I don't think so. I haven't seen ____________."
3. "These boots don't feel very nice." "How about these leather ____________?"
4. Here, wear my sunglasses. ____________ look good on you.
5. We stayed at a famous hotel in Las Vegas, but ____________ wasn't very nice.
6. This puzzle is too difficult. Let's do the easier ____________.
7. "Which cookies are the most delicious?" "The ____________ with coconut."

B. Complete the sentences with **one/ones** and the given words.

best	blue	dry	~~short~~	wild	wrong

1. *(the)* "Is Gary the tall boy?" "No. He's *the short one* ____________."
2. *(my)* "What color suit will you wear?" "________________________. What do you think?"
3. *(some)* I've only seen elephants in zoos. I hope to see ________________________ one day.
4. *(a)* "This towel is still wet. Can you get me ________________________?" "Sure."
5. *(his)* All of Evan's artwork is good, and these two statues are ________________________. Aren't they nice?
6. *(the)* These aren't the books I ordered! They sent me ________________________!

C. Look at the pictures and complete the sentences with **this/that/these/those** and the adjectives in *italics*. Add **one/ones** if neccessary.

There are so many ducks in the pond.

1. *(little)* I know. *Those little ones* ____________ are cute.

I like this sofa.
$1500
$500

2. *(expensive)* I don't like ________________________.

I can't find my gloves.

3. Are you looking for ________________________?

Which wallet is yours?
LOST and FOUND

4. *(brown)* ________________________ is mine.

D. Complete the sentences with **one/ones** and the words in *italics*. Add **the**.

1. *(in my neighborhood)* "Which gym do you go to?" "*The one in my neighborhood* ____________."
2. *(gold)* Don't wear those earrings. You look better in ________________________________.
3. *(cozy, on the hill)* "Did you find a house?" "Yes. I rented ________________________________."
4. *(big)* "Are all of those suitcases yours?" "Just ________________________________. I brought only two."
5. *(spicy, with chicken)* I'll order the pasta I had here before. It was ________________________________.
6. *(near the entrance)* "Which oranges are on sale?" "________________________________."

Answers **p.315** / Review Test 11 **p.254**

I have **some** tickets for a play. some and any

1 **some/any**

We can use **some/any** before *plural/uncountable nouns* or without a *noun*.

- I have **some tickets** for a play. Do you have **any plans** for tonight?
- Our new cereal is made with natural ingredients. Try **some** today!
- I'm thirsty. I haven't drunk **any water** today.

2 We usually use **some** in positive sentences and **any** in negative sentences and questions.

- **Some snacks** will be provided on the flight.
- "Does Amanda own **any pets**?" "No. She doesn't own **any**."
- The running shoes at that store are 60 percent off. You should get **some**!

But when we offer or request something, we usually use **some** in questions.

- Can I ask you for **some advice** on this project?

3 We usually use words with a negative meaning (hardly, without, etc.) with **any**.

- There's **hardly any room** in the drawer. It's almost full.
- The interview was quite easy. I finished it **without any difficulty**.

We also usually use **if** with **any**.

- **If** Ben has **any time** tomorrow, he'll help us with the research.
- Let me know **if** there are **any changes** to the schedule.

4 **someone/anything**/etc.

someone/somebody	something	somewhere
anyone/anybody	anything	anywhere

- **Someone** is waving at you. Do you know that person?
- Tommy didn't like the clothes at that store. He didn't buy **anything**.
- "Did you go **anywhere** last weekend?" "Yes. I went to the mountains."

We can use *adjectives* or **to . . .** after **someone/anything**/etc.

- You look beautiful! Are you going out with **someone special** tonight?
- I don't have **anything to hide**. I've always told you everything.

5 We can use **any** when there is more than one option and they are all OK. In this case, we use **any** in positive sentences.

- You can park your car in **any space** on this street.
- "What do you want to do today?" "**Anything** is OK with me."

When a *countable noun* is used after **any** in a positive sentence, we can use either a *singular* or *plural noun*.

- I'll treat you to dinner tonight. You may order **any dish** you want.
  OR I'll treat you to dinner tonight. You may order **any dishes** you want.
- I can answer **any question** you have. *OR* I can answer **any questions** you have.

PRACTICE

A. **Complete the sentences with some/any and the nouns in the box. Use the plural form if necessary.**

child	form	pill	time	~~towel~~	wind

1. I need to do laundry because I don't have *any towels* ______________ to use.
2. You have to fill out ____________________ to apply for health insurance.
3. The air was so calm after the storm. There wasn't ____________________ at all.
4. The doctor gave me ____________________. I hope they make me feel better.
5. "When are you free to meet with us?" "I have ____________________ on Tuesday."
6. "Do you have ____________________?" "Yes. We have a son and a daughter."

B. **Complete the sentences with some/any and the nouns in *italics*. Use the plural form if necessary.**

1. *(news)* "Have you heard *any news* ______________ from Jennifer?" "Not yet."
2. *(apple juice)* "Would you like ______________________?" "No, thank you."
3. *(drugstore)* "Are there ______________________ nearby?" "Yes. Pemberton Drugs is across the street."
4. *(candle)* The electricity is out. Do we have ______________________ at home?
5. *(salt)* "Can you get me ______________________ for my potatoes?" "Sure. Just a moment."
6. *(suggestion)* Professor Nelson gave me ______________________ for improving my writing.

C. Write **some/any** or **someone/anything**/etc.

1. Luke wanted to plant some seeds, so he bought *some* __________.
2. "I need ______________ to wear to the interview." "You can borrow my blue suit."
3. "Did Jack make that desk by himself?" "Yes. He did it without ______________ help."
4. Do we have any butter? I need ______________ for my toast.
5. This is a public library. It's open to ______________.
6. "I can't find my stapler." "Maybe ______________ took it."
7. Let's stop here. I want to take ______________ pictures.
8. "What did you do last night?" "I just stayed at home. I didn't go ______________."
9. Rosa likes ______________ activity that she can do outdoors. She enjoys being outside.
10. Have you heard? Treasure is hidden ______________ on this island!
11. I could hardly hear ______________ on the phone. The people beside me were so loud.
12. "Are you hungry?" "Yes, I am. Is there ______________ food?"

D. **The following is a radio advertisement for Frank's Outlet. Complete the sentences with some/any and the nouns in *italics*.**

Do you need a new sofa? Or a bed?
1. *(new furniture)* Come and buy *some new furniture* ______________!
Frank's Outlet is having a one-day sale this Sunday!
2. *(customer)* ______________________ visiting us that day will receive a gift.
We are offering a lot of great products at low prices.
3. *(item)* If you wait, there won't be ______________________ left!
4. *(sofa)* ______________________ will even be sold at half price!
So make sure to tell all of your friends.
5. *(trouble)* Take Highway 78, and you'll get here without ______________________.
6. *(question)* Call us today, and we'll answer ______________________ you have!

Quantity

LESSON 59

Answers **p.316** / Review Test 12 **p.256**

LESSON 60 There's **no** milk. no, none

1 **no** + *noun*

- "There's **no milk**." "I'll go to the store later today."
- **No visitors** may enter the building on the weekends.
- "Did you send Carrie an e-mail?" "Yes, but I got **no reply**."

We can use either *countable* or *uncountable nouns* after **no**. We usually use a *plural noun* when a *countable noun* is used after **no**.

- **No seats** were empty at Mr. Thompson's speech. It was very popular.
- "Is your company hiring?" "I don't know. There's **no information** about open jobs right now."

Note that we do not use **no** without a *noun*.

- That hair salon is never busy, so there's **no need** to make a reservation. (*NOT* there's no to make)

2 **no one** / **nobody** / **nothing** / **nowhere**

no one / nobody	nothing	nowhere

- **Nobody** knows where Louise went. She didn't tell anyone.
- You'll do fine on the test. You have **nothing** to worry about.
- There's **nowhere** quiet in this town. It's full of bars and shops.

3 We can use **not . . . any** + *noun* instead of **no** + *noun*.

- I do**n't** have **any trees** in my yard. *OR* I have **no trees** in my yard.
- After Sally took the medicine, she did**n't** feel **any pain**. *OR* After Sally took the medicine, she felt **no pain**.

We can also use **not . . . anything**/**anywhere**/etc. instead of **nothing**/**nowhere**/etc.

- We do**n't** have **anything** to do this Saturday. *OR* We have **nothing** to do this Saturday.
- This road does**n't** lead **anywhere**. *OR* This road leads **nowhere**.

We can use **no** + *noun* as the *subject* in a sentence, but we do not use **not . . . any** + *noun* as the *subject*.

- **No rain** fell this summer. The river is completely dry. (*NOT* Not any rain fell)
- "Excuse me, sir. **No pets** are allowed inside our restaurant." "Sorry. I didn't know." (*NOT* Not any pets are allowed)

4 We do not use **no** + *noun* / **nobody** / **nothing** / etc. with **not**.

- Shelly couldn't listen to the radio on the bus because she had **no earphones**. (*NOT* she didn't have no earphones)
- We chose Bill for the position because there was **nobody** better. (*NOT* there wasn't nobody)

5 We can also use **none** instead of **no** + *noun*.

- I did some experiments but **none** supported my ideas. (= no experiments)
- "Has any mail been delivered today?" "No. **None** has arrived yet." (= No mail)

Note that we do not use a *noun* after **none**.

- "How many foreign countries have you been to?" "**None**. I've never been overseas." (*NOT* None foreign countries)

P R A C T I C E

A. Complete the sentences with **no/any** and the nouns in the box.

advice	alcohol	energy	mistakes	~~patients~~	problem	secrets	snow

1. The doctor isn't seeing *any patients* this week. He's on vacation.
2. "Thanks for helping me yesterday." "Don't mention it. It wasn't __________ at all."
3. Max made __________ in his presentation. It was perfect.
4. I asked my teacher which college to choose, but she didn't offer me __________.
5. There was __________ last December. We didn't have a White Christmas.
6. My wife and I tell each other everything. There are __________ between us.
7. "I am so tired. I have __________ today." "You should get some rest."
8. "May I have a glass of red wine?" "Sorry. We don't serve __________ here."

B. Rewrite the sentences with **no/nobody**/etc. or **not . . . any/anybody**/etc.

1. The library contains no comic books. → *The library doesn't contain any comic books*.
2. This highway doesn't have any gas stations.
   → __________.
3. I planned nothing for today. I'm totally free.
   → __________. I'm totally free.
4. Aaron did no homework all afternoon.
   → __________.
5. There wasn't anybody at the gym this morning.
   → __________.
6. I didn't go anywhere last night. I was at home.
   → __________. I was at home.

C. Find and change any mistakes in each sentence. Put ✓ if the sentence is correct.

1. The ballet school has none boys in it. *none boys → no boys*
2. There's nowhere to stay. All of the hotels are full. __________
3. Not any flights were available, so we took the train. __________
4. There isn't nothing to eat in the fridge. Let's eat out. __________
5. Beth has to work this weekend. She has no choice. __________
6. I wanted to watch some movies, but no seemed interesting. __________
7. We don't know nobody in the neighborhood. We just moved here. __________

D. Complete the conversation with **some/any/no/none**.

MP3

LINDA

LINDA: What are you looking for?
JAMES: I want something to drink.
1. Maybe *some* milk, but there isn't __________.
LINDA: 2. I'm sure we have __________ in the refrigerator.
JAMES: I already looked. 3. We have __________. I think Chris drank all of it.
LINDA: Well, let me check just in case. Oh, you're right.
4. We have __________ milk left. 5. But we have __________ orange juice.
JAMES: 6. Is there __________ grape juice?
LINDA: No. 7. There are __________ other juices in the refrigerator.

JAMES

Quantity
LESSON 60
Grammar Gateway Intermediate

Answers p.316 / Review Test 12 p.256

LESSON 61 All people need exercise. all, every, each

MP3

1 We use **all**/**every** + *noun* to talk about the whole group or each person/thing in the group.

all + *plural/uncountable noun*

- **All people** need exercise.
- **All music** is interesting to me. I listen to **all types**.
- Laws should protect **all citizens**.

every + *singular noun*

- **Every person** needs exercise.
- **Every song** on this album is amazing.
- Jane is the fastest runner. She wins **every race**.

2 We use **each** + *singular noun* to talk about an individual person/thing in a group.

- **Each student** will choose a different essay topic.
- There is a computer at **each desk** in this room. Any library visitor can use them.

We can use **each** without a *noun*.

- "How much were these shirts?" "They were $14 **each**."
- This show consists of 10 episodes. **Each** is 30 minutes long.

3 Note that the *verb* form changes when **all**/**every**/**each** is used as the *subject* in a sentence.

We use *plural verbs* after **all** + *plural noun* and *singular verbs* after **all** + *uncountable noun*.

- **All countries have** their own unique cultures.
- **All bread** at Major Bakery **is** made from fresh ingredients.

We always use *singular verbs* after **every** + *singular noun* or **each** (+ *singular noun*).

- **Every building** in Rome **is** interesting. The city is lovely.
- There are two ways to get to the museum. **Each takes** about 10 minutes.

4 **everyone/everybody/everything/everywhere**

everyone/everybody	everything	everywhere

- They are at the beach. **Everyone** is having fun.
- I like **everything** about this cell phone. It has many useful functions.
- These mountains are beautiful in April. There are flowers **everywhere**.

We use **not** + **everyone**/**everything**/etc. to talk about just some parts of a group.

- **Not everyone** enjoys cooking, but some people love it.
- Our new store is opening soon. **Not everything** is ready yet, though.

Note that we use **not** + **everyone**/**everything**/etc. and **no one** / **nothing** / etc. in different ways.

- We bought some soda for the dinner party because **not everyone** drinks wine.
  (Some people drink wine, but some don't.)
  We didn't buy wine because **no one** in my family drinks it.
  (All of the people in my family don't drink wine.)
- **Not everything** in our living room is mine. Some things are Ruth's.
  Nothing in our living room is mine. Everything is Ruth's.

P R A C T I C E

A. Complete the sentences with **all/every** and the nouns in *italics*.

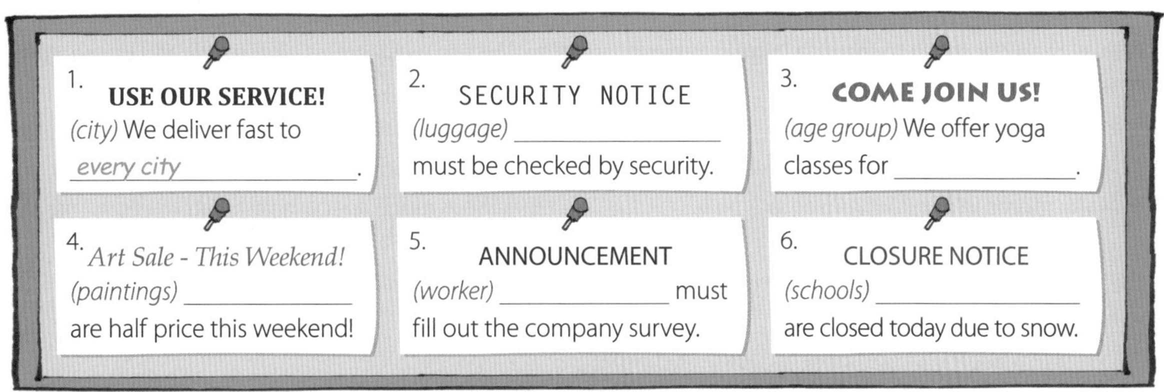

1. USE OUR SERVICE!
(city) We deliver fast to every city.
2. SECURITY NOTICE
(luggage) ______________ must be checked by security.
3. COME JOIN US!
(age group) We offer yoga classes for ______________.
4. Art Sale - This Weekend!
(paintings) ______________ are half price this weekend!
5. ANNOUNCEMENT
(worker) ______________ must fill out the company survey.
6. CLOSURE NOTICE
(schools) ______________ are closed today due to snow.

B. Look at the pictures and complete the sentences with **each** and the given words. Use the *present simple*.

~~ball~~	band member	can	chapter	piece of chocolate

1   2 Contents: Chapter 1 (Unit 1, Unit 2, TEST) Chapter 2 (Unit 3, Unit 4, Unit 5, TEST) Chapter 3 (Unit 6, Unit 7, Unit 8, TEST) Chapter 4 (Unit 9, Unit 10, TEST)   3 Chocolates   4 The hottest band: 3 BOYS — Kevin (guitar), Mike (synthesizer), Dave (drums)   5 SODA 355ml X 6 cans

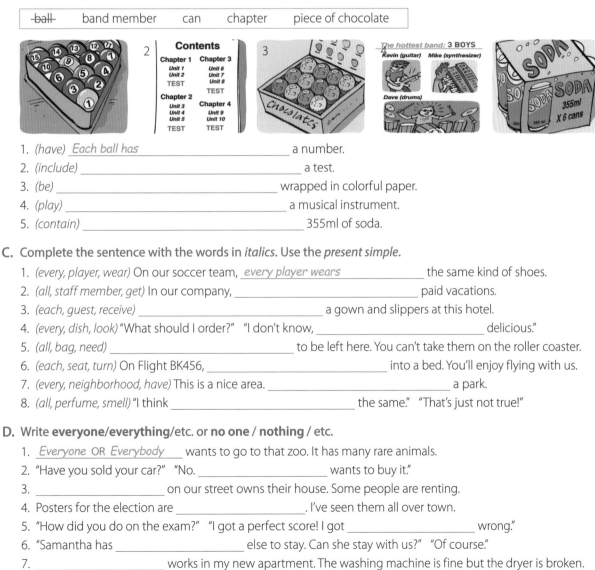

1. *(have)* Each ball has ______________ a number.
2. *(include)* ______________ a test.
3. *(be)* ______________ wrapped in colorful paper.
4. *(play)* ______________ a musical instrument.
5. *(contain)* ______________ 355ml of soda.

C. Complete the sentence with the words in *italics*. Use the *present simple*.

1. *(every, player, wear)* On our soccer team, every player wears ______________ the same kind of shoes.
2. *(all, staff member, get)* In our company, ______________ paid vacations.
3. *(each, guest, receive)* ______________ a gown and slippers at this hotel.
4. *(every, dish, look)* "What should I order?" "I don't know, ______________ delicious."
5. *(all, bag, need)* ______________ to be left here. You can't take them on the roller coaster.
6. *(each, seat, turn)* On Flight BK456, ______________ into a bed. You'll enjoy flying with us.
7. *(every, neighborhood, have)* This is a nice area. ______________ a park.
8. *(all, perfume, smell)* "I think ______________ the same." "That's just not true!"

D. Write **everyone/everything**/etc. or **no one / nothing** / etc.

1. Everyone OR Everybody ______________ wants to go to that zoo. It has many rare animals.
2. "Have you sold your car?" "No. ______________ wants to buy it."
3. ______________ on our street owns their house. Some people are renting.
4. Posters for the election are ______________. I've seen them all over town.
5. "How did you do on the exam?" "I got a perfect score! I got ______________ wrong."
6. "Samantha has ______________ else to stay. Can she stay with us?" "Of course."
7. ______________ works in my new apartment. The washing machine is fine but the dryer is broken.

Answers **p.316** / Review Test 12 **p.256**

LESSON 62 Many rooms in our dorm are empty now. many/much, a lot of / lots of, (a) few / (a) little

MP3

1 We use **many** or **much** to mean "a large number or quantity." We use *plural nouns* after **many** and *uncountable nouns* after **much**.

many + *plural noun*
- People don't send **many postcards** these days.
- **Many rooms** in our dorm are empty now.

much + *uncountable noun*
- The pasta didn't take **much time** to cook.
- Is there **much space** in your car? I need to bring a big suitcase.

We can use **a lot of / lots of** instead of **many/much**. We can use either *plural* or *uncountable nouns* after **a lot of / lots of**.
- We have **a lot of / lots of ideas** for Jill's birthday party. (= many ideas)
- I didn't get **a lot of / lots of rest** last night, so I'm tired. (= much rest)

2 We can use **many** or **a lot of / lots of** in positive/negative sentences and questions.
- "I have **many cousins**. Do you have **many cousins**?"
  "No, my family is small. I don't have **many cousins**."
- Krystal gets **a lot of / lots of homework**, so she doesn't have **a lot of/lots of free time**.
- "Do **a lot of / lots of theaters** close on Mondays?" "No. Just this one."

We usually use **much** in negative sentences and questions. We use **a lot of / lots of** rather than **much** in positive sentences.
- "I don't drink **much milk**. Do you drink **much milk**?" "Yes. I drink **a lot of / lots of milk**."

But we can use **much** in positive sentences when it is used with **so**/**too**/**very**/etc.
- There's **so much dirt** on the carpet. I need to clean it.
- Ms. Jenson wears **too much perfume**. It gives me a headache.

3 We can use **a few** or **a little** to mean "a small number or quantity." We use *plural nouns* after **a few** and *uncountable nouns* after **a little**.
- I have **a few things** to do before I leave.
- "I put **a little butter** on your toast for you." "Thanks!"

We use **few** or **little** to mean "almost none."
- **Few places** allow smoking these days.
- I have **little patience** when I am busy.

Note that we use **a few / a little** and **few/little** in different ways.
- I found **a few errors** in your essay. Please check my comments. (The essay has a small number of errors.)
  I found **few errors** in your essay. You did a good job. (The essay has almost no errors.)
- Edgar had **a little** money left. He didn't spend too much.
  Edgar had **little** money left. He shouldn't have spent so much.

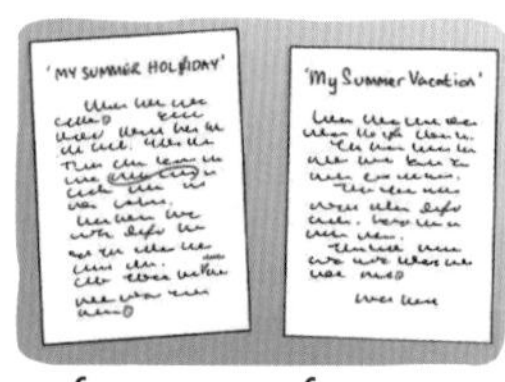

a few errors　few errors

4 We can use **many/much** and **(a) few / (a) little** without a *noun*.
- Hawaii has a lot of beaches, and **many** are very nice.
- "Do you want some pepper for your steak?" "Just **a little**, please."

We do not use **a lot of / lots of** without a *noun*. But we can use **a lot** without a *noun*.
- "Did you buy any clothes at the mall?" "Yes, **a lot**." (*NOT* a lot of)

P R A C T I C E

A. Complete the sentences with **many/much** and the nouns in the box.

advice	birds	clients	magazines	~~sugar~~	work

1. I didn't put *much sugar* in your iced tea. You can add more if you want.
2. "Did you do ____________ today?" "No. I wasn't very busy."
3. "Have ____________ requested refunds?" "Just a few."
4. ____________ live in this park. You can hear them sing in the morning.
5. "How was your meeting with your counselor?" "I didn't get ____________. It was too short."
6. This bookstore doesn't have ____________. Let's go to a different one.

B. Write **much / a lot (of)**.

1. There hasn't been *much* OR *a lot of* snow this winter. I hope there's more next winter.
2. I had ____________ time today, so I read a whole book.
3. "How many people came to the conference?" "____________. The hall was full of people."
4. Too ____________ food was left after the party, so we gave some to our neighbor.
5. Does this job require ____________ experience in marketing?
6. Doctors say it's important to drink ____________ water every day.
7. "How often do you go to the gym?" "I go ____________. Maybe 5 or 6 times a week."

C. Complete the sentences with **(a) few / (a) little** and the nouns in *italics*. Use the plural form if necessary.

1. *(damage)* Henry was in a car accident. Luckily there was *little damage* to his vehicle.
2. *(item)* ____________ will be left by tomorrow. The sale has been a huge success.
3. *(friend)* Greg has ____________ in Germany. He is going to see them this summer.
4. *(salad)* "Would you like ____________?" "Sure."
5. *(noise)* My apartment building is extremely quiet. There is ____________.
6. *(block)* "Excuse me. Where is the bank?" "It's ____________ away from here."
7. *(soup)* "What did you have for lunch?" "I had a sandwich with ____________."
8. *(train)* There are ____________ from here to Boston. In fact, on some days there are none.

D. The following is an e-mail from Amy to Kate. Choose the correct one.

Subject	Chicago trip?
To	kate77@gotmail.com
From	amy318@gotmail.com

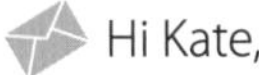 Hi Kate,

1. I was thinking of going to Chicago for (*a few* / *few*) days. Do you want to come with me?
2. There are (*so many* / *so much*) things to do there, like shopping or sightseeing.
3. I have (*much* / *a lot of*) good friends there, so we can stay with them.
4. I found a flight that doesn't cost very (*much* / *many*).
5. But there is (*few* / *little*) time to buy the tickets, so please let me know soon.

6. P.S. I can help if you need (*a little* / *little*) money for the ticket. It's no problem.

Amy 

Answers p.316 / Review Test 12 p.256

LESSON 63 Some of the flowers are yellow. some/many/all/etc. of

MP3

1 **Some of the flowers** are yellow.

There are six bunches of flowers. Three of them are yellow.
"Some of the flowers" describes a part of the group.

2 We can use the following expressions to talk about a part of the group or the whole group:

some/any/none many/much (a) few / (a) little all/most/half/each	of	the my/your/etc. this/that these/those	noun

- I invited **some of my neighbors** to the barbecue on Saturday.
- **Many of these cars** use electricity instead of gas.
- Tom showed me **a few of the poems** his students wrote. They were very funny.
- **All of our luggage** was lost during the trip, but **most of the bags** were found later.

We can leave out **of** after **all** or **half**.

- "Did you complete **all (of) your projects**?" "Yes, I just finished them today."
- "Your new coat looks nice." "Thanks. I got it for **half (of) the regular price**."

3 We can also use **it/us/you/them** after **some/any/(a) few/all**/etc. **of**.

- We still have some pizza left. Do you want **any of it**?
- **Each of us** is responsible for saving the Earth.

In this case, we do not leave out **of** after **all** or **half**.

- Kyle opened a bottle of soda and drank **all of it** by himself. (*NOT* all it)
- Please be careful when you deliver the eggs. **Half of them** were broken last time. (*NOT* Half them)

4 **some of** + *noun* and **some** + *noun*

We use **some/many**/etc. **of** + *noun* to talk about specific people/things in a group.

- I've been to **many of the museums** in Paris.
  (= specific museums in Paris)
- **Some of those trees** don't have flowers.
  (= those specific trees)

We use **some/many**/etc. + *noun* to talk about people/things in general.

- **Many museums** won't allow you to take pictures.
  (= museums in general)
- I want to plant **some trees** in my backyard.
  (= trees in general)

5 When **some/many**/etc. **of . . .** is the *subject*, we use *singular verbs* after *singular/uncountable nouns* and *plural verbs* after *plural nouns*.

- The storm was terrible. **Half of the city was** flooded.
- **Most of the countries** in Asia **have** long histories.

But we always use *singular verbs* when **each of . . .** is the *subject*.

- **Each of these mugs belongs** to a different person.

P R A C T I C E

A. Look at the pictures and complete the sentences with **all/most/some/none of** and the words in *italics*.

1-3

4-6

Appetizers		Main Dishes	
Chicken Soup	$8	Spaghetti and Meatballs	$12
Garlic Bread	$6	Lasagna	$15
Nachos	$7	Grilled Chicken	$22
Desserts		Pepper Steak	Not available
Brownie with coffee	$5	Lamb Chops	$38
Cheesecake with coffee	$6	Cheese Pizza	Not available

1. *(boys)* *All of the boys* are wearing caps.
2. *(girls)* ______________ have glasses on.
3. *(players)* ______________ are boys.
4. *(main dishes)* ______________ are not available.
5. *(appetizers)* ______________ are over $8.
6. *(desserts)* ______________ come with coffee.

B. Complete the conversations with **it/us/you/them** and the words in *italics*.

1. A: Did you receive many gifts for your birthday?
   B: *(all)* Yes. *All of them* were very nice.
2. A: Is everyone in your family tall?
   B: *(some)* No. Only ______________ are.
3. A: *(a little)* Is that fried rice? It looks delicious.
   Can I try ______________?
   B: Yes, but it's not very good.
4. A: *(any)* Are ______________ going out tonight?
   B: Bruce and Kim are, but I can't.
5. A: How was your trip?
   B: *(half)* Not great. I was sick for ______________.
6. A: Did your friends enjoy the movie?
   B: *(most)* ______________ enjoyed it, but a few didn't.

C. Put the words in *italics* in the correct order. Add **of** if necessary.

1. *(my classmates / none / Spanish / speak)* *None of my classmates speak Spanish*.
2. *(fish / all / in water / live)* ______________.
3. *(a little / with my pie / ice cream)* I want ______________.
4. *(most / us / Jenny / don't know)* ______________.
5. *(don't have / people / some / a mobile phone)* ______________.
6. *(them / made / a few / mistakes)*
   Most dancers were perfect, but ______________.
7. *(the cup / half / is filled)*
   Your drink will stay cold for a while. ______________ with ice.

D. Complete the sentences with the words in the box using the *present simple*. Add **of** if necessary.

(his fridge, be)	(my friends, own)	(the bedrooms, have)
(the snow, melt)	(their earrings, cost)	~~(these trees, appear)~~

1. Many *of these trees* *appear* to be burned. Was there a fire at this park?
2. All ______________ ______________ in March here, so we can't go skiing in April.
3. Each ______________ in this house ______________ its own bathroom.
4. Some ______________ ______________ cars. But most of them use public transportation.
5. That new shop sells some cheap jewelry. Most ______________ ______________ only $5.
6. Charlie likes to drink beer. Half ______________ ______________ filled with it.

Both houses are downtown. both, either, neither

1 We use **both/either/neither** (+ *noun*) to talk about two people/things.

both (+ plural noun)	either (+ singular noun)	neither (+ singular noun)

- Scott owns two houses. **Both houses** are downtown. (= Scott's two houses)
- "Who do you think will win the game?" "I'm not sure. **Either team** could win." (= Any one of the two teams)
- "Have you seen these movies?" "Yes, but **neither** was very good." (= none of the two movies)

There is the following difference in meaning between **both** and **either**.

- I want to visit Tahiti and Guam. Let's go to **both islands** when we are retired. (= We should go to Tahiti and Guam.)
  "Should we go to Tahiti or Guam?" "**Either island** would be great." (= We can go to Tahiti or Guam, and I don't care which one.)

2 We can use **not . . . either** instead of **neither**.

- I tried a swim class and a dance class at my gym, but I liked **neither**.
  OR I tried a swim class and a dance class at my gym, but I did**n't** like **either**.
- We called you twice, but you answered **neither time**.
  OR We called you twice, but you did**n't** answer **either time**.

Note that we do not use **neither** with **not**.

- My sister likes reading mystery and science fiction, but I like **neither**. (*NOT* I don't like neither)

3 We always use *plural verbs* when **both** (+ *plural noun*) is the *subject*. We use *singular verbs* when **either/neither** (+ *singular noun*) is the *subject*.

- "**Both shirts look** good on you!" "Thanks. But **neither shirt is** my style."
- "Do you want this table or that one?" "**Either seems** all right."

4 **both/either/neither of . . .**

both/either/neither	of	the/my/these/etc. + plural noun
		us/you/them

- **Both of my brothers** have blue eyes.
- I can't open the door with **either of these keys**.
- "Which of those hats is yours?" "**Neither of them** is mine."

We can leave out **of** before **the/my/these**/etc., but we do not leave out **of** before **us/you/them**.

- Pam wrote to **both (of) her best friends** last weekend. **Both of them** live abroad. (*NOT* Both them)

5 We always use *plural verbs* when **both of . . .** is the *subject*. We can use either *singular* or *plural verbs* when **either/neither of . . .** is the *subject*.

- **Both of Mila's roommates are** away this weekend, so she invited some friends to watch a movie.
- "Which do you prefer, jazz or classical music?"
  "**Neither of them interests** me." *OR* "**Neither of them interest** me."

PRACTICE

A. Write **both/either/neither**.

1. "Who brought these chairs?" "I'm not sure. *Both* ______ were here when I arrived."
2. "Should we turn left or right here?" "You can go ______ way. They'll both get you to the beach."
3. I think ______ bakeries are closed. Let's come back tomorrow.
4. "Do you want a black or a blue pen?" "It doesn't matter. ______ is fine."
5. Jenny suggested running in the park or going swimming. ______ sounded fun, so I stayed home.
6. "Which necklace is cheaper?" "______ are the same price."
7. "Let's buy some roses or lilies." "But I like ______ flower. How about some daisies?"
8. "Where shall we meet, at the bus stop or at the mall?" "______ place works for me, so you choose."
9. I complained to ______ managers. I still didn't get a refund, though.
10. We invited John and his sister to my exhibit, but ______ came. I was disappointed.

B. Look at the pictures and complete the sentences with both/either/neither and the nouns in the box. Use the plural form if necessary.

camera	drawing	girl	house	jacket	test	toy	~~woman~~

1. *Both women* ______ are riding horses.
2. He didn't pass ______.
3. ______ has buttons.
4. She hasn't started coloring ______ yet.
5. ______ are on sale.
6. ______ is wearing pants.
7. He doesn't like ______.
8. He wants ______.

C. Complete the sentences with the words in *italics* using the *present simple*. Add of if necessary.

1. *(both, TVs, be)* *Both TVs* ______ *are* ______ expensive. Let's look at the cheaper ones.
2. *(neither, the subway lines, go)* ______ ______ to city hall. We have to take a taxi.
3. *(both, us, look)* I have a twin sister. ______ ______ like our mother.
4. *(either, them, be)* "Do you want to watch the comedy or the drama?"
   "______ ______ OK with me."
5. *(neither, suit, fit)* ______ ______ me well. They are too small.
6. *(both, these flashlights, need)* ______ ______ a new battery.
7. *(either, event, sound)* "Should we go to the art exhibit or the concert?"
   "______ ______ good to me!"
8. *(neither, us, play)* Rita and I love music, but ______ ______ an instrument.

Answers **p.317** / Review Test 12 **p.256**

LESSON 65 She got a new camera. *Adjectives*

MP3

1 She got a **new** camera.

It's **small** and **light**.

"new," "small," and **"light"** describe the camera. **"new," "small,"** and **"light"** are *adjectives*.

2 We often use *adjectives* before *nouns* to describe someone or something.

- Tom is my neighbor. He's a **nice** person.
- "Would you like some **hot** tea?" "Sure. Thanks."
- That **old** couple looks so happy together.
- I watched a **sad** movie last night. I cried at the end.

We also often use *adjectives* after the following *verbs*:

be/get/become/seem	look/feel/sound/taste/smell

- The weather is **getting cold**. It'll be winter soon.
- Skydiving **looks dangerous**, but it**'s** quite **safe**.
- "Angela **seems tired**." "She just got back from a business trip."
- What did you put in this pasta sauce? It **tastes spicy**.

3 We always use the following *adjectives* before *nouns*:

former	indoor/outdoor	inner/outer	main	only	upper

- Abraham Lincoln is a **former president** of the United States. (*NOT* the president is former)
- "Can you meet me at the **main gate**?" "Sure. I'll see you then." (*NOT* the gate is main)
- "Does Pete have any brothers or sisters?" "No. He's the **only child**."

We usually use the following *adjectives* after **be/get/look**/etc. rather than before *nouns*:

afraid	alive	alone	asleep	glad	ill	sorry

- Sally heard a strange noise and **became afraid**. (*NOT* an afraid girl)
- Look! The lion **is asleep** in his cage. (*NOT* an asleep lion)
- I **feel ill**. I think I'm going to leave work early.

4 We can use two or more *adjectives* before a *noun*. In this case, they usually go in the following order:

Opinion →	Length, Size →	Age →	Color
beautiful, great, nice	short, big, large	young, old, new	black, blue, red

- I met a **beautiful young** woman on my trip to France.
- "Which boy is Evan?" "He's the boy in the **short black** jacket."
- My grandfather drives a **big old blue** truck. He has had it for 30 years.

PRACTICE

A. Complete the sentences with the given words.

dirty	~~happy~~	large	sweet	wrong

1. *(seems)* "Is your son enjoying college?" "I think so. He *seems happy* ."
2. *(tastes)* I ordered this coffee without sugar, but it ____________.
3. *(families)* ____________ aren't common these days. People aren't having many children.
4. *(answer)* Matt thought he got a perfect score on his test, but he had one ____________.
5. *(got)* My skirt ____________. I need to wash it.

familiar	fresh	long	strong	true

6. *(is)* I'm not telling you a lie. It ____________.
7. *(hair)* Jenny has always had ____________. I can't imagine her cutting it.
8. *(sounds)* "Have you heard this song?" "I think so. It ____________."
9. *(looks)* "This bread ____________." "It is. We just baked it."
10. *(wind)* During the storm, the ____________ blew down a lot of trees.

B. Put the words in *italics* in the correct order.

1. *(floor / the bedroom / the upper / on / is)* *The bedroom is on the upper floor* .
2. *(was / I / alone / not)* ____________ at home last night. I was with my mom.
3. *(this / the / train / only / is)* "____________ to Portland?" "Yes, it is."
4. *(feel / sorry / I)* ____________ about not going to your party.
5. *(became / The Beatles / famous)* ____________ in the 1960s.
6. *(pool / doesn't / have / outdoor / an / the hotel)* ____________.
7. *(the snake / alive / is)* ____________! I thought it was dead.
8. *(moved / the company's / office / main)* ____________ to New Zealand.
9. *(glad / to meet / I / you / am)* "This is my friend Eric." "____________, Eric."
10. *(important / is / day / tomorrow / an)*
____________ for me. I have several interviews.

C. Look at the pictures and put the words in the box in the correct order.

(nice / suit / gray / new)	~~(old / building / tall)~~	(puppies / cute / little)
(roses / pink / beautiful)	(table / large / white)	

1. There is a *tall old building* next to the post office.
2. She's holding some ____________.
3. There is a ____________ in the yard.
4. Three ____________ are sitting on the sofa.
5. He is wearing a ____________.

Adjectives and Adverbs

LESSON 65

Answers **p.317** / Review Test 13 **p.258**

66 crying baby, broken toy -ing and -ed (1)

1 The **crying** baby is Justin.

He is crying because of the **broken** toy.

"crying" describes the baby and **"broken"** describes the toy. **"crying"** and **"broken"** are *adjectives*.

2 We can also use -**ing** or -**ed** *(past participle)* before *nouns* to describe someone or something. In this case, -**ing** and -**ed** are used as *adjectives*.

We use -**ing** to say what a person/thing is doing at a certain time. -**ing** has an active meaning.

- The **departing passengers** are boarding the plane now. (the passengers are departing)
- "Do you see that **shining star** in the sky?" "Wow! It's so bright." (that star is shining)
- Be careful of **passing cars** when you cross the street.
- Our town is getting crowded because of the **growing population**.

We use -**ed** to say what has happened to a person/thing. -**ed** has a passive meaning.

- Only **invited guests** may attend the party. (certain guests are invited)
- The accident was caught on a **hidden camera**. The video provided good evidence. (a camera was hidden)
- If you have any questions, please ask our **trained staff**.
- "I'd like to request a refund for the **damaged goods**." "OK. Just a moment, please."

More about spelling rules: Appendix p.278

3 We can use various words after -**ing** or -**ed**. We use -**ing** or -**ed** with these words after *nouns* rather than before them.

	noun		
	The man	**carrying the suitcase**	looks like Mr. Jones.
	The river	**flowing through Paris**	is the Seine.
"Do you know	**those girls**	**sitting over there?"**	"No. Do you?"
"Who owns	**the cat**	**playing in the street?"**	"She's mine."

	noun		
	The articles	**published in that newspaper**	are usually interesting.
	The seats	**reserved for us**	are near the windows.
Your present is	**the box**	**wrapped in blue paper.**	
"Did you read	**the information**	**provided in the website?"**	"Yes. It was very helpful."

P R A C T I C E

A. **Complete the sentences with the verbs in the box.**

bark	~~fall~~	renovate	sign	sleep	steal

1. "I like to watch the *falling* __________ snow." "Me too. It's so peaceful."
2. The police arrested the man because he was carrying a __________________ passport.
3. Please be quiet in the hospital. Try not to disturb the __________________ patients.
4. That __________________ dog is so annoying. Make it stop.
5. We must receive your __________________ application by August 31.
6. The __________________ lobby is beautiful. I like it better now.

B. **Complete the conversations with the words from each box.**

all the songs	the boy
~~the dress~~	the flowers
the motorbike	the woman

\+

climb the tree	~~display in that store~~
grow in your garden	park over there
perform by the band	speak right now

1. A: *The dress displayed in that store* _____ is pretty.
   B: Why don't you try it on?
2. A: What are you looking at?
   B: __________________________________.
   I hope he doesn't fall.
3. A: __________________________________
   were great.
   B: I agree. The concert was fantastic.
4. A: Is __________________________________ Jake's?
   B: Yes. He rides it to work every day.
5. A: Who is your boss?
   B: __________________________________.
   She's practicing her speech.
6. A: What are __________________________________?
   They're getting so tall.
   B: Most of them are lilies.

C. **Put the words in *italics* in the correct order. Change the word form if necessary.**

1. *(stand / man)* "Is that your husband over there?" "No. He's the *man standing* ________ near the window."
2. *(use / computer)* Jack bought a __________________ because he couldn't afford a new one.
3. *(stare / woman)* "There's a __________________ at us. Do you know her?" "I don't think so."
4. *(tour / guide)* We went to Beijing on a __________________. We really enjoyed it.
5. *(crowd / cheer)* As the players entered the stadium, they waved at the __________________.
6. *(characters / describe)* The __________________ in the book weren't very interesting.

D. **Put the words in *italics* in the correct order. Change the word form if necessary.**

MP3

PAUL

PAUL: 1. What's that *picture hanging* ________ on the wall? *(hang / picture)*
AMY: 2. Oh, that's a __________________ by my grandmother. *(take / photo)*
PAUL: 3. Who's the __________________? *(cry / baby)*
AMY: That's Justin! 4. Can you see the __________________? *(toy / break)*
Ginger broke it! That's why he was crying.
PAUL: Oh, poor Justin! He looks so sad!
5. So who's the __________________ at Justin? *(laugh / girl)*
AMY: Ha ha, that's me!

AMY

Answers p.317 / Review Test 13 p.258

67 interesting vs. interested

-ing and **-ed** (2) *Adjectives* of feeling

1 Chris is telling a story.

The story is **interesting**.

They are **interested** in the story.

"interesting" describes the feeling that the story causes and **"interested"** describes how they feel. **"interesting"** and **"interested"** are *adjectives*.

2 We can use *adjectives* that end with **ing** or **ed** to talk about feelings or emotions. There is the following difference in meaning between **-ing** and **-ed**:

We usually use *adjectives* that end with **ing** to talk about feelings that a person/thing causes.

amazing	satisfying
exciting	relaxing
interesting	

- "John played really well at the music festival." "He was **amazing**." (He caused the amazement.)
- The breakfast at the hotel wasn't **satisfying**. (The breakfast caused the dissatisfaction.)
- I had a very **relaxing** weekend.

boring	depressing
tiring	disappointing
frustrating	annoying

- "Is that book good?" "No, it's **boring**." (The book caused the boredom.)
- Heavy traffic can be **frustrating**. (Heavy traffic can cause frustration.)
- Those people are **annoying**. They're too loud.

embarrassing	confusing
shocking	puzzling
surprising	frightening

- Dancing in front of people was **embarrassing**. (Dancing in front of people caused the embarrassment.)
- The test results were **surprising** to scientists. (The test results caused the surprise.)
- That rollercoaster was **frightening**.

We usually use *adjectives* that end with **ed** to talk about how a person feels.

amazed	satisfied
excited	relaxed
interested	

- I was **amazed** by John. He played the guitar so well. (I felt the amazement.)
- "Are you **satisfied** with your new car?" "Yes!" (Do you feel the satisfaction?)
- I feel **relaxed** when I'm lying on the beach.

bored	depressed
tired	disappointed
frustrated	annoyed

- If you're **bored**, let's go out somewhere. (You might feel the boredom.)
- My computer isn't working. I'm so **frustrated**. (I felt frustration.)
- We were **annoyed** because Tim was late again.

embarrassed	confused
shocked	puzzled
surprised	frightened

- Max was **embarrassed** after he fell on the stairs. (Max felt the embarrassment.)
- We were **surprised** by the price of the apartment. (We felt the surprise.)
- I was **frightened** by a bat. It flew right at me.

P R A C T I C E

A. Look at the pictures and complete the sentences with the correct word between the two in *italics*.

MR. and MRS. MILLER

1. *(relax / amaze)*
   Mr. and Mrs. Miller are amazed __________.
   The magic trick is __________.

2. *(satisfy / disappoint)*
   The Falcons' performance was __________.
   The players are __________.

3. *(confuse / surprise)*
   The map is __________.
   He is __________.

4. *(depress / frighten)*
   The kids are __________.
   The man is __________.

B. Complete the conversations with the words in *italics*.

1. A: *(tire)* Hiking was so tiring ______.
   B: Yes, but we got to the top of the mountain!

2. A: *(tire)* I'm really __________.
   B: *(relax)* Get a massage. It will be __________.

3. A: Bill made several mistakes in his speech.
   B: *(embarrass)* I heard. He seemed __________.

4. A: *(bore)* I think Bobby is __________.
   B: Not at all. He's actually a very fun person.

5. A: *(puzzle)* Many questions on the test were __________.
   B: *(puzzle)* I was __________ by them too. I couldn't answer many of them.

6. A: *(depress)* That was a __________ song!
   B: I agree. Now I feel sad.

7. A: Did you see that girl's jacket?
   B: *(shock)* Yes! The design was __________.

8. A: *(interest)* Is your roommate __________ ?
   B: *(bore)* Yes. I'm never __________ with her.

9. A: *(depress)* Mandy looks __________ today.
   B: I know. Let's go and cheer her up.

10. A: *(excite)* Are you __________ about moving abroad?
    B: *(interest)* Yes, I am. I've always been __________ in other cultures.

C. The following is Chris's review of an opera show. Complete the sentences with the words in *italics*.

A Night at the Opera

By Chris Wilson

Last night, I saw an opera with my girlfriend. It was called *The Quest for a Queen*.
1. *(interest)* The story was interesting ______. It was about a king who lived alone in a castle.
2. *(excite)* The opera was __________ from the opening scene.
The king traveled around the country to look for a beautiful woman to be his queen.
3. *(surprise)* But his final choice was __________.
4. *(shock)* In fact, I was __________ by it. The king fell in love with the ugliest girl in the country!
5. *(disappoint)* Although we enjoyed the opera, the acting was a little __________.
6. *(satisfy)* However, we were mostly __________ with it.

Answers p.317 / Review Test 13 p.258

LESSON

68 The car is moving **slowly**. *Adverbs*

MP3

1 The car is moving **slowly**.

They are **really** worried.

We might be late. I'm worried.

"slowly" describes how the car moves and **"really"** describes the degree of the feeling. **"slowly"** and **"really"** are *adverbs*.

2 We use *adverbs* to describe how something happens. We usually add -**ly** at the end of *adjectives* to make *adverbs*.

clear → **clearly**	easy → **easily**	terrible → **terribly**
excited → **excitedly**	automatic → **automatically**	

More about spelling rules: Appendix p.280

- There's so much fog this morning. I can't see **clearly**.
- Kim always tries her best. She never gives up **easily**.
- Our team played **terribly** at the game yesterday. We lost.
- The children talked **excitedly** about their field trip.

3 We usually use *adverbs* after *verbs*.

- The students **sat quietly** and listened to the teacher.
- "What time is it?" "I don't **know exactly**, but it's around noon."

When an *object* is used after a *verb*, we use an *adverb* after the *object*. Note that we do not use the *adverb* between the *verb* and *object*.

- Larry needs to **spend his money wisely**. He buys too much stuff. (*NOT* spend wisely his money)
- I think the mayor **answered the questions honestly**. (*NOT* answered honestly the questions)

4 We can use *adverbs* to talk about the degree of an *adjective* or another *adverb*. In this case, we usually use the *adverb* before the *adjective* or the other *adverb*.

- These pants seem **slightly long**. Do you have shorter ones?
- "Have you ever been to London?" "Actually, I was there **fairly recently**."
- "Your apartment looks **completely different**." "I replaced all the furniture."
- My presentation went **really badly**. I should have prepared more.

We can also use *adverbs* to talk about opinions. In this case, we often use the *adverb* at the beginning of a sentence.

- We hurried to the post office. **Luckily**, it was still open.
- **Hopefully**, I'll get a job soon. I've applied to several companies.
- I thought John couldn't ski. **Surprisingly**, he was very good at it!

5 The following words end with **ly**, but they are *adjectives* and not *adverbs*:

friendly	lovely	lively	elderly	likely	lonely	silly	ugly

- Your family is so **friendly**. It was great to meet them.
- I saw some **lovely** curtains at the store today. I might go back and buy them.
- Helen works with **elderly** people at a local hospital.
- "Will you be here before 10:30?" "It's not **likely**."

PRACTICE

A. Complete the sentences with the adjectives in the box.

careful	dramatic	~~fluent~~	kind	lazy	responsible

1. "Is Dave's German good?" "Yes. He speaks it *fluently* ______."
2. "The temperature has fallen ______ since yesterday." "I know. It's freezing now!"
3. Marco hasn't moved all day! He's been sitting ______ on the sofa and watching TV.
4. Mr. Jones always treats people ______. He's never rude to anyone.
5. "Could you show me how to use this photocopier?" "Sure. Watch ______."
6. Don't throw garbage on the street. You should always act ______.

B. Put the words in *italics* in the correct order. Change the adjectives into adverbs if necessary.

1. *(perfect / the fish)* The chef cooked *the fish perfectly* ______. It was delicious.
2. *(normal / complete)* Babies usually wake up a lot during the night. It's ______.
3. *(church / regular)* When I was a child, I attended ______.
4. *(total / different)* Rob and I rarely agree. We think ______.
5. *(loud / real)* "I just heard a ______ noise. Did you hear it?" "Yes. What was it?"
6. *(tight / the window)* Close ______. It's cold outside.
7. *(the new mall / rapid / surprising)* The workers built ______.
8. *(amazing / cheap)* "How much was your flight?"
   "It was ______. It was only $200."

C. Find and change any mistakes in each sentence. Put ✓ if the sentence is correct.

1. You should think serious before moving abroad. It's a big decision. *serious → seriously*
2. Read closely the instructions and answer the questions. ______
3. Our honeymoon was incredible. It was absolute wonderful. ______
4. "Did you catch the train?" "Yes. Luckily, it was delayed." ______
5. "Was the workshop successful?" "Yes. It went smoothly relatively." ______
6. What's wrong with Kevin? He shut the door angry and left the room. ______
7. We moved gently the furniture because we didn't want to damage it. ______
8. This town is lively on weekends. A lot of tourists come here. ______

D. Complete the conversation with the adjectives in the box.

~~complete~~	hopeful	immediate	patient	slight

MP3

AMY

AMY: Hurry up Kate! We're going to be late for the wedding!
[1.] The roads are *completely* ______ crowded on the weekends.
[2.] We need to leave ______.

KATE: OK. I'm almost ready. Is it cold outside? Do I need a coat?

AMY: [3.] It's ______ chilly, but not too bad.
Anyway, I can't wait to see Nancy in her wedding dress. She's going to look so lovely in it.

KATE: I think so too. I'm ready now.
[4.] Thank you for waiting ______.

AMY: Good, let's go. [5.] ______, we'll arrive on time.

KATE

Adjectives and Adverbs

LESSON 68

Grammar Gateway Intermediate

Answers p.317 / Review Test 13 p.258

LESSON 69

bright vs. brightly

Adjectives vs. Adverbs (1)

MP3

1

The sun is **bright**.

We use *adjectives* to describe someone or something.

- Ron and Betty look like a **happy couple**.
- "This singer has a **wonderful voice**." "I agree."
- My **alarm clock** was **loud**. It woke up everyone in the house.

The sun is shining **brightly**.

We use *adverbs* to describe how something happens.

- Ron and Betty are **smiling happily** in that photo.
- Sara is an excellent pianist. She **plays wonderfully**.
- Tom **snores loudly** when he sleeps. It's really hard to share a room with him.

2 We usually use *adjectives* in the following positions:

before *nouns*

- "I hope you have a **safe flight**." "Thank you."
- Simon is looking for a **new roommate.**
- Why don't you take a **warm bath**? It'll make you relax.

after **be**/**get**/**look**/**feel**/etc.

- That diamond is huge! **Is** it **real**?
- We should **get ready**. It's already 8:30.
- "I'm going bungee jumping this weekend." "That **sounds scary**!"

We usually use *adverbs* in the following positions:

after *verbs* (+ *objects*)

- "I'm leaving for Toronto now." "OK. **Drive safely**."
- If there's a fire, **leave the building quickly**.
- Larry **takes his job seriously**. It's the most important thing to him.

before *adjectives* or another *adverb*

- This soup is **really salty**.
- Elizabeth goes jogging **fairly regularly**.
- "Are you sure this is the right way?" "Yes. I'm **absolutely certain**."

3 We can use either *adjectives* or *adverbs* after **look**.

look + *adjective*

We use *adjectives* when **look** means "to have a particular appearance."

- "Greg **looks great** in his new suit." "I helped him pick it out."
- I think I'll get some of these grapes. They **look fresh**.

look + *adverb*

We use *adverbs* when **look** means "to see something."

- "I can't find my wallet." "**Look carefully**. It must be here somewhere."
- In some cultures, it's rude to **look directly** into other people's eyes.

PRACTICE

A. Put the words in *italics* in the correct order. Change the adjectives into adverbs if necessary.

1. *(skirt / colorful)* "Which woman is Ms. Dawson?" "The lady in the *colorful skirt* ."
2. *(surprising / strong)* Sean is a small boy, but he's ______.
3. *(getting / hungry)* Let's find a place to eat. I'm ______.
4. *(speakers / famous)* Were there any ______ at the conference?
5. *(extreme / rapid)* My hometown is growing ______. It will be a big city soon.
6. *(busy / normal)* "When can we meet?" "I'm ______ on weekdays. How about Saturday?"
7. *(popular / became)* This TV show ______ last year. Now all of my friends watch it.
8. *(automatic / open)* You don't have to open the garage door. It will ______.

B. Complete the sentences with the given words. Use the *present simple* or *past simple*.

anxious	brave	close	~~dizzy~~	sharp	sweet

1. *(feel)* "I *feel dizzy* ." "You should sit down and rest."
2. *(act)* The man jumped into the river and saved the boy. He ______.
3. *(smell)* Your perfume ______. The scent reminds me of honey.
4. *(look)* You should be careful with those scissors. They ______.
5. *(wait)* We ______ for our exam results. We were so nervous.
6. *(look)* The doctor ______ at my eyes and said there was nothing wrong.

C. Complete the sentences with the adjectives in *italics*. Change the adjectives into adverbs if necessary.

To	taylor77@fastmailco.com
From	bsmith@buildahouse.com

Dear Mr. Taylor,

I am writing to you about your order with our company.

1. *(recent)* It seems that you've decided to build a house *recently* .

You have asked for two different design ideas for your new house.

2. *(accurate)* I hope this is ______. We'll start the designs once you confirm your order.
3. *(incorrect, immediate)* If this is ______, please contact us ______.
4. *(glad)* We will be ______ to change your order.
5. *(short)* Anyway, the designs will be sent to you ______.
6. *(careful)* Please review them ______ when you receive them.

Thank you,

Brian Smith

D. Find and change any mistakes in each sentence. Put ✓ if the sentence is correct.

1. When you're doing this exercise, you should bend your knees slight. *slight → slightly*
2. "Dinner tasted deliciously. Thank you." "You're welcome." ______
3. Something's wrong with my phone. It's not working proper. ______
4. This is an easily video game. Anyone can play it. ______
5. When I become angrily, I take a deep breath and count to 10. ______
6. My kids are extreme excited about going back to school after vacation. ______
7. You're eating too fast. You should chew your food slowly. ______

Answers p.318 / Review Test 13 p.258

Nick is a **fast** learner. Nick learns **fast.** *Adjectives vs. Adverbs (2)*

MP3

1 We can use **fast**, **long**, and **early** as both *adjectives* and *adverbs*. We do not add **-ly** at the end of them.

fast	(adj.)	• Nick is a **fast** learner.
	(adv.)	• Nick learns **fast**. He's easy to teach.
long	(adj.)	• I haven't been camping for a **long** time.
	(adv.)	• Sorry I'm late. Have you been waiting **long**?
early	(adj.)	• Diane's flight lands in the **early** morning.
	(adv.)	• If we leave **early**, we can avoid the traffic.

2 We can also use **late**, **high**, **near**, and **hard** as both *adjectives* and *adverbs*. We can add **-ly** at the end of them, but they become *adverbs* with different meanings.

late	(adj.)	• "Are you hungry?" "No. I had a **late** lunch."
	(adv.)	• We arrived at the seminar **late**.
lately	(adv.)	• I've gained a lot of weight **lately**. (= "recently")
high	(adj.)	• That mountain is really **high**. It must have a great view at the top.
	(adv.)	• Bob hung the picture **high** on the wall.
highly	(adv.)	• Ms. Thomas is **highly** successful. She owns several businesses. (= "very")
near	(adj.)	• I hope to see you again in the **near** future.
	(adv.)	• Summer vacation is drawing **near**. I can't wait!
nearly	(adv.)	• Frank **nearly** fell when he was on the ladder. (= "almost")
hard	(adj.)	• Richard is a **hard** worker. He always does a good job.
	(adv.)	• Marcia studies **hard** every day.
hardly	(adv.)	• Tom is my classmate, but I **hardly** know him. (= "almost not")

3 We can also use **free** as both an *adjective* and an *adverb*.

free	(adj.)	• This is a **free** country. We can express our opinions openly. (= "without restrictions")
		• I have two **free** tickets to tomorrow's exhibition. (= "with no cost")
		• "Are you busy this weekend?" "No, I'm **free**. Why?" (= "not busy")
	(adv.)	• Children under five may travel **free** on the train. (= "at no cost")

We usually use **freely** (adv.) to talk about doing something without restrictions.

- Don't be shy. Please talk **freely** and share your ideas with us.

4 The *adverb* of **good** is **well**.

- Jack is a **good** athlete. He plays every sport **well**.

We can also use **well** as an *adjective* to mean "healthy."

- "I heard you were sick last week. But you look **well** now." "Yes. I feel much better."

PRACTICE

A. Complete the sentences with the words in the box.

comfortable	early	~~fast~~	hard	high	long	near	silent

1. The cheetah is a *fast* animal. It can run 100 meters in six seconds.
2. "Can you help me with something? It won't take ______." "Sure. What is it?"
3. I thought the jeans would be too small, but they fit ______.
4. You're too far away. Come ______ so I can hear you better.
5. "Why are you going to bed so soon?" "I've got an ______ meeting tomorrow morning."
6. Steve didn't say a word during dinner. He was ______ the whole time.
7. We've ______ had any rain this month. It has been so dry.
8. Bob hit the ball and it flew ______ over the fence.

B. Complete the sentences with the words in *italics*. Change the adjectives into adverbs if necessary.

1. *(long, late)* Janice has been working *long* hours ______, so she has been very tired.
2. *(late)* This morning she woke up ______.
3. *(near)* When she opened her eyes, it was ______ noon.
4. *(high)* The sun was already ______ in the sky.
5. *(immediate)* She jumped out of bed and called the office ______.
6. *(surprising)* ______, nobody answered the phone. Then she remembered it was a holiday!
7. *(happy)* So she went back to sleep ______.

C. Write free/freely or good/well.

1. You don't have to pay to get into the museum. Everyone can enter *free*.
2. The swimming pool closes at night, but you're ______ to use it during the day.
3. "This is a ______ book." "Yes. I enjoyed it too."
4. Marsha has been in the hospital for a while. I hope she gets ______ soon.
5. Our university provides many language courses, so you can choose ______.
6. My grandmother has bad eyesight. She can't read ______ without her glasses.
7. I can't go out tonight, but I am ______ tomorrow.

D. Find and change any mistakes in each sentence. Put ✓ if the sentence is correct.

1. I need a copy of this article fastly. *fastly → fast*
2. Lisa tried hard, but she failed to win the gold medal. ______
3. Mr. Collins is high intelligent. He's the smartest man I know. ______
4. "Have you been teaching longly?" "Yes, for over 10 years." ______
5. "Let's dance!" "I don't want to. I can't dance good." ______
6. We should go to the stadium early. I want to find good seats. ______
7. Fred paid the bill lately, so he had to pay an extra fee. ______
8. Buy one of our T-shirts and get the second one freely. ______

Answers p.318 / Review Test 13 p.258

LESSON 71

It's located downstairs.

Adverbs of place, time, and frequency

MP3

1 We usually use the following *adverbs* at the end of a sentence to talk about a place or time of an event:

Place	here/there	upstairs/downstairs	inside/outside
Time	now/then	soon	yesterday/today/tomorrow

- "Where's the restroom?" "It's located **downstairs**."
- The weather is beautiful **today**. We should do something **outside**.
- "Let's meet at 6." "I'll still be working **then**. How about 7?"

We can also use *adverbs* of time at the beginning of a sentence.

- **Yesterday**, I had a date with Matthew. We saw a musical.
- John is saving money for a bike. **Soon**, he'll be able to buy it.

We can use *adverbs* of place and time together. In this case, we use *adverbs* of place first.

- "Is Sally coming?" "Yes. She'll arrive **here tomorrow**."
- It's getting dark. We should go **inside now**.

2 We use the following *adverbs* to talk about the frequency of an event:

100% ←――――――――→ 0%

always	usually	often	sometimes	rarely/seldom	never

- I **always** wake up late, so I **never** have enough time for breakfast.
- We **sometimes** do our grocery shopping online.
- Our children **usually** play outside on weekends. They're **rarely** inside.

We usually use *adverbs* of frequency in the following positions:

before *verbs*
- I **sometimes forget** people's names.
- Ted doesn't **usually drive**. He **usually rides** the bus.

after **be**
- This park **is seldom** crowded.
- Ms. Walker **isn't usually** in town. She**'s often** away on business.

between **will**/**can**/etc. and **base form**
- Too much exercise **can sometimes cause** injury.
- You **won't often see** many stars at night in the city.

between **have**/**has**/**had** and **past participle**
- I**'ve never been** to Asia before.
- Gina **hasn't always lived** in LA. She lived in Dallas when she was young.

before **have to** or **used to**
- Do you **always have to** wear a suit to work?
- My sister and I **rarely used to** do anything together.

3 We usually use **just**, **really**, **hardly**, and **already** in the same positions as *adverbs* of frequency.

- "Have you seen Katie?" "Yes. She **just left**."
- "I**'m really** sorry about not attending your wedding." "Don't worry about it."
- We **could hardly see** the stage because our seats were so far away.
- "I need to wash the dishes." "Oh, I**'ve already done** them."

P R A C T I C E

A. Put the words in *italics* in the correct order.

1. *(to leave / need / soon)* Hurry up, Mitchell. We *need to leave soon* ________.
2. *(there / it / left / yesterday)* The file isn't on my desk, but I ________.
3. *(you / waiting for / downstairs)* "Someone is ________." "Oh, it's my cousin."
4. *(have / tomorrow / a doctor's appointment)* I ________.
5. *(you / then / can meet)* I have some free time at noon, so I ________.
6. *(now / upstairs / move / this sofa)* We want to ________. Can you help us?
7. *(outside / sit / today)* Let's ________. The weather is so nice.

B. Write sentences about yourself with **always/often/never**/etc. and the words in the box.

1. drink coffee at night
2. use public transportation
3. brush my teeth after meals
4. go jogging in the morning
5. travel to foreign countries
6. watch TV on weekends

1. *I often drink coffee at night* OR *I never drink coffee at night* ________.
2. ________.
3. ________.
4. ________.
5. ________.
6. ________.

C. Complete the conversations with the adverbs in *italics*. Write negative sentences if necessary.

1. Are Mr. Brown's tests easy? — *(seldom)* No. His tests *are seldom easy* ________.
2. Did Terry's flight arrive? — *(just)* Yes. It ________.
3. Is Mary friendly? — *(usually)* No. She ________.
4. Has Beth gone to work yet? — *(already)* Yes. She ________.
5. Can a hot shower help a cold? — *(sometimes)* Yes. It ________.
6. Have you seen Peter lately? — *(hardly)* No. We ________.
7. Do you go skiing in the winter? — *(often)* No. I ________.
8. Did you have to study a lot in college? — *(always)* Yes. I ________.

D. Put the words in *italics* in the correct order.

MP3

SANDY: 1. I *went hiking yesterday* ________. *(yesterday / hiking / went)*
2. I ________, but I enjoy it now. *(go / never / used to)*
How about you? Do you like hiking?

JUSTIN: No. 3. I don't like ________. *(anything / doing / outside)*
4. Also, I ________ taking long walks. *(hate / really)*

SANDY: But hiking is good for you.
5. You ________ for your health. *(often / exercise / should)*
6. By the way, I'm ________. *(going to / tomorrow / the mall)*
I need to buy hiking boots. Do you want to go together?

JUSTIN: Well . . . OK. How about tomorrow around 7?

SANDY: 7. Sure! Let's ________. *(meet / then / there)*

SANDY

JUSTIN

Answers **p.318** / Review Test 13 **p.258**

72 The water is too cold! too and enough

1 **too** + *adjective/adverb*

We use **too** (= "more than necessary") before *adjectives* or *adverbs* to emphasize their meanings.

- The water is **too cold**! I don't want to go in.
- Don't take Jimmy's words **too seriously**. He was just joking.
- How much do you earn? Or is that question **too personal**?

We can also use **very** instead of **too**. We can use **very** in any situations, but we usually use **too** in negative situations that would cause a problem.

- The exam questions were **very difficult**, but I answered all of them.
- The exam questions were **too difficult**. I wasn't able to answer all of them.

2 **too many/much** + *noun*

- There are **too many people** on the bus. Let's wait for the next one.
- I need a vacation. I've been under **too much stress** lately.

3 We can use **way/far**/etc. before **too** to emphasize the meaning even more.

- I can't wear this dress. It's **way too tight**.
- This school is strict. There are **far too many rules**.

4 *adjective/adverb* + **enough**

We use **enough** (= "equal to what is necessary") after *adjectives* or *adverbs* to emphasize their meanings.

- "Do you need more ice in your drink?" "No, thanks. It's **cold enough**."
- I can't usually understand Mr. Johns. He doesn't speak **clearly enough**.

We can use **enough** before *nouns*.

- I didn't get **enough sleep** last night, so I took a nap.
- "Does your bike have **enough air** in the tires?" "No. I think I need to add some."

We can also use **enough** alone.

- I don't want any more pizza. I've had **enough**.

5 We can use **for** + *person/thing* or **to . . .** after **too/enough**.

- I can't accept this money. It's **too much** **for me.**
- You're never **too old** **to learn.**
- There is **enough space** **for 120 cars** in this parking lot.
- I'm not **strong enough** **to carry** this box. Could you help me?

We can also use **for** + *person/thing* and **to . . .** together after **too/enough**.

- "Is it **too late for me to buy** tickets for the show?" "No. Tickets are still available."
- Don't worry. There's **enough gas for us to get** to a gas station.

PRACTICE

A. Look at the pictures and complete the sentences with **too/enough** and the words in the box.

beds	dirty	high	~~large~~	long	milk	slowly	small

1. The box isn't *large enough* ____________.
2. The towels are ____________.
3. She doesn't have ____________.
4. She can jump ____________.
5. He's eating ____________.
6. The sleeves aren't ____________.
7. The writing is ____________.
8. There are not ____________.

B. Complete the sentences with **too/enough** and the words in *italics*.

1. *(far, young)* "Do you remember your childhood in Canada?" "No. I was *far too young* ____________."
2. *(comfortable)* "Why didn't you buy those shoes?" "They weren't ____________."
3. *(many mistakes)* There were ____________ in Troy's article, so he had to write it again.
4. *(carefully)* "What did the boss say?" "I don't know. I wasn't listening ____________."
5. *(much homework)* Professor Edwards gives ____________. It's hard to finish all of it.
6. *(cash)* I don't have ____________. Could you lend me some?
7. *(suddenly)* The musical ended ____________. It seemed like the story hadn't finished.
8. *(way, short)* I cut my hair yesterday, and now it's ____________!
9. *(games)* I think you've played ____________ today. Please put them away.
10. *(far, early)* We arrived at the airport ____________. We waited for the flight for three hours.

C. Complete the sentences with **too/enough** and the words in the box. Add **for/to** if necessary.

(big, our living room)	(dark, read)	~~(expensive, me)~~	(loudly, us, have)
(safe, you, walk)	(sunlight, survive)	(time, me, go)	(well, you)

1. That car is *too expensive for me* ____________. I can't afford it.
2. "Is the steak cooked ____________?" "Yes. It's good."
3. "Is there ____________ to the bathroom?" "Sure. We'll wait for you."
4. It's ____________ the newspaper. Could you turn on the light?
5. My plant died. It didn't receive ____________.
6. The band is playing ____________ a conversation. It's impossible to hear.
7. I'll go with you. That street isn't ____________ alone.
8. That sofa is ____________. Let's find a smaller one.

Answers p.318 / Review Test 13 p.258

LESSON 73

Your dog is **so** cute! so and such

MP3

1 so + *adjective/adverb*

We use **so** (= "very") before *adjectives* or *adverbs* to emphasize their meanings.

- Your dog is **so cute**! What's her name?
- Brian is very smart. He solves these math problems **so easily**.
- "This mall is always **so crowded** on weekends."
  "Yes. There are too many people!"
- "Why did Jennifer go home **so early**?" "Oh, she had a headache."

Your dog is so cute!

2 We do not use a *noun* after so + *adjective*.

- "Have you met Leo's family?" "Yes. They're **so friendly**." (*NOT* so friendly people)
- The lecture lasted for three hours. It was **so boring**. (*NOT* so boring lecture)

But we can use a *noun* after **so many/much**.

- Robert travels a lot. He has been to **so many places**.
- This article has **so much information** about health. You should read it.

3 such (+ a/an) + *adjective* + *noun*

We can use **such** (= "very") before *adjective* + *noun* to emphasize the meaning of the *adjective*.

- They're **such cute dogs**.
- Getting married on a boat was **such an amazing experience**.
- This area has **such clean air**. I'd like to live here.
- "Cheer up. Everybody makes mistakes." "Thanks. You're **such a good friend**."

They're such cute dogs.

We can also use **such (+ a/an)** + *noun* to mean "that kind of person/thing."

- Mandy is an excellent skater. **Such talent** is rare.
- "Why are you in **such a hurry**?" "I have a presentation in 30 minutes."
- I can't believe Mike said that. **Such words** can be hurtful.

4 We can use so/such . . . that . . . In this case, we use so/such . . . to talk about the reason for something.

	so + adjective/adverb	*that + subject + verb*	
• The book was	so fun	that I read	it three times. (= Because the book was so fun, I read it three times.)
• I slept	so deeply	that I didn't hear	you come in. (= Because I slept very deeply, I didn't hear you come in.)
• My son plays	so loudly	that I can't rest	at home.
• David is	so tall	that it's	hard to find clothes in his size.

	such (+ a/an) + adjective + noun	*that + subject + verb*	
• It was	such a fun book	that I read	it three times.
• It's	such an important meeting	that I shouldn't be	late.
• Mia works	such long hours	that she has	little free time.
• We live in	such a small town	that everyone knows	one another.

PRACTICE

A. Complete the sentences with **so** and the words in the box. Add **many/much** if necessary.

animals	different	funny	~~long~~	often	pain

1. There were a lot of people at the ticket office. We had to wait in line *so long* ____________.
2. Fred had ____________ in his tooth. He had to see a dentist.
3. "You look ____________. I hardly recognized you." "Well, I've lost a lot of weight."
4. Harry must like Natalie. He talks about her ____________.
5. "Mom, we saw ____________ at the zoo!" "Which one was your favorite?"
6. Michael is ____________! His jokes make everyone laugh.

B. Complete the sentences with **so/such** and the words in *italics*. Add **a/an** if necessary.

1. *(beautiful, flowers)* I've never received *such beautiful flowers* ____________ before. They're lovely!
2. *(old, song)* This is ____________. I rarely hear it these days.
3. *(excited)* "I'm ____________ to meet your cousins!" "They can't wait either."
4. *(polite, children)* "You have ____________." "Thank you."
5. *(strange, dream)* "I had ____________ last night." "Oh? Tell me about it."
6. *(well)* Wendy could have been a chef. She cooks ____________.
7. *(great, news)* I have ____________! Tommy got promoted!
8. *(heavily)* We could hardly see the car in front of us. It was raining ____________!

C. Complete the sentences with **such** and the nouns in the box. Add **a/an** if necessary.

accidents	age	hobby	knowledge	~~places~~

1. "Stan went to a nightclub." "Why do people go to *such places* ____________? I don't get it."
2. I'm going to try scuba diving. Having ____________ must be fun.
3. Knowing how to fix a car is useful. ____________ can be very helpful in an emergency.
4. Babies sometimes swallow small objects. Watch them carefully to avoid ____________.
5. Joe became a CEO when he was 25. It's not easy to achieve success at ____________.

D. Rewrite the sentences with **so/such . . . that . . .**

1. Willy quit soccer because he had a very busy schedule.
   → *Willy had such a busy schedule that he quit soccer* ____________.
2. Because I was sick, I couldn't go to work.
   → ____________.
3. We left the café because the service was slow.
   → ____________.
4. People clapped at the end because it was an impressive movie.
   → ____________.
5. Because Michelle left quickly, I didn't have a chance to say goodbye.
   → ____________.
6. Because Rudy has really great style, people dress like him.
   → ____________.

Answers p.319 / Review Test 13 p.258

The backpack is smaller and more expensive.

Comparatives (1)

MP3

1 The backpack is **smaller** and **more expensive**.

"smaller" is used to compare the size of two bags, and **"more expensive"** is used to compare the price of them. **"smaller"** and **"more expensive"** are *comparatives*.

2 We use **faster**, **heavier**, etc. *(comparatives)* to compare two people/things. We make *comparatives* in the following ways:

+ -(e)r	one-syllable adj./adv.	fast → **faster**	nice → **nicer**	big → **bigger**
	two-syllable adj./adv. that end with **y**	heavy → **heavier**	early → **earlier**	funny → **funnier**
more +	two- or more- syllable adj./adv.	quickly → **more quickly**	comfortable → **more comfortable**	
	-ing/**-ed** adj.	interesting → **more interesting**	crowded → **more crowded**	
+ -(e)r or more +	quiet → **quieter** *OR* **more quiet**	simple → **simpler** *OR* **more simple**		
	lively → **livelier** *OR* **more lively**	polite → **politer** *OR* **more polite**		
Exceptions:	good/well → **better**	bad/badly → **worse**	far → **farther/further**	

More about spelling rules: Appendix p.280

- Take a taxi instead of the bus. It's **faster**, so you'll get home **more quickly**.
- We like our new sofa. It's **bigger** and **more comfortable**.
- The snow is getting **heavier** and the roads are becoming **worse**.
- "The park seems **livelier** / **more lively** today." "Yes, it's **more crowded** too."

3 We use **than** after *comparatives* to say what we are comparing someone or something with.

- "You're early today." "Yes. I finished work **earlier than** usual."
- Julie sang **more beautifully** in this concert **than** in the last concert.
- "Is Dan **older than** you?" "I think he's **younger than** me."
- That book was **more interesting than** I expected.

4 We use **less** + *adjective/adverb* to say that the degree of something is smaller.

- CD players are **less common** now. Not many people use them these days.
- I've been exercising **less often** lately. I haven't been feeling well.
- "How is your new job?" "Good. It's **less stressful** than my old one."
- Ben seems **less lonely** since he got a puppy.

5 We can use **more** as the *comparative* of **many/much** and **less** as the *comparative* of **little**. We can use **more** and **less** with or without *nouns*.

many/much → **more**	little → **less**

- I have many pairs of earrings, but Sarah has **more**.
- My grandmother used to go swimming a lot. Now she goes **less**.
- Our company is hiring **more people** this month. You should apply.
- We always buy this soda because it contains **less sugar**.

PRACTICE

A. Complete the sentences with the adjectives/adverbs in the box. Use the comparatives or add **less** if necessary.

carefully	~~close~~	difficult	hungry	painful	quiet	regularly	surprised

1. My cousins moved *closer* to our house. I see them every week now.
2. Finding a nice apartment was __________ than I thought. I found one quite quickly.
3. Mike used to talk a lot, but he's __________ these days.
4. I often have a big breakfast because I feel __________ in the morning than at night.
5. "Do you still write in your diary every day?" "No. I write in it __________ than before."
6. You need to use that knife __________ or you might hurt yourself.
7. "How is your leg?" "Better. It's __________ than it was before."
8. "I was shocked by Jenny's strange haircut." "I was __________ by the color! It was so shocking."

B. Complete the sentences with **than** and the words in *italics*.

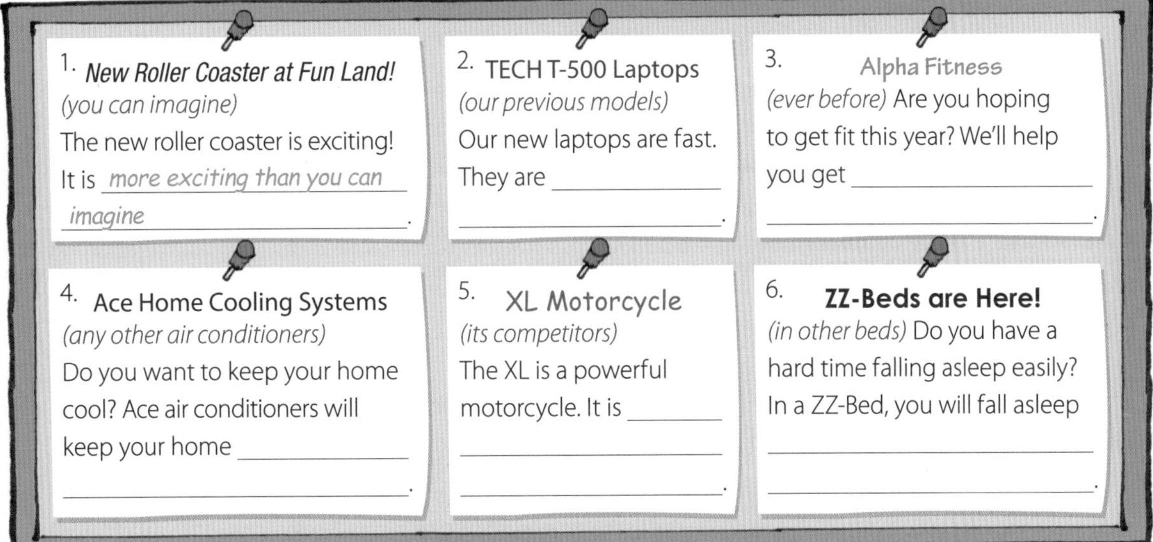

1. New Roller Coaster at Fun Land!
(you can imagine)
The new roller coaster is exciting! It is *more exciting than you can imagine*.

2. TECH T-500 Laptops
(our previous models)
Our new laptops are fast. They are __________.

3. Alpha Fitness
(ever before) Are you hoping to get fit this year? We'll help you get __________.

4. Ace Home Cooling Systems
(any other air conditioners)
Do you want to keep your home cool? Ace air conditioners will keep your home __________.

5. XL Motorcycle
(its competitors)
The XL is a powerful motorcycle. It is __________.

6. ZZ-Beds are Here!
(in other beds) Do you have a hard time falling asleep easily? In a ZZ-Bed, you will fall asleep __________.

C. Complete the sentences with **than** and the nouns in *italics*. Add **more/less**.

1. *(housework)* My mom had me do *less housework than* yesterday, so I'm free tonight!
2. *(customers)* Our store's grand opening was a success! There were __________ we expected.
3. *(clothes)* I'm buying __________ I used to these days. I'm trying to save money.
4. *(traffic)* There is __________ last weekend. I've never seen this many cars!
5. *(children)* I have four kids but Jo has __________ me. She has three sons and two daughters.
6. *(wine)* Daniel had __________ usual, but he still had a bad headache the next day.

D. Find and change any mistakes in each sentence. Put ✓ if the sentence is correct.

1. People live more long than in the past because of modern medicine. *more long → longer*
2. "Can we meet tomorrow? I'll be less busier then." "Sounds good." __________
3. The train station was farther than it looked on the map. __________
4. "This puzzle is simple than that one." "OK. Let's do that one." __________
5. I made many mistakes on my biology exam than my chemistry exam. __________
6. Mike and I both smoke, but I smoke less. __________

Answers **p.319** / Review Test 14 **p.260**

The water is much deeper than it looks! *Comparatives (2)*

MP3

1 We use **much** / **even** / **far** / **a lot** / etc. before *comparatives* to emphasize their meanings.

- Be careful! The water is **much deeper** than it looks!
- "My new project is **even more difficult** than the last one." "Really? It must be really hard."
- Both Mr. and Mrs. Mills can speak French. Mr. Mills speaks it **far more fluently**, though.
- The line at the bank was **a lot longer** than usual.

But we do not use **very** before *comparatives*.

- I live close to downtown, but Shawn lives **even closer**. (*NOT* very closer)
- Jack has more time these days, so he goes out with his friends **far more often** than before. (*NOT* very more often)

2 We use **a little** / **a bit** / **slightly** / etc. before *comparatives* to talk about a small difference in degree between two or more people/things.

- Could you turn up the radio **a little louder**?
- "This shirt is small. Do you have something **a bit larger**?" "Yes, we do."
- The price of gas in this part of town is **slightly lower** than in my neighborhood.
- We haven't practiced tennis much lately. We need to practice **a bit more regularly**.

3 **comparative + and + comparative**

We can use **comparative + and + comparative** to say that a person/thing gradually changes in some way.

- According to scientists, the earth is becoming **hotter and hotter** every year.
- **More and more** people are working from home these days.
- Cheryl's piano skills are improving. She's getting **better and better** every day.
- My heart began beating **faster and faster** before my presentation. I was so nervous.

We use **more and more + adjective/adverb** for *adjectives/adverbs* that have two or more syllables.

- That new TV show is becoming **more and more popular**.
- A storm must be coming. The wind is blowing **more and more strongly**.

4 **the + comparative . . ., the + comparative . . .**

We can use **the + comparative . . ., the + comparative . . .** to say that two people/things change together in some way.

the + comparative		*the + comparative*	
The bigger	the apartment is,	**the more costly**	rent is.
The more crowded	the café became,	**the slower**	the service got.
The busier	we are,	**the less**	we see each other.
The more frequently	I exercised,	**the healthier**	I became.

We often use **the + comparative + the better**.

- "When do you want to eat?" "**The sooner the better**. I'm really hungry."
- I'm looking for a cheap bicycle. In fact, **the cheaper the better**.
- "This sauce has hot pepper in it." "Good. **The spicier the better**."
- "How many balloons do we need for the event?" "**The more the better**."

P R A C T I C E

A. Look at the pictures and complete the sentences with the given words.

big	far	high	light	long	old	~~small~~	young

4 Bus Timetable

DESTINATION	DISTANCE (miles)	TRAVEL TIME
LAKEVIEW	140	1.5 hr
GREENVILLE	163	3.5 hr

1. *(slightly, much)* The chocolate bar is *slightly smaller*______, but its calorie count is __________.
2. *(a bit, even)* The Super S200 laptop is __________, but it's __________ than the Super S100.
3. *(far, much)* John is __________ than Tom, but he looks __________.
4. *(a little, a lot)* Greenville is __________ away, but it takes __________ to get there.

B. Complete the sentences with the adjectives/adverbs in the box. Use **comparative + and + comparative.**

afraid	~~clearly~~	close	quickly	tall

1. As the fog disappeared, we could see the road *more and more clearly*______.
2. Those sunflowers in my garden are getting __________. They used to be so short.
3. I'm scared of heights. I became __________ as the plane rose into the air.
4. My wedding is drawing __________. It's only a week away now.
5. The ice in the Arctic is melting __________ because of global warming.

C. Read the sentences and complete the new ones with **the + comparative . . ., the + comparative . . .**

1. When bread is fresh, it is tasty.
   → The fresher bread is, *the tastier it is*______.
2. We will be more successful if we work hard.
   → The harder we work, __________.
3. When a coin is rare, it becomes valuable.
   → The rarer a coin is, __________.
4. When kids are tired, they fall asleep fast.
   → The more tired kids are, __________.
5. People invest carefully if the economy is bad.
   → The worse the economy is, __________.

D. Complete the conversations with the adjectives/adverbs in the box. Use **the + comparative + the better.**

easy	many	scary	~~soon~~	sweet

1. When do you want the report? Do you need it quickly? — Yes. *The sooner the better*______.
2. Do you like sugar in your coffee? — Yes. __________.
3. It's a horror movie. Are you sure you want to see it? — Sure. __________.
4. I want to bring a lot of friends to the party. Is that OK? — Sure. __________.
5. Take Professor White's class. It isn't hard. — OK. __________.

Answers p.319 / Review Test 14 p.260

LESSON 76 The wallet is the smallest and the most expensive. *Superlatives (1)*

1 The wallet is **the smallest** and **the most expensive**.

"the smallest" is used to say that the wallet is smaller than all the others. **"the most expensive"** is used to say that it is more expensive than all the others. "**smallest**" and "**most expensive**" are *superlatives*.

2 We use **the + hardest/biggest**/etc. *(superlatives)* to compare a person/thing with all the others in a group. We make *superlatives* in the following ways:

+ (e)st	one-syllable adj./adv.	hard → **the hardest** big → **the biggest**	fast → **the fastest** nice → **the nicest**
	two-syllable adj./adv. that end with **y**	busy → **the busiest**	funny → **the funniest**
most +	two- or more- syllable adj./adv.	popular → **the most popular**	recently → **the most recently**
	-ing/-ed adj.	amazing → **the most amazing**	crowded → **the most crowded**
+ -(e)st or most +	quiet → **the quietest** *OR* **the most quiet** lively → **the liveliest** *OR* **the most lively**	simple → **the simplest** *OR* **the most simple** polite → **the politest** *OR* **the most polite**	
Exceptions:	good/well → **the best**	bad/badly → **the worst**	far → **the farthest/the furthest**

More about spelling rules: Appendix p.280

- Emily is **the busiest** person in our office. She also works **the hardest**.
- **The biggest** building in town was built **the most recently**.
- "Nancy can run **the fastest**." "Can she run **the farthest** too?"
- Our hotel has **the liveliest** / **most lively** bar and **the most amazing** view of the ocean.

We can leave out **the** when we use *superlatives* without a *noun*.

- I think this dress is **(the) prettiest**. What do you think?
- We love this golf course, so we come here **(the) most often**.

3 We use **the least** + *adjective/adverb* to say that the degree of something is the smallest.

- **The least crowded** park is Green Hills Park. Let's go there.
- There are a lot of buses that come by my house, but this one comes **the least frequently**.
- That report is **the least important**. We can do it last.

4 We can use **the most** as the *superlative* of **many/much** and **the least** as the *superlative* of **little**. We can use **the most** and **the least** with or without *nouns*.

many/much → **the most**	little → **the least**

- "Which café do you go to **the most**?" "City Café."
- In a band, the drummer usually gets **the least attention**.
- I caught **the most fish** of all of us. You should have come and watched.
- Let's just get the toothpaste that costs **the least**. I'm sure there's no difference.

P R A C T I C E

A. **Look at the pictures and complete the sentences with words from each box. Use the superlatives of the adjectives.**

high ~~long~~ many popular warm	+	~~coat~~ day people score song

1. Jen is wearing *the longest coat*.
2. ______________ is "A Lonely Heart."
3. Wednesday will be ______________ of the week.
4. There are ______________ in front of Pizza World.
5. Todd got ______________.

B. **Complete the sentences with the comparatives or superlatives of the adjectives/adverbs in the box. Leave out the if possible.**

comfortably dark early little ~~much~~ old polluted sad

1. "Do you miss your family much?" "Yes. I miss my mom *(the) most*. I really want to see her."
2. These shoes fit ______________ than the other pair. I think I'll buy these.
3. "What is ______________ time you can meet?" "Around 7:30. I won't be free until then."
4. It was sunny in the morning, but the sky has gotten ______________. There are a lot of clouds now.
5. "Does Mitchell have any younger sisters?" "No. He just has an ______________ one."
6. "This area of the river is ______________ of all." "I know. It smells really bad."
7. "I thought Mel's poetry was the best." "I disagree. I liked it ______________."
8. "I cried at the end of the documentary." "I did too. It was ______________ part."

C. **Complete the sentences with the adjectives/adverbs in *italics*. Use the superlatives or add the least if necessary.**

1. *(interesting)* We really enjoyed our trip to Ireland. They have *the most interesting* culture there.
2. *(short)* "Do you know ______________ way to the town center?" "Yes. That way is the quickest."
3. *(close)* Jeff is the one sitting ______________ to the exit. He's right next to the door.
4. *(frequently)* I see all of my friends often, but I see Julie ______________. We are best friends.
5. *(polite)* Nathan is ______________ boy in the neighborhood. He always says "thank you."
6. *(common)* ______________ blood type is AB. Only about 4 percent of people have it.
7. *(often)* I recommend Sun Airlines. Their flights are delayed ______________.
8. *(heavy)* "I'm looking for a light camera." "Here. This is ______________ one."

D. **Complete the sentences with the most / the least and the nouns in the box.**

experience ~~fans~~ interest money damage votes

1. Of all our basketball players, Scott has *the most fans*. He's loved by so many people.
2. "Who has ______________ in this school?" "Tom. He has taught here the longest."
3. My son shows ______________ in physics. He thinks it's the most boring subject.
4. I went shopping with my friends and spent ______________. I only bought a hairband.
5. Jenny became the class president because she received ______________.
6. The house that faced ______________ from the storm was built of bricks.

Answers **p.319** / Review Test 14 **p.260**

What's the tallest building in the world? *Superlatives (2)*

MP3

1 We usually use the following expressions after **the + superlative**:

in + *place/group*

- "What's **the tallest building in the world**?" "I'm not sure."
- I'm not **the oldest in my family**. I have two older sisters.
- Marie dances **the most wonderfully in our ballet class.**

of + *period of time*

- "How was your vacation?" "Great. I had **the best time of my life**."
- Getting out of bed is **the hardest part of the morning**.
- "Wow. That was **the most exciting game of the year**!" "I agree! Both teams played well."

of all (+ *plural noun*)

- The blue whale is **the largest of all animals**. It is nearly 30 meters long.
- I think roses are **the most beautiful flowers of all**.
- "Could you recommend a salad?" "Greek salad is **the tastiest of all our salads**."

I know

- Brian won the lottery twice! He's **the luckiest man I know**.
- This beach is **the most peaceful place I know**. I often come here to think.

I've (ever) + **met**/**taken**/etc. *(past participle)*

- Roy and Jane are **the smartest people I've met**.
- "How was your test?" "It was **the most difficult exam I've ever taken**."

2 We can use **by far** / **easily** / etc. before **the + superlative** to emphasize the meaning of the *superlative*.

- *War and Peace* is **by far the longest** book I've ever read.
- "College was **easily the most memorable** time of my life." "Me too."
- Our country's economy grew **by far the most rapidly** during the 1970s.
- The Hyde Hotel is **easily the nicest** hotel I've been to. I want to go there again one day.

3 We can use **the second**/**third**/etc. + **superlative** to talk about the rank of a person/thing in a group.

- On the history exam, I scored **the second highest** in the class!
- Manchester Airport is **the third busiest** airport in Britain.
- Olivia was **the fifth most common** name for baby girls in 2005.
- There was a big earthquake in the Atlantic yesterday. It was **the second strongest** in 20 years.

4 We often use **one of the** + **superlative** + **plural noun.**

- The New Year's party is **one of the biggest events** in our company.
- **One of the most famous astronauts** in America was Neil Armstrong.
- The Internet is **one of the greatest inventions** in history.
- "That was **one of the most interesting** movies I've ever seen." "I thought so too."

P R A C T I C E

A. **Put the words in *italics* in the correct order using the superlatives of the adjectives/adverbs. Add in/of if necessary.**

1. *(month / the year / short)* The shortest month of the year ______ is February.
2. *(quiet / town / street)* This is ______. There's rarely any traffic.
3. *(I've ever had / relaxing / holiday)* My trip to Hawaii was ______.
4. *(all materials / hard)* People thought diamonds were ______ until recently.
5. *(person / I know / honest)* Tim is ______. You can trust him.
6. *(composer / the 18th century / famous)* Mozart was ______.
7. *(our class / healthy / student)* Rick is ______. He's never sick.
8. *(all / slow)* There are a few slow runners on our football team, but I'm ______.
9. *(our museum / ancient / paintings)* Those are ______.
10. *(I've ever received / expensive / gift)* ______ was this necklace.

B. **Complete the sentences with the words in *italics*. Use the superlatives of the adjectives/adverbs.**

1. *(by far, popular)* "How about this model? It's by far the most popular ______ car we sell." "It looks nice."
2. *(by far, loudly)* Jo sings ______ of all our chorus singers. I can't hear the others.
3. *(easily, big)* "This park is huge!" "Yes. It's ______ park in the city."
4. *(by far, funny)* I never feel bored around Jimmy. He's ______ person I know.
5. *(easily, dangerous)* Hockey is ______ sport I've ever played.

C. **Look at the table and complete the sentences with the superlatives of the adjectives in *italics*. Add second/third if necessary.**

	House on Fifth Avenue	House on Acton Road	House in Lakeview Heights	House in Colton Village
Area (m^2)	175	140	240	200
Number of Rooms	6	4	8	7
Price ($)	550,000	390,000	470,000	890,000
Built	in 1988	in 2006	in 1990	in 2010

1. *(small)* The third smallest ______ house is the one in Colton Village.
2. *(large)* The house with ______ area is the one in Lakeview Heights.
3. *(expensive)* The house on Fifth Avenue is ______.
4. *(new)* ______ house is the one in Colton Village.
5. *(old)* The house on Acton Road is ______.
6. *(many)* The house in Colton Village has ______ rooms.

D. **Complete the sentences with one of the + superlative.**

1. This cake is very sweet. It's one of the sweetest cakes ______ we offer.
2. I have a noisy neighbor. He's ______ I've ever had.
3. Yesterday's meeting was so boring. It was ______ I've attended.
4. Picasso was a great artist. He was ______ of the 20th century.
5. Greg's job is extremely important. It's ______ at our company.

Answers p.319 / Review Test 14 p.260

LESSON 78

The backpack is **as expensive as** the belt. as . . . as (1)

MP3

1 The backpack is 150 dollars. The belt is 150 dollars.

The backpack is **as expensive as** the belt.

"as expensive as" is used to say that the price of the backpack and the belt are the same.

2 We use **as** + *adjective/adverb* + **as** to say that two people/things are the same in some way.

- "Your dog is **as friendly as** mine." "Yes. He likes people."
- Our new printer model is selling **as well as** the old one.
- Some of these statues look **as real as** people.
- I reviewed your essay **as carefully as** I could. I didn't see any mistakes.

We use **not as** + *adjective/adverb* + **as** to say that two people/things are not the same in some way.

- The strawberries were **not as fresh as** last week, so I didn't get any.
- William does**n't** jog **as regularly as** he used to.
- "Was the video game fun?" "Yes, but it was**n't as exciting as** I expected."
- Do**n't** close the jar **as tightly as** you did last time. It was hard to open.

3 We can also use **comparative** + **than** instead of **not as . . . as**.

- My sofa is **not as comfortable as** yours.
  OR Your sofa is **more comfortable than** mine.
- Yesterday's interview **didn't go as smoothly as** today's.
  OR Today's interview went **more smoothly than** yesterday's.
- Ms. Grace's lecture was **not as easy as** Mr. Mann's lecture.
  OR Mr. Mann's lecture **was easier than** Ms. Grace's lecture.

4 We use **as many/much** + *noun* + **as** to talk about the same degree or quantity.

- We invited **as many guests as** last time. It's going to be another big party!
- Tara doesn't have **as much time as** in the past. She's very busy these days.
- I got to the train station early because there weren't **as many cars as** usual.

5 We use **the same as** to mean "equal to."

- That suitcase is **the same as** mine. Where did you get it?
- "Are there any new movies?" "No, they're **the same as** last week."
- "How was school today?" "It was **the same as** always."

We can also use **the same** + *noun* + **as**.

- I'm **the same size as** my sister. We share our clothes.
- "We are staying at the Plaza Hotel." "Really? We are staying at **the same hotel as** you!"
- Tomorrow will be **the same temperature as** today.

PRACTICE

A. Complete the sentences with **as . . . as** and the given words.

badly	~~busy~~	calmly	famous	heavy	often

1. *(usual)* We just finished our exams, so we're not *as busy as usual*.
2. *(Kevin)* I practice football ____________, but he plays far better than I do.
3. *(they look)* "Do you need help with those grocery bags?" "No. They're not ____________."
4. *(the others in the city)* Only a few people visit this museum because it isn't ____________.
5. *(I could)* I was angry at Laura, but I spoke ____________.
6. *(we had feared)* Jeremy was in a car accident. Fortunately, he wasn't injured ____________.

B. Write sentences with the adjectives in *italics*. Use **not as . . . as** for 1-3 and **comparative + than** for 4-6.

The Brooklyn Bridge
- built in 1883
- 1,825 meters long
- 26 meters wide

1. *(long)* *The Brooklyn Bridge isn't as long as the Golden Gate Bridge*.
2. *(old)* ____________.
3. *(wide)* ____________.

The Golden Gate Bridge
- built in 1937
- 2,737 meters long
- 27 meters wide

4. *(long)* ____________.
5. *(old)* ____________.
6. *(wide)* ____________.

C. Read the sentences and complete the new ones with **as many/much . . . as** and the nouns in *italics*.

1. I drank two cups of tea. So did Mr. Hall.
   → *(tea)* I drank *as much tea as Mr. Hall*.
2. There are six men and two women on my team.
   → *(women)* There aren't ____________ on my team.
3. Ted has $50 in his wallet. I have the same amount.
   → *(cash)* I have ____________.
4. My brother's room gets a lot of light, but my room doesn't.
   → *(light)* My room doesn't get ____________.
5. This theater has 150 seats. The new theater has 300 seats.
   → *(seats)* This theater doesn't have ____________.

D. Complete the conversations with **the same . . . as** and the nouns in the box.

~~age~~	city	day	height	school	time

1. A: Fred is 10 years old.
   B: Really? My son is *the same age as him*.
2. A: I go to St. Mary's High School.
   B: My sister goes to ____________.
3. A: Stacy finishes work at 5 o'clock. What about you?
   B: I finish work at ____________.
4. A: I'm 6 feet tall.
   B: I'm ____________.
5. A: My checkup is on Monday. When is yours?
   B: Mine is on ____________.
6. A: Did you know that Henry and Jill were from Texas?
   B: Yes. We lived in ____________.

Answers **p.320** / Review Test 14 **p.260**

Sarah's cooking is **just as good as** her mother's. as . . . as (2)

MP3

1 We can use **just/nearly/almost** before **as** + *adjective/adverb* + **as**.

We use **just as . . . as** to say that people/things are exactly the same in some way.

- Sarah's cooking is **just as good as** her mother's.
- "Did you fail the driving test again?" "Yes. I did **just as badly as** last time."
- The author's newest novel is **just as exciting as** her other books. I finished it in two days.
- I can use a typewriter **just as easily as** I can use a computer.

We use **nearly/almost as . . . as** to say that people/things are similar but not exactly the same in some way.

- Brian is **nearly as old as** me.
- "Is it still raining?" "Yes. It's raining **almost as heavily as** it did yesterday."
- This book is **nearly as thick as** a dictionary.
- My math class is **almost as hard as** my history class.

2 We can use **twice / three times** / etc. before **as** + *adjective/adverb* + **as**.

- Vegetables are **twice as expensive as** last year because of the flood.
- The new train travels **three times as fast as** the old one.
- The Pacific Ocean is **12 times as large as** the Arctic Ocean.
- Cleaning the house took **twice as long as** I expected.

3 We can use **possible** after **as** + *adjective/adverb* + **as**.

- Our resort offers excellent service. We want our guests to feel **as comfortable as possible**.
- If you can't attend the meeting, please let me know **as soon as possible**.
- We parked **as close as possible** to the mall so we didn't have to walk far.
- The baby is sleeping, so we should talk **as quietly as possible**.

We can also use *subject* + **can** instead of **possible**.

- I'm on a diet, so I try to eat **as little as I can**.
  OR I'm on a diet, so I try to eat **as little as possible**.
- "Could you describe the thief **as clearly as you can**?"
  OR "Could you describe the thief **as clearly as possible**?" "Well, he was tall and thin."

4 We usually use **as far as** in the following expressions:

as far as I'm concerned (="in my opinion")	As far as I'm concerned, the best baseball team is the Knights.
as far as I know (="in my knowledge")	"Did Shirley graduate?" "**As far as I know**, she's still a student."
as far as I remember (="in my memory")	"Do people leave tips in China?" "**As far as I remember**, they don't."

PRACTICE

A. Complete the sentences with **as . . . as** and the given words.

confused	hungry	important	~~quickly~~	terribly	well

1. *(almost)* This tornado won't last long. It'll disappear *almost as quickly as* the last one.
2. *(just)* Getting enough exercise is ______________ eating healthy food.
3. *(nearly)* "Brandon's writing is awful." "I know. He writes ______________ I do!"
4. *(almost)* The breakfast at the hotel was too small. I'm ______________ before breakfast.
5. *(nearly)* Carl is still a good basketball player. He plays ______________ he did in college.
6. *(just)* "Do you understand the directions?" "No. I'm ______________ you."

B. Look at the pictures and complete the sentences with **twice / three times** / etc. **as . . . as** and the adjectives in *italics*.

1-3

100 years of tradition

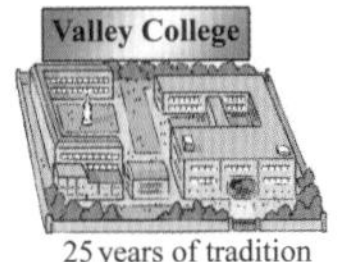

25 years of tradition

Area	4.5km^2	9km^2
Tuition Fee	$30,000	$10,000

4-6

Weight	40 tons	120 tons
Speed	3,200km/h	800km/h

1. *(old)* Hill College is *four times as old as* Valley College.
2. *(big)* Valley College's campus is ______________ Hill College's campus.
3. *(expensive)* Hill College's tuition fee is ______________ Valley College's.
4. *(long)* The A360 is ______________ the F71.
5. *(fast)* The F71 is ______________ the A360.
6. *(heavy)* The A360 is ______________ the F71.

C. Complete the sentences with **as . . . as** and the words in the box. Use **possible** for 1-3 and **subject + can** for 4-6.

loudly	often	soon	~~straight~~	truthfully	unique

1. Always try to sit *as straight as possible*. It's better for your back.
2. Tammy's art is very different. She tries to be ______________.
3. I answered all of your questions ______________. I was really honest.
4. Please reply to this e-mail ______________. I need your opinion right away.
5. "I can't hear you." "I'm talking ______________. Maybe something's wrong with your phone."
6. Stephen lives overseas, but he visits us ______________.

D. Give answers for each situation with **as far as** and the words in *italics*.

1. Someone asks you where the bank is. You think it's on 22nd Avenue.
   YOU: *(I know)* *As far as I know, it's on 22nd Avenue*.
2. Your roommate asks you when Donna is coming back from her trip. You think it's tomorrow.
   YOU: *(I remember)* ______________.
3. Your friend wants some advice on which dress to wear. You think the red dress looks best.
   YOU: *(I'm concerned)* ______________.
4. Your coworker wants to know where Mr. Brown is. You think he is in his office.
   YOU: *(I know)* ______________.

Answers **p.320** / Review Test 14 **p.260**

LESSON
80

He's watching the birds **at the window.** *Prepositions* of place **at**, **in**, **on** (1)

MP3

1 We use **at**, **in**, or **on** to talk about the place something happens or is located.

at + *point* (window, bus stop, etc.)

He's at the window.

at the window/door
at the bus stop
at the intersection
at the traffic light

in + *area* (box, living room, etc.)

He's in the box.

in the box
in the living room
in the building
in the town/city/country

on + *surface* (roof, table, etc.)

He's on the roof.

on the roof
on the table/sofa
on the floor/ground/wall
on my face/cheek

- "Rachel, what's your cat doing?" "He's watching the bird **at the window**."
- I saw you **at the bus stop**. Where were you going?
- There is a new shopping mall **at the intersection** of Main Street and Maple Road.

- "Where's your cat?" "He's sleeping **in the box** over there."
- "Did the children come home?" "Yes. They're playing **in the living room**."
- Hana Grill is one of the most popular restaurants **in New York City**.

- "Look! Your cat is **on the roof**." "Yes. He likes high places."
- After cleaning her house all afternoon, Rita sat down **on her sofa** to relax.
- Why are you staring at me like that? Is there something **on my face**?

2 There is the following difference in meaning between **at** and **in**:

- Can you drop me off **at the bank**? I need to get some cash. (**the bank** as a point)
  I waited for a long time **in the bank**. Many people were trying to pay their bills. (the inside of **the bank**)
- We're meeting Eric **at the station**. He's meeting us outside Exit 3.
  "Is the café outside the station?" "No. It's **in the station**."

3 There is the following difference in meaning between **at** and **on**:

- I went to talk to Ms. Jones, but she wasn't **at her desk**. (**her desk** as a point)
  "Did you give the report to Ms. Jones?" "I put it **on her desk**." (the surface of **her desk**)
- Someone left a package **at the door**. It's for you.
  The store's business hours are posted **on the door**.

4 There is the following difference in meaning between **in** and **on**:

- "What's **in the envelope**?" "It's a card from Kelly." (the inside of **the envelope**)
  Please write your address **on the envelope**. (the surface of **the envelope**)
- When I was crossing the bridge, I could see fish **in the river**.
  There were a lot of ducks **on the river** this morning.

PRACTICE

A. Write **at/in/on.**

1. This car key was *on* the table. Is it yours?
2. "Which way should I turn ____________ the traffic light?" "Left."
3. Let's take a picture ____________ that gate. It's a famous place for tourists.
4. Every night, Charlotte says good night to her son with a kiss ____________ the cheek.
5. Paco was born and raised ____________ village ____________ India.
6. "There are many schools ____________ this town." "There are a lot of children, too!"
7. The spider was ____________ the ceiling, and then it fell ____________ my shoulder. It was scary!
8. "Dan's house is ____________ the next intersection." "That's very close to my house."

B. Look at the pictures and complete the sentences with **at/in/on** and the words in the box.

the bus stop	the car	the car	the crosswalk	the desk	the desk
the door	the door	~~the lake~~	the tent	their bags	their faces

1-3 / 7-9 / 4-6 / 10-12

1. There is a boat *on the lake*.
2. Two people are ____________.
3. There is a bicycle ____________.
4. There is a poster ____________.
5. A man is sitting ____________.
6. He's looking at a picture ____________.
7. A man is getting off the bus ____________.
8. A dog is ____________.
9. Two girls are standing ____________.
10. Three children are ____________.
11. They have paint ____________.
12. They have candy ____________.

C. Complete the conversations with **at/in/on** and the words in *italics*.

1. A: *(the window)* Henry, why are you standing *at the window*?
   B: *(the door)* I'm looking outside. There's someone ____________.
2. A: *(the carpet)* What did you drop ____________?
   B: *(the sofa)* Jam. It's ____________ too. Sorry.
3. A: How do I get to the museum?
   B: *(the mall)* After you drive past the church, turn left ____________.
4. A: *(the library)* Excuse me, sir. Food isn't allowed ____________.
   B: *(the grass)* Sorry. I didn't know. Then, can I eat ____________ outside?
5. A: *(the floor)* The dog made a mess ____________.
   B: *(the yard)* We should keep him ____________.
6. A: *(his office)* Is Jim ____________?
   B: Yes. He's working on a report right now.

Answers p.320 / Review Test 15 p.262

We heard some wonderful music **at** the concert.

Prepositions of place
at, in, on (2)

MP3

1 We use **at** in the following expressions:

Event/Show	at a concert	at a party	at a football game	
Everyday place	at home	at work	at Tom's (house)	at the dentist's/doctor's

- We heard some wonderful music **at the concert**.
- "What are you going to do this weekend?" "I'll probably just stay **at home**."
- "I didn't see Betty **at the party**. Did you?" "Yes. She left early."
- Helen and I are having dinner **at Tom's** tonight.

2 We use **in** in the following expressions:

Nature/Environment	in the rain	in the sky	in the sea	in the ocean	in the woods	in the world
Line/Row	in (a) line	in a row	in a circle			
Printed material	in a book	in a newspaper	in a magazine	in a picture		
	Exceptions:	on a menu	on a page	on a list	on a map	

- When I was young, I liked playing outside **in the rain**.
- A lot of students were waiting **in (a) line** at the cafeteria.
- "Can pigs swim?" "Yes. I think I read that **in a book**."
- I'm trying to find the museum. Where is it **on this map**?

3 We use **on** in the following expressions:

Street/Floor	on the street	on the road	on the first/second/third floor	
Transportation	on a bus	on a train	on a plane	on a bicycle/bike
	Exceptions:	in a car	in a taxi	
Etc.	on the screen	on the platform	on the railway	

- There were musicians singing and playing guitars **on the street**.
- Joe left his gloves **in the taxi**. He realized it when he was **on the plane**.
- "The error message keeps appearing **on the screen**." "Try restarting the computer."
- "Do you know where Sophie's Closet is?" "It's **on the third floor**."

4 We also use **at/in/on** in the following expressions:

at the top/bottom of	in the middle of

- A man is sitting **at the top of** the stairs.
- **At the bottom of** the chart, you can see our sales records from last year.
- The fountain **in the middle of** the garden is beautiful.

at the top of

on the left/right (side of)

- Are you looking for the bathroom? Walk that way and it'll be **on the left**.
- **On the right side of** the post office, there is a hospital.
- There's a plant **on the left side of** my desk. Please give it water while I'm gone.

on the left

PRACTICE

A. Write **at/in/on**.

1. Dr. Kim's article was printed *in* the newspaper.
2. "Why are there so many cars ________ the road?"
   "It's probably because of the holiday."
3. We had fun ________ the football game last night.
4. Jack went to the store ________ his bicycle.
5. The Amazon is the widest river ________ the world.
6. "Where were you earlier?"
   "I was ________ the dentist's. I had a toothache."
7. We sat ________ a circle and listened to a story.
8. Never walk ________ the railway. It's too dangerous.

B. Complete the sentences with **at/in/on** and the words in the box.

Carrie's house	rows	the bus	the car	the eye doctor's	the menu	the ocean	~~the street~~

1. Don't throw your trash *on the street*. There's a garbage can around the corner.
2. "Why were you ________________ today?" "I needed glasses."
3. When I drive to work, I usually listen to music ________________.
4. "I don't see my favorite pasta dish ________________ anymore." "Let's ask about it."
5. The chairs in the conference room were arranged ________________ for the meeting.
6. We're going to be ________________ tonight for her graduation party. Can you come?
7. I fell asleep ________________ this morning. I almost missed my stop.
8. Sea turtles lay their eggs on land, but they live ________________.

C. Look at the pictures and complete the sentences with **at the top of / in the middle of** / etc. and the words in the box.

the door	the ladder	~~the letter~~	the poster	the table

1. Janet signed *at the bottom of the letter*.
2. A bowl of fruit is ________________.
3. A man is standing ________________.
4. There's a doorbell ________________.
5. The date of the concert is ________________.

D. The following is a letter from Paul. Find and change any mistakes in each sentence.

Dear Amy,

I am in Rome! 1. I am staying at a hotel ~~on~~ *in* the middle of the city.

2. My room is at the 15th floor. It has a great view.

3. In the plane, I met a girl named Giana. She invited me to a party last night.

4. I met so many people in the party and had a lot of fun.

5. The party was in her home. There was a big garden and I loved it.

6. Tomorrow, I'm going to pick out a few places in a map for sightseeing.

7. I think Rome is the most amazing city on the world.

I hope you can visit Rome someday.

From Paul

Answers **p.320** / Review Test 15 **p.262**

Let's meet at 8:30. *Prepositions* of time **at, on, in** (1)

MP3

1 We use **at** before a specific time or meal time.

at 8:30/6 o'clock/etc.	at breakfast/lunch/dinner

- Let's meet **at 8:30**. Don't be late.
- I didn't eat anything **at lunch**, so I'm really hungry.
- We're going to watch our favorite TV show **at 6 o'clock**.

2 We use **on** before a date, day, an anniversary, etc.

on September 27/March 15/etc.	on Saturday/Wednesday/etc.
on weekdays/weekends/weeknights/etc.	on your birthday/anniversary/etc.

- **On September 27**, we are having a huge sale. Visit our store!
- I go to bed early **on weeknights**. But **on Saturdays**, I stay up late.
- "What are we doing **on our anniversary**?" "We can do anything you want."

In everyday conversation, we can leave out **on** before a date and day.

- "When did you meet your boyfriend?" "I met him **(on) July 14**, two years ago."
- Sam didn't come to school **(on) Wednesday**. He wasn't feeling well.

We do not use **on** before **yesterday**, **today**, and **tomorrow**.

- "What are your plans tonight?" "I have to prepare for a meeting **tomorrow**." (*NOT* on tomorrow)
- I saw Cindy **yesterday**. She was talking to someone in the hallway. (*NOT* on yesterday)

3 We use **in** before parts of the day, a season, year, etc.

in the morning/afternoon/evening/etc.	in April/the summer/etc.
in 2012/the 19th century/etc.	in the past/the future

- "Did you go to Hawaii **in the summer**?" "No, we went **in April**."
- **In 2012**, Janice was very busy. She worked **in the afternoon** and attended classes **in the evening**.
- Our company only sold phones **in the past**, but we will offer other products **in the future**.

But we use **at** before **night**.

- This street is usually very quiet **in the morning**, but it's always crowded **at night**. (*NOT* in night)

4 We use **on** before **day** + **morning/afternoon**/etc. In everyday conversation, we can leave out **on**.

- My flight to London leaves **(on) Tuesday afternoon**.
- "When is the next soccer game?" "**(On) Monday evening**."
- I'm going to the movies **(on) Thursday night** with Jack. Do you want to join us?

5 We do not use **at/on/in** before **last/next/this**/etc. + *expression of time*.

- "What did you do **last weekend**?" "I went camping." (*NOT* on last weekend)
- Gabriel is retiring **next year**. He and his wife are moving to the country. (*NOT* in next year)
- Let's visit Joey **this Saturday**. We haven't seen him in a while.

PRACTICE

A. Write **at/on/in**.

1 **PARTY INVITATION!**
My party will be held _on_ May 20 ______ 6:00 p.m. There will be a singing competition ______ the party. I hope you can come!

2 *New Restaurant Opening!*
Casa Restaurant will have its grand opening ______ October 2 ______ 4:30 p.m. It's a great place for dinner ______ your anniversary.

3 *Concert Schedule: July*
A concert series will be held ______ July. ______ weekends, Jay Samson will perform each night ______ 8:00 p.m.

4 **Car for Sale:**
Dodger GT for sale. I bought it ______ 2008. For more information, call ______ the evening after 5:00 or come see it ______ a weekday.

5 **Memo:**
There will be a staff meeting ______ Thursday. We will meet in the conference room. Please be there ______ 1:30 ______ the afternoon.

6 Swimming Pool Open!
Escape the heat at Eaton Swimming Pool! It opens ______ 8:00 ______ the morning and closes ______ 9:00 ______ night.

B. Complete the sentences with **at/on/in** and the words in the box.

lunch	March 8	night	the 19th century	the future	the winter	~~weekends~~

1. _On weekends_, there aren't many trains. There are two on Saturdays, and none on Sundays.
2. "Did Lincoln live ______________?" "Yes. He was born in 1809."
3. "When can you call me today?" "Probably ______________, right after my morning classes."
4. Derek's birthday is ______________. He was born in the spring.
5. Tommy wants to be a pilot ______________. His dream is to have his own airplane.
6. I love cold weather. I especially enjoy ice fishing ______________.
7. "I have trouble sleeping ______________." "You should drink some hot tea."

C. The following is a reply from Amy. Write **at/on/in** or put – if nothing is necessary.

Dear Paul,

1. I got your letter _–_ yesterday! I am happy you are enjoying Rome.
2. Actually, I was there ______ 1997 with my family.
Anyway, I'm doing well. 3. I went to the beach with Justin ______ last weekend.
4. We went ______ Sunday morning, but it was so crowded.
5. So ______ lunch we left and went for some burgers downtown.
6. By the way, my family and I are going to visit my grandmother ______ Saturday.
7. We are all going to see a play ______ 2 o'clock ______ the afternoon.
It will be a fun day!

AIR MAIL

From Amy

Prepositions and Phrasal Verbs

LESSON 82

Grammar Gateway Intermediate

Answers **p.320** / Review Test 15 **p.262**

At first, I didn't like living in the city. *Prepositions* of time **at, on, in** (2)

MP3

1 We use **at** in the following expressions of time:

at first	at last	at that time	at the moment	at the end of

- **At first**, I didn't like living in the city. But now I enjoy it.
- You're here **at last**! I've been waiting for over an hour.
- "Why didn't you answer my call last night?" "Sorry. I was already in bed **at that time**."
- Carla is very interested in learning yoga **at the moment**.
- We finally solved the problem **at the end of** the discussion.

at the earliest	at the latest	at the same time	at once

- I have to work late tonight. I'll be home around 10 **at the earliest**.
- The show starts at 10:00. You should be here by 9:30 **at the latest**.
- Don't try to do too many things **at the same time**. It's better to focus on one thing.
- "In college, I had three part-time jobs **at once**." "Wow! You must have been busy."
- We'd better finish the report **at once**. Mr. Kim has been waiting for it.

2 We use **in** in the following expressions of time:

in advance	in the meantime	in the end	in years

- We should make a reservation **in advance**. That hotel is very popular.
- "Is dinner ready yet?" "No, but you can have a snack **in the meantime**."
- Finding a good job took a long time, but Travis got one **in the end**.
- "I haven't been on a vacation **in years**." "You need a break!"

Note that we use **in the end** and **at the end of** in different ways.

- In action movies, the hero always wins **in the end**. (="eventually")
  I cried **at the end of** the movie. (="at the final part of")
- Julie and Claire argued for a long time. **In the end**, they decided not to talk.
  At the end of the argument, Juile and Claire apologized to each other.

3 **in time** and **on time**

We use **in time** to say that something is done early enough.

- They arrived **in time** for the biology exam.
  (They arrived early enough for the exam.)
- Cindy got home **in time** to cook for her guests.
  (Cindy got home early enough to cook for her guests.)
- I didn't register for the class **in time**. Now it's full and I can't take it.

We use **on time** to say that something is done exactly at the right time.

- The biology exam started **on time**.
  (The exam started exactly at the right time.)
- Cindy's guests arrived **on time** for her dinner party.
  (Her guests arrived exactly at the right time.)
- "Timothy isn't **on time**."
  "He never is. We'll have to wait again."

P R A C T I C E

A. Complete the sentences with **at/in** and the words in the box.

once	~~the earliest~~	the latest	the meantime	the moment	years

1. "When can you call me?" "Around 2 p.m. *at the earliest* ________. I'll be in a meeting until then."
2. I did the laundry in the morning. My husband cleaned our car ________.
3. "We ate a lot." "I know. I'm feeling very full ________."
4. I haven't heard from Laura ________. I wonder how she is doing.
5. Thomas has to give his speech in 10 minutes. Tell him to come ________.
6. Please hand in your homework by Friday ________. After that, I won't accept it.

B. The following information is about the Eiffel Tower. Complete the sentences with **at/in** and the words in the box.

advance	first	the end	~~the end of~~	the same time

1. *At the end of* ________ the 1880s, Paris was preparing to host the World's Fair.
2. ________, architects were building the Eiffel Tower to celebrate the event.
3. To complete the construction on time, workers had started building it several years ________.
4. ________, the tower opened to the public in March of 1889.
5. ________, people thought it was ugly.

However, it quickly became a symbol of Paris.

C. Write **in the end / at the end of** or **in time / on time.**

1. I couldn't understand the assignment at first. But *in the end* ________, I finished it and got an A.
2. We couldn't begin the play ________. An actor showed up late, so it started 30 minutes later.
3. There was a chance to ask questions ________ the presentation.
4. Nancy tried on several dresses. ________, she chose none of them.
5. Some people aren't here yet, but we need to start ________. There's a lot to discuss.
6. I got to the violin contest ________. I had a chance to practice before it began.

D. Complete the conversation with **at/on/in** and the words in the box.

advance	~~last~~	that time	time	years

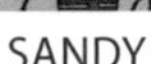

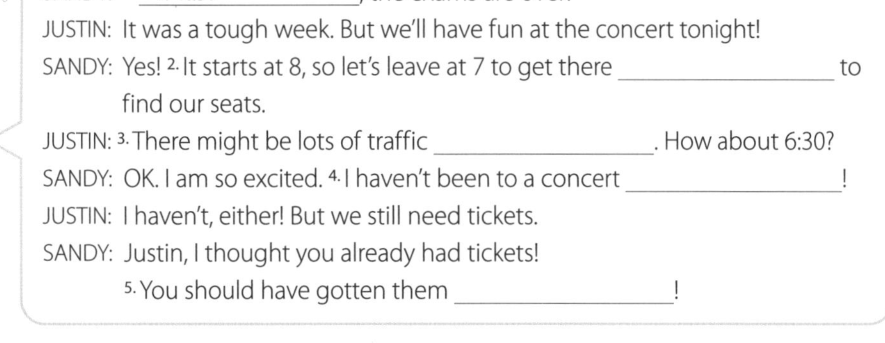

SANDY: 1. *At last* ________, the exams are over!
JUSTIN: It was a tough week. But we'll have fun at the concert tonight!
SANDY: Yes! 2. It starts at 8, so let's leave at 7 to get there ________ to find our seats.
JUSTIN: 3. There might be lots of traffic ________. How about 6:30?
SANDY: OK. I am so excited. 4. I haven't been to a concert ________!
JUSTIN: I haven't, either! But we still need tickets.
SANDY: Justin, I thought you already had tickets!
5. You should have gotten them ________!

Answers **p.321** / Review Test 15 **p.262**

She has been abroad for five years.

Prepositions of time **for, until, in,** etc.

1 for and during

We use **for** to say that something lasts over a particular time period.

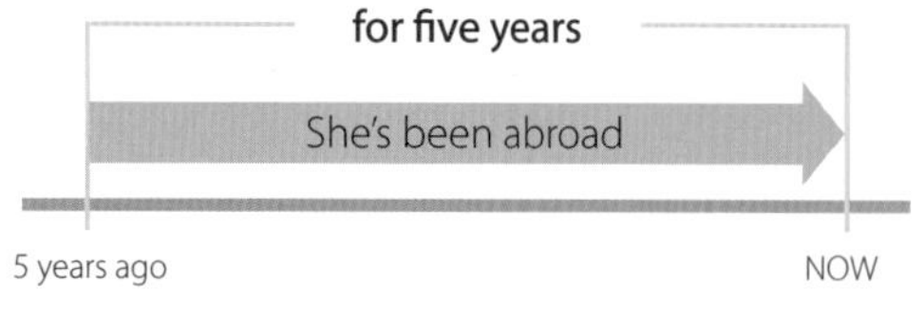

- "How long has Rebecca lived overseas?"
  "She has been abroad **for five years**."
- The baby cried **for 20 minutes**. I don't know why.
- I've been cleaning the house **for an hour**. I'm still not done.

We use **during** to say that something happens in a particular time period.

- "What did you do **during vacation**?"
  "I visited my friend Dave in San Diego."
- We do most of our shopping **during the weekend**.
- The doorbell kept ringing **during my phone conversation**.

2 until/till and by

We use **until/till** to say that something continues to a certain point in time.

- "Can I borrow your car **until/till Friday**?"
  "Sure. I don't need it."
- Joe exercises **until/till 10 p.m.** on weekdays.
- The sale will last **until/till the end of the week**.

We use **by** to say that something happens before a certain point in time.

- "You have to return this book **by Friday**."
  "OK. I won't forget."
- "Come home **by 7 p.m.**" "I'll try."
- We must complete the project **by the end of the month**.

We use **not . . . until . . .** to say that something does not happen before a certain point in time.

- Yesterday, I did**n't** go to sleep **until midnight**. I'll go to bed earlier today.
- "When does the workshop begin?" "It wo**n't** start **until 4 o'clock**."
- "Are you moving to Florida soon?" "No, **not until next month**."

3 in and within

We can use **in** to say that something happens after a particular time period has passed.

- Our lunch break is until 1 p.m. Please come back **in 10 minutes**.
- "I invited Julie to come over for drinks. She will be here **in half an hour**." "Great!"
- The new art museum opens **in two weeks**.

We use **within** to say that something happens before a particular time period has passed.

- I have to finish my lunch **within 10 minutes**. A client is coming to my office.
- "I got my driver's license **within two months**."
  "You must be a fast learner."
- You must finish this report **within the next hour**.

PRACTICE

A. Write **for/during.**

1. "I called you earlier, but you didn't answer." "Sorry, but you called *during* a meeting."
2. We have been taking dance classes ______ two months. We enjoy them a lot.
3. Julia fell asleep ______ the movie. She must have been so tired.
4. It snowed ______ about three hours this morning. Then it stopped around noon.
5. "Mike has been sick ______ five whole days." "I hope he feels better soon."
6. "Could you understand the speaker ______ the lecture?" "Only a little bit. He had a strange accent."
7. Please do not take pictures ______ the performance. There will be time for photos after the show.

B. Complete the sentences with **until/by** and the expressions of time in *italics.*

1. *(2 o'clock)* To avoid extra fees, you must check out of the hotel *by 2 o'clock*.
2. *(9 o'clock)* I have to work ______ today. I still haven't finished my report.
3. *(dinnertime)* I should be there ______, but there is a lot of traffic on the road.
4. *(next Saturday)* I'm staying at a friend's house ______. My apartment is being renovated.
5. *(the beginning of July)* "How long will you be in Florida?" "We'll be there ______."
6. *(August)* The design for the new building will be decided ______.
7. *(the end of the week)* You must register for the seminar ______. Next week will be late.

C. Read the sentences and complete the new ones with **not . . . until . . .** and the words in *italics.*

1. Leo will move to England next year. → *(move to England)* Leo *won't move to England until next year*.
2. I will hand in my essay this Friday.
   → *(be submitted)* My essay ______.
3. The company pays the staff the last day of every month.
   → *(pay the staff)* The company ______.
4. We picked the winner of the contest at 5 o'clock.
   → *(be chosen)* The winner of the contest ______.
5. Ms. Cruz gave the students the test results yesterday.
   → *(receive the test results)* The students ______.

D. The following is a news report about James's restaurant. Choose the correct one.

James's Restaurant Grand Opening!

By Sam Davis of *Restaurant Reviews*

1. James Wilson worked at a bank *(by / during / for)* 30 years.
2. *(After / Until / In)* his retirement last month, he opened a restaurant.
3. *(For / During / In)* my visit last night, I was very surprised because my food came out so quickly.
4. It was served *(for / until / within)* 15 minutes of ordering, and the food tasted excellent.
5. If James keeps serving delicious meals like last night, I'm sure his restaurant will be famous *(by / in / for)* a few months!
6. To celebrate the grand opening, all noodle dishes will be half price *(by / in / until)* the end of this month.

Please visit James's Restaurant! You will have an unforgettable experience.

Answers **p.321** / Review Test 15 **p.262**

LESSON 85

We're going to Italy **by train!**

Other *prepositions* **by, with, in, for, on**

MP3

1 by

Transportation	by plane by train	by subway *Exception*: on foot	by car/taxi	by bus
Communication	by phone	by e-mail	by mail	by fax
Payment	by credit card	by check	*Exception:* in cash	
Etc.	by mistake	by accident	by chance	

- We're going to Italy **by train**! I sent you the schedule **by e-mail**.
- I wanted to pay the deliveryman **by credit card**, but he asked me to pay **in cash**.
- "Why is Jerry's phone in the fridge?" "He must have left it there **by mistake**."

2 with

Person/Animal	with my dog	with a friend	with my parents	with me
Tool	with a knife	with a pen	with a stick	
Appearance	with blond hair	with blue eyes	with glasses	
Emotion	with excitement	with joy	with fear	with anger

- When I go to the park **with my dog**, he always jumps **with excitement**.
- Julia prefers writing **with a pen**. She doesn't like to type on a keyboard.
- "Which child is your son?" "The boy **with blond hair**."

3 in

Clothes/Shoes/etc.	in a suit/dress	in shorts/jeans	in sneakers/boots	in glasses
Word/Number/etc.	in writing	in words	in capital letters	in numbers
Etc.	in a hurry in danger	in general in love	in use in my opinion	

- "Brent was **in a suit** and in a hurry when I saw him." "Oh, he had an interview today."
- All refund requests must be made **in writing**.

4 for

Meal	for breakfast	for lunch	for dinner
Sale/Rent	for sale	for rent	

- Jim and I had Thai food **for lunch**. It was so good.
- Our neighbors must be moving. Their house is **for sale**.

5 on

Period	on holiday/vacation on the phone	on a trip/a tour on a diet	on sale on (a) strike	on (the) air
Etc.	on business	on purpose	on the whole	

- "Is Bob **on vacation?**" "No. He's away **on business.**"
- Ms. Wallace is **on the phone** right now. She's talking to a client.

PRACTICE

A. Look at the pictures and complete the sentences with **by/with/in** and the words in the box.

a tour guide	boots	~~bus~~	capital letters	chopsticks	glasses	love	phone	shorts	taxi

1. They are traveling to Sydney *by bus* ____________.
2. The man ____________ is riding a motorcycle.
3. He went to the airport ____________.
4. The woman ____________ is the manager.
5. The children are walking ____________.
6. The warning is written ____________.
7. She is making a reservation ____________.
8. The boy ____________ is very tall.
9. She is ____________ with him.
10. He is eating ____________.

B. Write the appropriate prepositions.

1. Ann didn't have dessert because she was *on* ________ a diet.
2. Jenny's Wedding Shop has dresses and tuxedos ________ rent.
3. Sometimes I have trouble expressing my thoughts ________ words.
4. I saw an old friend ________ chance on the street this morning.
5. That girl ________ the dark brown eyes is really pretty. She looks like a model.
6. "Peter didn't invite me to his party." "He's so forgetful. I'm sure it was not ________ purpose."

C. Read the sentences and complete the new ones with the words in the box and the appropriate prepositions.

air	anger	fax	~~my opinion~~	use

1. I think Julie should win the essay contest. → *In my opinion* ________, Julie should win the essay contest.
2. Chuck's face was red. He was angry. → Chuck's face was red ________.
3. That meeting room is being used. → That meeting room is ________.
4. I sent my application with a fax machine. → I sent my application ________.
5. You can listen to the radio program every morning. → The radio program is ________ every morning.

D. The following is an advertisement for the Schwann bicycle. Complete the sentences with the words in *italics* and the appropriate prepositions.

SCHWANN

1. *(car)* Traveling *by car* ________ costs a lot of money.
2. *(a hurry)* But you don't have time to walk because you're always ________.
So what will you do? Come and get a Schwann bicycle!
3. *(sale)* Our bicycles are now ________. They're 20 percent off the regular price!
Don't wait! Buy today! 4. *(check)* You can pay ________ or credit card.
5. *(e-mail)* For further details, contact us ________ at info@schwann.com.

Prepositions and Phrasal Verbs

LESSON 85

Grammar Gateway Intermediate

Answers p.321 / Review Test 15 p.262

Tara chose the bag **because of** its color.

Prepositions of two or more words

MP3

1 because of

- Tara chose the bag **because of its color**. She loves pink.
- "They play some good songs at this bar!" "I know! I come here **because of the music**."
- Gina couldn't go to the movies **because of her younger sister**. She had to take care of her.

We can also use **due to** or **owing to** instead of **because of**.

- **Due to the traffic jam**, I was late for my appointment.
  OR **Because of the traffic jam**, I was late for my appointment.
- Oranges grow well in Florida **owing to its warm climate**.
  OR Oranges grow well in Florida **because of its warm climate**.

2 thanks to

- **Thanks to our customers**, our business has improved every year.
- "**Thanks to your help**, the presentation was a success." "Thank you for saying that."
- I can easily communicate with my family from abroad **thanks to the Internet**.

3 instead of

- Let's get fish **instead of chicken**. I had chicken for lunch.
- Why don't we walk **instead of driving**? It's not that far.
- "Can we record the lecture **instead of taking** notes?" "We should ask."

We can also use **instead** alone.

- Jack didn't want to go shopping, so we went to a coffee shop **instead**.
- "Will your brother go to college after graduation?" "I think he'll get a job **instead**."

4 in spite of

- **In spite of his efforts**, the repairman couldn't fix the dishwasher.
- Karen hurt her ankle. **In spite of the injury**, she finished the race.
- **In spite of arguing** a lot, Brad and Mark are still best friends.

We can also use **despite** instead of **in spite of**. Note that we do not use **of** after **despite**.

- **Despite living** in China for years, Susan speaks very little Chinese. (*NOT* Despite of living)
  OR **In spite of living** in China for years, Susan speaks very little Chinese.
- Jerry is a fantastic basketball player **despite his small size**. (*NOT* despite of his small size)
  OR Jerry is a fantastic basketball player **in spite of his small size**.

P R A C T I C E

A. Rewrite 1-3 using **because of** and 4-6 using **thanks to** with the words in *italics*.

1. Ben had to attend a friend's wedding, so he couldn't go to the concert.
   → *(his friend's wedding)* Because of his friend's wedding, Ben couldn't go to the concert.
2. Maria had a headache, so she had to go home early.
   → *(her headache)* ______________________.
3. My grandparents have bad hearing, so they rarely hear the phone ring.
   → *(their bad hearing)* ______________________.
4. Betty took a computer class, so she knows computers better than I do.
   → *(her computer class)* ______________________.
5. Helen and Ryan had made a reservation, so they didn't have to wait.
   → *(their reservation)* ______________________.
6. Jim had a map, so he was able to find his hotel without any problem.
   → *(the map)* ______________________.

B. Write **instead / instead of.**

1. "Did you go to the beach?" "No. We went to the mountains instead."
2. __________ paper cups, use mugs. It's better for the environment.
3. "This credit card doesn't work." "Why don't you try this one __________?"
4. We should ask Mom for her pasta recipe __________ looking for one on the Internet.
5. Let's move closer to the intersection __________ standing here. It'll be easier to get a taxi there.
6. You don't need to call me. __________, just send a text message!

C. Complete the sentences with **in spite of** and the words in the box.

being nervous	her busy schedule	taking vitamins
the darkness	~~the icy roads~~	washing my shirt

1. "The car didn't slow down in spite of the icy roads." "That sounds dangerous!"
2. __________________ three times, I couldn't get the ink out.
3. Lucy has two jobs. She also volunteers at a hospital __________________.
4. It was getting late at night. __________________, the police kept searching for the child.
5. Don tried to look confident during his speech __________________.
6. __________________, Jamie often gets a cold.

D. The following information is about Mozart. Write **because of / instead (of) / despite.**

Mozart was a great musician from a very young age.
1. Because of his talents, he was often asked to perform in front of the king.
2. He became popular in Salzburg, especially __________ his young age.
But Mozart did not want to stay there. 3. He moved to Vienna __________.
4. In Vienna, he focused on creative music __________ traditional styles and became even more famous.
5. __________ his fame, he did not become wealthy during his lifetime.
However, he was one of the best musicians that has ever lived.

Prepositions and Phrasal Verbs

LESSON 86

Grammar Gateway Intermediate

Answers p.321 / Review Test 15 p.262

LESSON 87

Let's talk about it later. *Verb + preposition*

MP3

1 We can use *verbs* and *prepositions* together in the following expressions:

about

talk about	think about	complain about
worry about	forget about	learn about

- I don't have time to chat now. Let's **talk about** it later.
- "I hope I pass my test!" "I'm sure you will. Don't **worry about** it so much."

at

stare at	point at	shout at
smile at	laugh at	wave at

- "What are you **staring at**?" "Those flowers. They are so colorful."
- My baby **smiled at** me for the first time today. I feel so happy.

for

wait for	leave for	pay for
care for	apply for	apologize for

- Gary had to **wait for** his wife while she shopped for clothes.
- "Is Adam the oldest child?" "Yes. He often **cares for** his younger sisters."

to

object to	lead to	reply to
stick to	belong to	happen to

- Most citizens **object to** the tax increase.
- If we want to meet the deadline, we must **stick to** the schedule.

2 The meanings usually change when we use different *prepositions* after the *verbs* as in the following ways:

look	at	• **Look at** this menu! Everything looks delicious. (= "see")
	for	• Kevin is **looking for** a roommate. (= "search")
	after	• David is going to **look after** our dog while we're traveling. (= "care for")

ask	for	• Brian **asked for** a ride, so I drove him home. (= "request")
	about	• Gina **asked about** your brother. I think she wants to meet him. (= "ask questions about")

More about phrasal verbs: Appendix p.289

3 We do not usually use *prepositions* after the following *verbs*:

answer	call	enter
discuss	marry	resemble

- Someone is ringing the doorbell. Could you **answer** it, please? (*NOT* answer to it)
- Let's **discuss** our travel plans at dinner. (*NOT* discuss about our travel plans)
- Jim **resembles** his father. They look exactly alike.

PRACTICE

A. Look at the pictures and complete the sentences with the given words and the appropriate prepositions. Use the *present progressive*.

learn	pay	point	think	~~wait~~	wave

1. *(the elevator)* He *'s waiting for the elevator* ________.
2. *(geography)* They ________________.
3. *(a sign)* He ________________.
4. *(the newspaper)* She ________________.
5. *(chocolate cake)* She ________________.
6. *(the cameras)* They ________________.

B. Complete the sentences with the words in the box. Use the *present simple* or *past simple*.

(apologize, losing)	~~(apply, a job)~~	(belong, Monica)
(forget, appointments)	(lead, many health problems)	(shout, each other)

1. Two hundred people *applied for a job* ________ at our company last week.
2. A lot of research shows that smoking ________________.
3. Angela and Gabby ________________ loudly. Lisa told them to stop.
4. Ted ________________ my umbrella, but he didn't offer to buy me a new one.
5. "Whose shoes are those?" "They ________________."
6. Ron ________________ easily. You should remind him.

C. Complete the sentences with **look/ask** and the appropriate prepositions.

1. Mary will *look for* ________ a new apartment before she moves to Manchester.
2. I'm trying to take a picture of you! Please ________________ me.
3. I called the gym to ________________ their weekend hours.
4. "Did you ________________ another bottle of wine?" "Yes. The waiter is going to bring it."
5. Susan's job is to ________________ patients. She works as a nurse.
6. "I can't find my cell phone." "Let's ________________ it together."

D. Find and change any mistakes in each sentence. Put ✓ if the sentence is correct.

1. The air conditioner wasn't working, so we complained at it. *complained at → complained about*
2. Please answer to my question. I'm still waiting. ________
3. "What's so funny?" "I'm laughing at this magazine article." ________
4. Aaron married with his wife at a beautiful church. ________
5. "When do the speeches begin?" "Look after the schedule." ________
6. The crowd cheered when the boxer entered the stadium. ________
7. "Did you hear from Jill?" "No. She hasn't replied for my message." ________
8. Let's call to Taco Factory and order dinner. ________

Answers p.321 / Review Test 15 p.262

LESSON 88 Paul is working out. *Phrasal verbs*

1 Chris is working.

Paul is **working out**.

"work" and **"out"** are used together to say that Paul is exercising.
"work out" is a *phrasal verb* that means "exercise."

2 *Phrasal verbs* are *verb + preposition/adverb*. *Phrasal verbs* usually have different meanings from the original *verbs*.

work out (= "exercise")	get along (= "be friendly")	hang out (= "spend time with")
hold on (= "wait")	calm down (= "relax")	run away (= "leave without permission")
show up (= "appear")	break up (= "end a relationship")	look around (= "explore a place")

- "Do your children **get along**?" "Yes. They rarely argue."
- "Bob, hurry up! We're late." "**Hold on**! I'm coming."
- I **showed up** on time for our meeting, but my counselor was late.
- Please **calm down** and listen to me. I can explain everything.
- "That shop seems interesting." "Well, do you want to **look around**?"

3 We can use *prepositions* after *phrasal verbs*.

- "Do you **hang out** with Rob much?" "Not really. He's always busy."
- In my dream, I was in a jungle. I was **running away** from a tiger.
- Ashley **broke up** with her boyfriend. She regrets it.
- I **get along** with my roommates very well. They're nice people.
- "I want to go home." "Me too. Let's **get out** of here."
- We **ran out** of paper for the fax machine.
- Brian is going to **sign up** for tennis classes.

4 We can use an *object* before or after the *preposition/adverb* of the following *phrasal verbs*:

turn on/off	put off	pick up	throw away
put on	take off	clean up	take away
try on	turn down	make up	point out

	object				*object*
• We **put**	the deadline	**off**.	*OR*	We **put off**	the deadline.
• Please **take**	our dishes	**away**.		Please **take away**	our dishes.
• Susie **turned**	my proposal	**down**.		Susie **turned down**	my proposal.
• Mr. Lee **pointed**	some errors	**out**.		Mr. Lee **pointed out**	some errors.

But we do not use **it**/**them**/etc. *(pronouns)* after the *preposition/adverb*.

- If you like the shirt, you should **try it on**. (*NOT* try on it)
- "Why are the lights on?" "Sorry, I forgot to **turn them off**." (*NOT* turn off them)

More about phrasal verbs: Appendix p.289

P R A C T I C E

A. Complete the sentences with the phrasal verbs in the box.

calm down	hold on	~~look around~~	show up	work out

1. "I don't know where I put my wallet!" "Let's *look around* the house."
2. Brenda drank some hot tea to ________________ after a hard day at work.
3. Julia is always really popular. So many people ________________ to her parties.
4. Let's ________________ for a bit before we start. Not everyone is here.
5. My plan to go to Europe didn't ________________. Maybe I can go next year.

B. Look at the pictures and complete the sentences with the words from each box. Use the *present progressive*.

clean	~~pick~~	run	take	turn

\+

away	down	off	~~up~~	up

1. She *'s picking up* a puzzle piece.
2. He ________________ his socks.
3. They ________________ the garage.
4. He ________________.
5. She ________________ the invitation.

C. Complete the sentences with the phrasal verbs in the box and the appropriate prepositions.

break up	get along	get out	~~hang out~~	run out	sign up

1. Karen usually *hangs out with* her friends on Friday nights.
2. I've tried everything to stop the baby from crying. I have ________________ ideas!
3. My sister and I used to fight a lot when we were young. Now, we ________________ each other.
4. "Did Stella ________________ John?" "No. They just had an argument. They'll be OK soon."
5. I ________________ the crowded bar because I needed some fresh air.
6. Marshall ________________ a class at the art gallery. He is excited to learn about modern art.

D. Put the words in *italics* in the correct order.

1. *(going to / your coat / are / on / you / put)*
   "*Are you going to put your coat on* OR *Are you going to put on your coat*?" "No. I'm not cold."
2. *(turn / the TV / why / on / you / did)* ________________? I'm trying to sleep.
3. *(made / it / she / up)* "Do you believe Lauren's story?" "Yes. I don't think ________________."
4. *(these shoes / on / have to / try / you)* ________________. They're perfect for the dance!
5. *(want to / I / it / away / throw)* I hate that lamp. ________________, but my husband likes it.
6. *(can't just / you / take / away / them)*
   Jimmy, these are your little brother's toys. ________________!
7. *(the mistake / out / pointed / Susan)*
   ________________ in your charts.

Answers p.322 / Review Test 15 p.262

I'm curious about this book. *Adjective + preposition*

MP3

1 We can use *adjectives* and *prepositions* together in the following expressions:

about

curious about	concerned about	crazy about

- I'm **curious about** this book. The title sounds interesting.
- George watches a lot of soccer and baseball on TV. He's **crazy about** sports.

at

shocked at	excellent at	terrible at

- Carry was **shocked at** the price of the purse. It was really expensive.
- In high school, I was **terrible at** science.

for

sorry for	responsible for	late for
ready for	eager for	suitable for

- I feel **sorry for** shouting at Thomas. I think I should apologize.
- I'm **ready for** the interview tomorrow. I'm really **eager for** this job.
- Jane was **late for** class on the first day because she couldn't find the classroom.

of

scared of	fond of	full of
short of	aware of	capable of

- Nina used to be **scared of** birds. But now she is **fond of** them.
- We're **short of** toilet paper. We need to go to the store soon.
- Max dove into the sea to save the boy even though he was **aware of** the danger.

to

similar to	related to	close to
rude to	polite to	kind to

- "Andrea looks **similar to** Jill."
  "I think so too. Maybe they're **related to** each other."
- "Sometimes Frank is **rude to** people." "Really? He's always **polite to** me."
- England is really **close to** Germany. I'll show you on a map.

2 The meanings usually change when we use different *prepositions* after the *adjectives* as in the following ways:

good	at	"Are you **good at** yoga?" "Not really. I just like it." (= "skilled at")
	for	Eating vegetables is **good for** you. (= "beneficial to")
	to	Roy is so **good to** his friends. He always helps them. (= "nice to")
familiar	to	The *Mona Lisa* is **familiar to** everyone. (= "known to")
	with	Carl just moved here, so he isn't **familiar with** the area. (= "know well about")

More about adjective + preposition expressions: Appendix p.298

P R A C T I C E

A. Complete the sentences with the adjectives in the box and the appropriate prepositions.

~~aware~~	close	curious	eager	fond	related	suitable	terrible

1. "Andy is selling his house." "Really? I wasn't *aware of* ________ that. When did he decide to sell it?"
2. "Are you staying at a hotel?" "Yes. It's very ________ the city center."
3. Many bees are dying these days. The problem might be ________ global warming.
4. Could you tell me your name again? I'm ________ remembering names.
5. I need to change my shoes. These aren't ________ wearing in the rain.
6. Rita isn't ________ yogurt. She has never liked its flavor.
7. My sister is so ________ good grades. She's always studying.
8. "I don't want to watch the rest of this movie." "Aren't you ________ the ending?"

B. Put the appropriate prepositions and the words in *italics* in the correct order.

1. *(crazy / fashion)* Melissa is *crazy about fashion* ________. She is always buying new clothes.
2. *(shocked / the news)* "Phil got into law school." "I heard. I was ________!"
3. *(sales / responsible)* "What does John do at your company?" "He's ________."
4. *(similar / limes)* Lemons are ________. You can use them instead.
5. *(Sue's performance / concerned)* I'm ________ at work lately.
6. *(the noise / scared)* When there's a thunderstorm, my dog gets ________.
7. *(people / full)* The elevator is ________. Let's take the stairs.

C. Complete the sentences with good/familiar and the appropriate prepositions.

1. I'm quite *good at* ________ cooking. All of my friends think my food is delicious.
2. We should go outside. Taking a break will be ________ us.
3. "Do you know Harry Parsons?" "No. I'm not ________ that name."
4. Be ________ strangers. You might need someone's help one day.
5. "Have you been to that museum before?" "I think so. It seems ________ me."

D. The following is a recommendation letter for Amy. Complete the sentences with the adjectives in *italics* and the appropriate prepositions.

Dear Sir or Madam,

I'd like to recommend Amy Wilson for the Future Leaders Scholarship.
1. *(suitable)* I am confident that she is definitely *suitable for* ________ it.
2. *(excellent)* She is ________ her studies and has strong leadership skills.
3. *(capable)* Last summer, she showed that she is ________ organizing large social events.
4. *(kind)* She is also ________ her classmates. She has helped them study for exams.
5. *(late)* Furthermore, Amy has never been ________ class.
She has been a great student of mine, and I strongly believe that she should get this scholarship.

Yours sincerely,
Professor Carol Yang
Department of Law

Answers **p.322** / Review Test 15 **p.262**

Can you find the **difference between** these two pictures? *Noun + preposition*

MP3

1 We can use *nouns* and *prepositions* together in the following expressions:

between

difference between	relationship between	conversation between

- Can you find the **difference between** these two pictures?
- This article talks about the **relationship between** regular exercise and good health.
- "What were you talking to Eric about?" "Nothing much. It was just a **conversation between** friends."

for

need for	demand for	search for
reason for	responsibility for	respect for
room for	desire for	request for

- Don't throw away the receipt. There might be a **need for** it later.
- One **reason for** water pollution is the use of chemicals.
- "Is there **room for** my luggage in your car?" "I think so."
- Kevin has a lot of **respect for** Thomas Edison, because he never gave up until he succeeded.

in

interest in	success in	belief in
increase in	decrease in	change in

- My son has a strong **interest in** music. He wants to be a professional musician.
- "We had an **increase in** sales last month." "That's good news!"
- Professor Reynolds has achieved great **success in** his research.
- There has been a **change in** the schedule. The meeting will be at 1:30, not 1 o'clock.

of

cause of	example of	cost of	lack of
idea of	advantage of	knowledge of	way of

- Stress is one **cause of** illnesses.
- "What's your **idea of** the perfect date?" "A romantic dinner and a movie."
- The big swimming pool is the main **advantage of** this gym.
- Every culture has a different **way of** greeting people.

to

answer to	key to	solution to
reply to	reaction to	damage to

- Henry probably knows the **answer to** the math problem. You should ask him for help.
- "Have you sent a **reply to** Sue's e-mail?" "Yes, I sent it yesterday."
- The **key to** success is hard work.
- "What was Simon's **reaction to** the news?" "He wasn't even surprised."

More about noun + preposition expressions: Appendix p.300

PRACTICE

A. Write the appropriate prepositions.

1. The bookshelf is full. I have no room *for* ______ more books.
2. Steve has a lot of success ______ his toy car business. Nobody expected it.
3. The cause ______ your skin condition is simple. It's a reaction ______ peanuts.
4. The storm did a lot of damage ______ the crops. We have to find a solution ______ this.
5. The relationship ______ language and culture has been studied for many years.
6. "Your idea ______ going fishing next weekend sounds like fun." "Great. Let's do it."
7. Our store needs more customers. Last month, we had a decrease ______ sale by 20 percent.

B. Complete the sentences with the words from each box.

change	cost	difference	example
key	~~respect~~	responsibility	

\+

between	~~for~~	for	in
of	of	to	

1. Many people have *respect for* ______ that movie director. He has made some meaningful films.
2. "How much is the ______ delivery?" "It's already included in your payment."
3. My grandmother says that the ______ a happy life is to make lots of friends.
4. "Mr. Watson got fired. I feel bad." "Yes, but everyone has to take ______ their mistakes."
5. Notre Dame is a good ______ a European church.
6. The biggest ______ the twins is their hair. One has short hair and the other has long hair.
7. It was sunny in the morning, but there was a ______ the weather. It's raining now.

C. Put the appropriate prepositions and the words in *italics* in the correct order.

1. *(seeing that movie / any interest)* "Do you have *any interest in seeing that movie* ______?" "Not really."
2. *(thanking people / a good way)* ______ is to write them letters.
3. *(belief / Santa Claus)* ______ is common among children.
4. *(a desire / wealth)* Many people have ______.
5. *(your suggestion / Mary's reply)* "What was ______?" "She said yes."
6. *(the conversation / Chuck and Arnold)* I heard ______. They seemed upset.
7. *(a vegetarian meal / a request)* Tim made ______ on his flight.

D. The following is a page from Stanley City's local newspaper. Complete the sentences with the words in *italics* and the appropriate prepositions.

THE STANLEY DAILY

July 02, 2019

1. *(an advantage, a great need)* *An advantage of* ______ an engineering degree is that there's always ______ it. Research shows that employers want more engineers.

2. *(an answer)* The concerned people of Stanley City requested safer parks for children. The mayor still hasn't given ______ this request.

3. *(the search, knowledge)* ______ the robber has continued since last night, but the police say they have no ______ where he is now.

4. *(the demand, an increase)* ______ houses has gone up recently because there's been ______ the city population.

5. *(the lack, the reason)* ______ public transportation is surely ______ the bad traffic on 5th Avenue.

Answers p.322 / Review Test 15 p.262

While he was playing outside, he broke the window. while, until, by the time

1 while

We use **while** to say that an action happens during another action. We use *subject + verb* after **while**.

- **While he was playing outside**, he broke the window.
- "Are you going to visit the Great Wall **while you are in China**?" "Yes."

In this case, we can also use **when** instead of **while**.

- **When I wasn't looking**, the baby spilled his milk. (= While I wasn't looking)

We also use **while** to say that two actions are in progress at the same time.

- I listen to the radio **while I'm cooking**.
- **While Harry was waiting in the lobby**, he read a magazine.

We can also use **during** to say that two actions are in progress at the same time. But we always use *nouns* after **during**.

- We slept on the plane **during our flight** to Phoenix.
  We slept on the plane **while we were flying** to Phoenix.

2 until

We use **until** to say that an action continues to a certain point in time. We use *subject + verb* after **until**.

- **Until everyone left**, he stayed in the room.
- Andrea is taking care of our plants **until we come back from our trip**.

We can also use *nouns* after **until**.

- The store will be closed **until next week**. They are renovating the store.
  The store will be closed **until the renovations are completed**.

3 by the time

We use **by the time** to say that an action has already happened before another action. We use *subject + verb* after **by the time**.

- **By the time he finished his work**, it was dark outside.
- I'm on my way. Will you still be at the mall **by the time I get there**?

We can use **by** to say that an action has already happened before a certain point in time. But we always use *nouns* after **by**.

- **By winter**, all of the leaves will have fallen off the trees.
  By the time winter comes, all of the leaves will have fallen off the trees.

4

Note that we use the *present simple* after **while**, **when**, **until**, or **by the time** to talk about future events. We do not use **will** or **am/is/are going to**.

- "May I speak to Mr. Jones?" "Sure. Please wait **while I connect** you." (*NOT* while I'll connect)
- Sally isn't allowed to go out **until she apologizes** to her brother. (*NOT* until she's going to apologize)
- **By the time we're** home, the babysitter will have fed the kids.

More about **when** for future events: Lesson 21

PRACTICE

A. Look at the pictures and write sentences with **while** and the words from each box. The order is A → B.

A		B	
he brushed his teeth	he fell	he was snowboarding	he watched the news
she played the guitar	~~the phone rang~~	she sang	they saw a deer
they were walking in the forest		~~they were having coffee~~	

1. *The phone rang while they were having coffee*.
2. ______.
3. ______.
4. ______.
5. ______.

B. Rewrite the two sentences as one with **until / by the time**. Do not change the order of the two sentences.

1. Travelers searched for an oasis. They found one. → *Travelers searched for an oasis until they found one*.
2. Frank called Julie back. She was already asleep. → ______.
3. Max applied for jobs. He finally got one. → ______.
4. Hans kept studying Russian. He became fluent. → ______.
5. We were already back in the hotel. It began to rain. → ______.
6. Our seminar ended. Everyone was pleased with it. → ______.

C. The following is Mike's voice mail. Complete the sentences with the words in *italics*. Use the *present simple* or add **will**.

1. TIM: There's a party on Friday. When I *find* out the time, I ______ you know. *(find, let)*
2. KEVIN: We ______ anything until you ______ at the restaurant. *(not order, arrive)*
3. TINA: By the time you ______ this message, I ______ on my way to London. *(hear, be)*
4. JOHN: ______ you ______ my dog while I ______ away? *(feed, be)*
5. MICHELLE: I had fun tonight. Take care of yourself until we ______ again. *(meet)*
6. BRAD: When your brother ______ from school, ______ you ______ him to call me? *(return, tell)*

D. Find and change any mistakes in each sentence. Put ✓ if the sentence is correct.

1. When I will go to France, I will visit the Louvre Museum. *When I will go → when I go*
2. In just one day, Steve read the long book until the end. ______
3. By Selena got to the platform, the train had left. ______
4. You can't vote until you are going to be 18. ______
5. Ben checked the weather during he was getting ready. ______
6. By the time Helen finished all of her laundry, she was very tired. ______

Conjunctions and Clauses
LESSON 91
Grammar Gateway Intermediate

Answers p.322 / Review Test 16 p.264

As I was surfing the Internet, I read an interesting article. as

MP3

1 We use **as** to say that an action happens during another action. We can also use **while** instead of **as**.

- **As I was surfing the Internet**, I read an interesting article. (= While I was surfing the Internet)
- Bella followed the recipe really carefully **as she was cooking**. Her chicken was perfect. (= while she was cooking)
- Jimmy fell off the bed **as he was sleeping**. He woke up right away.

We also use **as** to say that two actions happen at the same time.

- **As the thief entered the house**, the dog started barking.
- Everyone clapped **as the pianist bowed to the audience**.
- We got excited **as we discussed starting a business together**. We're going to be great partners.

We also use **as** to say that two situations develop or change together over a long period of time.

- **As Stan grew older**, he looked more and more like his father.
- "You seem happy these days." "I am! I get more excited **as the holidays get closer**."
- **As the seasons changed**, our friendship became stronger.

Note that we use the *present simple* after **as** to talk about future events. We do not use **will** or **am/is/are going to.**

- You will see the mall **as you drive** through the next intersection. (*NOT* as you'll drive)
- **As you leave** the plane, please remember to take all of your belongings. (*NOT* As you're going to leave)

2 We can also use **as** to say that something is already known or has already been discussed.

- **As you know**, wasting water has become a serious issue.
- "I don't know what to order." "**As I said**, all the food here is good."
- **As I mentioned during our last class,** we will have a test next Friday.
- "Here's your steak, **as you requested**." "Thank you."
- "Are you sure you can give me a ride?" "**As I said** before, it's no trouble."
- **As we agreed,** the time of the meeting will be changed to 1:30.
- **As you know**, life is full of challenges. We should learn to enjoy them.

3 We can also use **as** to talk about reasons. In this case, we use **as** in formal situations rather than in everyday conversation.

- **As sales have decreased sharply**, the company plans to advertise more.
- You'll have to wait **as we are still preparing to open our store**.
- Please keep the restroom clean, **as it is used by other customers too**.

We can also use **because** or **since** to talk about reasons.

- "Did you find the office building?" "No. I couldn't find it **because the roads were too confusing**."
- **Since you love jazz music**, I'll take you to a jazz club tonight.

P R A C T I C E

A. Look at the pictures and complete the sentences with **as** and the words in the box.

he crossed the finish line	~~he was using a hammer~~	she was looking through her bag
she was pouring it	they introduced themselves	

1. He hurt himself *as he was using a hammer*.
2. She dropped some money on the ground ______.
3. He raised his arms ______.
4. She spilled the coffee ______.
5. They shook hands ______.

B. Complete the sentences with **as** and the words in the box.

gas becomes more expensive	Melissa drank more water	the population grows
~~the sun came out~~	we went up the mountain	

1. *As the sun came out*, it started to get hot. By the afternoon, the temperature had reached 36°C.
2. People drive less ______. They use public transportation more.
3. ______, she noticed that her skin felt smoother.
4. ______, the city will build more schools and parks.
5. We had great view ______. From the top, we could see everything.

C. Put **as** and the words in *italics* in the correct order.

1. *(told you / be late / I / am going to / I)* *As I told you, I'm going to be late* for dinner tonight.
2. *(can't park / says / your car / the sign / you)* ______ here.
3. *(promised / I / bought / my wife / I)* ______ a diamond ring.
4. *(is giving / mentioned / Sandra / I / on the phone)*
   ______ a speech at the science academy.
5. *(in the e-mail / explained / I / has / Mr. Jennings)*
   ______ the day off tomorrow.

D. Read the sentences and complete the new ones with **as** and the words in *italics*.

1. Nobody answered the door. So I left a note. → *(nobody)* *As nobody answered the door*, I left a note.
2. A lot of fruit is grown in this area. That's because it has a warm climate.
   → *(this area)* ______, a lot of fruit is grown here.
3. Because the elevator was broken, I had to take the stairs.
   → *(the elevator)* ______, I had to take the stairs.
4. Claire asked for help. That's because she didn't understand the instructions.
   → *(Claire)* ______, she asked for help.
5. Our products are high quality. That's the reason people trust our brand.
   → *(our products)* ______, people trust our brand.

Answers **p.323** / Review Test 16 **p.264**

LESSON 93

She studies law **so that** she can become a lawyer. so that

MP3

1 She studies law **so that she can become a lawyer**.

She wants to be a lawyer in the future. It is her purpose for studying law.
"so that" describes the purpose for studying law.

2 We use **so that** to talk about the purpose for doing something. We often use **can/could/will/would**/etc. after **so that**.

- We rented a car **so that we could travel more comfortably during our trip**.
- I woke John up **so that he wouldn't miss his flight**.
- "Can you take my suit to the cleaners **so that it will be ready tonight**?" "No problem."

We can use the *present simple* after **so that** to talk about future events.

- Keep your passport in a safe place **so that you don't lose it**.
  (= so that you won't lose it)
- Let's all introduce ourselves **so that everyone knows each other's names**.
  (= so that everyone will know each other's names)

In everyday conversation, we often leave out **that**.

- "Should we meet **so (that) we can go to the exhibit together**?" "OK."
- It's getting late. Let's call Mom and Dad **so (that) they don't worry about us**.

3 We can also use **to . . .** or **for + noun/-ing** to talk about a purpose.

- "We need to turn here **to go** to the beach!" "Are you sure? I think it's the next street." (= so that we can go)
- Mr. Barry will be in Vancouver tomorrow **for a seminar**. (= so that he can attend a seminar)
- I bought a pan **for frying**. It's big but not heavy.

Note that we use **so that**, **to**, and **for** in different structures.

so that + subject + verb	• Can we use that closet **so that we can store** our luggage?
to . . .	• Can we use that closet **to store** our luggage?
for + noun/-ing	• Can we use that closet **for (storing) our luggage**?

4 Note that we use **so that** and **so +** *adj./adv.* **+ that** in different ways. **so +** *adj./adv.* **+ that** describes a reason and its result.

so that

- Andy stayed up all night **so that** he could read the book.
  (The purpose for staying up all night was to read the book.)
- I wrapped the baby in a blanket **so that** she wouldn't feel cold.
  (The purpose for wrapping the baby was to make her not feel cold.)
- Anthony has been practicing the song **so that** he will be able to sing it at Jim's wedding.

so + *adjective/adverb* **+ that**

- The book was **so long that** Andy had to stay up all night to read it.
  (Because the book was long, Andy had to stay up all night.)
- The speaker spoke **so quietly that** few people could hear her.
  (Because the speaker spoke quietly, few people could hear her.)
- This package is **so heavy that** I can't carry it.

More about **so + adjective/adverb + that**: Lesson 73

PRACTICE

A. Read what each person says and complete the sentences with **so that** and the verbs in *italics*. Write negative sentences if necessary.

1 I plan to visit my family more often. I want to spend more time with them.	4 I'm going to work hard. I hope to get a promotion.
2 I'm going to exercise every day. I don't want to gain any more weight.	5 I plan to get a bigger apartment. I want to have more space for my children.
3 I plan to study Spanish. I want to speak it fluently.	6 I'm going to get up early. I don't want to be late for school again.

1. *(can)* He plans to visit his family more often *so that he can spend more time with them*.
2. *(will)* She is going to exercise every day ______________________.
3. *(can)* She plans to study Spanish ______________________.
4. *(will)* He is going to work hard ______________________.
5. *(can)* She plans to get a bigger apartment ______________________.
6. *(will)* He is going to get up early ______________________.

B. Complete the sentences with **so that / to . . . / for** and the words in the box.

drinks	I won't forget	make some extra money	running
send Mom's birthday card	~~we could go camping~~	your hands don't get cold	

1. "Did you buy a tent *so that we could go camping*?" "Yes, I'm so excited for our trip."
2. Marcia got a part-time job ______________________. Her rent has increased.
3. These shoes are ______________________. I wear them to jog every morning.
4. Wear your gloves today ______________________.
5. "Do you want to go out ______________________ tonight at the bar?"
   "Sorry, but I have to wake up early tomorrow."
6. I need to go to the post office ______________________.
7. I'm going to take notes ______________________ the important parts of the lecture.

C. Put the words in *italics* in the correct order.

1. *(could / so / help / that / I)* I became a doctor *so that I could help* sick people.
2. *(loud / I / couldn't / that / so / concentrate)*
   The music was ______________________ on my homework.
3. *(get / can / so / he / that)*
   Alex eats an orange every morning ______________________ some vitamin C.
4. *(bright / that / so / need / I)*
   It's ______________________ sunglasses.
5. *(that / skate / so / couldn't / we / thin)*
   The ice on the lake was ______________________.
6. *(so / be / that / we / won't)*
   We should leave soon ______________________ stuck in traffic.

Answers p.323 / Review Test 16 p.264

LESSON 94 Although the food was spicy, she liked it. although, though, etc.

MP3

1

Although the food was spicy, she liked it.

It's spicy, but I like it.
MENU

The food was spicy, but she liked it. **"Although"** connects two contrasting ideas: **"the food was spicy,"** and **"she liked it."**

2

We use **although** to connect two contrasting ideas.

- **Although the bus was crowded**, we were able to get on it.
- Janice enjoys living overseas, **although she sometimes misses her family**.
- **Although I went to bed early last night**, I woke up late this morning.
- The documentary was good, **although it was a bit too long**.

3

We can also use **though** instead of **although**.

- **Though the resort is expensive**, it isn't very nice. (= Although the resort is expensive)
- I love the style of that dress **though I don't like the color**. (= although I don't like the color)
- **Though I didn't win a prize**, I think the contest was a good experience.

We can use **though** at the end of a sentence.

- "How was the exam?" "It was really hard. I think I passed, **though**."
- "Did you go to the Metropolitan Museum of Art?" "Yes. It wasn't open, **though**.

4

We can also use **even though** instead of **although/though** for emphasis.

- **Even though I want to stay longer**, I can't. I have an appointment.
- I had fun at the party **even though I didn't know anyone there**.
- **Even though Johnny is a chef**, he doesn't cook at home.

5

We can also use **in spite of** or **despite** to connect two contrasting ideas. Note that we use *nouns* or -**ing** after **in spite of / despite**.

- Zoe arrived at work on time **in spite of the traffic jam**. (= although there was traffic jam)
- **Despite being** a terrible singer, Jillian sang for Tim on his birthday. (= Although she's a terrible singer)
- **In spite of playing** for hours, the children weren't tired.
- The mayor did not try to explain **despite all of the rumors**.

Note that we use **although** and **in spite of / despite** in different structures.

although + subject + verb	• **Although Cassie had** a cold, she went to school.
in spite of / despite + noun/-ing	• **In spite of / Despite (having) a cold**, Cassie went to school.

We can also use **the fact (that)** + *subject* + *verb* after **in spite of** or **despite**.

- **In spite of the fact (that) the weather was** bad, we went camping.
- Karen's necklace looks great **despite the fact (that) it didn't cost** much.

P R A C T I C E

A. Connect the two sentences and rewrite them as one with **although**.

1. Carla lives in the United States.	It works perfectly.
2. My computer is old.	He plays golf really well.
3. I washed my sneakers twice.	They're still very active.
4. I didn't put much salt on the food.	The smell didn't disappear.
5. Greg is just a beginner.	Sam said it was too salty.
6. My grandparents are over 70 years old.	She has never been to Washington, DC.

1. *Although Carla lives in the United States, she has never been to Washington, DC*.
2. ______.
3. ______.
4. ______.
5. ______.
6. ______.

B. Complete the sentences with the given words.

failing the test	I've been on a diet for a month
she isn't famous	Terry practiced his speech many times
the flight's delayed departure	~~Tom is interested in winter sports~~

1. *(though)* *Though Tom is interested in winter sports*, he's never learned to ski.
2. *(in spite of)* Some passengers still missed the plane ______.
3. *(although)* ______, he forgot what he was going to say.
4. *(despite)* I feel good ______. I tried my best.
5. *(even though)* The singer's song is quite popular ______.
6. *(in spite of the fact that)* ______, I haven't lost any weight.

C. The following is an e-mail from Nancy to a restaurant manager. Write **although / though / in spite of.**

Subject	Unhappy with my recent visit
To	customerservice@therosegarden.com
From	nancy@gomail.com

Dear Manager,

I recently went to your restaurant with a friend for dinner.

1. *In spite of* having a reservation for 6:30, we had to wait 30 minutes to be seated.
2. Also, we were served the chicken pasta, even ______ we had ordered the seafood pasta.
3. ______ the fact that the waiter had made a mistake, he did not apologize.
4. So ______ the food was very good, we were very unhappy with the service.

Since the service was so bad, we were expecting a discount.

5. We had to pay our entire bill, ______.
6. We really enjoy your food, but ______ that, we might not return.

You should train your staff better, or you could lose more customers.

Nancy Lewis

Answers p.323 / Review Test 16 p.264

LESSON 95

Cleaning his room, he found some money. -ing

1 **Cleaning his room,** he found some money.

He was cleaning his room. During this time, he found some money under the bed. **"Cleaning his room"** expresses when he found some money.

2 We use **-ing** to say that an action happens during another action.

- **Walking to the supermarket**, Rebecca realized she'd forgotten her wallet.
  (= While she was walking to the supermarket)
- **Running to catch the taxi**, I heard someone yell my name.
  (= While I was running to catch the taxi)
- **Reaching the top of the mountain**, we could see the whole city.

We also use **-ing** to say that two actions happen or are in progress at the same time.

- I hurt my back **picking up a heavy box**.
  (= when I picked up a heavy box)
- John always listens to music **packing his bag in the morning**.
  (= when he packs his bag in the morning)
- Melanie got a flat tire **driving down the road**.

In this case, we can use **when**, **while**, etc. before **-ing**.

- **While living** in Malaysia, Pam traveled around Asia a lot.
- Make sure to wear a mask **when entering** the factory.

3 We also use **-ing** to talk about the reason why something happens.

- **Feeling hungry**, Daniel went to the café to buy a bagel. (= Because he felt hungry)
- Becky usually comes home late **working as a bartender**. (= because she works as a bartender)
- **Being retired**, my grandparents have a lot of free time.
- We saved a lot of money **traveling by train**.
- **Being injured**, Ben couldn't play soccer for six months.

4 **not + -ing** *(negative)*

- **Not having** her glasses on, Jane wasn't able to read the road sign.
  (= Because she didn't have her glasses on)
- My house was a mess when my friends arrived. I hadn't cleaned up **not expecting guests**.
  (= because I didn't expect guests)
- The directions were very confusing. **Not understanding** them, I asked the teacher to explain.
- Phil went outside with no umbrella **not thinking** it was going to rain.
- **Not knowing** where to stay, we searched the Internet for a hotel recommendation.

P R A C T I C E

A. **Look at the pictures and complete the sentences with the words in the box.**

look at himself in the mirror	open the window	put pepper in her soup
receive the award	~~shop at the mall~~	

1

2

3

4

5

1. *Shopping at the mall* ________, she saw her friend Terry.
2. She sneezed ________________.
3. ________________, he noticed it was raining.
4. ________________, she said "thank you."
5. He put on his necktie, ________________.

B. **Rewrite the sentences with -ing.**

1. While she waited for Peter, Lisa checked her text messages.
   → *Waiting for Peter, Lisa checked her text messages* ________.
2. Because Shelly needed to borrow a blouse for an interview, she asked her sister.
   → ________________.
3. Because we noticed the smoke from the building, we called 911.
   → ________________.
4. When Max ate his burger, he dropped some ketchup on his pants.
   → ________________.
5. As I'm married to a pilot, I don't see my husband every day.
   → ________________.
6. When I rode my bicycle around the neighborhood, I saw many of my friends.
   → ________________.

C. **Complete the sentences with the words in the box. Add not if necessary.**

be old enough	be stuck	feel refreshed after our vacation	own my house
~~remember his doctor's appointment~~		ride on the boat	want to argue anymore

1. Bob said goodbye and left suddenly, *remembering his doctor's appointment* ________.
2. I have to pay rent every month, ________________.
3. ________________, we were ready to go back to work.
4. Chad hung up the phone ________________.
5. ________________, Laura could smell the sea.
6. I was late for work, ________________ in traffic.
7. ________________, Mandy wasn't allowed to watch that movie.

Answers **p.323** / Review Test 16 **p.264**

If Chris is busy, she'll be at home. *if + present simple*

1 **If Chris is** busy, **she'll be** at home.

If Chris isn't busy, **she'll have** dinner with him.

Chris might be busy, and she will stay at home in this case. Chris might not be busy, and she will go out to dinner with him in this case. **"If Chris is/isn't"** describes a thing that is possible in the future.

2 We use **if** + *present simple* to talk about things that are possible in the future. In this case, we use the following structure:

If . . . + *present simple*, . . . will/can/etc. + base form

- **If you stay** up longer, **you'll be** tired tomorrow.
- **If Maggie doesn't have** time to finish the assignment, **I can help** her.
- **Jack and Paula might not take** a trip to Italy **if they don't save** enough money.
- "**Can we make** a snowman **if it snows** a lot?" "Yes, of course!"

Note that we use the *present simple* after **if** to talk about future situations. We do not use **will** or **am/is/are going to.**

- **If you go** near that dog, it might bite you. (*NOT* If you'll go)
- Roger's team won't play in the final match **if it doesn't win** the next game. (*NOT* if it isn't going to win)

More about **if** for future events: Lesson 21

3 We can use **if** + *present simple* with *imperative sentences*.

- **If you want** to speak to customer service, please **press** 2.
- **Take off** your coat **if you are** hot.
- **If you don't understand** the instructions, **don't hesitate** to ask me.

4 We can also use **if** + *present simple* to say that a specific action always follows after something happens. In this case, we use the following structure:

If . . . + *present simple*, . . . + *present simple*

- **If water reaches** 100°C, **it boils**.
- **If lightning strikes, thunder follows**. That's because light travels faster than sound.
- Dan has allergies. **He sneezes if he is** near flowers.
- **Cindy does not have** breakfast **if she wakes up** late.

5 We can also use **unless** instead of **if . . . not.**

- **Unless you come** home soon, I will fall asleep. (= If you don't come home soon)
- We might get lost **unless we ask** for directions. (= if we don't ask for directions)
- Staff can't use the conference room **unless they reserve** it.

Note that **unless** means "if not." We do not use **not** after it.

- **Unless that shirt is** on sale, I won't buy it. (*NOT* Unless that shirt isn't on sale)
- I won't date you **unless you shave** that beard. (*NOT* unless you don't shave that beard)

PRACTICE

A. Complete the sentences with **if** and the given words.

~~be not too cloudy~~	be nothing interesting on TV	get a scholarship
hurry to the theater	not reply	not pay the electricity bill

1. *(the sky)* The full moon will be visible tonight *if the sky isn't too cloudy*.
2. *(he)* I really need Don to answer my e-mail. I'll call him ______________ soon.
3. *(Emma)* ______________, she can quit her part-time job.
4. *(there)* I might just go to sleep ______________.
5. *(I)* The lights might go out ______________ by next week.
6. *(we)* ______________, we can see the movie from the beginning.

B. Tina wants to do a lot of things in the future. Write sentences about her plans with **if**.

buy a sports car ← get my driver's license ←1

open a children's hospital ← become a doctor ←2

3→ move to France 4→ learn to paint → have an exhibit

5→ graduate college → work at the UN

TINA

1. *If I get my driver's license, I'll buy a sports car*.
2. ______________.
3. ______________.
4. ______________.
5. ______________.

C. Complete the sentences with the words in *italics*. Add **will** if necessary.

1. *(not be, not take)* If the traffic *isn't* heavy, it ______________ long to get to the mall.
2. *(send, travel)* I love postcards. ______________ me one if you ______________ somewhere this summer.
3. *(open, eat)* You're such a good cook! If you ______________ a restaurant, I ______________ there every day.
4. *(lock, leave)* Please ______________ the door if you ______________ before I come back.
5. *(mix, not get)* If you ______________ red and blue, you ______________ green. The result would be purple.
6. *(not order, not be)* If we ______________ these swimsuits today, they ______________ here until next week.
7. *(take, hurt)* ______________ a break from the computer if your eyes ______________.
8. *(pour, sink)* If you ______________ water into oil, the water ______________.

D. Rewrite the sentences with **unless**.

1. We can't go into the museum if we don't pay a fee.
→ *We can't go into the museum unless we pay a fee*.
2. If Sarah doesn't have an important appointment, she doesn't wear makeup.
→ ______________.
3. You can't borrow new DVDs if you don't return the old ones first.
→ ______________.
4. If Rick doesn't call his mom back, she will keep worrying.
→ ______________.
5. If you're not interested, I'm not going to ask you again.
→ ______________.

Answers **p.323** / Review Test 17 **p.266**

LESSON 97

If she felt well, she'd visit her friend.

if + *past simple*

MP3

1

If she felt well, **she'd visit** her friend.

She wants to visit her friend, but she doesn't feel well. So she is not visiting her friend now. **"If she felt"** describes a thing that is not real now.

2 We use **if** + *past simple* to talk about things that are not real or not possible now. In this case, we use the following structure:

If . . . + *past simple*, . . . would/could/etc. + base form

- Laura is such a nice person. **If you knew** Laura, **you would like** her.
  (= You don't know Laura now, so you don't like her.)
- **If Bob worked** in a team, **he wouldn't be** so stressed. He has to do everything by himself.
  (= Bob doesn't work in a team now, so he's so stressed.)
- **Charlotte would enjoy** African music **if she listened** to it.
- I never have time for the gym. **I would exercise** every day **if I wasn't** so busy.

Note that we use the *past simple* after **if** to talk about present situations and not past situations.

- **If I understood** Chinese, I could translate this document for you.
- Fiona is a vegetarian. We would take her to a steakhouse **if she ate** meat.

We usually use **were** after **if** + **I**/**he**/**she**/**it**/etc. But we can also use **was** in everyday conversation.

- **If I were/was** an actress, I'd be rich and famous.
- We could go to the park **if the weather weren't/wasn't** rainy.

3 We also use **if** + *past simple* to talk about things that are unlikely to happen in the future.

- "**If you had** only one more day to live, how **would you spend** it?" "I'd go skydiving."
  (It's unlikely that you'll have only one more day to live.)
- **If I won** the lottery, **I wouldn't work** anymore.
  (It's unlikely that I'll win the lottery.)
- What would you do **if there were/was** a fire in the building?
- I would climb up a tree **if I met** a wolf in the forest.

4 Note that we use **if** + *past simple* and **if** + *present simple* in different ways.

We use **if** + *past simple* to talk about things that are not real or not possible now or in the future.

- **If my boyfriend drove**, we would go on road trips.
  (My boyfriend doesn't drive now.)
- I would end poverty in our country **if I became** president. (It's unlikely that I'll become president.)

We use **if** + *present simple* to talk about things that are possible in the future.

- **If my boyfriend drives**, we can go on road trips.
  (It's possible that my boyfriend will drive in the future.)
- I'll hire more staff **if I become** manager.
  (It's possible that I'll become manager in the future.)

PRACTICE

A. **Complete the sentences with if.**

1. Howard doesn't have hair. *If he had hair*____________, he'd look younger.
2. You live near me. I couldn't visit you often ________________.
3. I'm so shy. I'd ask Sally on a date ________________.
4. I don't draw well. ________________, I could draw your portrait.
5. My brother owns a garden. ________________, he wouldn't grow all these vegetables.
6. Sharon doesn't have glasses. She could read the menu ________________.

B. **Read the sentences and complete the new ones.**

1. The company doesn't sell a lot of products because it doesn't advertise.
   → If *the company advertised*________, *it would sell a lot of products*________.
2. Daniel doesn't read many books because he plays so many video games.
   → ________________ if ________________.
3. Eric will not attend the wedding because he's on a business trip.
   → If ________________, ________________.
4. We have to call the repairman because our heater doesn't turn on.
   → If ________________, ________________.
5. Cindy won't go dancing tonight because she doesn't have a partner.
   → ________________ if ________________.

C. **Complete the sentences with the words in *italics*. Add will/would if necessary.**

1. *(pay, do)* Jen doesn't focus in class. If she *paid*______ attention, she ________ better on her exam.
2. *(take, not be)* If you ________ a taxi to the airport right now, you ________ late for your flight.
3. *(arrive, mail)* ________ this package ________ tomorrow if I ________ it today?
4. *(not ask, not be)* I really need your help on my homework. I ________ if it ________ difficult.
5. *(have, go)* It's too bad you're not going camping. We ________ more fun if you ________ with us.
6. *(get, give)* "Could you call me later?"
   "I'll try. If I ________ home before midnight, I ________ you a call."

D. **Complete the conversation with the verbs in *italics*. Add will/would if necessary.**

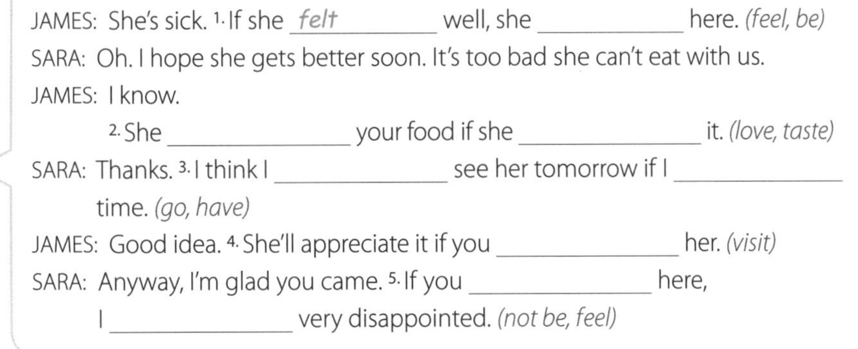

MP3

SARA: Thanks for coming, James. Where's Linda? Isn't she coming?
JAMES: She's sick. 1. If she *felt*______ well, she ________ here. *(feel, be)*
SARA: Oh. I hope she gets better soon. It's too bad she can't eat with us.
JAMES: I know.
2. She ________ your food if she ________ it. *(love, taste)*
SARA: Thanks. 3. I think I ________ see her tomorrow if I ________ time. *(go, have)*
JAMES: Good idea. 4. She'll appreciate it if you ________ her. *(visit)*
SARA: Anyway, I'm glad you came. 5. If you ________ here, I ________ very disappointed. *(not be, feel)*

SARA

JAMES

Answers p.324 / Review Test 17 p.266

LESSON 98 If she had had a camera, she would've taken a photo. if + *past perfect*

1 **If she had had** a camera, **she would've taken** a photo.

She wanted to take a photo, but she didn't have a camera. So she couldn't take a photo yesterday. **"If she had had"** describes a thing that was not real.

Yesterday

2 We use **if** + *past perfect* to talk about things that were not real in the past. In this case, we use the following structure:

If . . . + had + past participle, . . . would/could/etc. + have + past participle

- **If Anna had worn** a coat, **she would have been** warm. (= Anna didn't wear a coat, so she wasn't warm.)
- **If I hadn't attended** that seminar, **I couldn't have met** professor Jones. (= I attended the seminar, so I met professor Jones.)
- **You would have enjoyed** the show **if you had gone** with me.
- **Luke might have paid** less for the stereo **if he had ordered** it online.

Note that we use the *past perfect* after **if** to talk about past situations. We do not use the *past simple*.

- **If Sandra had told** me she had plans, I would have understood. (*NOT* If Sandra told)
- I would have missed the meeting **if Jamie hadn't reminded** me about it. (*NOT* if Jamie didn't remind)

3 Note that we use **if** + *past perfect* and **if** + *past simple* in different ways.

We use **if** + *past perfect* to talk about past situations.

- I had roommates when I was in college. **If I had lived** alone, I would have been very lonely. (I didn't live alone when I was in college.)
- The car appeared suddenly! **If Peter hadn't stopped** so quickly, he could have hit it. (Peter stopped the car quickly.)

We use **if** + *past simple* to talk about present or future situations.

- **If I lived** alone, I'd be very lonely. I'm glad I have roommates. (I don't live alone now.)
- **If we bought our own airplane**, we could travel around the world. (It's unlikely that we'll buy an airplane.)

4 We also use **if** + *past perfect* to say how the present situation would be different if something had or had not happened in the past. In this case, we use the following structure:

If . . . + had + past participle, . . . would/could/etc. + base form

- **If Valerie had saved** John's phone number, **she could call** him. (= Valerie didn't save his number, so she can't call him now.)
- I'm angry that Tim took my bike. **If he had asked** me first, **I wouldn't feel** upset.
- **We would be** at the gallery by now **if we had left** before rush hour.

There is the following difference between using **base form** and **have + past perfect** after **would/could**/etc.:

- **If I had cleaned** my room this morning, **it wouldn't look** so messy now. (= I didn't clean my room this morning, so it's messy now.)

  If I had cleaned my room this morning, **it would have looked** clean when I came home from work. (= I didn't clean my room this morning, so it was messy when I came home.)

PRACTICE

A. Complete the sentences with if.

1. Sally didn't review the article. *If Sally had reviewed the article*______, she could've fixed the errors.
2. Ben studied business in college. He would have studied math ____________________.
3. We didn't work hard. ____________________, we could have finished the project by now.
4. Tom scored three goals. ____________________, we would have lost.
5. I had a bad dream. I wouldn't have woken up at night ____________________.
6. We didn't return the book on time. ____________________, we could've avoided the late fee.

B. Rewrite the sentences with if.

1. I was late for work because I didn't hear the alarm.
   → *If I had heard the alarm, I wouldn't have been late for work*______.
2. Lucy didn't practice enough, so she didn't do well in her speech.
   → ______________________________.
3. Greg drank too much wine, so he got a headache.
   → ______________________________.
4. Mike and Jenny fell because they ran on the icy sidewalk.
   → ______________________________.
5. We didn't know about Claire's birthday, so we didn't send her a present.
   → ______________________________.
6. I didn't complete my report because my computer broke.
   → ______________________________.

C. Complete the sentences with the words in *italics*. Add would if necessary.

1. *(ask, give)* We gave our sofa to Jill. If you *had asked*____ about it earlier, we __________ it to you.
2. *(lock, not get)* If Max __________ his office, his wallet __________ stolen.
3. *(know, tell)* "Who's that girl?" "I don't know. If I __________ her name, I __________ you."
4. *(not be, come)* I'm sorry I missed your graduation. If I __________ out of town, I __________.
5. *(have, buy)* I don't like the color. If the store __________ these shoes in black, __________ them.
6. *(not use, be)* I __________ that cup if I __________ you. It looks dirty.

D. Read what Jay says and write sentences about it.

JAY

1. I can't listen to music because I gave my earphones to Joe.
2. I didn't go to the bank, so I don't have cash.
3. I can cook Spanish food well because I grew up in Spain.
4. I don't feel hungry because I had a big lunch.
5. I can't get in my car because I forgot my keys.

1. If *he hadn't given his earphones to Joe, he could listen to music*______.
2. If ______________________________.
3. If ______________________________.
4. If ______________________________.
5. If ______________________________.

Answers **p.324** / Review Test 17 **p.266**

LESSON 99 I wish I had blue eyes like Caroline. I wish

MP3

1 I wish + *past simple*

We use **I wish ... +** *past simple* to talk about things that are not real now that we want to happen.

- **I wish I had** blue eyes like Caroline. I think her eyes are really pretty. (I don't have blue eyes.)
- "**I wish Steve wasn't** so angry with me." "Don't worry. Just give him some time." (Steve is angry with me.)
- I like these suits, but they're too expensive. **I wish they didn't cost** so much.
- **I wish we knew** the answer to this math question. It's so hard.

We use **were** after **I wish** when **I**/**he**/**she**/**it**/etc. is the *subject*. But we can also use **was** in everyday conversation.

- I'm too lazy. **I wish I were/was** more active.
- **I wish my interview weren't/wasn't** tomorrow. I'm not ready for it.

2 I wish + *past perfect*

We use **I wish ... +** *past perfect* to talk about things that were not real in the past that we wanted to have happened.

- **I wish I had gone** on the trip with my friends last weekend. They said they had a lot of fun. (I didn't go on the trip last weekend.)
- I think this road takes longer. **I wish I had taken** the other road. (I took the road that takes longer.)
- "There's still so much to do!" "I know. **I wish we had started** earlier."
- **I wish you had come** to class today. We had an excellent guest speaker.

There is the following difference in meaning between using the *past perfect* and *past simple* after **I wish ...**

- It was raining when I got off the bus. **I wish I had had** an umbrella! (I didn't have an umbrella when I got off the bus.)
  It's raining! **I wish I had an umbrella** right now! (I don't have an umbrella now.)

3

We also use **I hope** to talk about situations that we want to happen. Note that we use **I wish** and **I hope** in different ways.

We use **I wish** to talk about wishes that are unreal or impossible.

- **I wish** she liked my gift. I shouldn't have picked it myself. (She didn't like the gift.)
- **I wish** we had seen Andy when we were in LA. But we ran out of time. (We didn't see Andy.)
- **I wish** I played the violin. It sounds so beautiful.

We use **I hope** to talk about things that are possible.

- **I hope** she likes my gift. I picked it myself. (It's possible that she likes my gift.)
- **I hope** we will see Andy when we go to LA. Let's call him when we arrive. (It's possible that we'll see Andy.)
- **I hope** I win. I prepared a lot for this competition.

4 If only

We can also use **If only** to talk about unreal situations that we want to happen or wanted to have happened. **If only** is stronger than **I wish.**

- Jennifer could show me how to use this program. **If only she were** here. (Jennifer isn't here now.)
- My favorite band is performing at 7 p.m. **If only I didn't** have to work late tonight.
- **If only I had done** laundry yesterday! I have nothing to wear today. (I didn't do the laundry yesterday.)
- College wasn't fun for me. **If only I had chosen** a different major.

P R A C T I C E

A. Look at the pictures and write sentences with **I wish** and the words in the box. Write negative sentences if necessary.

he is so busy	I am alone	I am stronger
I can ski like him	~~my kids eat more vegetables~~	we have more space

1. *I wish my kids ate more vegetables*.
2. ____________________.
3. ____________________.
4. ____________________.
5. ____________________.
6. ____________________.

B. Complete the sentences with the verbs in *italics*. Use the *past simple* or *past perfect*.

1. *(not order)* I wish I *hadn't ordered* the fish at the restaurant. It wasn't good.
2. *(visit)* I rarely see my aunt. I wish she __________ us more often.
3. *(go)* Strawberries were sold out at the market. I wish we __________ earlier.
4. *(live)* I wish I __________ near the ocean. I would go to the beach every day.
5. *(not be)* I wish this café __________ so loud. I can't have a conversation here.
6. *(not read)* I wish I __________ the book before I saw the movie. I already knew the ending.

C. Write **I wish / I hope**.

1. A: *I hope* you'll write me often while you're overseas.
   B: Don't worry. I will.
2. A: Thanks for the cake. It looks delicious.
   B: __________ you enjoy it.
3. A: __________ my husband didn't snore.
   B: I understand. My husband snores too.
4. A: The dry cleaner closes at 5 p.m.
   B: __________ you had told me sooner. It's 5:30 now.
5. A: I hear you're going to take an art class.
   B: Yes. __________ it's interesting.
6. A: __________ I had worn a suit.
   B: I know. It seemed like a formal event.

D. Read the sentences and write sentences with **If only**.

1. Jill can't go to the bar with us because she is not old enough. *If only she was/were old enough*.
2. Andrew wasn't nice to Judy, and now she's crying. ____________________.
3. I left the cookies in the oven too long and they burned. ____________________.
4. Mike is so scared that he can't go on the roller coaster. ____________________.
5. Sandra is mad at us because we didn't visit her in the hospital. ____________________.
6. I have a stomachache so I can't go to my yoga class tonight. ____________________.

Answers p.324 / Review Test 17 p.266

LESSON 100 She met a man who had a beard. *Relative pronouns (1)* **who/which/that** *as subjects*

MP3

1

She met a man. He had a beard.

She met a man who **had a beard.**

"who" connects the sentence that identifies **"a man"** with the first sentence. **"who"** is a *relative pronoun*.

2 We use **who/which/that** *(relative pronouns)* after a *noun* to identify it.

	noun	*who/which/that*	
• Do you know	**the person**	who **didn't sign** this form?	
• I'm looking forward to	**the picnic**	which **will be** on June 5th.	
•	**The dancers**	that **aren't performing right now**	can take pictures with you.
•	**The flight**	which **goes to Madrid**	departs from Gate 6.

We use **who** to talk about people and **which** to talk about things. We can use **that** to talk about people/things.

- Gandhi is **a person** who/that **fought for peace in India**.
- "Is that **the road** which/that **leads to Paradise Resort**?" "Yes, it is."

3 We can use **who/which/that** as the *subject* of a *verb*.

> Ben knows a girl. She is from France.
> *subject verb*
> Ben knows a girl who is from France.

	noun	*who/which/that*	
• Ms. Walker is	**the nurse**	who **took care of my grandmother.**	(**the nurse** took care of my grandmother.)
• I prefer	**desserts**	which **aren't too sweet.**	(**desserts** aren't too sweet.)
•	**The guest**	that **hasn't checked in yet**	is Mr. Thompson.
•	**The mail**	which **must be sent today**	is on your desk.

We use a *singular verb* when **who/which/that** refers to a *singular* or an *uncountable noun* and a *plural verb* when it refers to a *plural noun*.

- **A secretary** who **doesn't speak** Japanese won't be very helpful. We do a lot of business in Japan.
  (**A secretary** doesn't speak Japanese.)
- Are there any **restaurants** that **are** open on Thanksgiving Day? (**restaurants** are open on Thanksgiving Day.)
- That advertisement had a lot of **information** which **wasn't** correct.

4 When we use **who/which/that** as a *subject*, we do not use it with other *subjects* such as **he**/**it**/etc.

- **The boy** who **is riding** a bicycle is my cousin. (*NOT* The boy who he is)
- I see **a sign** which **says** "Chicago 21 miles." We are getting close. (*NOT* a sign which it says)
- "Were there **any items** that **were** damaged during your move?" "Luckily, no."

P R A C T I C E

A. Look at the picture and complete the sentences with **who/which**.

1. Harriet is a woman _who owns two dogs_ ______.
2. Paula bought some shoes ______.
3. Bob has a brother ______.
4. Molly is a girl ______.
5. Alan has a car ______.

B. Complete the sentences with **who/which** and the verbs in *italics*. Use the *present simple*.

1. *(grow)* Plants _which grow_ ______ in the desert don't need much water.
2. *(not want)* Visitors ______ beer can have wine or soda.
3. *(play)* I'm looking for someone ______ badminton because I need a partner.
4. *(be)* Regina writes poems ______ difficult to understand.
5. *(go)* The subway line ______ to the city center is the blue line.
6. *(not lie)* Ted is a person ______. He always tells the truth.
7. *(not have)* The rings ______ a sale tag are regular price.
8. *(understand)* Our team needs a new coach ______ soccer better.

C. Rewrite the two sentences as one with **that**.

1. Mr. White is the mailman. He delivers our mail.
   → Mr. White _is the mailman that delivers our mail_ ______.
2. I have a leather bag. It doesn't get dirty easily.
   → I ______.
3. This is the music album. It has sold over one million copies.
   → This ______.
4. The clerk brought Samantha a shirt. It wasn't her size.
   → The clerk ______.
5. The artist is famous. He created this painting.
   → The artist _that created this painting is famous_ ______.
6. The room is on the top floor. It provides the best view.
   → The room ______.
7. The actress has only been in two movies. She won the big award.
   → The actress ______.
8. Our friends invited us to dinner on Friday. They are chefs.
   → Our friends ______.

Answers **p.324** / Review Test 18 **p.268**

He is the man who she saw in the newspaper.

Relative pronouns (2)
who/which/that *as objects*

MP3

1 We can use **who/which/that** *(relative pronouns)* as the *object* of a *verb*. In this case, we can leave out **who/which/that**.

> He is the man. She saw him in the newspaper.
> (saw = *verb*, him = *object*)
>
> He is the man (who) **she saw in the newspaper**.

	noun	who/which/that	
• Is there	**anyone**	(who) **I can help?**	(Can I help **anyone**?)
• Summer is	**the season**	(which) **Elise likes best.**	(Elise likes **the season** best.)
•	**The letters**	(that) **you wrote**	were very long.
•	**The person**	(that) **Steve has interviewed**	got hired.

But we cannot leave out **who/which/that** when it is the *subject*.

- **People** who **don't exercise** every day may feel more tired. (*NOT* People don't exercise . . .)
- The museum has **a statue** which **is** more than 500 years old. (*NOT* a statue is . . .)

We can use **whom** instead of **who** when we use it as the *object*. In everyday conversation, we use **who** more often.

- Isn't that **the boy** (who/whom) **we met at the park earlier**?

2 We can also use **who(m)/which/that** as the *object* of a *preposition*. In this case, we can leave out **who(m)/which/that**.

> Ms. Brown is the boss. Paul works for her.
> (for = *preposition*, her = *object*)
>
> Ms. Brown is **the boss** (who/whom) **Paul works for**.

	noun	who/which/that	
• Science is	**a subject**	(which) **I'm not interested in.**	(I'm not interested in **a subject**.)
• Did you buy	**the house**	(that) **you looked at?**	(you looked at **the house**.)
•	**The travelers**	(that) **we rode the train with**	told us funny stories.
•	**The man**	(who) **Anna has talked about all week**	is a famous poet.

We can use *prepositions* before *relative pronouns*. In this case, we use **whom/which**, but not **who/that**.

- Nora is **the friend** with whom **I took dance lessons**. (*NOT* with who)
- **The land** on which **we stand** used to be a golf course. (*NOT* on that)

When we use *prepositions* before *relative pronouns*, we cannot leave out the *relative pronouns*.

- Ms. Nelson is **the neighbor** to whom **I gave some of my tomatoes**. (*NOT* the neighbor to I gave . . .)
- Everyone must follow the rules of **the society** in which **they live**. (*NOT* the society in they live)

3 When we use **who(m)/which/that** as an *object*, we do not use it with other *objects* such as **her**/**it**/etc.

- **The woman** who **I voted for** didn't win the election. (*NOT* The woman who I voted for her)
- "Do you have **a pen** that **I can borrow**?" "Sure." (*NOT* a pen that I can borrow it)

P R A C T I C E

A. Complete the sentences with **that** and the words in the box.

I've ever seen	you might wear	~~my younger brother read~~
she hasn't met before	we attended today	William can cook

1. A book *that my younger brother read* recently is *Jungle Jim*. He really enjoyed it.
2. The only dish ______________ is spaghetti. He's never made anything else.
3. Tina doesn't go to many parties. She doesn't like talking to people ______________.
4. This is a nice dress. Is this the one ______________ to the opera?
5. The lecture ______________ was very popular. There were no empty seats.
6. This is the best movie ______________. I really love the story.

B. Look at the pictures and complete the sentences with the words from each box.

~~a box~~	a person	a place
a plant	a tool	

\+

you can get medicine from	you can make beer with
you can open a wine bottle with	~~you can store valuable things in~~
you can wash your clothes at	

1 a safe　2 a pharmacist　3 barley　4 a laundromat　5 a corkscrew

1. A safe is *a box you can store valuable things in*.
2. ______________ is a pharmacist.
3. Barley is ______________.
4. ______________ is a laundromat.
5. A corkscrew is ______________.

C. Rewrite the two sentences as one with **who/which**. Leave out **who/which** if possible.

1. The bowl broke. I dropped it. → The bowl *I dropped broke*.
2. These are photos. They were taken last week. → These ______________.
3. Sarah has two sisters. She shares a bedroom with them. → Sarah ______________.
4. Fred's cousins are traveling abroad. They write to him. → Fred's cousins ______________.
5. Mark is a VIP member of the gym. He exercises at it. → Mark ______________.
6. The bus was crowded. Christina got on it. → The bus ______________.

D. Find and change any mistakes in each sentence. Put ✓ if the sentence is correct.

1. The boy from who I received this chocolate is Greek. *from who → from whom*
2. The song you sang at the concert was perfect. ______________
3. The building in I am living was constructed last year. ______________
4. I always love the cookies that Antonio makes them. ______________
5. Taylor High School is the school I go to. ______________
6. Claire is the girl with that I went hunting. ______________
7. I visited a park had the biggest lake in Canada. ______________

Answers p.325 / Review Test 18 p.268

LESSON 102

Amy is the girl whose hair is blond.

Relative pronouns (3) **whose** and **what**

MP3

1 We can use **whose** to talk about possession. In this case, **whose** replaces **her**/**his**/etc., and a *noun* always comes after it.

Amy is the girl. Her hair is blond.
possessive *noun*

Amy is the girl whose hair is blond.

	noun	*whose + noun*	
• Charles owns	a dog	whose name is Charlie.	(His name is Charlie.)
• I have	friends	whose lockers are messy.	(Their lockers are messy.)
•	The player	whose nose Harry broke	is in the hospital.

2 We can use **whose** + *noun* as the *subject* or *object* of a *verb*.

- **The author** whose novel **sold the most this year** is Ian Riley. (**The author's novel** sold the most this year.)
- Is there **any language** whose grammar **is similar to English**?
- **The woman** whose bag **I found** thanked me. (I found **the woman's bag**.)
- Switzerland **is a country** whose scenery **you must see**. It's amazing.

When **whose** + *noun* is the *subject*, we use a *singular verb* for a *singular* or an *uncountable noun* and a *plural verb* for a *plural noun*.

- I have **a friend** whose brother **works** at City Hall. (**a friend's brother** works at City Hall.)
- **The yoga teacher** whose classes are the most popular is Helen. (**The yoga teacher's classes** are the most popular.)
- Fiona lives in **a city** whose public transportation **is** very convenient. I want to move there.

3 We can use **what** to mean "the thing(s) that."

- I'm enjoying our new project, but what **worries me** is the deadline. (= the thing that worries me)
- I can't remember what **I wore yesterday**. I am so forgetful these days! (= the things that I wore yesterday)
- What **Sam brought** was doughnuts. I was expecting something else.

We can use **what** as the *subject* or *object* of a *verb*.

- What **confused me** about the movie was the ending. Can you explain it? (**The thing** confused me)
- Selena didn't do very well, but what **impressed us** was her effort.
- Did you find what **you needed** at the mall? (you needed **the thing**)
- "What are the children talking about?" "Oh, they're talking about what **they learned** at school today."

4 We usually use **who**/**which**/**that** after a *noun*, but we do not use **what** after it.

- **The dinner** that **you prepared** was delicious.
  What **you prepared** was delicious. (*NOT* The dinner what you prepared)
- "This is **the ring** which **I got** from Pete." "Wow. It's nice!"
  "This is what **I got** from Pete." "That's a nice ring!" (*NOT* the ring what I got)

P R A C T I C E

A. Look at the characters from the movie *Space Battle*. Complete the sentences about them with **whose**.

MALACHI - *King*
His dream is to control all of the planets.

DORN - *Teacher*
His school trained all of the fighters!

JAKE - *Pilot*
Malachi killed his parents.

DAN VIVO - *Warrior*
His leg was injured during battle.

LULU - *Princess*
Malachi attacked her planet.

1. Malachi is *the king* *whose dream is to control all of the planets*.
2. Dorn is ______ ______.
3. Jake is ______ ______.
4. Dan Vivo is ______ ______.
5. Lulu is ______ ______.

B. Put **whose** and the words in *italics* in the correct order. Use the *present simple*.

1. *(score / be / the team)* *The team whose score is* the highest will get a $500 prize.
2. *(a garden / look / flowers)* Jessica has ______ really pretty.
3. *(seeds / have / a vegetable)* A pumpkin is ______ many vitamins.
4. *(a country / be / oil industry)* Saudi Arabia is ______ famous.
5. *(not be / a company / employees)* ______ satisfied won't succeed.
6. *(a store / not cost / furniture)* Jim's Home Design is ______ a lot.

C. Complete the sentences with **what** and the words in the box.

attracts me to Jenny	caused Kevin's illness	scares Patrick
she learned	~~you said~~	you wear

1. Could you repeat that? I couldn't hear *what you said*.
2. ______ is her smile. It's the most beautiful smile I've seen in my life.
3. ______ to the interview is important. You should dress nicely.
4. Erica attended a boxing class last week, and she's been practicing ______.
5. The doctors aren't sure ______. They need to do more tests.
6. ______ about flying is the height. He's afraid that he might fall.

D. Write **whose/what/that**.

1. A vacuum is a machine *that* helps people clean floors.
2. The building ______ roof is damaged is the bookstore.
3. Ms. Lawrence is the woman ______ called 911. She saw the accident first.
4. ______ made Amanda so angry was the way her husband talked to her while they were fighting.
5. Everything on the menu looks great. I can't decide ______ I want.
6. The museum ______ we visited was built in 1820.
7. I bought another balloon for the little girl ______ balloon flew away.
8. Tim wants to know ______ happened at the party after he left.

Answers **p.325** / Review Test 18 **p.268**

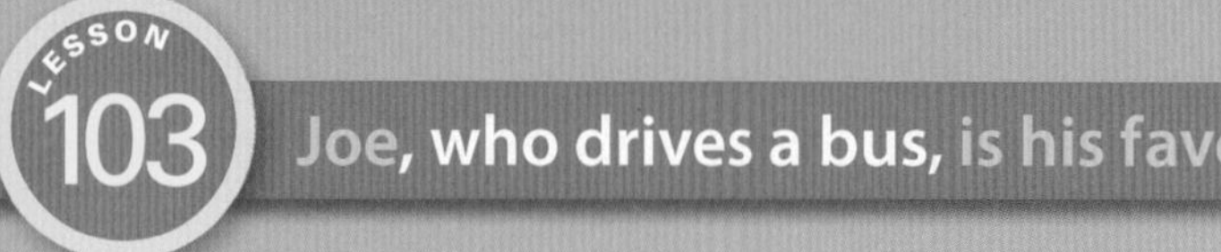

LESSON 103 Joe, who drives a bus, is his favorite uncle.

Relative pronouns (4) **who/which** for additional information

1 Joe, who **drives a bus**, is his favorite uncle.

Joe is my favorite uncle.
He drives a bus.
JOE

", who drives a bus" is used after **"Joe"** to give additional information about him. But Joe can still be identified as his favorite uncle without **", who drives a bus."**

2 We can use **who/which** to give additional information about a person/thing that is already identified. In this case, we always use a comma (,) before **who/which.**

- **Tom**, who **married my cousin**, seems nice.
- **My old house**, which **was on Easton Street**, didn't have a balcony.
- Gina bought that new phone, which **she broke in two days**.
- Mr. Johnson introduced me to his two sons, who **he always talks about**.

But we cannot use **that** to give additional information about the person/thing.

- I'll connect you to **Hilary**, who **can answer your questions**. (*NOT* Hilary, that can answer . . .)
- **These chairs**, which **I designed**, are now sold at furniture stores. (*NOT* These chairs, that I designed . . .)

We can also use **who/which/that** to give necessary information that identifies a person/thing. In this case, we do not use a comma (,).

- The doctor who/that **performed my surgery** is Dr. Kim.
  (**who/that performed . . .** is necessary information that identifies the doctor.)
  Dr. Kim, who **performed my surgery**, was great.
  (**who performed . . .** is additional information about Dr. Kim.)
- We stayed at the resort which/that **you recommended**.
  Aloha Resort, which you recommended, was a great place to stay.

3 We can also use **which** to give additional information about an entire sentence. In this case, we always use a comma (,) before **which.**

George closed the door loudly. That woke up the baby.
George closed the door loudly, which **woke up the baby**.

- I was up very late the day before the test, which **wasn't a smart idea**.
- We went skiing in Colorado last winter, which **was a fun experience**.
- The team's best player got hurt, which **made the team lose**.

But we cannot use **that** to give additional information about an entire sentence.

- I couldn't remember if I locked my door, which **made me nervous**. (*NOT* my door, that made me nervous)

In this case, we always use a *singular verb* after **which.**

- Our office recycles all paper products, which **is** good for the environment.
- Amber wanted to surprise Jim, which **explains** her strange behavior.

P R A C T I C E

A. Rewrite the two sentences as one with **who/which** and a comma (,).

1. Lyon is a beautiful city. It is in France.
   → *Lyon, which is in France, is a beautiful city*.
2. My English professor is very intelligent and friendly. I won't ever forget her.
   → ______________________.
3. Tracey had already decorated a room for her twins. They weren't born yet.
   → ______________________.
4. Everyone enjoyed Annie's chocolate cookies. She baked them yesterday.
   → ______________________.
5. Matt owns that small car. His friends always joke about it.
   → ______________________.
6. Kevin's parents will retire soon. They've been working as lawyers.
   → ______________________.

B. Connect the two sentences and rewrite them as one with **which**.

1. Ms. Marsh prepares a lot for her class.	•	• That worried her whole family.
2. My neighbors painted their fence yellow.	•	• That wasn't good news for the fans.
3. Lisa didn't eat anything at the family dinner.	•	• That made their garden look bright.
4. Kevin showed up late for the meeting.	•	• That isn't normal for him.
5. The final match was canceled due to rain.	•	• That helps her students learn better.
6. I took a vacation last week.	•	• That was very relaxing.

1. *Ms. Marsh prepares a lot for her class, which helps her students learn better*.
2. ______________________.
3. ______________________.
4. ______________________.
5. ______________________.
6. ______________________.

C. Write **who/which/that.** Add a comma (,) if necessary.

1. **Two People** *Who* OR *That* **Are Important to Me**

By Justin Wilson

2. Joe __________ is a bus driver, is my favorite uncle.
3. And his wife Betty __________ is my mom's sister, is always very kind to me.
4. Since I was young, I've often visited their house __________ is close to mine.
5. The memories __________ we have created together are very special.

They both have taught me many things.

6. Betty __________ is a great advisor, solved many of my problems while I was growing up.
7. She taught me how to be confident __________ is still very valuable.
8. Joe and I have discussed a lot of topics __________ has helped me to become an excellent speaker.
9. Joe and Betty are two of the people __________ I love most. I hope I grow up to be like them.

Answers **p.325** / Review Test 18 **p.268**

I'm thinking about the time **when I first met you.** *Relative adverbs* **when/where/why**

MP3

1 We use **when/where/why** *(relative adverbs)* to identify a specific time, place, or reason.

the time/day/etc. + **when**

- I'm thinking about **the time** when **I first met you**.
- Next Monday is **the day** when **we vote for a new president**.
- 1988 was **the year** when **the Seoul Olympics were held**.
- **The summer** when **I worked as a lifeguard** was many years ago.

the place/zoo/etc. + **where**

- I'd like to visit **the place** where **Jerry took these pictures**. It looks amazing.
- **The zoo** where **we saw polar bears** has closed down.
- Do you know **a store** where **I can get rain boots**?
- "Is this **the church** where **you got married**?" "Yes, it is."

the reason + **why**

- Melanie told me **the reason** why **she couldn't meet Josh**.
- "Are you on a diet?" "Yes. That's **the reason** why I've been eating less."

2 In everyday conversation, we often leave out **when/where/why** after the following *nouns*:

the time/day/year	the place	the reason

- "Do you remember **the time** (when) **we went scuba diving**?" "Yes. It was so much fun!"
- "Is this **the place** (where) **you lost your wallet**?" "Actually, I'm not sure."
- **The reason** (why) **Carrie moved out** was that her roommate was so messy.

We can also use **that** instead of **when/where/why**. In this case, we can also leave out **that**.

- **The year** (that) **Kevin started working for the airline** was 2001.
  (= The year (when) Kevin started working for the airline)
- Last weekend, Morris and I visited **the place** (that) **he grew up**.
  (= the place (where) he grew up)
- Dr. Clark is **the reason** (that) **I chose this college**. He is a famous biology professor.

3 We use **the way (that)** to identify a method or process. In everyday conversation, we often leave out **that**.

- **The way** (that) **you're holding your chopsticks** isn't correct.
- I think **the way** (that) **this café makes coffee** is great. It smells good and it's strong.

We can also use **how** instead of **the way (that)**. Note that we do not use **how** and **the way** together.

- Celia isn't happy about **the way** (that) **her haircut looks**, but I think it's cute.
  OR Celia isn't happy about how **her haircut looks**, but I think it's cute. (*NOT* the way how her haircut looks)
- **The way** (that) **Kim sings** is unique.
  OR How **Kim sings** is unique. She has her own style. (*NOT* The way how Kim sings)

P R A C T I C E

A. Complete the sentences with **when/where/why** and the words in the box.

a lot of accidents happen	Andy didn't take	I buy my groceries
~~I had to speak~~	my daughter was born	she's so tired all the time

1. I was so nervous that morning *when I had to speak* in front of the whole school.
2. The reason __________ that job was the company's location. It was too far.
3. This intersection is dangerous. It's a place __________.
4. Flora is taking too many classes. That's the reason __________.
5. The day __________ was the happiest moment of my life. I love being a dad.
6. The prices are usually lower at the store __________. That's why I shop there.

B. Complete the sentences with **when/where/why** and the words in *italics*. Leave out **when/where/why** if possible.

1 ***Construction Ahead***
The bridge will be closed for repair work.

2 **Best Pizza in Town!**
Sophia's Pizzeria! You can get the city's best pizza here!

3 ***Summer Vacation!***
Summer vacation begins on Wednesday!

4 **Concert Canceled**
The concert is canceled because of the singer's illness.

5 **Warning!**
Swimming at Glory Coast is not allowed.

6 *Wild Animal Safari*
Some animals start to hunt after sunset.

1. *(the reason)* Repair work is *the reason (why) the bridge will be closed*.
2. *(the restaurant)* Sophia's Pizzeria is __________.
3. *(the day)* Wednesday is __________.
4. *(the reason)* The singer's illness is __________.
5. *(the beach)* Glory Coast is __________.
6. *(the time)* After sunset is __________.

C. Find and change any mistakes in each sentence. Put ✓ if the sentence is correct.

1. The library I got these books is closed on Sundays. *The library → The library where*
2. I'm looking forward to the day which I can travel more. __________
3. I'm proud of the way my children behaved today. __________
4. This is the stadium the basketball game will be held. __________
5. I like the way how Ralph talks. He has an interesting accent. __________
6. The reason Matt went to the hospital was his broken leg. __________

D. Write **when/where/why** or **who/which**.

MP3

AMY

AMY: [1] Do you remember the time *when* we went to London?
CHRIS: Oh yes! [2] The week __________ we were there is my favorite memory. [3] Do you remember the boy __________ we met there?
AMY: I do. [4] He showed us all of the pictures __________ he had taken.
CHRIS: Right. [5] I also liked the hotel __________ we stayed.
AMY: Me too. [6] The reason __________ it was so nice was the garden.
CHRIS: That's right! I'd like to go back to London one day.

CHRIS

Answers **p.325** / Review Test 18 **p.268**

Kim **said that** Gina's house was huge. *Reported speech (1)*

MP3

1 We use **said that** to report what someone said. If what someone says is in the present tense, we change it to the past tense.

Present simple		*Past simple*
Kim: "Gina's house is huge!"	→	• Kim **said that** Gina's house **was** huge.
Nick: "I don't read mystery books."	→	• Nick **said that** he **didn't read** mystery books.
Present progressive		*Past progressive*
Molly: "Tim and Ann are taking a walk."	→	• Molly **said that** Tim and Ann **were taking** a walk.
Jason: "I'm not sleeping."	→	• Jason **said that** he **wasn't sleeping**.
Present perfect		*Past perfect*
The reporter: "The government has made a new law about education."	→	• The reporter **said that** the government **had made** a new law about education.
Rita: "I haven't heard from Jeff in weeks."	→	• Rita **said that** she **hadn't heard** from Jeff in weeks.

We can leave out **that**.

- "Where is Ms. Brown?" "She **said (that)** she was almost here."

2 In reported speech, we use **would/could** for **will/can**.

Jake: "I will see you at the party."	→	• Jake **said (that)** he **would see** us at the party.
Mr. Jones: "You can borrow my car."	→	• Mr. Jones **said** I **could borrow** his car.
Kelly: "I won't be home until 8 o'clock."	→	• Kelly **said** she **wouldn't be** home until 8 o'clock.

3 If what someone said is still true now, we can also use the present tense instead of the past tense.

Denise: "I exercise every day."

→ • Denise **said (that)** she **exercised** every day.
OR Denise **said (that)** she **exercises** every day. (She still exercises every day.)

Mr. and Mrs. Smith: "We travel somewhere new every summer."

→ • Mr. and Mrs. Smith **said** they **traveled** somewhere new every summer.
OR Mr. and Mrs. Smith **said** they **travel** somewhere new every summer. (They still travel every summer.)

But we use the past tense if it is not true now.

Sam: "It's cold." → • Sam **said** it **was** cold yesterday, but it has gotten warmer today. (It's not cold now.)

4 If what someone said is in the *past simple*, we can either use the *past simple* or change to the *past perfect*.

Ray and Jacob: "We washed the carpet."

→ • Ray and Jacob **said (that)** they **washed** the carpet.
OR Ray and Jacob **said (that)** they **had washed** the carpet.

Liz: "I didn't have anything for dinner."

→ • Liz **said** she **didn't have** anything for dinner.
OR Liz **said** she **hadn't had** anything for dinner.

PRACTICE

A. Report what Jack says with **said that**.

1. I've met a famous actress before.
2. I'm trying to lose weight.
3. My parents haven't been to Europe.

4. I don't like the food at that restaurant.
5. My neighbor's dogs bark too much.
6. Cindy and Julie aren't paying their rent.

1. *He said that he had met a famous actress before* .
2. ______________________________ .
3. ______________________________ .
4. ______________________________ .
5. ______________________________ .
6. ______________________________ .

B. Report what each person says with **said**.

1
I will finish the report by Friday.
2
I can't watch scary movies alone.
3
I need to buy a new wallet.
4
I'll call Derek later.
5
The mall won't be open this month.
6
We have lived in Toronto for 10 years.
7
Monica can sing beautifully.
8
Max and Sue aren't dating anymore.

1. *He said he would finish the report by Friday* .
2. ______________________________ .
3. ______________________________ .
4. ______________________________ .
5. ______________________________ .
6. ______________________________ .
7. ______________________________ .
8. ______________________________ .

C. Report what people say in each situation with **said**. Use the *present simple* or *past simple*.

1. SEAN: "I feel great." *(But he feels tired now.)*
   YOU: *Sean said he felt great* .
2. JANE: "Robert doesn't like jazz music." *(And he still doesn't like jazz music.)*
   YOU: ______________________________ .
3. DANA: "I studied English literature in college."
   YOU: ______________________________ .
4. BILL: "I won't be attending Joel's presentation." *(But later he attended.)*
   YOU: ______________________________ .
5. SYLVIA: "My office is too small." *(And it is still too small.)*
   YOU: ______________________________ .
6. TED: "Roger can draw portraits well." *(And he can still draw portraits well.)*
   YOU: ______________________________ .
7. MR. PHILLIPS: "The clock wasn't broken when I left."
   YOU: ______________________________ .

Answers **p.326** / Review Test 19 **p.270**

LESSON 106

The doctor **told Tim that** he was very healthy.

Reported speech (2)

MP3

1 We can also use **told** to report what someone said. We use *person* + **that** after **told**.

- The doctor **told Tim that** he was very healthy.
- "Did you leave some cake for Dorothy?" "No. She **told us that** she didn't want any."
- Mr. Potter **told his students that** the assignments had been uploaded on his website.

We can leave out **that**.

- The mechanic **told me (that)** my car would be ready in a week.

2 There is the following difference between **told** and **said**:

told + *person* (+ **that**)

Note that we always use *person* after **told**.

- John **told his boss (that)** he needed a break.
  (*NOT* John told that he needed)
- "Is Tina coming to the meeting?"
  "No. She **told me** she couldn't come."
  (*NOT* She told she couldn't come)

said (+ **that**)

Note that we do not use *person* after **said**.

- John **said (that)** he needed a break.
  (*NOT* John said his boss that he needed)
- Rebecca **said** she couldn't go out with us this weekend. She has a bad cold.
  (*NOT* Rebecca said us she couldn't go)

But we can use **to** + *person* after **said . . .**

- Has Matt **said anything to you** about last night?
- You should **say "thank you" to people** when they help you.

3 We use **tell/ask** + *person* + **to . . .** to report an order or a request from someone.

Mike: "Billy, put on your seat belt." → • Mike **told Billy to put** on his seat belt.
Sally: "Could you give me a ride, Phil?" → • Sally **asked Phil to give** her a ride.

We use **not** before **to . . .** when the order or request is about not doing something.

Ellen: "Don't talk so loudly, Jim." → • Ellen **told Jim not to talk** so loudly.
George: "Tara, please don't bother me." → • George **asked Tara not to bother** him.

4 We use **ask** / **wonder** / **want to know** / etc. to report a question from someone in the following ways:

We use *question word* + *subject* + *verb* to report a question with a *question word*.

Hugh: "Where is the post office?" → • Hugh **asked where the post office was**. (the post office = *subject*, was = *verb*)
Sue: "When does the library close?" → • Sue **wondered when the library closed**. (the library = *subject*, closed = *verb*)

We use **if/whether** + *subject* + *verb* to report a question without a *question word*.

Ms. Tyler: "Has Gary called me?" → • Ms. Tyler **wondered if/whether Gary had called** her. (Gary = *subject*, had called = *verb*)
Bob: "Are those pants on sale?" → • Bob **wanted to know if/whether those pants were** on sale. (those pants = *subject*, were = *verb*)

More about indirect questions: Lesson 31

PRACTICE

A. Report what each person says with **told**.

1. I don't drive to the office.
2. You look like twins.
3. You can't smoke in the building.
4. We haven't cleaned the bathroom yet.
5. I'm learning to cook Thai food.

YOU

1. *He told her he didn't drive to the office*.
2. ______________________.
3. ______________________.
4. ______________________.
5. ______________________.

B. Put the words in *italics* in the correct order. Add **to** if necessary.

1. *(her friends / got / told / she)* Wendy *told her friends she got* a scholarship.
2. *(his brother / said / goodbye)* Jeremy ______________________ on the platform.
3. *(Joey / he / told / wait / should)* Cassie ______________________ for her after school.
4. *(said / me / nothing)* Lucy ______________________ because she was angry with me.
5. *(Nate / it / told / that / was snowing)* Frank ______________________ outside.
6. *(the concert / had been canceled / that / said)*
   Last week, the band ______________________.

C. Janet is making requests. Report what she says with the verbs in *italics*, and add **not** if necessary.

1. Barbara, could you close the door? *(ask)* *She asked Barbara to close the door*.
2. Don't turn on the radio, Harry. *(tell)* ______________________.
3. Would you take out the garbage, Laura? *(ask)* ______________________.
4. Beth, get some rest. *(tell)* ______________________.
5. Christine, don't open the present yet. *(tell)* ______________________.
6. Roy, please don't leave too early. *(ask)* ______________________.

JANET

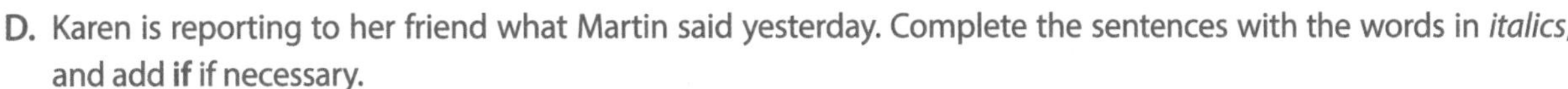

D. Karen is reporting to her friend what Martin said yesterday. Complete the sentences with the words in *italics*, and add **if** if necessary.

Yesterday

1. Do you like spicy food?
2. Who's your favorite actor?
3. Do you have any hobbies?
4. Where are you from?
5. Are you interested in sports?

Today

1. *(ask)* He *asked if I liked spicy food*.
2. *(want to know)* He ______________________.
3. *(ask)* He ______________________.
4. *(want to know)* He ______________________.
5. *(wonder)* He ______________________.

It is said that elephants have good memories.

MP3

1 We use **It is said that . . .** to talk about generally accepted ideas.

People say that elephants have good memories.
It is said that elephants have good memories.

People say that women live longer than men. → • **It is said that women live** longer than men.
People say that money can't buy happiness. → • **It is said that money can't buy** happiness.

- **It is said that children learn** languages faster than adults.
- **It is said that chocolate gives** you energy right away.

We can also use the following expressions to talk about generally accepted ideas:

It is	believed/thought/known/expected	that . . .

• It is	believed	that the earth is	over four billion years old.
• It is	thought	that fireworks were	invented in China.
• It is	known	that air pollution causes	some types of cancer.
• It is	expected	that you don't wear	shoes inside the house in some countries.

2 We can also use **. . . is/are + said to . . .** to talk about generally accepted ideas.

People say that elephants have good memories.
Elephants are said to have good memories.

People say that warm milk helps you sleep. → • **Warm milk is said to help** you sleep.
People say that almonds are the healthiest nut. → • **Almonds are said to be** the healthiest nut.

- **Colors are said to** greatly **influence** people's feelings.
- **The president is said to be** a big basketball fan.

We can also use **believed/thought/known/expected** in the following ways:

. . . is/are	believed/thought/known/expected	to . . .

• The number 13 is	believed	to bring	bad luck.
• Some plants are	thought	to grow	well in the shade.
• New Zealand is	known	to have	beautiful mountains.
• Thousands of people are	expected	to attend	the music festival.

PRACTICE

A. The following are generally accepted ideas in some countries. Complete the sentences about them with **that** and the words in *italics*.

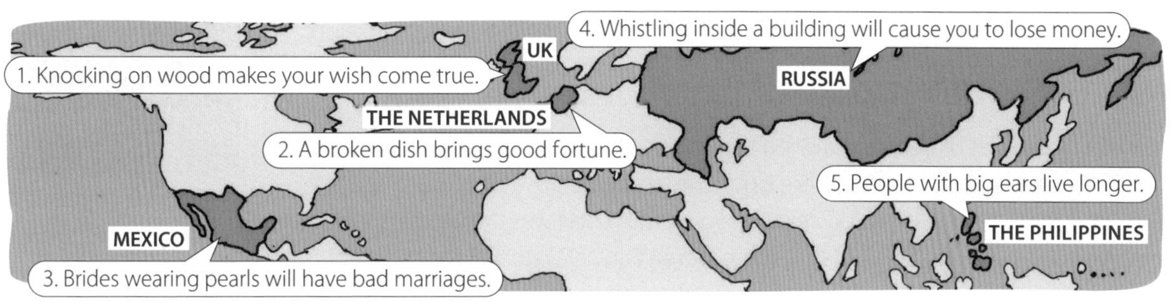

4. Whistling inside a building will cause you to lose money.
UK
1. Knocking on wood makes your wish come true.
RUSSIA
THE NETHERLANDS
2. A broken dish brings good fortune.
5. People with big ears live longer.
THE PHILIPPINES
MEXICO
3. Brides wearing pearls will have bad marriages.

1. *(said)* In the UK, *it is said that knocking on wood makes your wish come true*.
2. *(believed)* In the Netherlands, __________.
3. *(said)* In Mexico, __________.
4. *(thought)* In Russia, __________.
5. *(believed)* In the Philippines, __________.

B. Read what people say and write sentences about them with **to . . .** and the words in *italics*.

1. Lander Hotel has good service.
2. Dogs feel emotions.
3. Exercise reduces stress levels.

4. Carrots are good for eyesight.
5. That house on the hill belongs to a famous singer.
6. The rose is the flower of love.

1. *(known)* *Lander Hotel is known to have good service*.
2. *(believed)* __________.
3. *(known)* __________.
4. *(thought)* __________.
5. *(said)* __________.
6. *(thought)* __________.

C. The following is Justin's article for the school paper. Put **that/to . . .** and the words in *italics* in the correct order.

Choose Us, Harry!

By Justin Wilson

Big news this week!

1. The famous CEO Harry Crow is *known to visit* high schools often. *(visit / known)*
2. It is __________ to meet young people and listen to their stories. *(he / said / likes)*
3. Mr. Crow is __________ a good example to students because he does a lot of charity work. *(be / thought)*
4. It is __________ which high school to visit. *(will soon decide / believed / Mr. Crow)*
5. On Thursday, it is __________ everyone his decision. *(expected / will tell / he)* Hopefully, we will get a chance to meet him.
6. Mr. Crow is __________ in our town, so I hope that means he'll come! *(said / have lived)*

Answers **p.326** / Review Test 19 **p.270**

LESSON 108 There are a lot of people watching the fashion show. there + be

MP3

1 We use **there + be** to say that someone or something exists.

(Present simple)	there	is/are	(not)
(Past simple)		was/were	

- **There are** a lot of people watching the fashion show.
- The game is about to start. **There isn't** time to get snacks.
- "**Was there** anyone in the office when you left?" "No. I was the last person to leave."
- We had to use the stairs because **there weren't** any elevators in the building.

(Present perfect)

there	have/has	(not)	been

- **There have been** three accidents this month at that intersection.
- Recently, **there hasn't been** enough snow to ski on the slopes.
- "It has been colder than usual lately." "I know. **There's been** so much damage to the crops."

2 We use the singular form of **be** when we use a *singular* or an *uncountable noun* after **there + be** and the plural form for a *plural noun*.

- Look! **There's a dolphin** near that boat.
- Our store just opened. **There haven't been any visitors** so far.
- **There is not enough oil** in the pan. We need to add some more.

3 We use **there + be** with **will/may/must**/etc. or **used to** in the following structures:

there	will/may/must/etc.	(not)	be

- **There'll be** a cocktail party on Friday at 7 o'clock.
- A staff member said that **there may be** a delay in tonight's show.
- This soup is not spicy at all. **There must not be** any pepper in it.

there	used to	be

- **There used to be** nothing here. But now, there are many tall buildings.
- "I think **there used to be** more dishes on the menu." "I think so too."

4 We use **there seem/appear to be** to mean "I think there might be . . ." Note that we use **there seems/appears to be** when we use a *singular* or an *uncountable noun* after it.

- **There seems to be** an error with this program. Can you check?
- I can't find anything useful in this book. **There doesn't appear to be** any information about the war.
- Which resort do you want to stay at? **There seem to be** many resorts on that island.

5 We often use **there + be** with the following expressions of quantity:

some/any/no many/much/a lot of two/three/etc.	(noun)

- **There were some empty seats** near the window, so we sat there.
- I'm trying to decide between these two phones. **Is there much difference**?
- "**Were there any people** at the park?" "Yes, but **there were** only **two**."

P R A C T I C E

A. Complete the sentences with **there + be**. Write negative sentences if necessary.

1. *There is* __________ some orange juice in the fridge. Have some.
2. __________ any job openings at the company since 2005, but there might be some this year.
3. "Do we have any shampoo?" "I'm looking now. No, __________ any."
4. "__________ any scary movies at the theater?" "Yes. There's one I really want to see."
5. We were relieved because __________ any problems with our grandmother's health.
6. Since the road construction started, __________ so much noise. It's horrible.
7. Our office isn't usually busy, but __________ a lot of calls from customers yesterday.
8. "__________ a delivery for me last week? I was on vacation." "No, nothing came."

B. Complete the sentences with **there + be** and the given words. Write negative sentences if necessary.

a fire	~~a lot of traffic~~	any live music	cheap clothes
enough copies	many fish	much snow	

1. *(could)* "Why is Dad late?" "*There could be a lot of traffic* __________. I think he'll be home soon."
2. *(may)* __________ of the poster. Maybe we should make some more.
3. *(will)* "__________ at the dinner?" "Yes. There'll be a band."
4. *(used to)* "The prices at this store have increased!" "I know. __________ here."
5. *(could)* __________ on the street. It snowed only for a few minutes.
6. *(must)* "Look at all that smoke!" "__________ somewhere."
7. *(used to)* __________ in this lake. Now, it's too polluted.

C. Rewrite the sentences with the verbs in *italics*.

1. I think you cooked enough food for everyone. → *(seem)* *There seems to be enough food for everyone* __________.
2. I think we have some problems with the project. → *(seem)* __________.
3. I guess there is a concert at city hall. → *(appear)* __________.
4. I think someone put flowers on your desk. → *(seem)* __________.
5. I guess there is no mail today. → *(appear)* __________.

D. Complete the conversation with **there + be** and the words in *italics*. Write negative sentences if necessary.

MP3

LINDA: Why did you come home so late?
AMY: I went to see a fashion show.
1. And when it was over, *there were no* __________ buses. *(no)*
2. So __________ people trying to get taxis. *(a lot of)*
LINDA: 3. Well, you know __________ buses after 11 p.m. *(any)*
Why didn't you leave sooner?
AMY: There was a party after the show!
4. You know, __________ time for fun activities next week. *(any)*
LINDA: Oh, that's right. You'll have final exams. Well, did you eat dinner?
AMY: 5. No. __________ food there. *(no)* They just had drinks.
LINDA: You should eat something!
6. __________ snacks in the cabinet. *(might, some)*

LINDA

AMY

Answers p.326 / Review Test 20 p.272

LESSON

109 So do I, I think not

so, neither, not

MP3

1 We use **so** to mean "also" and **neither** to mean "also not." We use **so** and **neither** before *verb + subject*.

	verb	*subject*
so neither	am/is/are/etc. do/does/did have/has/had will/can/etc.	I/we/you/they he/she/it my mom/Jacob/etc.

- "I'm ready to leave." **"So am I."** (= I'm also ready.)
- "My parents don't like dogs." "Really? **Neither do my parents.**" (= My parents also don't like dogs.)
- "I have been taking the subway to school." **"So has Jacob.** He said it's very convenient."
- "I couldn't believe Stacy won the contest." **"Neither could she.** It was a big surprise for everyone."

2 We can use the following expressions with **so** or **not** to avoid repeating an earlier statement:

I	think/hope/guess/suppose/believe/am afraid	so

- "I forgot where Tom lives. Was it 7th Avenue?" **"I think so."** (= I think it was 7th Avenue.)
- "Do you think we'll do well in this match?" **"I hope so."** (= I hope we'll do well in this match.)
- "I was going to take the 7 o'clock shuttle. Did I miss it?" **"I believe so."**

I	think/hope/guess/suppose/believe/am afraid	not

- "I don't think Sam is coming." **"I guess not."** (= I guess Sam isn't coming.)
- "Nobody will be on time. It won't matter if we're five minutes late."
  "I suppose not." (= I suppose it won't matter if we're five minutes late.)
- "Is parking allowed here?" **"I'm afraid not.** It's only for fire trucks."

We can also use **think/guess/suppose/believe** with **I don't . . . so.**

- "Is the post office still open?" **"I don't think so.** It's past 5 o'clock." (= I think not.)
- "Will we get our exam results back today?" **"I don't believe so."** (= I believe not.)

But for **hope** and **am afraid**, we use **I hope not** and **I'm afraid not** only.

- "Do we have to work this weekend?" **"I hope not."** (*NOT* I don't hope so.)
- "Is there any more coffee?" **"I'm afraid not."** (*NOT* I'm not afraid so.)

3 **if so/not**

- "I might be free this afternoon." "Well, **if so**, let's watch a movie." (= if you're free this afternoon)
- Are there any questions? **If not**, we can end the meeting now. (= If there aren't any questions)

4 **why not?**

We can use **why not?** to ask the reason for someone's negative statement.

- "I don't want to stay at that hotel." **"Why not?** It looks OK."

We can also use **why not?** to willingly accept a suggestion or proposal.

- "Do you want to order a pizza?" "Sure. **Why not?"**

P R A C T I C E

A. Complete the conversations with **so/neither** and the subjects in *italics*.

TINA

	ALISON
1. My family is from Italy.	*(my father)* So is my father. He was born in Rome.
2. We haven't lived here long.	*(we)* ____________. We moved here last year.
3. My daughter plays tennis.	*(my son)* ____________. He's really good at it.
4. My son isn't taking art lessons now.	*(my kids)* ____________. They take ski classes instead.
5. My mom has been a teacher for a long time.	*(my husband)* ____________. He's been teaching since 1985.
6. My family didn't travel last summer.	*(my family)* ____________. We were too busy.
7. I should call home.	*(I)* ____________. My family might worry about me.
8. I can't stay out much longer.	*(I)* ____________. We should go home soon.

B. Write Lynn's answers to Philip's questions with **so/not** and the words in *italics*.

PHILIP

1. Is that man's name Thomas?
2. Are you coming home late again?
3. Will they serve pork for dinner?
4. Will Alice sell her car?
5. Are you attending the seminar?
6. Did you get some eggs from the store?
7. Will you get a new dress for the party?

LYNN

Lynn thinks	Lynn says
1. I think that man's name is Thomas.	1. *(think)* I think so.
2. I have to work late again.	2. *(am afraid)* ____________.
3. I hate pork.	3. *(hope)* ____________.
4. Alice said she probably won't sell her car.	4. *(believe)* ____________.
5. My boss told me I should attend it.	5. *(guess)* ____________.
6. I didn't buy any groceries today.	6. *(am afraid)* ____________.
7. I'll probably get a new dress for the party.	7. *(suppose)* ____________.

C. Complete the conversation with **so/neither/not**.

MP3

PAUL

CHRIS

PAUL: Are Amy and Kate coming on the fishing trip?
CHRIS: 1. I don't think *so*. Amy said they're not coming.
2. ____________ are Justin and Sandy.
PAUL: 3. Why ____________? I thought everybody liked fishing.
CHRIS: 4. ____________ did I. But they all wanted to stay home. It'll still be a good trip, though.
PAUL: 5. I suppose ____________. But I heard it might rain on Sunday.
CHRIS: Really? 6. If ____________, we won't be able to catch a lot of fish.
PAUL: But it would be so much fun anyway. And maybe it won't rain!
CHRIS: 7. I hope ____________!

Answers **p.327** / Review Test 20 **p.272**

LESSON 110 He thinks that she is beautiful. *Verb/Adjective* + **that . . .**

1 He **thinks that she is** beautiful.

He saw her wearing a wedding dress. She was beautiful in his opinion.
"thinks that she is" describes his opinion.

2 We can use **that . . .** after the *verbs* that express thoughts, feelings, opinions, etc. In everyday conversation, we usually leave out **that**.

think	believe	know	learn	feel	notice	suppose	hope

- That woman over there looks familiar. I **think (that) I've seen** her somewhere before.
- "Did you **know (that) Ron moved** to Seattle?" "No. When did he move?"
- "I **noticed you don't drive** to work." "No. I don't have a car."
- I didn't bring my socks. I don't **suppose you have** extra socks, do you?

We can also use **that . . .** after the *adjectives* that express emotions. In this case, **that . . .** describes the reason for the emotion.

happy	glad	proud	surprised	afraid	sorry	disappointed

- We weren't **happy (that) we had to wait** in line for so long.
- Monica's parents were **proud (that) she received** a scholarship.
- Tom and Doris seemed like a perfect couple. Everyone was **surprised they broke** up.
- I'm **afraid I can't come** to your birthday party. I'll be out of town.

3 We can also use **that . . .** after the *verbs* that express requests, demands, suggestions, etc. In this case, we use **base form** after **that**.

demand	propose	suggest	recommend	insist	advise

- The teacher **demanded (that) everyone be** quiet during the test.
- "Would you **recommend (that) I wear** the red tie or the blue tie?" "The red one."
- "We should leave now." "Please, I **insist you stay** a bit longer."

We can also use **that . . .** after **It is essential/important/necessary/vital**/etc. In this case, we also use **base form** after **that**.

- If you don't do well in the interview, you won't get the job. **It's essential that you be** prepared.
- "**Is it necessary that I read** all of the instructions?" "Well, it's probably a good idea."
- **It's vital that Jack take** his medicine at the same time every day. He'll feel better much sooner.

When we use a negative sentence after **that**, we use **not** before **base form**.

- The lawyer **advised that his client not say** anything in court.
- **It's important that you not forget** what you've learned. Keep practicing!

PRACTICE

A. Read what each person thinks and write sentences about their thoughts with the verbs in *italics*.

1. *(think)* *She thinks (that) Hannah is smart* ________.
2. *(suppose)* ________.
3. *(feel)* ________.
4. *(know)* ________.
5. *(believe)* ________.

B. Read what each person says and write sentences about them with the verbs in *italics*.

1. *(recommend)* *He recommended (that) she watch the movie* ________.
2. *(insist)* ________.
3. *(demand)* ________.
4. *(propose)* ________.
5. *(suggest)* ________.
6. *(advise)* ________.

C. Rewrite the two sentences as one with **that**.

1. Denny can play the drums. We are surprised. → *We are surprised that Denny can play the drums* ________.
2. Lesley canceled our date. I'm disappointed. → ________.
3. The music festival isn't sold out. Pam is glad. → ________.
4. You should drink enough water. It's important. → ________.
5. Schools must teach history. It's vital. → ________.
6. People should exercise regularly. It's essential. → ________.

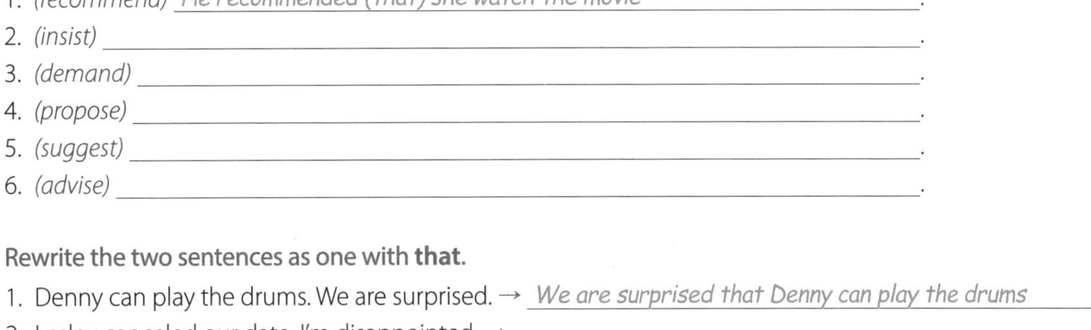

D. Complete the sentences with the verbs in the box. Add **not** if necessary.

climb	learn	lower	miss	~~visit~~	wait

1. It's essential that you *visit* ________ the doctor immediately if you have any more pain.
2. It is necessary that you ________ the deadline. Late applications will not be accepted.
3. I'd recommend that you ________ that tree. You might fall.
4. It's important that kids ________ manners. They need them to live with other people.
5. The citizens demanded that the city ________ taxes. They think they are paying too much.
6. Cindy advised that we ________ for her, so we left without her.

Answers **p.327** / Review Test 20 **p.272**

GRAMMAR GATEWAY INTERMEDIATE

The Review Test can help you check what you learned in the lessons. If you are not sure about the answer to a question, go back to the lessons and review them.

Test 01

 Put the words in *italics* in the correct order. Write negative sentences if necessary.

1. *(is / far / Boston)*
   Boston isn't far ______ from New York. It's only a few hours by bus.
2. *(socks / I / wear)*
   ______ at home because they're uncomfortable.
3. *(in the kitchen / they / are)*
   "I made some sandwiches for you." "Thank you! ______?"
4. *(Mike and Kim / preparing / are)*
   ______ for their exams these days. They're studying very hard.
5. *(always / breakfast / eat / you)*
   "______?" "Not every day."
6. *(is / it / raining)*
   You don't need an umbrella. ______ anymore.

 Complete the conversations with the words in *italics*. Use the *present simple* or *present progressive*.

7. Can I talk to Diane, please?	*(she, take)* She's taking ______ a shower now.
8. I really enjoy my history class.	*(you, learn)* Really? What ______ these days?
9. I love the park next to the city hall.	*(I, not go)* Me too, but ______ there often.
10. Is Derek's house near yours?	*(he, live)* Yes. ______ across the street.
11. Jessica wants to live in France.	*(she, speak)* ______ French?
12. Are you on vacation?	*(I, not work)* Yes. ______ this week.

 Complete the sentences with the words in *italics*. Use the *present simple* or *present progressive*.

To	billnelson@fastmail.com
From	lisamoore@fastmail.com

Hi Bill,

How is everything going? All is OK here.

13. *(my sister, not stay)* My sister isn't staying ______ with me this week.
14. *(she, visit)* ______ our cousin, Jamie, in New York.
15. *(Jamie and I, not see)* ______ each other often.
16. *(we, talk)* However, ______ on the phone almost every day.
17. *(I, listen)* Anyway, ______ to Jim King's music at the moment.
18. *(you, know)* ______ him?
19. *(his voice, sound)* ______ so peaceful. Listen to him when you have the chance.

Well, I have to go now. I'll talk to you soon.

Lisa

Choose the correct one.

20. "__________ cold?" "Yes. Could you turn on the heater, please?"
a) Are you feeling b) Are you feel c) Does you feel d) Do you feeling

21. "__________ a basketball player." "Is she tall?"
a) Mary are b) Mary does c) Mary is d) Is Mary

22. Mr. Thompson is a professor. He __________ math at a university.
a) is teach b) teaching c) teaches d) does teaches

23. My leg is hurt, so __________ at all this week.
a) I don't jog b) I'm not jogging c) I'm jogging d) I jog

24. __________ in the office at the moment. Please leave a message.
a) I'm not b) I am c) I don't d) I doesn't

25. Water __________ most of the earth. The rest is land.
a) covers b) is covering c) cover d) is cover

26. Jessica is in the garden. __________ the flowers now.
a) She isn't smelling b) She is smelling c) She smells d) She smell

Choose the incorrect one.

27. "Is this your jacket?" "No, it doesn't mine. I think it's Jane's."
a) b) c) d)

28. This milk isn't tasting good. When did you buy it?
a) b) c) d)

29. My house is very old, so I am plan to move into a new house.
a) b) c) d)

30. "Are you and your brother like sports?" "Yes. We play hockey every Sunday."
a) b) c) d)

31. Jill is in Hawaii on vacation. She has a good time with her family there.
a) b) c) d)

32. "Are you be honest right now?" "Yes. I'm not lying to you."
a) b) c) d)

Answers p.328

If you are not sure about some answers, go back to the following lessons:

Question	1	2	3	4	5	6	7	8	9	10	11	12	13	14	15	16
Lesson	1	3	1	2	3	2	5	5	5	5	5	5	5	5	5	5
Question	**17**	**18**	**19**	**20**	**21**	**22**	**23**	**24**	**25**	**26**	**27**	**28**	**29**	**30**	**31**	**32**
Lesson	5	4	4	4	1	3	5	1	5	4	1	4	2	4	4	2

Test 02

 Complete the conversations with the words in *italics*. Use the *past simple* or *past progressive*.

1. A: *(you, see)* *Did you see* ______ Christine at the party last Friday?
   B: *(she, dance)* Yes. ______ with someone when I saw her.
2. A: *(you, not work)* ______ when I got to the shop two hours ago.
   B: *(I, have)* I ______ dinner.
3. A: *(you, get)* I sent you an e-mail yesterday. ______ it?
   B: *(I, not check)* ______ my e-mail yesterday. Was it important?
4. A: *(you, turn off)* Why ______ the radio?
   B: *(you, listen)* Sorry. ______ to it?
5. A: *(I, meet)* ______ Tara at the mall by chance this morning.
   B: *(she, shop)* ______ again?
6. A: *(Mark, not visit)* ______ me when I was at the hospital.
   B: *(he, want)* ______ to see you, but he was really busy that week.

 Complete the sentences with the verbs in the box using **used to** or the *present simple*. Write negative sentences if necessary.

drink	~~have~~	play	prepare	spend	wear

7. I *used to have* ______ a lot of comic books, but I lost most of them.
8. Karen always ______ dinner for us, and I always wash the dishes.
9. Timothy ______ glasses, but now he can't see well without them.
10. "______ Mr. Lopez ______ guitar in the band?" "No. He's the drummer."
11. I ______ alcohol because it gives me a headache.
12. "______ you and Julia ______ a lot of time together when you were little?" "Not really, but we do a lot of things together now.

 Find and change any mistakes in each sentence. Put ✓ if the sentence is correct.

Aaron's Diary May 5, 2019

By Aaron Rogers

13. I ~~was waking~~ *woke* up at 6 o'clock this morning.
14. Helen did yoga when I went to the living room.
15. She's used to jogging every day, but now she practices yoga instead.
16. I was hungry, so I was making some breakfast in the kitchen.
17. While I was cooking eggs, Helen set the table.
18. After breakfast, I was wanting to go for a walk.
19. However, when I opened the door, it was raining. So I stayed inside with Helen.

Choose the correct one.

20. "Jake ________________ at Anna on the street last night." "Why? Did Anna do something wrong?"
   a) was shouting b) were shouting c) is shouting d) shouts

21. "Why were you running this morning?" "________________ late for school."
   a) I did b) I didn't c) I wasn't d) I was

22. I ________________ anything when I went to the auction a week ago.
   a) didn't buy b) bought c) don't buy d) wasn't buying

23. Maria ________________ in Japan when she had her daughter. She was in Beijing.
   a) was living b) lived c) wasn't living d) not living

24. When Joseph ________________ up suddenly, everyone looked at him.
   a) stands b) is standing c) wasn't standing d) stood

25. I ________________ well yesterday, so I didn't go to work.
   a) was feeling b) wasn't feeling c) felt d) don't feel

26. I tried to call you several times around 10 o'clock. What ________________ then?
   a) do you do b) did you do c) are you doing d) were you doing

Choose the incorrect one.

27. "Were you in town last weekend?" "No, I traveled in Canada."
   a) Were b) you c) traveled d) in

28. I saw a bear while I was hiking. I told Daniel, but he wasn't believing me.
   a) saw b) was hiking c) told d) wasn't believing

29. Somebody called my name while Betty and I walked across the street this morning.
   a) called b) while c) walked d) across

30. "There were some difficult questions during my job interview." "What were they ask you?"
   a) were b) during c) were d) ask

31. "Did Sarah and Jason at the meeting this afternoon?" "No, they weren't."
   a) Did b) at the meeting c) they d) weren't

32. My wife and I moved to Atlanta in 2009, and we was buying this house in 2010.
   a) moved b) in c) we d) was buying

Answers **p.328**

If you are not sure about some answers, go back to the following lessons:

Question	1	2	3	4	5	6	7	8	9	10	11	12	13	14	15	16
Lesson	7	7	7	7	7	7	9	9	9	9	9	9	7	8	9	7
Question	17	18	19	20	21	22	23	24	25	26	27	28	29	30	31	32
Lesson	8	7	8	7	6	7	7	8	7	7	7	7	8	6	6	7

 Complete the sentences with the given words using the *present perfect* or *past simple*. Write negative sentences if necessary.

eat	hurt	play	rain	read	~~see~~

1. *(we)* *We didn't see* ______________ Tony at the office last night. He wasn't there.
2. *(I)* "______________ golf since I was 12 years old."
   "You must be really good."
3. *(you)* "______________ a lot of books when you were young?"
   "Yes. I loved books."
4. *(it)* ______________ for months. It's very dry.
5. *(Mr. Young)* ______________ his leg a week ago, but he's OK now.
6. *(she)* I'm making a hamburger for Jenny. ______________ dinner yet.

 Complete the sentences with the words in *italics*. Use the *present perfect* or *present perfect progressive*.

7. *(Allison, try)* *Allison has tried* ______________ sushi twice. She liked it both times.
8. *(Jack, work)* ______________ at the bank since 2012. He really enjoys it.
9. *(you, stay)* "How many times ______________ at this hotel?" "This is my second time."
10. *(I, not study)* ______________ Spanish very long, but I'm improving every day.
11. *(you, live)* "How long ______________ in this apartment?" "About six months."
12. *(I, not travel)* "Let's go to Paris this summer."
    "That sounds like fun. ______________ to Europe before."

Complete the sentences with the verbs in *italics*. Use the *past perfect* or *past simple*.

My Trip to Denver

By Sam Carter

13. *(go)* I *went* ______________ to Denver in December for a ski trip.
14. *(arrive)* When I got there, my friend Tom ______________ at the resort already.

We skied together for three days.

15. *(meet)* On our last day there, we ______________ some interesting people.
16. *(move)* They ______________ to Denver two years before.

They said they were really enjoying their lives there.

17. *(take)* They ______________ us to the Cherry Tree Shopping Center that night.
18. *(do, have)* We ______________ some shopping at the mall and ______________ dinner together.
19. *(return, leave)* We ______________ to the hotel by taxi because the last bus ______________ already.

Anyway, Tom and I had a lot of fun in Denver. We are planning to go there again next year.

Choose the correct one.

20. "I ________________ to Jacob's house before. How about you?" "I've visited him a few times."
a) haven't gone b) haven't been c) don't go d) hadn't go

21. Edison ________________ the light bulb in 1879.
a) invented b) had invented c) has invented d) has been inventing

22. ________________ the street already when Terry called my name. I didn't hear him.
a) I have crossed b) I haven't crossed c) I have been crossing d) I had crossed

23. "Where are our drinks?" "The waiter ________________ them yet."
a) has brought b) had brought c) hadn't brought d) hasn't brought

24. Ian and Laura ________________ the house when we got home. It was very neat.
a) have cleaned b) have been cleaning c) had cleaned d) are cleaning

25. "________________ well last night?" "Not at all. I had a nightmare."
a) Did you sleep b) Have you slept
c) Have you been sleeping d) Had you slept

26. "You look very fit. ________________ out since I saw you last time?" "Yes. Every evening after work."
a) Did you work b) Have you been working
c) Do you work d) Had you worked

Choose the incorrect one.

27. That film is(a) very good. Maria and I had(b) seen(c) it(d) several times.

28. I haven't(a) climbed a mountain before(b) I hiked(c) Mt Fuji. It was(d) my first time.

29. Daniel didn't spend(a) much(b) money lately. He's(c) saving(d) to buy a new car.

30. Have(a) you talked(b) to Professor Lim since(c) you have graduated(d) from college?

31. "Is(a) Mr. Jackson in his office?" "He has(b) been(c) to the bank. He'll be(d) back in a few minutes."

32. Ms. Green makes(a) amazing pies! They are(b) the best(c) pies I ever taste(d).

Answers p.328

If you are not sure about some answers, go back to the following lessons:

Question	1	2	3	4	5	6	7	8	9	10	11	12	13	14	15	16
Lesson	12	12	12	12	12	12	14	14	14	14	14	14	15	15	15	15
Question	17	18	19	20	21	22	23	24	25	26	27	28	29	30	31	32
Lesson	15	15	15	11	12	15	12	15	12	13	11	15	14	10	11	11

Put the words in *italics* in the correct order. Use **will** or the *present simple.*

1. *(with my parents / live / I)*
   I'll live with my parents ______ until I get a job.
2. *(the fashion show / after / watch / we)*
   ______, we are going to shop at the mall.
3. *(the children / I / take / not)*
   ______ to the doctor if they feel better this afternoon.
4. *(lose / he / 10 pounds / until)*
   Jim will exercise every day ______.
5. *(tell / you / me)*
   "______ when my package arrives?" "Of course."
6. *(red wine / the restaurant / sell / if / not)*
   ______, we'll go to a wine bar after dinner.

Complete the conversations with the words in *italics* using **will** or the *future progressive*. Write negative sentences if necessary.

7. A: I think I'll arrive around 5.
   B: *(I, wait)* OK. *I'll be waiting* ______ for you in the lobby at that time.
8. A: I'm already full. I don't want these french fries.
   B: *(I, eat)* Are you sure? Then ______ them.
9. A: Can I call you at 6?
   B: *(I, drive)* ______ home then. Please call me at 7.
10. A: *(you, swim)* ______ already when I get to the hotel?
    B: Yes. Come and see me at the pool.
11. A: Did you win the competition?
    B: *(we, know)* I hope so, but ______ until next week.
12. A: *(Mr. Perez, teach)* ______ us in May.
    B: Is he quitting?

Complete the sentences with the words in *italics*. Use **will** or the *future perfect*.

Hello Cindy,

AIR MAIL

How are you these days?

13. *(I, finish)* I'm busy doing my graduation work now, but *I'll have finished* ______ it by next week.
14. *(I, graduate)* As you know, ______ from college next month.
15. *(I, study)* By the time I graduate, ______ in Korea for five years!

Anyway, I met a man here and his name is Eric.

16. *(we, get)* ______ married next year.
17. *(we, date)* ______ for six months by the end of this month.

He's always nice to me.

18. *(Eric and I, leave)* By the time you get this letter, ______ for a trip to Japan.
19. *(I, send)* ______ you a postcard there.

Catherine

Choose the correct one.

20. ______________ to this store again. The staff is so rude.
a) I think I'll come b) I don't think I won't come
c) I don't think I come d) I don't think I'll come

21. "Do you and Dan need a ride to the airport?" "No, thanks. ______________ a taxi."
a) We take b) We'll take c) We'll have taken d) Will we take

22. You should fasten your seatbelt. The plane ______________ land.
a) will be about to b) be about to c) is about to d) is to about

23. ______________ for a walk tonight. I'm really tired.
a) I'll go b) I'll have gone c) I won't go d) I won't have gone

24. "When ______________?" "At 9 a.m."
a) does the bank open b) will the bank have opened
c) is the bank be opening d) is the bank open

25. All of the leaves ______________ by the time winter comes.
a) will be falling b) will have fallen c) are going to fall d) will fall

26. We ______________ 10 songs at the concert, but we only did five.
a) are going to perform b) will perform c) will be performing d) were going to perform

Choose the incorrect one.

27. "Jake and I are going to the cinema tonight." "Great. What movie do you watch?"
a) Jake and I b) are c) going d) do you watch

28. Janice wasn't going to return to work until next Friday because she is on summer vacation.
a) wasn't b) going to c) return d) is

29. "Will you be believing me if I tell you a true story?" "Yes. I promise."
a) Will b) be believing c) tell d) promise

30. "Sam went to medical school." "Really? I thought he will be going to become a lawyer."
a) went b) thought c) will be d) to become

31. "While you are going to make the salad, I'll set the table." "Thanks. That will help a lot."
a) are b) going to make c) I'll set d) will

32. Brian has an appointment at noon today, so he won't have joined us for lunch.
a) has b) won't c) have joined d) for lunch

Answers p.328

If you are not sure about some answers, go back to the following lessons:

Question	1	2	3	4	5	6	7	8	9	10	11	12	13	14	15	16
Lesson	21	21	21	21	21	21	19	19	19	19	19	19	20	20	20	20
Question	**17**	**18**	**19**	**20**	**21**	**22**	**23**	**24**	**25**	**26**	**27**	**28**	**29**	**30**	**31**	**32**
Lesson	20	20	20	16	16	18	16	18	20	17	18	17	19	17	21	19

Put the words in *italics* in the correct order.

1. *(right / may / you / be)*
   "I think the movie starts at 7, not 8."
   " You may be right ______. Let me check."
2. *(submit / have / do / my résumé / I / to)*
   " ______ online?" "You can also send it by mail."
3. *(a bike / be / to / I / able / ride / will)*
   ______ soon. Sam promised to teach me.
4. *(we / meet / should)*
   "Where ______?" "Let's meet at the café downtown."
5. *(much time / Tony / been / has / able / spend / to)*
   ______ with you since he quit his job?
6. *(open / not / the windows / better / had / we)*
   ______. It's raining harder now.

Complete the sentences with the correct words in *italics* and the verbs in the box. Write negative sentences if necessary.

be	buy	~~drive~~	get up	pass	turn off

7. *(had better / have to)* You 'd better not drive ______ so fast or you might get a speeding ticket.
8. *(could / was able to)* The math test was very difficult, but I ______ it.
9. *(had better / should)* We ______ that sofa. It looks very comfortable.
10. *(could / might)* "Is this your key?" "It ______ mine. Mine's in my pocket."
11. *(might / must)* You ______ your cell phone. The plane is about to take off.
12. *(must / have to)* Jeff ______ now because he has only afternoon classes.

Complete the sentences with the given words. Use **have + past participle** if necessary.

ask	~~be~~	forget	get	make	read	start

Dear Dan,

Did you get your essay score?

13. *(could not)* My score is too low, so it couldn't be ______ right.

I made some good points.

14. *(might)* I think Professor Reed ______ a mistake when he graded my essay.
15. *(should)* ______ I ______ him about it?

I've attached my essay. Please let me know your opinion.

Dear Cindy,

16. *(must not)* You ______ his comments carefully.

Your score was low because you did not have a conclusion.

17. *(should not)* You ______ to include a conclusion next time.
18. *(might)* Or you ______ another low score.
19. *(could)* And you ______ with a better introduction before you mentioned your main point. I hope you do better next time.

Choose the correct one.

20. "__________ speak Chinese?" "Yes. They took classes when they were young."
    a) Can your children be able to b) Can your children to
    (c) Are your children able to d) Are able your children to

21. This bag is very light. It __________ many things in it.
    a) must have b) must not have c) must have had d) must not have had

22. Sam __________ an umbrella this morning. He got wet because he didn't have one.
    a) should have taken b) shouldn't have taken c) should take d) shouldn't take

23. I __________ at the hospital for a few days last month because I got hurt in a car accident.
    a) have to stay b) don't have to stay c) had to stay d) didn't have to stay

24. Our team didn't practice very much. We __________ the game.
    a) have to lose b) were able to lose c) could lose d) had better lose

25. Sandra's boss is in an important meeting right now. She __________ disturb him.
    a) had better not b) had better c) should d) doesn't have to

26. Melanie __________ here last week. She was in Canada.
    a) might not have been b) may not have been c) shouldn't have been d) couldn't have been

Choose the incorrect one.

27. "Laura could (a) find (b) her purse. It's gone." "She must (c) have been (d) very upset." — (a)

28. "Tanya must (a) be very angry at Aaron." "I think (b) so. He may (c) not have damaged (d) her car."

29. Eric might not (a) clean (b) his room yesterday. He had to (c) do (d) his homework.

30. "I just heard (a) that Steve is sick, so I'll must (b) visit him tonight." "Can (c) I come (d) with you?"

31. "Where's (a) Lynn?" "She could leave (b) for lunch. Do you have to (c) see (d) her now?"

32. You don't have to (a) run (b) around the swimming pool. You may (c) fall down and get (d) hurt.

Answers p.329

If you are not sure about some answers, go back to the following lessons:

Question	1	2	3	4	5	6	7	8	9	10	11	12	13	14	15	16
Lesson	24	26	22	27	22	28	28	22	28	24	26	26	23	24	27	25
Question	17	18	19	20	21	22	23	24	25	26	27	28	29	30	31	32
Lesson	27	24	23	22	25	27	26	23	28	23	22	27	24	26	23	26

Test 06

Complete the sentences with the words in *italics*. Use the *present simple* or *past simple*.

1. *(the bus, stop)* Does the bus stop ____________ near my house?
2. *(what, you, study)* ____________ in college?
3. *(you, come)* ____________ to this restaurant often?
4. *(when, the bank, open)* ____________?
5. *(I, call)* ____________ you too late?
6. *(where, you, go)* ____________ shopping for clothes?

No. It goes the opposite direction.
I majored in politics.
Yes. I usually eat here.
At 9 o'clock on weekdays.
No. I was awake.
I often go to the department store.

Put **what/who/which** and the words in *italics* in the correct order.

7. *(the flight / has / delayed)*
"What has delayed the flight ____________?" "There is a lot of fog outside."
8. *(give / we / should)*
"____________ a tip to?" "That waiter with glasses. He was so nice."
9. *(is / computer / yours)*
"____________, this one or that one?" "This one."
10. *(order / you / are / to / going)*
"____________ for dinner?" "What about Chinese noodles?"
11. *(you / helped)*
"____________ with your assignment?" "Dan. He was very helpful."
12. *(enjoy / sport / does / Tom)*
____________ more, basketball or tennis?

Put the words in *italics* in the correct order.

To	dawncollins@fastmail.com
From	terryallen@fastmail.com

Hello. I have some questions about your dance classes. I hope you can help.
My main goal is to lose some weight.
13. *(which / is / dance)* So can you tell me which dance is ____________ the best for losing weight?
14. *(should / class / whose / I / take)* Also, I wonder ____________.
I've heard good things about Ms. Wright.
15. *(she / does / what / teach / kind of dance)* ____________?
16. *(her class / be / will / if)* I'm not sure ____________ too difficult for me.
17. *(I / must / when / register)* And ____________ for a class if I want to start in September?
18. *(open / you / are)* Oh, and one more question. ____________ on Sundays?
Thank you in advance!
Terry Allen

Choose the correct one.

19. "________ your dress for the party?" "Yes. I'm going to wear the blue one."
a) Have you choose b) Have chosen you c) Have you chosen d) You chosen have

20. "________ from here?" "It takes 20 minutes on foot."
a) How your school is b) How far is your school
c) How far your school is d) How your school is far

21. "________ my wedding invitation?" "Yes. I just received it this morning."
a) Did you get not b) Don't you got c) Didn't get you d) Didn't you get

22. "________ do you usually listen to?" "Bruno Dars's."
a) Whose songs b) What songs c) Which songs d) How songs

23. "I'd like to know ________ an ATM on this floor." "There's one near the elevator."
a) if is there b) if there is c) where there be d) where is there

24. "Gary and Louise were at the meeting, ________ they?" "I'm not sure."
a) weren't b) didn't c) were d) did

25. Can you tell me ________ improve my writing?
a) how can I b) what can I c) how I can d) what I can

Choose the incorrect one.

26. "Why you did stay home last weekend?" "I wasn't feeling very well."
a) b) c) d)

27. "The cookies are ready. Who do you want one?" "I do!"
a) b) c) d)

28. "Charlie didn't wake up until late, does he?" "No. He got up after lunch time."
a) b) c) d)

29. "Aren't your parents in town this weekend?" "Yes, they aren't."
a) b) c) d)

30. "To where do I have to send this package to?" "To Jacob's office in New York."
a) b) c) d)

31. "How do you go to the movies?" "About once a week. How about you?"
a) b) c) d)

32. "Is Kevin at school now?" "I'm not sure whether did he go to school today."
a) b) c) d)

Answers p.329

If you are not sure about some answers, go back to the following lessons:

Question	1	2	3	4	5	6	7	8	9	10	11	12	13	14	15	16
Lesson	29	29	29	29	29	29	30	30	30	30	30	30	31	31	30	31
Question	**17**	**18**	**19**	**20**	**21**	**22**	**23**	**24**	**25**	**26**	**27**	**28**	**29**	**30**	**31**	**32**
Lesson	29	29	29	29	32	29	31	32	31	29	30	32	32	29	29	31

Test 07

 Complete the conversations with the verbs in *italics* using the active or passive. Use the *present simple* or *past simple*.

1. Whose hat is that? — *(find)* I don't know. I *found* ________ it under the sofa.
2. Is Teresa single? — *(marry)* No. She ________.
3. How was your job interview? — *(not ask)* It was OK. I ________ many questions.
4. Your house is always tidy. — *(clean)* Peter ________ it every day.
5. Those buildings look very old. — *(build)* They ________ 50 years ago.
6. Is John at the airport now? — *(not arrive)* No. His flight ________ until 8 o'clock.

Put the words in *italics* in the correct order.

7. *(chosen / not / Mr. Clark / be / might)*
   " *Mr. Clark might not be chosen* ________ as the mayor of this city." "Why do you say that?"
8. *(being / the package / shipped / is)*
   " ________ by airmail?" "Yes. So you'll get it soon."
9. *(the meeting / been / had / arranged)*
   ________ for 6 o'clock, but Dan didn't appear.
10. *(will / the renovations / not / be / completed)*
    " ________ until next month." "It's taking longer than I expected."
11. *(were / menus / being / handed)*
    ________ out by the waiters.
12. *(have / postponed / all of today's games / been)*
    ________ due to bad weather?"
    "Yes. They announced it about 10 minutes ago."

 Complete the sentences with the words in *italics* using the active or passive. Use the *present simple* and add **to** if necessary.

Mr. Miller's Cooking School

By Jacob Gardeners

13. *(Mr. Miller, own)* *Mr. Miller owns* ________ a cooking school.
14. *(various classes, offer)* ________ the students there.
15. *(the students, teach)* ________ both traditional and modern cooking styles.
16. *(some scholarships, give)* ________ the top students.
17. *(the school, send)* Also, ________ the top student to a famous restaurant for an internship after graduation!
18. *(the intern, not pay)* ________ any money, but he or she gets valuable experience.
19. *(Mr. Miller, hope)* Because of the school's success, ________ to open another cooking school within the next five years.

Choose the correct one.

20. Those clothes are beautiful. __________ by a famous designer?
    a) Did they design b) Did they designed c) Were they design d) Were they designed

21. The music festival __________ yet. It lasts until Sunday night.
    a) isn't finished b) isn't finish c) wasn't finished d) doesn't finish

22. At the Christmas celebration, all of the children __________.
    a) were given to presents b) were given presents
    c) were given by presents d) were giving to presents

23. "I like this song, but it __________ at tonight's concert." "Why not?"
    a) won't be performed b) won't perform c) will be performed d) will perform

24. "I heard you had an accident. Are you OK?" "I'm fine. I __________."
    a) didn't be injured b) didn't injure c) didn't get injured d) didn't injured

25. __________ when nobody was inside?
    a) Did the robbery occurred b) Did the robbery occur
    c) Was the robbery occurred d) Was the robbery occur

26. That website is very popular. It __________ by millions of people.
    a) has visited b) hasn't visited c) has been visited d) visited

Choose the incorrect one.

27. "This food tastes really good." "All the dishes were prepared of my wife."
    a) tastes b) were c) prepared d) of

28. I received a letter but I couldn't read it. It didn't write in English.
    a) received b) couldn't read c) didn't write d) in English

29. "Are these your pens?" "No. They are belonged to Peter."
    a) Are b) these c) They d) are belonged

30. "Did you be invited to Tom's birthday party?" "Yes. Are you going too?"
    a) be b) invited c) Tom's d) Are you

31. The actor didn't know by a lot of people five years ago, but now he is very famous.
    a) didn't know b) a lot of people c) five years ago d) he is

32. "Are you still working?" "No. I did. I'm leaving in a minute."
    a) Are b) working c) did d) leaving

Answers p.329

If you are not sure about some answers, go back to the following lessons:

Question	1	2	3	4	5	6	7	8	9	10	11	12	13	14	15	16
Lesson	33	34	35	33	33	33	33	33	33	33	33	33	33	35	35	35
Question	**17**	**18**	**19**	**20**	**21**	**22**	**23**	**24**	**25**	**26**	**27**	**28**	**29**	**30**	**31**	**32**
Lesson	33	35	33	33	34	35	33	34	34	33	34	33	34	34	33	34

 Put the words in *italics* in the correct order using **-ing** or **to** . . .

1. *(read / I / it / not / suggest)*
   "Look! Here's Marie's diary." "I suggest not reading it ______. She'll be very upset."
2. *(for / it / her / is / get up / difficult)*
   "Why is Janet always late?" "I think ______ in the morning."
3. *(you / decide / did / study / not)*
   "I'm not taking Japanese classes." "Why not? ______ in Japan?"
4. *(are / busy / they / prepare)*
   I haven't seen Tom and Sarah for days. ______ for their wedding.
5. *(order / the last train / in / not / miss)*
   You should leave soon ______.
6. *(you / would / make / not / mind)*
   ______ so much noise? Jessica is sleeping.

Complete the sentences with the verbs in *italics*. Use **-ing** / **to + base form** or **being + past participle** / **to be + past participle**.

7. *(retire)* "Do you hope to be retired ______ when you're 60?" "Yes, I do."
8. *(sing)* I'm too shy. I can't imagine ______ at a party.
9. *(wash)* My pants are so dirty. They need ______.
10. *(quit)* "Jake promised ______ smoking." "That's good news."
11. *(catch)* The thieves avoided ______, so they got away with the money.
12. *(choose)* "Dan looks depressed." "He failed ______ as the captain of the hockey team."

Complete the sentences with the words in *italics*. Use the *present simple*.

To	terryallen@fastmail.com
From	dawncollins@fastmail.com

Hi Terry. Thank you for your e-mail.

13. *(want, lose)* If you want to lose ______ some weight, the Tango is your best option.
14. *(invite, you, attend)* So we ______ one of our three new Tango classes this fall.
15. *(recommend, take)* If you're a beginner, we ______ the Tuesday night class. No experience is necessary for that one.
16. *(consider, sign)* If you already have some experience, then ______ up for our class on Wednesday night. That one is taught by Ms. Wright.
17. *(decide, join)* If you ______ her class, you'll receive a 10% discount.
18. *(remember, register)* Please ______ before August 20 if you want to start in September.

And yes, we are open on Sundays.

19. *(learn)* You can visit our website ______ more about these great opportunities.

Best wishes,
Dawn Collins, Uptown Dance Studios

Choose the correct one.

20. "It was a pleasure ________ you." "Me too. Let's meet again soon."
a) for meeting b) meet c) to meet d) to meeting

21. "I'll ________ me up after work. You don't have to give me a ride." "Oh, OK."
a) get Sharon pick b) get Sharon picked
c) get Sharon picking d) get Sharon to pick

22. "What is that man doing on the roof?" "He appears ________ something."
a) to be fixed b) to be fixing c) being fixed d) being fixing

23. I have a cold, but it isn't bad. It won't stop me ________ out tonight.
a) going b) to go c) of going d) from going

24. Something was wrong with my computer, so I ________ at it for me.
a) had Steven looking b) had Steven looked
c) had Steven look d) had Steven to look

25. The boy admitted ________ the vase. He promised to be more careful.
a) having broken b) having breaking c) to have broken d) to break

26. "Is it ________ the cookies out of the oven?" "Not yet."
a) time taking b) time to take c) to take time d) taking time

Choose the incorrect one.

27. "I'm not sure where(a) hanging(b) this picture." "I feel like(c) hanging(d) it on that wall."

28. I bought(a) this knife to cut(b) vegetables, but it isn't very good(c) for cut(d) them.

29. "Did you get(a) the wall paint(b)?" "Yes. It took(c) two days to get(d) it done.

30. I always set(a) my alarm before(b) going(c) to bed not to oversleep(d) in the morning.

31. "I couldn't help(a) to notice(b) your dress. It's beautiful." "It's very kind of you(c) to say(d) that."

32. We can't(a) afford to having(b) breakfast today. We need to attend(c) a meeting(d) at 7 a.m.

Answers **p.329**

If you are not sure about some answers, go back to the following lessons:

Question	1	2	3	4	5	6	7	8	9	10	11	12	13	14	15	16
Lesson	37	43	38	46	42	37	38	37	39	38	37	38	38	40	37	37
Question	**17**	**18**	**19**	**20**	**21**	**22**	**23**	**24**	**25**	**26**	**27**	**28**	**29**	**30**	**31**	**32**
Lesson	38	39	42	36	41	38	40	41	37	42	44	45	41	42	46	46

Test 09

Put the words in *italics* in the correct order using the *present simple*. Change the word forms if necessary.

1. *(person / visit / many)*
   Busan is one of the most beautiful places in Korea. *Many people visit* the city every year.
2. *(hair / a few / be)*
   "__________ on the floor." "Really? I'll vacuum the floor then."
3. *(help / the news)*
   I like watching the news. __________ us understand what is happening in the world.
4. *(cost / of / two / cake / piece)*
   This bakery is so expensive. __________ $15.
5. *(wood / be)*
   __________ used to make many kinds of furniture.
6. *(some / contain / juice)*
   __________ a lot of sugar. For example, grape juice is sweeter than orange juice.

Complete the sentences with the nouns in the box. Add **a/an** or use the plural form if necessary.

article	flower	furniture	picture	~~travel~~

7. Jason and I really enjoy *travel*. We take many __________ of the sights we visit.
8. Jim gave us __________ for our wedding gift. He bought us a bed and two chairs.
9. There's __________ about gardening in this magazine. It explains how to grow __________.

assignment	glass	e-mail	ice	team

10. "May I have __________ of water, please?" "Sure. Do you want some __________ in it?"
11. My __________ won first prize in the competition. We received congratulations from many people.
12. I got __________ from Jenny. I haven't replied to it yet because I have a lot of __________ to do.

Find and change any mistakes in each sentence. Put ✓ if the sentence is correct.

The Daily News

October 15, 2018

Robbery at the Lakeview Mall

13. Two ~~thief~~ *thieves* broke into the Lakeview Mall last weekend.
14. The robbery happened when the staffs had already gone home.
15. The thieves stole a lot of money and some jewelries.
16. They also took an antique lamp and a pair of binoculars.
17. Fortunately, the thieves were caught by the polices yesterday.
18. And the stolen items was found in a room in their house.

Choose the correct one.

19. "Why are you so late?" "__________ on the road."
    a) There were too much traffic
    b) There were too much traffics
    c) There was too much traffic
    d) There was too much traffics

20. "Does our room have __________ of the beach?" "Yes, it does."
    a) view b) a view c) a scenery d) sceneries

21. "Was Kathy interested in __________ from an early age?" "Not really."
    a) politic b) a politic c) some politics d) politics

22. Julie added __________ to the mixing bowl to make some cookies.
    a) three cups of flours b) three cup of flours c) three cup of flour d) three cups of flour

23. "__________ on this website might be helpful for your essay." "Thanks. I'll check it out."
    a) the information b) an information c) informations d) the informations

24. __________ very important for growing plants. They can't grow without it.
    a) Lights are b) A light are c) Light is d) A Light is

25. "__________ very soft and comfortable." "They are. They're made of cotton."
    a) Your pajamas look b) Your pajama look c) Your pajamas looks d) Your pajama looks

Choose the incorrect one.

26. "Do you have(a) any baggages(b), sir?" "Yes. I have two small(c) suitcases(d)."

27. It's easy to learn vocabularies(a), but it's hard to speak(b) complete sentences(c) fluently(d).

28. "What did you buy(a) at the mall(b) yesterday?" "I bought two pairs(c) of pant(d)."

29. Frank didn't have(a) times(b) to repair his(c) glasses(d).

30. The beautiful(a) surrounding(b) of Mount Fuji are(c) great for taking photos(d).

31. The audiences(a) cheered(b) at the concert while the rock band(c) was performing its music(d).

32. Don't forget your belonging(a) in the airport(b). Cell phones(c) are(d) often left behind.

Answers p.330

If you are not sure about some answers, go back to the following lessons:

Question	1	2	3	4	5	6	7	8	9	10	11	12	13	14	15	16
Lesson	47	48	48	48	48	47	49/47	49	49/47	48	50	49	47	50	49	50
Question	17	18	19	20	21	22	23	24	25	26	27	28	29	30	31	32
Lesson	50	47	47	49	48	48	48	48	50	49	49	50	48	50	50	50

 Complete the sentences with **a/an** or **the** and the nouns in the box.

essay	manager	pharmacist	radio	table	~~umbrella~~

1. It's raining heavily outside. Did you bring _an umbrella_ ____________?
2. "Are you listening to ____________?" "No. You can turn it off."
3. ____________ is someone who sells medicine.
4. "Who is ____________ of your department?" "His name is Peter West."
5. "What are you writing?" "It's ____________. It's for my English class."
6. Sarah bought me ____________. I think I'll use it in my dining room.

 Put the words in *italics* in the correct order. Add **the** if necessary.

7. *(on / fell / ground)* A lot of trees _fell on the ground_ ____________ because of the storm.
8. *(TV / watch)* I usually ____________ on Sundays, but I'm seeing a friend tonight.
9. *(that hotel / at / rooms)* ____________ were very clean. I'd like to go there again.
10. *(breakfast / some cereal / for)* Jane had ____________ this morning.
11. *(were / my neighbors / Smiths)* ____________ until last month. Now they live in Seattle.
12. *(church / attend)* I didn't use to ____________ very often, but I go every week now.

Find and change any mistakes in each sentence. Put ✓ if the sentence is correct.

To	sallyscott@fastmail.com
From	tinaevans@fastmail.com

Hi, Sally!

I haven't heard from you in a long time. How are you?

13. I met ~~the friend~~ _a friend_ on the street yesterday by chance.

14. We used to go to a same school.

15. She's the engineer and works for the government.

16. We decided to go to movies tomorrow. Do you want to go with us?

17. And what are you doing on Saturday?

18. I'm planning to go downtown to buy the present for my mother.

Her birthday is next week. If you can go with me, let me know.

Tina

Choose the correct one.

19. Scientists disagree on how ________________ formed. It's still a mystery.
    a) universe b) the universe c) a universe d) an universe

20. "Did the thief get caught?" "Yes. He's in ________________ now."
    a) prison b) the prison c) a prison d) prisons

21. I don't have any brothers or sisters. I'm ________________ in my family.
    a) only child b) a only child c) the only child d) child only

22. "How do people celebrate ________________ in Korea?" "We spend time with our family."
    a) a New year's Day b) New Year Day c) the New Year's Day d) New Year's Day

23. When I ________________ from work, there was a package on the doorstep.
    a) came home b) came a home c) came to home d) came the home

24. "I bought a laptop yesterday." "What model is ________________? Is it a good one?"
    a) a laptop b) the laptop c) laptop d) laptops

25. ________________ consists of 12 months, which is 365 days.
    a) The year b) Year c) A year d) Years

Choose the incorrect one.

26. "Do you go to the work by bus?" "Yes. It's the most convenient way."
    a) the b) work c) the d) way

27. "I need money to pay the parking fee. Where is nearest bank?" "It's just around the corner."
    a) money b) the parking fee c) nearest bank d) the

28. A health is very important to me, so I eat right and go to the gym every day.
    a) A health b) right c) the gym d) every day

29. Jack always visits his grandparents in a summer. They live in Toronto.
    a) always b) his c) a summer d) in Toronto

30. "Nate will be joining an army in June." "Really? Is he the first soldier in your family?"
    a) an army b) June c) the d) your family

31. Cello is a string instrument like a violin. It makes a lower sound than the violin.
    a) Cello b) a c) a violin d) the violin

32. "Is Jenny in the bed already?" "Yes. She was tired from school."
    a) Is b) the bed c) was d) from school

Answers p.330

If you are not sure about some answers, go back to the following lessons:

Question	1	2	3	4	5	6	7	8	9	10	11	12	13	14	15	16
Lesson	51	53	52	51	52	51	53	53	51	54	54	54	51	53	52	53
Question	**17**	**18**	**19**	**20**	**21**	**22**	**23**	**24**	**25**	**26**	**27**	**28**	**29**	**30**	**31**	**32**
Lesson	54	51	53	54	53	54	54	51	52	54	53	51	54	53	52	54

 Choose the correct one.

1. Have you seen *(mine / my / me)* phone? I think I've lost it.
2. "Which shoes are yours?" "The *(some / ones / them)* over there."
3. "I found this umbrella by the door." "Melissa has one like that. I think it's *(her / she / hers)*."
4. "Can you recommend a watch for my mom's birthday present?" "This pink *(ones / one / it)* is very popular."
5. We've cooked plenty of food for everyone, so please help *(yourselves / yours / you)*.
6. "I hope Pete remembers the meeting time."
   "Laura sits next to Pete. I'm sure she will remind *(him / herself / himself)*."

Put **-'s/of** and the words in *italics* in the correct order.

7. *(this poem / the title)* The title of this poem is "A Summer in Tokyo."
8. *(this month / magazine)* My article will be published in __________. I'm so excited!
9. *(classmate / mine / a)* __________ won a national art contest.
10. *(our house / the roof)* __________ was leaking, so we had it repaired.
11. *(husband / Katie)* __________ is a doctor. He's a very nice man.
12. *(my / necklace / sister)* "I like your jewelry!" "Thank you. This is __________."

Complete the sentences with **her/him**/etc. or **herself/himself**/etc. and the words in *italics*. Leave out **herself/himself**/etc. if possible.

Success Through Hard Work

By Cathy Lewis

When Mark Davis was growing up, his family was very poor.

13. *(take care of)* His parents were always working, so he had to take care of himself.
14. *(look after, cared for)* His sister was too young to __________, so he __________ too.

After high school, he was accepted into college. But his parents couldn't afford the tuition.

15. *(paid for school)* So he found a part-time job and __________.

Even though his life wasn't easy, he never gave up.

Today, he is a famous speaker. He travels around the world giving presentations to teenagers.

16. *(helped)* He says the hardships __________ to become successful.

He even met the president.

17. *(gave him an award)* He __________ for inspiring young people.
18. *(believe in)* At the awards ceremony, he said, "If you __________, you can be successful too!"

Choose the correct one.

19. Mary has to leave work early this afternoon. She has to go to ________________.
    a) dentist's office b) the dentist's c) the dentist office d) dentist

20. "Have fun on your honeymoon!" "Thanks. I'm sure we'll ________________."
    a) enjoy ourselves b) enjoy themselves c) enjoy us d) enjoy yourselves

21. I wanted to drink some milk, but we didn't have ________________ in the fridge.
    a) one b) it c) any d) its

22. "Did you travel to Florida ________________?" "Yes. I went alone."
    a) yourself b) by yourself c) all yourself d) yourselves

23. My new apartment has ________________. It's very convenient.
    a) own its parking space b) its parking space own
    c) parking space own its d) its own parking space

24. The old paintings in this museum are OK, but I prefer ________________ the other museum.
    a) the modern ones in b) the ones modern in c) modern ones in d) modern the ones in

25. "Is that Ryan and Helen's suitcase?" "No. ________________ black, but that one is brown."
    a) Theirs are b) Theirs is c) Their is d) Their are

Choose the incorrect one.

26. "I like your new table." "Thanks. My parents bought it for we."
    a) your b) My parents c) it d) we

27. Cats can be easier to keep than dogs because they can clean them.
    a) can be b) than c) they d) them

28. A your car is blocking the road. Can you move it, please?
    a) A your car b) the road c) you d) it

29. When we were in Bolivia, we visited La Paz. It is Bolivia capital city.
    a) we b) It c) Bolivia d) capital city

30. "The Lees bought a house downtown. I've seen theirs house and it's huge." "I'd like to see it myself."
    a) Lees b) downtown c) theirs d) myself

31. Those pants don't look good on Joel. I think he should wear his black one.
    a) Those b) on Joel c) he d) his black one

32. "Whose briefcase is that? Is it Mr. Roberts?" "I don't know. I'll ask him."
    a) Whose b) that c) Mr. Roberts d) him

Answers p.330

If you are not sure about some answers, go back to the following lessons:

Question	1	2	3	4	5	6	7	8	9	10	11	12	13	14	15	16
Lesson	55	58	55	58	57	57	56	56	56	56	56	56	57	57	57	57
Question	**17**	**18**	**19**	**20**	**21**	**22**	**23**	**24**	**25**	**26**	**27**	**28**	**29**	**30**	**31**	**32**
Lesson	57	57	56	57	58	57	55	58	55	55	57	55	56	55	58	56

Test 12

 Complete the sentences with **some/any/no** and the nouns in the box.

advice	milk	movies	plans	room	~~students~~

1. There are _some students_ ______ on the playground. They are playing football.
2. Katie bought me a new sofa, but my house has ______ for it.
3. "We don't have ______ for the cereal." "Really? I'll go to the store and get some."
4. ______ seemed interesting, so we decided not to watch one.
5. "Have you made ______ for the holidays?" "Yes. I'm visiting my parents."
6. I really need your opinion. Could you give me ______?

Complete the sentences with the words in *italics* using the *present simple*. Add **of** if necessary.

7. *(every, car, need)*
   Every car needs ______ a parking pass to park in this garage.
8. *(either, the parks, seem)*
   ______ perfect for our picnic. I like both.
9. *(all, paper, come)*
   "______ from trees, right?" "Actually, that's not true."
10. *(half, them, be)*
    I bought these apples today, but ______ spoiled.
11. *(both, my children, go)*
    ______ to that high school.
12. *(each, these boxes, cost)*
    "______ $10." "OK. I'll take two of them, please."

 Choose the correct one.

The First Sports News

April 06, 2019

Big Game Next Weekend

13. ((Many) / Any / Much) people are looking forward to the game between the Panthers and the Bears.

It's going to be a great game because they're the strongest teams.

14. *(Both / Neither / Either)* of them has lost a game this season.
15. So it seems that *(either / both / neither)* team could win.
16. Unfortunately, *(each / every / some)* of the players from the Bears are injured.
17. But Bears fans don't have *(some / any / no)* doubt that the Bears will win.

The tickets are selling fast.

18. If you want to see this game, you must hurry because *(few / some / little)* tickets remain.

Choose the correct one.

19. "If you have any problems, you can call me ________." "That's so nice of you."
    a) some time　　b) any time　　c) no time　　d) both time

20. Ronald bought two pairs of shoes, and he paid $50 for ________.
    a) each　　b) many　　c) no　　d) much

21. ________ was in the swimming pool, so we couldn't swim.
    a) Not any water　　b) No water　　c) Not water　　d) None water

22. When Sam arrived at the birthday party, we had already eaten ________.
    a) none cake　　b) any cake　　c) most cake　　d) most of the cake

23. My wife and I come to this café ________. It's our favorite.
    a) a lot of　　b) lots of　　c) a lot　　d) a lots of

24. "I left my phone ________, and I don't remember where." "Did you check in your car?"
    a) somewhere　　b) anywhere　　c) nowhere　　d) everywhere

25. ________ in the store is on sale, but most products are.
    a) Not everything　　b) Nothing　　c) No one　　d) Not everyone

Choose the incorrect one.

26. You eat salad for breakfast every day. You should try different something.
    a) salad　b) every　c) day　d) different something

27. There are over a hundred applicants for the job and each of them are well qualified.
    a) a hundred　b) the job　c) are　d) qualified

28. Tim missed the meeting because nobody didn't tell him about it.
    a) the meeting　b) didn't tell　c) him　d) it

29. We have gotten hardly some rain in weeks. A lot of farmers are worried.
    a) some　b) weeks　c) A lot of　d) farmers

30. I had two exams today, but I didn't do well on neither. Both were so difficult.
    a) exams　b) do well　c) neither　d) Both

31. Judy has to travel a lot on business. That's why she has none pets.
    a) a lot　b) business　c) why　d) none

32. "We have few cheese left. There's not enough for a sandwich." "I ate most of it yesterday."
    a) few　b) not　c) most of　d) it

Answers p.331

If you are not sure about some answers, go back to the following lessons:

Question	1	2	3	4	5	6	7	8	9	10	11	12	13	14	15	16
Lesson	59	60	59	60	59	59	61	64	61	63	64	63	62	64	64	63
Question	**17**	**18**	**19**	**20**	**21**	**22**	**23**	**24**	**25**	**26**	**27**	**28**	**29**	**30**	**31**	**32**
Lesson	59	62	59	61	60	63	62	59	61	59	63	60	59	64	60	63

Test 13

Complete the sentences with the words in the box. Change the adjectives into adverbs if necessary.

~~expensive~~	melting	outdoor	perfect	sudden	surprised

1. "That purse looks *expensive*!" "Actually, it was cheap."
2. "Alice didn't expect to receive the award, but she did." "She must have been very ________."
3. The pianist performed the music ________, so everyone in the audience was impressed.
4. "Do you enjoy playing soccer?" "Not really. I don't like ________ sports."
5. Scientists warn that the ________ ice will cause sea levels to rise.
6. "Where's Cathy?" "I don't know. She left the room ________."

Put the words in *italics* in the correct order. Change the adjectives into adverbs if necessary.

7. *(you / warm / enough / for)*
   "Is the room *warm enough for you*?" "Actually, I feel a little cold."
8. *(us / go / for / too / heavy / to)*
   It's raining ________ on a picnic today. Let's go tomorrow.
9. *(garden / beautiful / such / a)*
   "You have ________, Ms. Taylor." "Thank you."
10. *(that / want / didn't / deep / so / I)*
    Kevin was sleeping ________ to wake him up.
11. *(long / to / too / Katie / for / wear)*
    I think this skirt is ________. Do you have any shorter ones?
12. *(polite / always / Ellie / so / talks)*
    "________ to everyone." "I know. She's never been rude to anyone."

Find and change any mistakes in each sentence. Put ✓ if the sentence is correct.

To	toddbaker@fastmail.com
From	samadams@fastmail.com

Hello Mr. Baker,

I bought a sofa from your store last year.

13. It has been an ~~excellently~~ *excellent* sofa for me. Also, I liked your staff too.

14. I have never met so friendly staff!

15. So the experience was highly satisfied.

16. Anyway, I'm looking for a new table for my dining room.

17. Could you recommend me a suitably table for me?

Oh, and if I decide to buy one, can you deliver it on the weekend?

18. I'm asking this because I usually am at work on weekdays.

I hope I hear from you soon.

Sincerely,

Sam Adams

Choose the correct one.

19. "Look at that __________ sports car!" "Wow. That seems very expensive!"
    a) red nice   b) nice red   c) red nicely   d) nicely red

20. "Do you know who __________ is?" "Yes. That's Emily Brown."
    a) the girl singing on the stage   b) the singing on the stage girl
    c) the girl sung on the stage   d) singing the girl on the stage

21. I'm a twin, but I look __________ from my twin brother.
    a) complete different   b) different complete
    c) differently complete   d) completely different

22. It is __________ by yourself. I'll drive you home.
    a) to walk too dark   b) too walk to dark   c) too dark to walk   c) too darkly to walk

23. "I'm looking for Ms. Green." "She's gone out for lunch. She'll __________."
    a) be soon here   b) be here soon   c) here soon be   d) soon here be

24. I can't study here because there is __________.
    a) too much noise   b) too many noise   c) very much noise   d) very many noise

25. "How was your exam?" "It was __________. Everyone got an A."
    a) so easily test   b) so easy test   c) so easy   d) so easily

Choose the incorrect one.

26. "Jake works so good that I don't need to train him." "That's very convenient."
    a) so b) good c) very d) convenient

27. "Did you receive the signing contract from the buyer?" "Yes. I got it late last night."
    a) receive b) signing c) late d) last

28. Mr. Jones usually lets us speak free during class discussions.
    a) usually lets b) speak c) free d) class discussions

29. "You don't look happily. Is something wrong?" "I'm just too tired."
    a) look b) happily c) too d) tired

30. I accidentally spilled red wine on the carpet. Bring me a towel fastly.
    a) accidentally b) red c) Bring d) fastly

31. "Did you have time enough to finish the test?" "No. The test was so long."
    a) time enough b) to finish c) so d) long

32. Our old house was too small, so we moved to a bigger house recent.
    a) old b) too c) small d) recent

Answers p.331

If you are not sure about some answers, go back to the following lessons:

Question	1	2	3	4	5	6	7	8	9	10	11	12	13	14	15	16
Lesson	69	67	68	65	66	68	72	72	73	73	72	73	69	73	67	65
Question	**17**	**18**	**19**	**20**	**21**	**22**	**23**	**24**	**25**	**26**	**27**	**28**	**29**	**30**	**31**	**32**
Lesson	69	71	65	66	68	72	71	72	73	70	66	70	69	70	72	68

 Complete the sentences with the adjectives/adverbs in the box. Use the comparatives/superlatives or add **as** if necessary.

cold	exciting	little	~~polite~~	smoothly	soon

1. You are *the politest* ______ person I know. You're always kind to everyone.
2. "Which car should I buy?" "The red car. It runs a lot ______ than the black one."
3. Mary cooks with ______ salt than before. She is trying to eat healthy.
4. You'd better finish the report ______ you can, or you won't meet the deadline.
5. My trip to Alaska was fun, but it was ______ place I've ever been to.
6. The end of the musical wasn't ______ the beginning. I was a little disappointed.

Put the words in *italics* in the correct order.

7. *(than / a little / tidier / usual)*
   "Your room looks *a little tidier than usual* ______." "I cleaned it this morning."
8. *(the smartest / one / animals / of)* The dolphin is ______ in the world.
9. *(as / calls / many / as)* The office received ______ it normally do.
10. *(the most / experience / amazing)*
    Riding an elephant was by far ______ I've ever had.
11. *(the other days / twice / as / crowded / as)*
    There are so many people at the restaurant today. It is ______.
12. *(you / the more / will sing / the better / practice / you)*
    "I want to be good at singing." "______."

Complete the sentences with the adjectives/adverbs in *italics*. Use the comparatives/superlatives if necessary.

To	samadams@fastmail.com
From	toddbaker@fastmail.com

Hello Mr. Adams,

As you wanted me to recommend a table, I picked three different tables for you.

	TABLE 1	TABLE 2	TABLE 3
Size	1.5m X 1m	1.2m X 1m	1.4m X 1m
Price	$300	$250	$500
Material	wood	plastic	steel

13. *(cheap)* If price is most important to you, table 2 is *(the) cheapest* ______ of all.
14. *(small)* However, it's slightly ______ than the other two tables. And it's made of plastic.
15. *(expensive)* Table 3 is stronger than the others as it's made of steel, but it's much ______.
16. *(much)* If you want a cheaper one, table 1 doesn't cost as ______ as table 3.
17. *(large)* And it is ______ in our store.
18. *(heavy)* Also, it's not as ______ as table 3 because it's made of wood.

Please call me if you need any more information.

Sincerely,

Todd Baker, Sales Manager

Choose the correct one.

19. Our neighbors are ________________ people in the neighborhood. They have loud parties every night.
    a) the noisiest   b) the noisier   c) the most noisy   d) noisiest

20. I arrived at the café ________________ than Tom, so I ordered our drinks.
    a) a bit early   b) a bit earlier   c) by far early   d) by far earliest

21. I can run almost ________________ as Jack, but he always wins the races.
    a) faster   b) fastest   c) as fast   d) quickly

22. "Who scored ________________ during the soccer game?" "I did."
    a) most goals   b) the more goals   c) the most many goals   d) the most goals

23. Our town was chosen as ________________ city in the country.
    a) the third safest   b) the third safe   c) third the safest   d) the third most safe

24. "Where did you get that wallet? It's ________________." "Janet gave it to me for my birthday."
    a) the same than mine   b) the same mine as   c) the mine same as   d) the same as mine

25. Mr. Jones is popular among students because he's ________________ the other teachers.
    a) less strict as   b) less stricter as   c) less strict than   d) less stricter than

Choose the incorrect one.

26. The sunflowers in my garden have grown (a) very (b) taller than my son. They used to (c) be very short (d).

27. "The math test was as (a) just (b) easy as the science test." "Really? I thought (c) it was more difficult (d)."

28. Jamie can (a) speak (b) Chinese, English, and Korean, but she speaks Chinese the less (c) fluently (d) of all.

29. "Did you enjoy (a) your trip?" "Yes. It was (b) the best (c) vacation in (d) my life."

30. The weather gets (a) warm and warm (b) as (c) spring comes nearer (d).

31. "Is tomorrow's meeting at the same time (a) than (b) the last one?" "No. It starts (c) an hour earlier (d)."

32. The supermarket is having (a) a sale. Food prices are slightly (b) lowest (c) than (d) last week.

Answers p.331

If you are not sure about some answers, go back to the following lessons:

Question	1	2	3	4	5	6	7	8	9	10	11	12	13	14	15	16
Lesson	77	74	74	79	77	78	75	77	78	77	79	75	76	75	75	78
Question	17	18	19	20	21	22	23	24	25	26	27	28	29	30	31	32
Lesson	76	78	77	75	78	76	77	78	74	75	79	77	77	75	78	75

Test 15

 Put **at/on/in** and the words in *italics* in the correct order.

1. *(the world / great places)*
   There are many great places in the world.
2. *(dinner / anything)*
   Janet didn't say ________. Is something wrong with her?
3. *(Friday / the baseball game)*
   "Do you want to watch ________?" "Sure. What time is the game?"
4. *(something / my face)*
   Is there ________? People keep looking at me.
5. *(the hairdresser's / her)*
   "Where did you see Sherry yesterday?" "I saw ________."
6. *(my hometown / years)*
   "I haven't visited ________." "Why not? Is it far from here?"

 Complete the sentences with the words from each box.

concerned	~~difference~~	excellent
look	replied	search

\+

about	after	at
~~between~~	for	to

7. "Is there any difference between these two shirts?" "No. They're the same."
8. Is Sarah busy these days? She hasn't ________ my e-mails for days.
9. Jerry has been sick for a week. We're very ________ him.
10. "Would you ________ my baby while I'm away?" "Sure. I'll take care of him."
11. The ________ the missing dog has been going on for three days.
12. Robin is ________ learning languages. She speaks five languages now.

Choose the correct one.

Welcome to Pan Music School!

13. Are you wondering what to do *(during / with / by)* summer vacation?
Come and learn to play the guitar at Pan Music School!
14. You will perform like a professional *(at / within / until)* two months.
15. *(Thanks to / In spite of / By)* our great instructors, many of our students have been able to play the guitar after only four weeks of training!
16. Or if you want to learn a different instrument *(despite / instead / instead of)*, we'll find a perfect class for you!
17. If you apply for a class *(until / by / in)* the end of this month, you'll get a 10 percent discount.
18. So hurry! This offer is only available *(till / by / on)* August 31.
For directions to our location, please visit www.panmusic.com/location.
19. We are easy to find, and you can come here *(in / by / with)* bus or subway.

Choose the correct one.

20. Is someone cooking __________ the kitchen? I smell something delicious.
    a) at   b) on   c) in   d) within

21. Katie was late for the meeting. She must not have been aware __________ the meeting time.
    a) about   b) at   c) for   d) of

22. I didn't __________ before going to bed last night. I was so sleepy.
    a) turn my clothes on   b) turn my clothes down
    c) take my clothes off   d) put my clothes off

23. "I think the cost __________ entrance to the zoo was $20." "It's $30 now."
    a) between   b) for   c) in   d) of

24. Jim shouted on the phone __________ anger. He might have been fighting with someone.
    a) by   b) with   c) to   d) for

25. "What did you complain __________ at the restaurant?" "The waiter was so rude to me."
    a) about   b) at   c) by   d) to

26. I'd like to go shopping on the weekend __________ watching a movie.
    a) instead of   b) instead   c) due to   d) because of

Choose the incorrect one.

27. "I like that guy singing(a) on(b) the middle of(c) the stage." "Oh, I saw him on(d) TV!"

28. "Do you exercise at(a) the gym on every(b) evening(c)?" "No. Every(d) morning."

29. Timothy came(a) to(b) my wedding despite of(c) his broken(d) leg.

30. I wasn't good for(a) painting before(b) taking(c) lessons in(d) the summer.

31. When(a) we entered to(b) the church, we could(c) see a huge cross on(d) the wall.

32. "Where(a) are my old toys?" "I threw away them(b). You're too(c) old to play with(d) them."

Answers p.331

If you are not sure about some answers, go back to the following lessons:

Question	1	2	3	4	5	6	7	8	9	10	11	12	13	14	15	16
Lesson	81	82	82	80	81	83	90	87	89	87	90	89	84	84	86	86
Question	17	18	19	20	21	22	23	24	25	26	27	28	29	30	31	32
Lesson	84	84	85	80	89	88	90	85	87	86	81	82	86	89	87	88

Put the given words in the correct order.

~~as~~	as	by the time	even though	so that	until

1. *(got / the holidays / closer)*
   I become more excited *as the holidays get closer* ______.
2. *(sit down / can / I)*
   "Would you move your bag ______?" "Oh, sorry. Have a seat."
3. *(on a diet / Lisa / was)*
   ______, she ate lots of food. She was so hungry.
4. *(set / the sun)*
   "Why do the children look so tired?" "They played in the park ______."
5. *(Christmas presents / I / buy)*
   ______ for everyone, I won't have much money left.
6. *(on the phone / was / Tim / talking)*
   ______, the doorbell rang.

Complete the sentences with the words in the box. Add not if necessary.

be scared	know how to cook curry	~~live with my sister~~
travel in Europe	want to gain any more weight	watch the animal show

7. *Living with my sister* ______, I usually have dinner with her.
8. ______, I visited many cities. Paris was the most exciting.
9. Heather joined a running club, ______.
10. ______ of heights, I didn't go skydiving with my friends.
11. "We had a good time ______ at the zoo." "Did you take pictures?"
12. ______, I searched the Internet to find a recipe.

Find and change any mistakes in each sentence. Put ✓ if the sentence is correct.

Follow Your Dreams

By Timothy White

Mary Williams has always been interested in fashion.

13. However, she majored in education ~~while~~ *during* college, and she became a teacher.

14. Despite she was successful as a teacher, she decided to quit and study fashion.

15. By she graduated Parsons Fashion School, she had opened her first fashion design business.

16. As her brother majored in marketing, he helped her to start the business.

17. Mary is busy so that she stays at her office until midnight these days.

18. However, she seems very happy when design clothes.

19. By the time this year will end, she'll start her second business.

Choose the correct one.

20. ________________ Kenneth was walking in the forest, he saw a snake.
    a) Until b) By the time c) Although d) While

21. ________________ a bicycle, you should wear a helmet.
    a) While ride b) Not riding c) When riding d) When ride

22. ________________ the hot weather, we went hiking.
    a) Until b) In spite of c) During c) Although

23. "Could you check the oven ________________ the table?" "OK."
    a) though I set b) while I set c) while I'll set d) though I'll set

24. ________________ the teacher told us yesterday, we don't have class today.
    a) While b) When c) By the time d) As

25. "How does Matt like college?" "He enjoys it ________________ he says it's hard."
    a) in spite of b) despite c) although d) while

26. Sharon is very angry at me. Should I keep apologizing ________________ me?
    a) until she forgives b) until she'll forgive
    c) by the time she forgives d) by the time she'll forgive

Choose the incorrect one.

27. I read(a) many books while(b) my vacation because(c) I had a lot of(d) free time.

28. By(a) Jasmine woke(b) up, everybody had(c) gone out. She watched TV until(d) they came back.

29. Can you look for(a) spelling(b) mistakes as(c) you will check(d) the reports?

30. Charlie's shoes are dirty(a) so(b) that you can't(c) see what(d) color they actually are.

31. There(a) was some traffic as(b) we were going(c) to work. We weren't late, although(d).

32. This money is(a) so that(b) paying the rent. I didn't spend it although(c) I wanted(d) to buy a new bag.

Answers p.332

If you are not sure about some answers, go back to the following lessons:

Question	1	2	3	4	5	6	7	8	9	10	11	12	13	14	15	16
Lesson	92	93	94	91	91	92	95	95	95	95	95	95	91	94	91	92
Question	17	18	19	20	21	22	23	24	25	26	27	28	29	30	31	32
Lesson	93	95	91	91	95	94	91	92	94	91	91	91	92	93	94	93

Test 17

Complete the sentences with the words in *italics*. Add **will** if necessary.

1. *(not find, buy)* Michael lost his wallet. If he *doesn't find* it, he *'ll buy* a new one.
2. *(have, book)* We ________ to wait a long time unless we ________ a table. That restaurant is very popular.
3. *(catch, drink)* If Jamie ________ cold, she always ________ lemon tea.
4. *(ask, accept)* If Ted ________ me on a date, I ________ his offer. I have a boyfriend.
5. *(make, be)* "I'm hungry." "I ________ you some toast if there ________ some bread."
6. *(not go, not feel)* "________ to the party if you ________ well."
   "Well, I might feel better later."

Read the sentences and complete the new ones.

7. I didn't bring my jacket, so I feel cold.
   → *I wouldn't feel cold* if *I had brought my jacket*.
8. I won't go jogging because it's snowing.
   → If ________, ________.
9. Brian forgot about the meeting because I didn't remind him.
   → ________ if ________.
10. We can't send Sam a wedding gift because we don't know his address.
    → ________ if ________.
11. Angela broke her leg, so she is at the hospital.
    → If ________, ________.
12. Timothy didn't study hard, so he couldn't pass the English test.
    → If ________, ________.

Complete the sentences with the words in *italics*. Add **will/would** if necessary.

Hello Kathy,

AIR MAIL

I'm in Osaka now. I'll be here for a couple of days.
I almost missed my flight this morning because I arrived at the airport late.
13. *(not stay, not wake)* If I *hadn't stayed* up so late, I ________ up late.
14. *(not call, miss)* If my dad ________ me, I ________ my flight!
15. *(not rain, visit)* Anyway, if it ________ tomorrow, I ________ the Osaka Market.
16. *(buy, go)* I ________ you a present if I ________ there.
By the way, I ate sushi for dinner. It was very good.
17. *(come, like)* If you ________ with me, you ________ it too.
18. *(be)* I wish we ________ here together. There are lots of interesting places in Osaka.
I hope you have a nice holiday too.

Julia

Choose the correct one.

19. "Ken ________________ this show if he watched it." "I think so too. It's very funny."
a) will enjoy b) enjoy c) would have enjoyed d) would enjoy

20. If ________________ the president, what would you say?
a) you will meet b) you meet c) you met d) you had met

21. I'll ask Jennifer to help me with my assignment if ________________ busy.
a) she isn't b) she wasn't c) she won't be d) she hadn't been

22. Exercise more ________________ to be healthier.
a) if you wanted b) if you want c) if you will want d) if you had wanted

23. I wish I ________________ Spanish. It's a very beautiful language.
a) spoke b) speak c) will speak d) had spoken

24. If your office were closer to mine, I ________________ you a ride every morning. But it's far away.
a) can give b) could give c) could have given d) give

25. If I ________________ a nightmare last night, I could have slept well.
a) had had b) didn't have c) don't have d) hadn't had

Choose the incorrect one.

26. If you'll wash the dishes, I'll do the laundry.
a) you'll b) wash c) 'll do d) laundry

27. Unless the salad isn't fresh, I won't eat it.
a) the salad b) isn't c) won't d) eat

28. It's very hot in here because the air conditioner is broken. If only I had it fixed in advance.
a) because b) If c) only d) I had

29. If Chloe visited her parents last month, they could have celebrated her birthday together.
a) If b) visited c) could d) have celebrated

30. I wish I attended class yesterday. I think Mr. Thomson said something important about the exam.
a) wish b) attended c) think d) said

31. Tom would make fewer mistakes if he listens to his brother's advice.
a) make b) fewer c) if d) listens

32. "If you're free Saturday night, will you have joined us for dinner?" "Sure."
a) If b) you're c) will d) have joined

Answers p.332

If you are not sure about some answers, go back to the following lessons:

Question	1	2	3	4	5	6	7	8	9	10	11	12	13	14	15	16
Lesson	96	96	96	96	96	96	98	97	98	97	98	98	98	98	96	96
Question	**17**	**18**	**19**	**20**	**21**	**22**	**23**	**24**	**25**	**26**	**27**	**28**	**29**	**30**	**31**	**32**
Lesson	98	99	97	97	96	96	99	97	98	96	96	99	98	99	97	96

Test 18

Put the words in *italics* in the correct order.

1. *(studies / her cousin / who)*
   Kim introduced me to her cousin who studies ______ in New York.
2. *(can / a restaurant / we / have / where)*
   "Would you recommend ______ both seafood and steak?"
   "There's one on 6th Avenue."
3. *(stories / I / whose / the novelist / like)*
   "I sent a letter to ______ so much." "Who is that?"
4. *(makes / what / angry / me)*
   ______ is Tom's behavior. He's being very rude these days.
5. *(from / I / the library / borrowed / which)*
   ______ this book is too far. Can you drive me there?
6. *(the way / cook / I)*
   Jack likes ______ pasta. I put a lot of garlic and pepper in it.

Complete the sentences with **who/which/that/what** and the words in the box. Add a comma (,) if necessary.

caused the fire	~~Christine gave to me~~	I went to Paris
still live in my hometown	stole your bag	was very fun

7. This cup , which Christine gave to me ______, is my favorite. I always use it for coffee.
8. "Do you know ______?" "I heard lightning started it."
9. "Did you find the thief ______?" "Not yet."
10. Yesterday, I took my kids to the amusement park ______.
11. Aaron and Ken ______, are my oldest friends.
12. "The time ______ was exciting." "What did you do there?"

Find and change any mistakes in each sentence. Put ✓ if the sentence is correct.

Hello Jennifer,

13. Yesterday, I found an old photo ~~which took~~ which we took together years ago.

AIR MAIL

Since I saw it, I've missed you so much.

14. And that's the reason I'm writing this letter.

15. Do you remember the river we went fishing?

16. We met a man which name was Patrick. He was really good at fishing.

17. And the woman came with Patrick was a really good cook.

18. I can't forget the delicious fish which she cooked it. Let's go fishing again when you have time.

Love,
Sharon

Choose the correct one.

19. "Is that the dancer __________ the first prize in the dance contest?" "Yes. His name is Jonny."
    a) which won b) which he won c) who won d) who he won

20. The man __________ last week for the manager position was really impressive.
    a) whom I interviewed b) whom interviewed c) who interviewed d) which I interviewed

21. The city __________ my childhood has a great night view.
    a) which I spent b) in which I spent c) in I spent d) I spent

22. "What's this?" "It's __________ I bought my mom for her birthday. Do you think she'll like it?"
    a) who b) which c) that d) what

23. Ms. Collins, __________ me Japanese, is getting married next month.
    a) who taught b) that taught c) who she taught d) that she taught

24. Can you tell me __________ I can turn on this air conditioner? It's very hot in here.
    a) the way how b) how c) the way what d) which

25. The little girl __________ eyes are brown is very cute.
    a) who b) whom c) whose d) that

Choose the incorrect one.

26. This is the briefcase, that was in the conference room. Whose is it?
    a) b) c) d)

27. I know two brothers whose father work as an editor at this company. They also want to become editors.
    a) b) c) d)

28. Did you see the man to who I was talking earlier? That's Professor Anderson.
    a) b) c) d)

29. The thing what the mailman delivered this morning is a postcard Jake sent from LA.
    a) b) c) d)

30. I own a house which it has five rooms. It's big enough for our family.
    a) b) c) d)

31. The way how Terry deals with customers is rude. Some people who shopped here complained.
    a) b) c) d)

32. Karen has the flu, which stop her from going to school.
    a) b) c) d)

Answers **p.332**

If you are not sure about some answers, go back to the following lessons:

Question	1	2	3	4	5	6	7	8	9	10	11	12	13	14	15	16
Lesson	100	104	102	102	101	104	103	102	100	103	103	104	101	104	104	102
Question	**17**	**18**	**19**	**20**	**21**	**22**	**23**	**24**	**25**	**26**	**27**	**28**	**29**	**30**	**31**	**32**
Lesson	100	101	100	101	101	102	103	104	102	103	102	101	102	100	104	103

Report what each person says with the verbs in *italics*. Add **if** if necessary.

1. SARAH: "Tim passed the driving test."
   YOU: *(said)* Sarah said (that) Tim passed (OR had passed) the driving test.
2. DR. TURNER: "Nancy, you'll feel much better."
   YOU: *(told)* ________________.
3. RICHARD: "Is the bathroom on the first floor?"
   YOU: *(asked)* ________________.
4. JAKE: "Annie, I'm writing a letter to John."
   YOU: *(told)* ________________.
5. HELEN: "Can I use the computer?"
   YOU: *(asked)* ________________.
6. JEFF: "I haven't tried bungee jumping."
   YOU: *(said)* ________________.

Report what Vicky says with the verbs in *italics*. Add **not** if necessary.

7. Bill, please don't touch my phone.	*(told)* She told Bill not to touch her phone.
8. Lisa, could you make some toast for me?	*(asked)* ________________.
9. Mike, stop playing video games.	*(told)* ________________.
10. Sam, please don't talk loudly.	*(asked)* ________________.
11. Janice, don't be late for class.	*(told)* ________________.
12. Kim, would you lend me some money?	*(asked)* ________________.

VICKY

Put the words in *italics* in the correct order. Add **that/to . . .** if necessary.

Amazing Animal Behaviors

Some animal behaviors are so amazing.

13. *(are / lay / some birds / known)*
For example, some birds are known to lay their eggs in another bird's nest.

14. *(cows / face / believed / are)*
And ________________ north while eating in the field.

15. *(some penguins / is / known / dance / it)*
In addition, ________________ when they are trying to attract females.

16. *(thought / like / cats / are)*
And, ________________ people who don't like them.

17. *(eating stones / it / said / helps / is)*
Also, ________________ crocodiles swim.

18. *(don't / is / it / sleep / believed / dolphins)*
Finally, ________________ for months after their babies are born.

It's hard not to be surprised by these behaviors. So, next time you see an animal, watch it carefully.

Choose the correct one.

19. Don't get onions on the pizza. Daniel said his daughter __________ onions.
    a) is hating b) hated c) to hate d) hate

20. Professor Lim __________ be very strict to his students.
    a) is known to b) is known c) know to d) know

21. Jennifer __________ not good at math. So I decided to teach her.
    a) told she was b) told she is c) said she was d) said to she was

22. Mr. Young asked __________ help him paint the wall.
    a) whether could I b) whether I could c) that I could d) to

23. In that restaurant, it is __________ only in cash.
    a) expected customers pay b) expected to customers pay
    c) expected customers that pay d) expected that customers pay

24. Whenever Karen is angry with me, I always __________ first.
    a) say sorry to her b) say sorry her c) told sorry to her d) told sorry her

25. Ronald __________ he was practicing dancing.
    a) told that b) said me c) told me that d) said me that

Choose the incorrect one.

26. "Ms. Carter said her husband that she wanted to buy a new car." "Did they buy one?"
    a) said b) that c) wanted d) Did

27. Betty said she lives in Hong Kong before she moved to Beijing a few years ago.
    a) said b) lives c) moved d) a few years

28. The president is speaking at the seminar. He is expected that he will arrive soon.
    a) He b) expected c) that d) he will

29. "Donna wondered why George calls her last night." "I have no idea. I'll ask him."
    a) wondered b) why c) calls d) have

30. It is said to that Mt. Everest is very hard to climb.
    a) It is said b) to c) is d) to climb

31. "I like dogs." "Me too. They believed to understand people's feelings very well."
    a) like b) Me too c) They d) to understand

32. Michael asked to Jessie go camping with him last weekend, but she was too busy then.
    a) to Jessie b) camping c) was d) then

Answers p.333

If you are not sure about some answers, go back to the following lessons:

Question	1	2	3	4	5	6	7	8	9	10	11	12	13	14	15	16
Lesson	105	106	106	106	106	105	106	106	106	106	106	106	107	107	107	107
Question	**17**	**18**	**19**	**20**	**21**	**22**	**23**	**24**	**25**	**26**	**27**	**28**	**29**	**30**	**31**	**32**
Lesson	107	107	105	107	106	106	107	106	106	106	105	107	106	107	107	106

Test 20

Complete the conversations with **so/neither/not** and the words in *italics*.

1. I've never watched that TV show before.	*(I)* Neither have I. But Janice said it's funny.
2. I'm hungry. Is there anything to eat?	*(I'm afraid)* ________. Let's order a pizza.
3. Sarah can speak Spanish very well.	*(Jake)* ________. He can also speak Italian.
4. Is our boss in his office?	*(I think)* ________. It's lunchtime now.
5. My parents didn't let me go to the party.	*(mine)* ________. So I stayed home.
6. Are you going to get vacation time in August?	*(I hope)* ________. I want to go to Cebu City this summer.

Put the words in *italics* in the correct order. Add **not** if necessary.

7. *(space / there / be / might / some)*
   "Where should I put these boxes?" "There might be some space in the garage."
8. *(so / do / I / think)*
   "Is Tony working hard these days?" "________. He's being a little lazy."
9. *(eggs / are / enough / there)*
   ________ in the fridge? We will need three to make the cookies.
10. *(have / any / new employees / been / there)*
   ________ at the company for years. But they're hiring some this year.
11. *(Aaron / were / we / asked / surprised / that)*
   ________ Sharon to marry him. We thought they were just friends.
12. *(was / much / there / traffic)*
   ________ on the road, so it took less time than usual to get here.

Complete the sentences with the verbs in the box. Add **not** if necessary.

~~be~~	be	go	join	miss	read	talk

Tips for Freshmen from the President of the Student Council

13. Some freshmen think that getting good grade is difficult.
So here are some tips for doing well in your first year.

14. First, it's essential that students ________ any classes.
15. And I suggest you ________ with your professors if you have any problems.
16. Also, I recommend that you ________ study groups on campus, which can be helpful.
17. And it's important that college students ________ as many books as possible.
18. Lastly, I advise that you ________ to too many parties. Many students' grades have dropped for this reason.
19. I hope that these tips ________ helpful for you.

Choose the correct one.

20. "Have the Andersons come back from Japan?" "I ________________. I called but nobody answered."
    a) don't believe   b) don't believe so   c) believe so   d) don't believe not

21. "________________ coins on the desk. Have you seen them?" "Kathy might have taken them."
    a) There is some   b) There are some   c) There was some   d) There were some

22. We demand that ________________ in the river. It's very dangerous.
    a) kids don't swim   b) kids swim   c) kids not swim   d) kids swim not

23. "I might not be able to go to your wedding." "________________? Will you be out of town?"
    a) Why no   b) Why so   c) Why not   d) Not why

24. Was Carol ________________ a teacher?
    a) proud that Jill became   b) proud that became Jill
    c) proud became Jill   d) proud Jill became that

25. "I have my haircut at the Alexis Hair Salon downtown." "________________."
    a) Neither have I   b) Neither do I   c) So have I   d) So do I

26. Are you driving to school tomorrow? ________________, let's take the bus together.
    a) If so   b) If not   c) If neither   d) If don't

Choose the incorrect one.

27. When you're pregnant, it's important you don't be upset. It's harmful to your baby.
    a) b) c) d)

28. There be should enough sunlight for plants, or they might die.
    a) b) c) d)

29. "Is it essential that we finish this essay today?" "I don't hope so. I have another assignment."
    a) b) c) d)

30. "I'm surprised that Jim get a scholarship." "So am I. He didn't study very hard."
    a) b) c) d)

31. "The fireman insisted that everyone went outside quickly." "I suppose there was a big fire."
    a) b) c) d)

32. "I have been very busy these days." "So was I. I'm afraid I haven't slept for two days."
    a) b) c) d)

Answers p.333

If you are not sure about some answers, go back to the following lessons:

Question	1	2	3	4	5	6	7	8	9	10	11	12	13	14	15	16
Lesson	109	109	109	109	109	109	108	109	108	108	110	108	110	110	110	110
Question	**17**	**18**	**19**	**20**	**21**	**22**	**23**	**24**	**25**	**26**	**27**	**28**	**29**	**30**	**31**	**32**
Lesson	110	110	110	109	108	110	109	110	109	109	110	108	109	110	110	109

GRAMMAR GATEWAY INTERMEDIATE

The appendix can help you understand basic essentials for learning English and organize what you have learned in the lessons. It also introduces commonly used phrases.

1. Parts of Sentences

English sentences consist of basic elements, such as subjects and verbs, but they also consist of additional elements like modifiers. Let's take a look at the following explanations and examples to get familiar with them.

A. Subject and verb

Subject + Verb

She drives.
subject *verb*

Every English sentence needs a subject and verb. The subject is a person/thing that is being discussed or performs an action. The verb expresses an action or the state of person/thing. In the sentence above, **She** is the subject and **drives** is the verb.

Subject-Verb Agreement

A bird is in the tree.
singular noun *singular verb*

Water flows under the bridge.
uncountable noun *singular verb*

Three cows are in the field.
plural noun *plural verb*

When we use a singular or an uncountable noun as the subject, we use a singular verb. When we use a plural noun as the subject, we use a plural verb. In the sentence above, **A bird** is the singular noun and **Water** is the uncountable noun, so we use the singular verbs **is** and **flows**. **Three cows** is a plural noun, so we use the plural verb **are**.

B. Object

Subject + Verb + Object

He teaches **math**.
subject *verb* *object*

Some sentences only need a subject and verb, such as **She drives**. However, for other sentences, we use an object after the verb. The object is a person/thing that receives the action of the verb. In the sentence above, the object **math** is used to show what he teaches.

Subject + Verb + Indirect Object + Direct Object

She gave **the girl a present**.
subject verb indirect object direct object

Some sentences need two objects. The indirect object is a person/thing that receives what is being given or sent, while the direct object is a person/thing that is being given or sent. In the sentence above, the indirect object **the girl** is used to show who received a present, while the direct object **a present** is used to show what was given.

C. Complement

Subject + Verb + Complement

He is **a police officer**.
subject verb complement

Some sentences need a complement. The complement is used to describe or identify the subject. In the sentence above, the complement **a police officer** is used after the verb **is** to describe the subject **He**.

Subject + Verb + Object + Complement

The story made her **sad**.
subject verb object complement

The complement can also describe or identify the object. In the sentence above, the complement **sad** is used to describe the object **her**.

D. Modifier

Every evening, he watches TV.
modifier subject verb object

He watches TV **with Helen**.
subject verb object modifier

In addition to basic elements of sentences, there are also modifiers. The modifier is an element that adds details to sentences to make them more vivid and comprehensive. In the first sentence, the modifier **Every evening** is used to explain when the subject watches TV. In the second sentence, the modifier **with Helen** is used to describe who the subject watches TV with.

2. Spelling Rules

English verbs, nouns, adjectives, and adverbs can change forms. Let's take a look at the following charts to see how they change.

A. Spelling rules for verbs (Lesson 2-20, 33, 36)

Adding -(e)s (when the subject is **he**/**she**/**it**/etc. in the present simple)

+ -s	speak → speak**s** laugh → laugh**s**	care → care**s** know → know**s**	clean → clean**s** ride → ride**s**
-ss/-sh/-ch/-x + -es	miss → miss**es** rush → rush**es** mix → mix**es**	pass → pass**es** touch → touch**es** fix → fix**es**	wash → wash**es** catch → catch**es** relax → relax**es**
-o + -es	go → go**es**	do → do**es**	
Consonant + -y → change **y** to **i** + -es	worry → worr**ies** reply → repl**ies**	fly → fl**ies** rely → rel**ies**	hurry → hurr**ies** dry → dr**ies**
Vowel + -y → + -s	stay → stay**s**	pay → pay**s**	buy → buy**s**

Adding -ing

+ -ing	cook → cook**ing**	grow → grow**ing**	join → join**ing**
-e → remove **e** + -ing	dance → danc**ing** use → us**ing** change → chang**ing**	drive → driv**ing** hope → hop**ing** save → sav**ing**	write → writ**ing** decide → decid**ing** invite → invit**ing**
-ee + -ing	agree → agree**ing**	see → see**ing**	
-ie → change **ie** to **y** + -ing	die → d**ying**	lie → l**ying**	tie → t**ying**
Words ending with single vowel + single consonant	Add the same consonant + **-ing** for 1-syllable words. stop → sto**pping** plan → pla**nning** get → ge**tting**	 knit → kni**tting** dip → di**pping** chat → cha**tting**	 rub → ru**bbing** run → ru**nning** jog → jo**gging**
	Add the same consonant + **-ing** for 2 or more syllable words only when the last syllable is stressed. begin [bigín] → begi**nning** permit [pərmít] → permi**tting** admit [ædmít] → admi**tting**	refer [rifə́ːr] → refe**rring** prefer [prifə́ːr] → prefe**rring** regret [rigrét] → regre**tting**	

Adding -(e)d

+ -ed	ask → ask**ed** reach → reach**ed**	allow → allow**ed** call → call**ed**	order → order**ed** rain → rain**ed**
-e/-ee/-ie + -d	create → create**d** die → die**d**	believe → believe**d** tie → tie**d**	agree → agree**d** lie → lie**d**
Consonant + **-y** → change **y** to **i** + **-ed**	try → tr**ied** bury → bur**ied**	apply → appl**ied** copy → cop**ied**	study → stud**ied** carry → carr**ied**
Vowel + **-y** → + **-ed**	enjoy → enjoy**ed** *Exceptions*: **pay** → **paid**	delay → delay**ed** **lay** → **laid**	stay → stay**ed** **say** → **said**
Words ending with single vowel + single consonant	Add the same consonant + **-ed** for 1-syllable words. drop → dro**pped** jog → jo**gged**	beg → be**gged** grab → gra**bbed**	rub → ru**bbed** shop → sho**pped**
	Add the same consonant + **-ed** for 2 or more syllable words only when the last syllable is stressed. **occur** [əkə́ːr] → occu**rred** **permit** [pərmít] → permi**tted** **regret** [rigrét] → regre**tted**	**equip** [ikwíp] → equi**pped** **prefer** [prifə́ːr] → prefe**rred** **control** [kəntróul] → contro**lled**	

* Consonant: **b**, **c**, **g**, **y**, etc. / Vowel: **a**, **e**, **i**, **o**, **u**
* Syllable: a unit of sound with one vowel sound. (**cheap** = one syllable, **mar·ket** = two syllables)

B. Spelling rules for nouns (Lesson 47, 56)

Adding -(e)s (Plural nouns)

+ -s	idea → idea**s**	museum → museum**s**	street → street**s**
-s/-ss/-ch/-x + -es	bus → bus**es** match → match**es**	dress → dress**es** lunch → lunch**es**	brush → brush**es** box → box**es**
-f(e) → change **f** to **v** + **-es**	leaf → lea**ves** thief → thie**ves**	wolf → wol**ves** life → li**ves**	shelf → shel**ves** knife → kni**ves**
Consonant + **-y** → change **y** to **i** + **-es**	lady → lad**ies** city → cit**ies**	family → famil**ies** penny → penn**ies**	story → stor**ies** secretary → secretar**ies**
Vowel + **y** → + **s**	holiday → holiday**s**	toy → toy**s**	journey → journey**s**
Consonant + **-o** → + **-es**	potato → potato**es** *Exceptions*: **kilo** → **kilos**	tomato → tomato**es** **piano** → **pianos**	hero → hero**es** **photo** → **photos**
Vowel + **-o** → + **-s**	video → video**s**	radio → radio**s**	zoo → zoo**s**

Adding 's (Possessive nouns)

Singular noun + -'s	the **doctor's office** my **boss's car**	the **bird's nest** the **elephant's nose**	**John's address** **Charles's birthday**
Plural nouns not ending with **s + -'s**	the **women's clothes**	the **children's books**	the **people's feelings**
Plural nouns ending with **s + -'**	the **clients' needs**	the **dogs' houses**	the **giraffes' necks**

C. Spelling rules for adjectives/adverbs (Lesson 68, 74-77)

Adding -ly to adjectives (Adverbs)

+ -ly	cheap → cheap**ly** safe → safe**ly**	careful → careful**ly** extreme → extreme**ly**	excited → excited**ly** similar → similar**ly**
-y → change **y** to **i** + **-ly**	lazy → laz**ily** hungry → hungr**ily**	noisy → nois**ily** happy → happ**ily**	heavy → heav**ily** easy → eas**ily**
-le → remove **e** + **-y**	probab**le** → probably possib**le** → possibly	incredib**le** → incredibly simp**le** → simply	terrib**le** → terribly reasonab**le** → reasonably
-ic + **-ally**	fantast**ic** → fantastic**ally** automat**ic** → automatic**ally**	romant**ic** → romantic**ally** dramat**ic** → dramatic**ally**	

Adding -(e)r/-(e)st (Comparatives/Superlatives)

1-syllable adj./adv. → + **-er/-est**	deep - deep**er** - the deep**est** bright - bright**er** - the bright**est** *Exceptions*: fun - **more** fun - the **most** fun	fast - fast**er** - the fast**est** hard - hard**er** - the hard**est**
1-syllable adj./adv. ending with **e** → + **-r/-st**	larg**e** - large**r** - the large**st** saf**e** - safe**r** - the safe**st**	wid**e** - wide**r** - the wide**st** lat**e** - late**r** - the late**st**
1-syllable adj./adv. ending with single vowel + single consonant → add the same consonant + **-er/-est**	h**ot** - ho**tter** - the ho**ttest** f**it** - fi**tter** - the fi**ttest**	f**at** - fa**tter** - the fa**ttest** s**ad** - sa**dder** - the sa**ddest**
2 or more syllable adj./adv. ending with **y** → change **y** to **i** + **-er/-est**	funn**y** - funn**ier** - the funn**iest** angr**y** - angr**ier** - the angr**iest**	dirt**y** - dirt**ier** - the dirt**iest** earl**y** - earl**ier** - the earl**iest**

Adding more/most

2 or more syllable adj./adv.	famous - **more** famous - the **most** famous quickly - **more** quickly - the **most** quickly	popular - **more** popular - the **most** popular clearly - **more** clearly - the **most** clearly
adj. ending with **-ing/-ed**	boring - **more** boring - the **most** boring tired - **more** tired - the **most** tired	relaxing - **more** relaxing - the **most** relaxing annoyed - **more** annoyed - the **most** annoyed

3. Irregular Verbs (Lesson 6, 10-15, 20, 33)

In English, some verbs change forms in an irregular way, such as **eat** (present) - **ate** (past) - **eaten** (past participle). Let's take a look at the list of common irregular verbs.

Present	Past	Past Participle
am/is/are (be)	was/were	been
arise	arose	arisen
awake	awoke	awoken
beat	beat	beaten
become	became	become
begin	began	begun
bend	bent	bent
bite	bit	bitten
blow	blew	blown
break	broke	broken
bring	brought	brought
build	built	built
burn	burned/burnt	burned/burnt
burst	burst	burst
buy	bought	bought
catch	caught	caught
choose	chose	chosen
come	came	come
cost	cost	cost
cut	cut	cut
deal	dealt	dealt
dig	dug	dug
dive	dived/dove	dived
do	did	done
draw	drew	drawn
dream	dreamed/ dreamt	dreamed/ dreamt
drink	drank	drunk

Present	Past	Past Participle
drive	drove	driven
eat	ate	eaten
fall	fell	fallen
feed	fed	fed
feel	felt	felt
fight	fought	fought
find	found	found
fit	fit	fit
fly	flew	flown
forbid	forbade	forbidden
forget	forgot	forgotten
forgive	forgave	forgiven
freeze	froze	frozen
get	got	got/gotten
give	gave	given
go	went	gone
grow	grew	grown
hang	hung	hung
have	had	had
hear	heard	heard
hide	hid	hidden
hit	hit	hit
hold	held	held
hurt	hurt	hurt
keep	kept	kept
know	knew	known
lay	laid	laid
lead	led	led

Present	Past	Past Participle
lean	leaned/leant	leaned/leant
learn	learned/learnt	learned/learnt
leave	left	left
lend	lent	lent
let	let	let
lie	lay	lain
light	lit	lit
lose	lost	lost
make	made	made
mean	meant	meant
meet	met	met
pay	paid	paid
prove	proved	proved/proven
put	put	put
quit	quit	quit
read [riːd]	read [red]	read [red]
ride	rode	ridden
ring	rang	rung
rise	rose	risen
run	ran	run
say	said	said
see	saw	seen
seek	sought	sought
sell	sold	sold
send	sent	sent
set	set	set
shake	shook	shaken
shine	shined/shone	shined/shone
shoot	shot	shot
show	showed	showed/shown
shut	shut	shut
sing	sang	sung
sit	sat	sat

Present	Past	Past Participle
sleep	slept	slept
slide	slid	slid
speak	spoke	spoken
spell	spelled/spelt	spelled/spelt
spend	spent	spent
spill	spilled/spilt	spilled/spilt
spin	spun	spun
split	split	split
spread	spread	spread
spring	sprang	sprung
stand	stood	stood
steal	stole	stolen
stick	stuck	stuck
strike	struck	struck
sweep	swept	swept
swim	swam	swum
swing	swung	swung
take	took	taken
teach	taught	taught
tear	tore	torn
tell	told	told
think	thought	thought
throw	threw	thrown
understand	understood	understood
upset	upset	upset
wake	woke	woken
wear	wore	worn
win	won	won
write	wrote	written

4. Tenses (Lesson 2-20)

Throughout the lessons, we have learned how to use various tenses. Let's take a look at the following charts to see how verbs change according to tense.

A. Present

		Negative	Question
Present Simple **do/does**	Tom **exercises.**	Tom **doesn't exercise.**	**Does** Tom **exercise**?
Present Progressive **am/is/are doing**	Tom **is exercising.**	Tom **isn't exercising.**	**Is** Tom **exercising**?
Present Perfect **have/has done**	Tom **has exercised.**	Tom **hasn't exercised.**	**Has** Tom **exercised**?
Present Perfect Progressive **have/has been doing**	Tom **has been exercising.**	Tom **hasn't been exercising.**	**Has** Tom **been exercising**?

B. Past

		Negative	Question
Past Simple **did**	Tom **exercised.**	Tom **didn't exercise.**	**Did** Tom **exercise**?
Past Progressive **was/were doing**	Tom **was exercising.**	Tom **wasn't exercising.**	**Was** Tom **exercising**?
Past Perfect **had done**	Tom **had exercised.**	Tom **hadn't exercised.**	**Had** Tom **exercised?**

C. Future

		Negative	Question
Future **will do** *OR* **am/is/are going to do**	Tom **will exercise.** *OR* Tom **is going to exercise.**	Tom **won't exercise.** *OR* Tom **isn't going to exercise.**	**Will** Tom **exercise**? *OR* **Is** Tom **going to exercise**?
Future Progressive **will be doing**	Tom **will be exercising.**	Tom **won't be exercising.**	**Will** Tom **be exercising**?
Future Perfect **will have done**	Tom **will have exercised.**	Tom **won't have exercised.**	**Will** Tom **have exercised**?

5. Short Forms

In English, we use short forms such as **He's** and **We can't** more often than **He is** and **We cannot**. Let's take a look at the following ways to make short forms.

		Negative
be **(am/is/are, was/were)**	am → **'m** is → **'s** are → **'re**	am not → **'m not** is not → **'s not** *OR* **isn't** are not → **'re not** *OR* **aren't**
	-	was not → **wasn't** were not → **weren't**
do **(do/does/did)**	-	do not → **don't** does not → **doesn't** did not → **didn't**
have **(have/has/had)**	have → **'ve** has → **'s** had → **'d**	have not → **'ve not** *OR* **haven't** has not → **'s not** *OR* **hasn't** had not → **'d not** *OR* **hadn't**
will/would	will → **'ll** would → **'d**	will not → **'ll not** *OR* **won't** would not → **'d not** *OR* **wouldn't**
modal verbs	-	cannot → **can't** could not → **couldn't** might not → **mightn't** must not → **mustn't** should not → **shouldn't**

's is the short form of **is** or **has**, but there are no short forms of **was** or **were**.

- Kelly**'s** good at Spanish because she**'s** lived in Mexico. (= Kelly is good at Spanish because she has lived in Mexico.)
- Jack **was** sleeping while we **were** watching TV. (*NOT* Jack's sleeping while we're watching TV.)

'd is the short form of **had** or **would**.

- Sara wasn't at the party when we arrived. She**'d** already left. (= She had already left.)
- If I won the lottery, I**'d** buy a new car. (= I would buy a new car.)

We do not use short forms in short answers with **yes**.

- "Is Mr. Bradley in his office?" "Yes, **he is**." (*NOT* Yes, he's)
- "Are these shoes on sale?" "Yes, **they are**." (*NOT* Yes, they're)

6. Modal Verbs (Lesson 22-28)

Throughout the lessons, we have learned various modal verbs. Let's look at the following charts to review the forms and meanings of modal verbs.

A. Modal verb + base form

Ability

can	Melissa **can play** the piano very well.
can't	My grandmother **can't see** without her glasses.
could	I **could run** fast when I was young.
couldn't	Henry **couldn't drive** a motorcycle, so I taught him.

Possibility / Certainty

might/may	Be quiet! You **might wake** the baby.
might/may not	I **might not move** to Miami. I just got a job offer in Dallas.
could	It's cloudy and cold today, so it **could snow**.
couldn't/can't	This sweater **couldn't fit** Maria. It's too big.
must	Larry worked all night. He **must be** tired.
must not	Tim never plays cards with us. He **must not enjoy** it.

Necessity

must	You **must fill** out this form to register for the course.
must not	"Excuse me, sir. You **must not smoke** here." "Oh. Sorry."
have/has to	I **have to write** an essay for my history class.
don't/doesn't have to	I did the dishes. You **don't have to do** them.

Advice / Suggestion

should	We **should try** that new restaurant. My friend said it's great.
shouldn't	The floor is very slippery. You **shouldn't run**.
had better	I**'d better go** to bed soon. I have an interview tomorrow morning.
had better not	You**'d better not be** late or you'll miss your flight.

B. Modal verb + have + past participle

could have + past participle (something was possible in the past)	• Eric **could have baked** a cake, but he bought one instead. • "Joe is not answering his doorbell." "He **could have left** home."
couldn't/can't have + past participle (something was certainly not possible in the past)	• Rita **couldn't/can't have gone** to the wedding. She had to work that day.
might/may (not) have + past participle (something was possible in the past)	• "I can't find my purse." "You **might have lost** it." • Mr. Porter wasn't at the meeting. He **might not have known** about it.
must have + past participle (It is certainly true that something happened in the past)	• All of the cookies are gone. Somebody **must have eaten** them.
must not have + past participle (It is certainly not true that something happened in the past)	• The mailbox is empty. The mailman **must not have come** yet.
should have + past participle (It is regretful that something didn't happen)	• My computer crashed. I **should have saved** the files I was working on.
shouldn't have + past participle (It is regretful that something happened)	• I **shouldn't have drunk** so much wine. I have a headache now.

7. Names of Locations (Lesson 53-54)

We use **the** before some names of locations, but for others we do not. Let's take a look at the following explanations and charts to know whether to use **the** or not.

We usually do not use **the** with the names of cities, islands, countries, and continents.

City/Island	Tokyo	Washington DC	Prague	Long Island	Jeju Island	Bermuda
Country/Continent	Brazil	Russia	Canada	Europe	Africa	Asia

- When we were living in **Tokyo**, we visited many sushi restaurants.
- "Have you ever been to **Brazil**?" "No. But I plan to go next year."
- **Russia** is the largest country in **Europe**.

But we use **the** with the names of countries that contain Republic, Kingdom, or States and are in the plural form.

the Czech Republic	the United Kingdom	the United States of America	the United Arab Emirates

- "Is Prague the capital of **the Czech Republic**?" "Yes, that's right."
- **The United Arab Emirates** has the tallest building in the world.

We usually do not use **the** with the names of mountains, but we use **the** with mountain ranges.

Mountain	Mount St. Helens	Mount Everest	Mount Fuji	Mount Seorak
Mountain Range	the Himalayas	the Rocky Mountains	the Alps	the Andes

- **Mount St. Helens** is an active volcano. It is between Portland and Seattle.
- I've never been to **the Himalayas**, but I want to go someday.

We usually do not use **the** with the names of lakes, but we use **the** with the names of rivers, seas, and oceans.

Lake	Lake Superior	Lake Michigan	Lake Victoria	Lake Titicaca
River	the Thames	the Nile	the Amazon	
Sea/Ocean	the Caribbean	the Mediterranean	the Pacific	the Arctic

- "Have you ever been ice fishing?" "Yes. I tried it once at **Lake Superior**."
- We relaxed by **the Thames** after a long day of sightseeing.
- **The Caribbean** is famous for its clear water. It's popular among scuba divers.

We usually do not use **the** before the names of public buildings and universities.

Public Building	Waterloo Station	Union Station	Narita Airport	JFK Airport
University	Harvard University	Oxford University		

- Meet me at **Union Station** at 4 p.m. My train will arrive then.
- **Harvard University** was founded in 1636. It is one of the oldest universities in North America.

But we use **the** if the names contain an adjective or **of**.

the White House	the Open University	the University of Florida

- Our history class toured **the White House** last year. It was very interesting.
- Do you know anyone who attends **the University of Florida**?

We usually do not use **the** with the names of roads, streets, parks, and squares.

Road/Street	76th Street	Main Road	Park Avenue	Wilshire Boulevard	
Park/Square	Central Park	Hyde Park	Stanley Park	Times Square	Trafalgar Square

- We live near **Central Park**. Our house is on **76th Street**.

8. Phrasal Verbs (Lesson 87, 88)

There are many phrasal verbs in English, such as **talk about**. Let's take a look at the following lists of common phrasal verbs along with examples.

A. Two-Word Phrasal Verbs

about	bring about (="produce")	The invention of the train **brought about** a huge change in transportation.
	care about	I don't **care about** celebrity gossip.
	come about	"How did the accident **come about**?" "The other car didn't stop at the red light."
after	go after	My cat saw a mouse and **went after** it.
	take after (="resemble")	Ted **takes after** his father. Their personalities are very similar.
along	come along	The train already left, but another one will **come along** soon.
apart	tell apart	The twins are difficult to **tell apart**. They look just alike.
around	move around	My suitcase is easy to **move around**. It has four wheels.
	play around	"Can we **play around** in the pool for a while?" "Sure."
	turn around	There's Katie over there. Let's wave at her if she **turns around**.
at	aim at	The store **aims at** increasing sales this year.
	glance at	Scott **glanced at** his watch many times during the meeting.
	grin at	I like when Tina **grins at** me. She has a beautiful smile.
	shoot at	The hunter **shot at** the bird, but it flew away too fast.
away	drive away	Mark tried to **drive away**, but he couldn't start his car.
	fly away	Oh no! My balloon is **flying away**!
	give away (="donate")	The rich man **gave away** most of his money to charity.
	go away	Why did Jeff **go away**? I had a question for him.
	put away	Your room is so messy! **Put away** all your clothes that are on the floor.
back	answer back	Mrs. Lee's children are well behaved and never **answer back**.
	bring back	You must **bring back** this book by next week.
	call back	Henry isn't in the office right now. Please **call back** later.
	cut back (="reduce")	"I've been drinking too much coffee lately." "I agree. You should **cut back**."
	get back	Dad **gets back** from China tomorrow. He's been gone a week.

back	**go back**	Jan was born in France. She wants to **go back** someday.
	pay back	When I graduate from university, I will **pay back** my loans.
	put back	"Did you **put back** the milk?" "Yes. It's in the fridge."
	sit back	Tom **sat back** in his chair and relaxed as the movie began.
	take back	I **took back** my headphones that Mike borrowed.
	walk back	I forgot to lock the door. Can you **walk back** home and lock it?
	wave back	The people on the boat waved, so I **waved back**.
	write back	Liz wrote me a letter, but I haven't **written back** yet.
behind	**fall behind**	Max studies hard so that he doesn't **fall behind** in school.
down	**bend down**	Kim **bent down** and picked a flower from the garden.
	blow down	The wind **blew down** the old bridge.
	break down	"Why were you late this morning?" "My car **broke down**."
	bring down	Emily took medicine to **bring down** her fever.
	burn down	There was a fire last night and two houses **burned down**.
	close down	I was sorry to see that my favorite café had **closed down**.
	cut down	My dad **cut down** the maple tree in the yard.
	fall down	Mr. Harris **fell down** on the ice. Thankfully, he's OK.
	go down	The price of gas has **gone down** a lot recently.
	knock down (="cause to fall over")	The goal in bowling is to **knock down** all the pins.
	let down (="disappoint")	I can't be late for dinner. I don't want to **let down** my wife.
	put down	Christina finished her drink and **put down** the glass.
	slow down	**Slow down**! You're driving too fast.
	take down	After the garage sale was over, I **took down** the posters.
	tear down (="destroy")	The workers **tore down** the old factory to build a gallery.
	write down	"Let me **write down** my phone number for you." "Thanks."
for	**fall for**	"Did you **fall for** the trick?" "Yes. It was very clever."
	feel for	Diane lost all of her money. I really **felt for** her, so I let her borrow some.
	qualify for	A friend of mine **qualified for** the Olympics. We're so proud of her.
	search for	I **searched for** a good cookbook at the bookstore.
	stand for (="represent")	ASAP **stands for** "as soon as possible."
in	**believe in**	My little sister **believes in** Santa Claus.
	bring in	It's raining, so we had better **bring in** the laundry.

in	call in	Phil couldn't fix his computer, so he **called in** a technician.
	check in	Bob went to the hotel's front desk to **check in**.
	come in	Our flight **came in** 30 minutes early.
	fill in	You need to **fill in** all the blanks on the form to apply for a credit card.
	fit in (="get along")	"Do you like your new school?" "Yes. At first it was hard to **fit in**, but now I really enjoy it."
	get in	I'll give you a ride. **Get in** the car.
	give in (="surrender")	Henry tried to win the chess game, but after several hours he just **gave in**.
	hand in (="submit")	Please **hand in** your reports on Friday.
	join in	There were some people playing volleyball on the beach, so we **joined in**.
	let in	Close the window! You'll **let in** mosquitoes!
	look in	"I can't find my coat." "Did you **look in** the closet?"
	move in	The new neighbors **moved in** last month.
	plug in	You should **plug in** the laptop because the battery is low.
	result in	The flood in New Orleans **resulted in** a lot of damage.
	specialize in (="be expert in")	This restaurant **specializes in** sushi.
	stay in	"Let's **stay in** tonight. I'll cook for us." "OK. That sounds good."
	succeed in	Mr. Lee gave me some advice about how to **succeed in** business.
	take in (="absorb")	Our bodies need to **take in** vitamins every day.
	turn in (="submit")	Please **turn in** your résumé when you apply for the job.
into	break into	An alarm rang when someone **broke into** the building.
	bump into (="hit")	While Dave was playing in his room, he **bumped into** the wall and hurt his head.
	crash into	The Titanic **crashed into** an iceberg and sank to the bottom of the ocean.
	get into	After graduating from college, Emily **got into** a good company.
	look into	My uncle will **look into** the problem with the kitchen sink.
	run into (="meet by chance")	I **ran into** my friend from high school at the mall.
	turn into	During heavy rain, small streams can **turn into** large rivers.
like	feel like (="want to do") (="want to eat")	I don't **feel like** going shopping. I'll just stay home. I'm tired of my usual lunch. I **feel like** a pizza today.
	look like	The students decorated the gym to **look like** a dance hall.

of	approve of	• Lena's parents don't **approve of** her new boyfriend.
	complain of	• Some passengers on the flight **complained of** bad service.
	consist of	• The US **consisted of** 13 states when it was formed in 1776.
	die of	• The movie director passed away. He **died of** cancer.
	dream of	• Beth **dreams of** having a long vacation. She has worked overtime a lot lately.
	hear of	• "Do you know Dave Akers, the author?" "No. I've never **heard of** him before."
	talk of	• The factory workers **talked of** asking for higher pay.
	think of	• "I miss Mary." "Me too. I **think of** her often."
off	call off (="cancel")	• The weather was bad, so we **called off** the baseball game.
	cut off	• Do you have any scissors? I want to **cut off** the tag of my new shirt.
	doze off (="start sleeping")	• I **dozed off** during the lecture. It was quite boring.
	drive off	• The bus **drove off** after all the tourists were seated.
	drop off	• Ms. Smith **drops off** her kids at school every morning.
	fall off	• All of the books **fell off** the shelf during the earthquake.
	get off	• "Is this the stop for the museum?" "No. You should **get off** at the next stop."
	lay off (="fire")	• Five employees were **laid off** after the management changed.
	let off	• The city **let off** fireworks during the parade. They were beautiful.
	nod off (="fall asleep")	• William was so tired that he **nodded off** during the movie.
	pay off (="finish paying") (="achieve")	• Janet **paid off** her credit card bill this morning. • My team's hard work **paid off**. We won the championship.
	set off (="begin traveling")	• "Let's leave for the beach early in the morning." "OK. What time shall we **set off**?"
	show off	• Tracy **showed off** her new dress to her friends.
	shut off	• "Did you remember to **shut off** the stove?" "Of course."
	stop off	• We **stopped off** at a local coffee shop on our way home.
	switch off	• **Switch off** the light when you leave the room.
	tear off	• Jake **tore off** the wrapping paper to get to his present.
	wear off	• The pain medicine is **wearing off**. My leg is hurting again.
	work off (="get rid of")	• Running is a great way to **work off** extra calories.
on	add on	• When Sally and Ron had a baby, they had to **add on** a room to the house.

on	carry on	• Pat **carried on** studying despite the noise.
	catch on	• The teacher tried explaining the lesson clearly, but the students didn't **catch on**.
	come on	• When I turned on the TV, the evening news **came on**.
	concentrate on	• Please be quiet. I can't **concentrate on** my homework.
	count on	• I will finish the assignment before the deadline. You can **count on** me.
	decide on	• Mia and John haven't **decided on** a date for their wedding yet.
	depend on	• Children **depend on** their parents for food and clothing.
	drive on	• My son wanted me to stop at the toy store, but I **drove on**.
	get on	• Tom and Rick **got on** the train at the Low Valley station.
	go on	• Susie's story sounded interesting, so I asked her to **go on**.
	insist on	• Beth wanted to leave the party early, but Dawn **insisted on** staying.
	keep on	• Lena **kept on** practicing the piano. She improved a lot.
	leave on (="keep wearing")	• "May I **leave on** my shoes in the house?" "Sure."
	live on	• My grandmother died years ago, but her memory **lives on**.
	move on	• After 12 years at the law office, Peter decided to **move on** and do something new.
	pass on	• "Mr. Smith wants to see Jack." "OK. I'll **pass on** the message."
	plan on	• "Do you **plan on** going to Jill's wedding?" "Yes. What about you?"
	play on	• Tim hurt his ankle during the game, but he **played on**.
	rely on	• Many people **rely on** public transportation.
	settle on (="make a choice for")	• I've **settled on** the black car. It looks nicer than the red one.
	spend on	• "How much money did you **spend on** those clothes?" "Around $500."
	switch on	• I can't see in here. Please **switch on** the light.
	take on (="undertake")	• I'm too busy to **take on** any extra work.

out	ask out	"Kyle **asked out** my sister." "Really? Is she going to go out with him?"
	block out	I use curtains to **block out** the light in my room.
	blow out	**Blow out** the candles on your cake and make a wish.
	break out (= "occur")	"Did you hear about the fight at school?" "Yes. It **broke out** at lunch."
	carry out	We need to **carry out** our plan to clean the basement.
	check out (= "leave") (= "borrow")	The tourists **checked out** and went to the airport. I'm going to **check out** this book from the library.
	come out	It **came out** that Mary will become the department manager.
	cross out	Just **cross out** the wrong word and write in the correct one.
	cut out (= "remove")	My doctor told me to **cut out** red meat from my diet.
	drop out	Tom didn't have enough time to practice for the singing contest, so he **dropped out**.
	empty out	The fire department **emptied out** the building because of a gas leak.
	fall out	My keys were in my pocket earlier, but I think they **fell out**.
	figure out	Something is wrong with my car, but the mechanic can't **figure out** the problem.
	fill out	Donna **filled out** the form to register for the tennis class.
	find out	"Did you **find out** when the exam starts?" "Yes. It's at 2:30."
	give out	The grocery store **gave out** free samples of cheese.
	hand out	The restaurant **handed out** coupons to the first 100 customers.
	help out	I **help out** my grandparents with their garden every Sunday.
	keep out	We got our windows repaired in order to **keep out** the flies in the summer.
	knock out	The fighter **knocked out** the other boxer with one punch.
	lay out (= "arrange")	Lucy **laid out** all the fruit and let the guests help themselves.
	leave out	I thought I'd invited everyone to the party, but I **left out** Ben!
	let out	Julie **let out** a scream when the bee flew toward her.
	lock out	My sister had to bring an extra set of keys because I left mine in the car and got **locked out**.
	look out (= "be careful")	**Look out**! There's a dog running across the road.
	move out	"Doesn't Lily live next to you?" "No. She **moved out**."
	pass out (= "black out")	Tim's fever became so high that he **passed out**.

out	**pick out**	I have to **pick out** the perfect gift for our anniversary.
	print out	I **printed out** the list of words so I could study at home.
	put out	The firemen **put out** the fire. They saved the building.
	run out (= "use all")	"Is there any tea left?" "No, we **ran out** yesterday."
	send out	Gina **sent out** invitations to her wedding last month.
	set out (= "start")	I packed a lunch and **set out** for a hike up the mountain.
	sort out	You have to **sort out** the bottles from the cans for recycling.
	take out	Please **take out** the trash. The trash can is full.
	tear out	Alison **tore out** a photo from the magazine. It was a picture of her favorite actor.
	throw out	I bought some new towels, so I **threw out** my old ones.
	turn out	A large crowd **turned out** for the parade.
	watch out	**Watch out**! You're about to step in a puddle.
over	**check over**	My mom used to **check over** my homework before bedtime.
	get over (= "overcome")	It took two weeks for Megan to **get over** the flu.
	go over	You should **go over** used cars carefully before you buy them.
	hand over	I felt sad when we **handed over** the keys to our old house. I had lived there all my life.
	look over	Mary always **looks over** her reports very carefully.
	run over (= "drive over")	If you drive too fast, you might **run over** a pedestrian.
	start over	The computer crashed and I forgot to save my file. Now I have to **start over**.
	talk over	Let's **talk over** our options with the salesperson.
	think over	We're still **thinking over** the contract. We haven't signed it yet.
	turn over	Don't forget to **turn over** the form. There's writing on the back side, too.
through	**get through** (= "finish")	We finally **got through** all of our exams. Let's celebrate!
	(= "be connected")	I tried to call Jackie twice earlier, but I didn't **get through**.
	see through	I can **see through** Kelly's lies. Her story is clearly false.
to	**admit to**	Rick **admitted to** the mistake and said he caused the car accident.
	apologize to	The server **apologized to** us for spilling the wine.
	get to	I **got to** the bus stop just as the bus was arriving.
together	**get together**	Jeremy **got together** all his tools to fix the fence.
	put together	"I **put together** a list of my favorite movies." "Great. Let's watch some of them."

up	**back up** (= "move backwards") (= "support")	• If you see a snake, **back up** slowly so you don't scare it. • Nobody **backed up** Ed's proposal. It wasn't a good idea.
	bring up (= "mention") (= "raise")	• I hate to **bring up** the issue, but you still owe me money. • I want to **bring up** my children in the country.
	cover up (= "hide")	• Lenny tried to **cover up** the fact that he didn't go to class.
	dress up	• Let's **dress up** and go to a dance club tonight!
	end up	• It's cold outside. You should wear your coat or you might **end up** sick.
	fill up	• "Did you **fill up** the tank with gas?" "Yes. I stopped at the gas station after work."
	give up	• You can finish the race, Steve! Don't **give up**!
	go up (= "increase") (= "be built")	• The temperature has **gone up** a lot since this morning. • A new apartment will **go up** on this street. It'll get busy.
	hang up	• Every Christmas, my kids **hang up** stockings on the fireplace.
	hurry up	• **Hurry up** or we're going to be late for the concert.
	keep up	• The heavy snow **kept up** for several days.
	look up	• Kathy **looked up** Alex's phone number in the phone book, but it wasn't in there.
	set up (= "prepare")	• I've **set up** the chess board and I'm ready to play now.
	sign up	• "There's an art class starting next week." "Are you going to **sign up**?"
	speak up	• Please **speak up**. We can't hear you.
	split up	• The two owners of the shop **split up** the profits every month.
	stay up	• I want to **stay up** until 11:00 so I can watch the show.
	turn up	• **Turn up** the sound on the television. I can't hear it.
	use up	• Jennifer **used up** all the butter to bake her cake.
	walk up	• You have to **walk up** a lot of stairs to get to Jim's apartment.
with	**deal with**	• "Who handles refund requests?" "Maria **deals with** those."
	stick with	• Although Fred wasn't good at basketball at first, he decided to **stick with** it.

B. Three-Word Phrasal Verbs

break out of	• The prisoners tried to **break out of** jail, but the guards caught them.
catch up with	• The runner tried to **catch up with** the people in front of him.
come down with (= "become ill")	• I've **come down with** a terrible cold, so I'm staying in bed today.
come up with	• How do you **come up with** your brilliant fashion designs?
cut back on	• I have to **cut back on** my spending if I want to buy a new car.
cut down on	• Larry's eyes get tired easily. He should **cut down on** computer time.
do away with (= "quit")	• I'm going to **do away with** all my bad habits and make a fresh start.
drop out of	• Tom **dropped out of** band and decided to play soccer instead.
end up with	• Gina barely studied, so she **ended up with** a bad score on the exam.
get away with	• The thieves **got away with** lots of expensive jewelry.
go up to	• We should **go up to** the pop star and ask for an autograph.
hang on to	• Can you **hang on to** my bag? I need to tie my shoes.
hold on to	• I don't need that book, so you can **hold on to** it.
keep away from	• Please **keep away from** the fire. It's dangerous.
live up to (= "keep") (= "fulfill")	• You need to finish college and **live up to** the promise you made. • The comedian's show definitely **live up to** our expectations.
look forward to	• Everyone in class was **looking forward to** summer vacation.
look out over	• From the top of the hill, you can **look out over** the whole village.
make up for (= "compensate for")	• To **make up for** missing your graduation, I'll take you out for dinner.
miss out on	• Karen **missed out on** Bill's surprise party.
put up with (= "endure")	• I can't **put up with** Mike's bad attitude. He never seems happy.
run away from	• "Jeremy **ran away from** home." "His parents must be worried."
step down from	• Mr. Park **stepped down from** his position as the CEO of the company.
watch out for	• **Watch out for** children on the road. We're near a school.

9. Adjective + Preposition Phrases (Lesson 89)

There are many adjective + preposition phrases in English, such as **kind to**. Let's take a look at the following list of common adjective + preposition phrases along with examples.

about	angry about	Mr. Meyer is **angry about** the mistakes in the report.
	excited about	"Are you **excited about** your trip to Europe?" "Yes! I've never been there before."
	nervous about	"Are you **nervous about** your first day at work?" "Not really."
	sad about	Kristy is **sad about** moving. She'll miss her friends.
	sorry about	"Excuse me, I'm still waiting for my food. It's been an hour." "**Sorry about** that. I'll go and ask the chef."
	sure about	I asked how much the car was, but the salesman wasn't **sure about** the price.
	upset about	We had a party, and our neighbors were **upset about** the noise.
	worried about	"I can't sleep." "Why? Are you **worried about** something?"
at	amazed at	We were **amazed at** your performance. Your voice is beautiful.
	angry at	I'm **angry at** Betty for ignoring my phone calls.
	mad at	My wife is **mad at** me for forgetting our anniversary.
	surprised at	John hadn't studied at all, so he was **surprised at** his high score on the test.
for	bad for	"Is sugar **bad for** health?" "Only if you eat too much."
	crazy for	Monica is absolutely **crazy for** romance novels.
	famous for	This restaurant has become **famous for** its wonderful desserts.
	prepared for	Thomas did so well during the interview because he was **prepared for** it.
from	different from	"How is this apartment **different from** the other one?" "This one has an extra bathroom."
in	dressed in	All of the men were **dressed in** tuxedos at the party.
	interested in	I'm **interested in** art, so I often go to galleries.
	involved in	Jacob is very busy because he's **involved in** many school activities.
of	afraid of	You don't have to be **afraid of** my dog. He won't bite.
	ashamed of	I was **ashamed of** Bill's behavior. He was rude to the waitress.

of	certain of	Erica loves me. I'm **certain of** it.
	conscious of	Drivers need to be **conscious of** people crossing the street.
	convinced of	A lot of people take vitamins these days. They seem **convinced of** their benefits.
	guilty of	The man wasn't **guilty of** theft. He didn't have to go to jail.
	jealous of	A lot of people are **jealous of** Kenny. He's so popular.
	proud of	I'm so **proud of** you for winning the tennis tournament.
	sick of	I'm **sick of** the snow. I wish it would stop.
	terrified of	Hannah is **terrified of** spiders.
	tired of	Brent was **tired of** waiting for his friend, so he went home.
to	accustomed to	Dorothy isn't **accustomed to** living with roommates.
	clear to	"The instructions for my new camera aren't **clear to** me." "Let me see them. Maybe I can explain them to you."
	dedicated to	Tony is a hard worker. He is very **dedicated to** his job.
	engaged to	Jackie is **engaged to** my younger brother.
	equal to	A mile is **equal to** 1.6 kilometers.
	identical to	"What do you think of this new cap?" "It looks **identical to** the one that Jim has."
	married to	Jeff has been **married to** his wife for six years.
	nice to	Matt, you should be **nice to** your younger sister.
	opposed to	My wife is **opposed to** taking a vacation this summer.
with	angry with	I'm sorry I broke your glasses. Please don't be **angry with** me.
	careful with	Be **careful with** that plate. It's hot.
	crowded with	The stadium was **crowded with** people who were excited to see the boxing match.
	happy with	Thomas is very **happy with** his new bicycle.
	impressed with	All of the guests were **impressed with** Danny's speech.
	pleased with	Rita was **pleased with** her exam results. She did a good job.
	satisfied with	I'm **satisfied with** our president. He's leading the country well.
	wrong with	What's **wrong with** the TV? It's not turning on.

10. Noun + Preposition Phrases (Lesson 90)

There are many noun + preposition phrases in English, such as **reason for**. Let's take a look at the following list of common noun + preposition phrases along with examples.

about	argument about	My parents and I had an **argument about** staying up late.
	discussion about	Let's have a **discussion about** the new marketing project.
	information about	"Do you have any **information about** tours in London?" "Yes. I'll give you some brochures."
between	connection between	There's a **connection between** hard work and success.
	link between	The professor discussed the **link between** history and culture.
for	advertisement for	I saw an **advertisement for** the art exhibit in the paper. Why don't we go tomorrow?
	cure for	Researchers are working hard to find a **cure for** AIDS.
	hope for	There's still **hope for** the patient. His condition has improved recently.
	recipe for	Could you give me the **recipe for** this pasta? It's so good!
	sympathy for	I feel a lot of **sympathy for** Eric. He's had a difficult year.
in	difficulty in	My grandfather has some **difficulty in** remembering names.
	drop in	There will be a **drop in** temperature later today, so don't forget your coats.
	reduction in	The **reduction in** tuition made all of the students very happy.
	rise in	I'm expecting a **rise in** income next year.
of	beginning of	School will start around the **beginning of** August.
	experience of	I've never had the **experience of** bungee jumping.
	importance of	I teach my children the **importance of** saving money.
	method of	My company is looking for a new **method of** attracting customers.
	opinion of	"What's your **opinion of** Jeffery?" "I think he's very nice."
	plan of	Ken's **plan of** traveling across Mexico sounds fun!
	price of	The **prices of** airline flights are going up. I'm glad I bought my ticket last month.
on	advice on	This article has some good **advice on** how to prepare for a new baby.

on	agreement on	After many hours, we finally reached an **agreement on** the contract.
	attack on	David took photos of the tiger's **attack on** the deer.
	comment on	Randy didn't make any **comments on** my article.
	decision on	I haven't made a **decision on** a name for my new business yet.
	effect on	Exercising every day has a good **effect on** my health.
	expert on	Professor Williams is an **expert on** Russian history.
to	approach to	My friend Lisa has a very positive **approach to** life.
	introduction to	Have you read the **introduction to** the book? It's interesting.
	invitation to	Did you get an **invitation to** Erin's birthday dinner?
with	contact with	I lost **contact with** Jessica. I wonder how she is.
	conversation with	Jim enjoys having **conversations with** his grandfather.
	problem with	There's a **problem with** the printer. It's out of ink.
	trouble with	I'm having **trouble with** my phone. Can I borrow yours?

GRAMMAR GATEWAY INTERMEDIATE

Answers

PRACTICE Answers

Review Test Answers

PRACTICE Answers

Lesson 1

A

2. Sarah and Julia are nurses. They're in a cafeteria *OR* They are in a cafeteria
3. Betty is a reporter. She's in a helicopter *OR* She is in a helicopter
4. Marvin is a soldier. He's at the airport *OR* He is at the airport
5. Jim and Alan are baseball players. They're on a bench *OR* They are on a bench

B

2. 're not in my bag *OR* aren't in my bag *OR* are not in my bag
3. 'm not happy *OR* am not happy
4. is at the theater
5. are twins
6. isn't Chinese *OR* is not Chinese

C

2. Johnny and Robert are in Seattle
3. is the bathroom
4. I'm not familiar *OR* I am not familiar
5. Are you a photographer
6. This necklace isn't expensive *OR* This necklace is not expensive

D

2. Is; in his room
3. 's busy *OR* is busy
4. is at school; isn't back from the library *OR* is not back from the library
5. Are; hungry
6. 'm OK *OR* am OK

Lesson 2

A

2. is reading a book
3. is holding a cup
4. are riding bikes
5. are moving a plant
6. is cleaning the desk
7. is fixing a photocopier
8. are standing at the door

B

2. I'm not acting *OR* I am not acting
3. I'm taking *OR* I am taking
4. are you doing
5. I'm teaching *OR* I am teaching
6. Is he studying
7. he's not attending *OR* he isn't attending *OR* he is not attending
8. He's learning *OR* He is learning

C

2. I'm listening *OR* I am listening
3. Are they dating
4. She's not sleeping *OR* She isn't sleeping *OR* She is not sleeping
5. we're not hiring *OR* we aren't hiring *OR* we are not hiring
6. Is Mom baking
7. I'm not spending *OR* I am not spending
8. The leaves are changing

Lesson 3

A

2. see
3. wake
4. travels
5. cost
6. teaches
7. fixes
8. eat

B

2. don't have flowers *OR* do not have flowers
3. doesn't mix with water *OR* does not mix with water
4. falls in the rainforest
5. fly south in the winter

C

1. I bring
2. do you and your friends go
3. Does this bus stop; It turns
4. Does Jennifer enjoy
5. do you spell
6. Does Peter send; he calls

D

2. usually helps
3. often answers
4. Does; like
5. doesn't talk *OR* does not talk
6. always meets

Lesson 4

A

2. don't agree
3. 's planting
4. Does; have
5. are; going
6. doesn't belong
7. isn't lying
8. are having

B

2. sounds
3. Do; feel *OR* Are; feeling
4. doesn't taste
5. don't smell
6. is tasting

C

2. have → are having
3. ✓
4. tastes → is tasting
5. ✓
6. I'm not believing → I don't believe
7. is possessing → possesses
8. ✓

D

2. know
3. look *OR* 're looking
4. are; doing
5. 'm searching
6. sounds

Lesson 5

A

2. Do; bring
3. Is; shopping
4. runs

5. are singing
6. Does; smoke
7. freezes
8. Are; looking

B
2. 'm practicing
3. see
4. 's growing
5. 're staying
6. plays

C
2. are
3. is being
4. 's
5. 're being
6. 'm being

D
2. 'm watching
3. meet
4. 're taking
5. want
6. 'm being

Lesson 6

A
2. exercised at a gym
3. got a haircut
4. watched a movie
5. went to a restaurant

B
2. joined
3. didn't hear *OR* did not hear
4. were
5. didn't swim *OR* did not swim
6. wrote
7. wasn't *OR* was not

C
1. Was it
2. Were you; I arrived
3. Did Roy play; he was
4. I worked; did you leave

D
2. was
3. met; fell
4. didn't give up *OR* did not give up
5. got
6. live; visit

Lesson 7

A
2. was attending
3. was holding
4. wasn't giving *OR* was not giving
5. were sitting
6. was talking
7. was looking
8. weren't eating *OR* were not eating

B
2. weren't wearing *OR* were not wearing
3. wasn't paying *OR* was not paying
4. were; carrying
5. was arguing
6. Was; hiding

C
1. He was meeting
2. Were you driving; I was going
3. You weren't exercising *OR* You were not exercising; I was walking
4. Did you know; We were
5. did you turn; Were you watching
6. Did you show; They liked

D
2. was reading
3. came; wanted
4. didn't hear
5. was listening
6. were sleeping

Lesson 8

A
2. jumped; was swimming
3. paid; left
4. lost; was jogging
5. landed; got
6. was snowing; went

B
2. got; was cooking
3. was preparing; put
4. was sleeping; went
5. was ringing
6. had

C
2. while I was giving my presentation
3. when the rain stopped
4. While I was parking
5. while we were watching TV
6. When Maria woke up
7. when his computer shut down
8. When the child dropped the glass

Lesson 9

A
2. didn't use to wear
3. used to be
4. didn't use to grow

B
2. Did; use to drink
3. didn't use to have
4. used to bake
5. Did; use to be
6. didn't use to check
7. used to belong

C
2. 'm used to running
3. used to be
4. 'm used to taking
5. used to ski

D
2. used to spend
3. costs
4. have
5. used to take
6. miss
7. need

Lesson 10

A
2. Has; worked
3. 've not visited *OR* haven't visited *OR* have not visited
4. have made
5. hasn't checked *OR* has not checked
6. have; had

B
2. 've not brushed my hair since last week *OR* haven't brushed

my hair since last week *OR* have not brushed my hair since last week
3. 's taught here since last semester *OR* has taught here since last semester
4. 've not done the laundry for a month *OR* haven't done the laundry for a month *OR* have not done the laundry for a month
5. hasn't come for 30 minutes *OR* has not come for 30 minutes
6. 's driven that car since 1995 *OR* has driven that car since 1995

C
1. 's become *OR* has become
2. 've not gone *OR* haven't gone *OR* have not gone
3. have been; was
4. 's sold *OR* has sold
5. 've not listened *OR* haven't listened *OR* have not listened; broke

D
2. hasn't smoked since he got married *OR* has not smoked since he got married
3. 've met many people since we moved to LA *OR* have met many people since we moved to LA
4. haven't spoken since they had an argument *OR* have not spoken since they had an argument

Lesson 11

A
2. hasn't lived
3. Have; listened
4. haven't used
5. 's received
6. Has; given

B
2. I've (never) broken a bone
3. I've (never) tried scuba diving
4. I've (never) made bread at home
5. Have you ever studied Chinese
6. Have you ever broken a bone
7. Have you ever tried scuba diving
8. Have you ever made bread at home

C
2. 's gone
3. Have; been
4. Have; gone
5. 's been

D
2. Have you ever done
3. I've volunteered
4. I've been to Africa once
5. I've ever had
6. I've never thought

Lesson 12

A
2. Has; lost
3. woke
4. visited
5. Did; paint
6. has wanted
7. have; played
8. did; go

B
2. Have you chosen a wedding dress yet *OR* Did you choose a wedding dress yet
3. I bought
4. Have you already found a place *OR* Did you already find a place
5. We've just made reservations *OR* We just made reservations

C
2. exercised → have exercised
3. ✓
4. didn't smoke → hasn't smoked
5. ✓
6. Have you gone → Did you go

D
2. were
3. have; worked
4. started
5. haven't told *OR* didn't tell

Lesson 13

A
2. have been listening to
3. has been cleaning the windows
4. has been painting a picture
5. has been sitting
6. have been running

B
2. She's been cooking dinner since 5 o'clock *OR* She has been cooking dinner since 5 o'clock
3. They've been building a bridge for six months *OR* They have been building a bridge for six months
4. They've been playing tennis since noon *OR* They have been playing tennis since noon
5. He's been using his laptop for an hour *OR* He has been using his laptop for an hour

C
2. 've been climbing *OR* have been climbing
3. 's been sleeping *OR* has been sleeping
4. 's been swimming *OR* has been swimming
5. 've been packing *OR* have been packing

D
2. How long have you been watching
3. Where has John been staying
4. Have you been enjoying
5. How long has Lucy been planning

Lesson 14

A
2. 's driven 90 miles
3. 've baked eight muffins
4. 's picked a basket of oranges
5. 's had three cups of coffee

B
2. 's been keeping a diary since she was 10
3. have been sleeping for an hour
4. 's been wearing glasses for five

years
5. have been renovating the house since May

C
2. I've called her
3. I've read this book
4. It's sold *OR* It's been selling
5. Sandra has spent *OR* Sandra has been spending
6. Sue has visited
7. Ken and Mark haven't worked *OR* Ken and Mark haven't been working
8. They've had
9. have you gone out for drinks
10. have you been designing clothes *OR* have you designed clothes

Lesson 15

A
2. had broken the lamp
3. had gone to bed
4. had left a note
5. had eaten all the cookies

B
2. 'd not seen *OR* hadn't seen *OR* had not seen
3. had ordered
4. 'd not expected *OR* hadn't expected *OR* had not expected
5. hadn't opened *OR* had not opened
6. 'd practiced *OR* had practiced

C
2. had answered
3. 'd saved *OR* had saved
4. watched
5. reached
6. 'd gone *OR* had gone

D
2. arrived; had already left
3. got; 'd already gone *OR* had already gone
4. did; get
5. drank *OR* 'd drunk *OR* had drunk

Lesson 16

A
2. will call
3. Will; be
4. won't hurt *OR* will not hurt
5. will have
6. will; arrive
7. 'll help *OR* will help
8. won't buy *OR* will not buy

B
2. won't play *OR* will not play
3. won't eat *OR* will not eat
4. 'll explain *OR* will explain

C
2. I (don't) think I'll get a haircut next week
3. I (don't) think I'll see a movie next weekend
4. I (don't) think I'll travel abroad next year
5. I (don't) think I'll go to the beach next summer

D
2. I'm sure you'll become *OR* I'm sure you will become
3. Will you take
4. I guess I'll study *OR* I guess I will study
5. You won't be *OR* You will not be
6. I'll think *OR* I will think

Lesson 17

A
2. are going to fall into the box
3. 's going to sleep on the sofa
4. 're going to wash the dog
5. is going to melt

B
2. 'll help *OR* 's going to help
3. 's going to have
4. 'll find *OR* 're going to find
5. 'll learn *OR* 'm going to learn
6. 're going to complete

C
2. He's going to visit
3. I'll be
4. I won't order
5. She's not going to be

D
2. were going to give
3. was going to attend
4. were going to wait

Lesson 18

A
2. They're meeting
3. She's opening a bakery
4. He's running in a marathon
5. They're getting married

B
2. arrives at 11:40 a.m.
3. starts at 7:00
4. departs on February 5
5. play on Thursday

C
2. The class begins
3. she's not joining
4. does the musical end
5. Alex and I are going
6. The bus doesn't leave

D
2. is about to close
3. 'm about to check
4. is about to break
5. are about to announce

Lesson 19

A
2. 'll be packing
3. 'll be painting the new house
4. 'll be buying some furniture
5. 'll be moving into the new house

B
2. won't remember
3. Will; be sleeping
4. 'll go
5. 'll be preparing
6. won't be attending
7. Will; show
8 will be playing

C
2. won't be coming
3. 'll be volunteering
4. will; be staying

D
2. I won't be going
3. will you be doing
4. I'll be having
5. I won't be doing
6. I'll be waiting

Lesson 20

A
2. will have saved
3. will have produced
4. will have dropped
5. will have lost

B
1. finds
2. won't have finished
3. 'll have melted; get
4. reach; 'll have walked
5. won't have read; return
6. 'll have waited

C
2. Will; pass
3. 'll call
4. 'll have cleaned
5. will have lived
6. 'll pay

D
2. I'll have completed college
3. I'll have directed several movies
4. I'll have won a big award

Lesson 21

A
2. When I move to New York City
3. when he gets a bonus next month
4. when Lisa and Jake feel hungry
5. When Mr. Harris retires next year

B
1. make
2. don't pay; will charge
3. travel; 'll study
4. 'll be; doesn't come
5. buys; 'll give
6. won't start; arrive
7. Will; become; receives

C
2. ✓
3. won't be using → isn't using
4. ✓
5. will return → returns
6. will have completed → have completed

D
1. leave
2. fixes; 'll pick
3. Will; stop; go
4. have; will; do
5. 'll ask; comes

Lesson 22

A
2. can't reach
3. Can; do
4. can play
5. Can; pay
6. can't eat

B
2. I could type
3. they couldn't get
4. I can't run
5. he can throw
6. Josh can't afford
7. You could read
8. Kelly couldn't ski

C
2. was able to
3. couldn't *OR* weren't able to
4. were able to
5. couldn't *OR* wasn't able to
6. could *OR* was able to

D
2. can *OR* 'm able to speak
3. been able to learn
4. couldn't understand *OR* wasn't able to understand
5. be able to sing

Lesson 23

A
2. couldn't see
3. could have
4. could tell
5. couldn't join
6. could be

B
2. couldn't fly
3. couldn't have done
4. couldn't know
5. couldn't have written
6. couldn't have gotten
7. couldn't eat
8. couldn't have arrived

C
2. We could have visited the Great Wall
3. Bill and Helen could have sold their old car
4. You could have gone shopping with me

D
2. could have dropped
3. couldn't have done
4. could belong

Lesson 24

A
2. She might not help Jo with her presentation
3. He might not buy that shirt
4. The package might arrive today
5. She might not go to the festival next week
6. They might have dinner with Tom

B
2. might know
3. might not wear
4. might not have heard
5. might have ordered
6. might not attend
7. might have missed
8. might not have left

C
2. might not have felt
3. couldn't be
4. couldn't have
5. might not provide
6. couldn't have begun
7. might not work
8. might not have woken

Lesson 25

A

2. must not cook
3. must know
4. must play
5. must not be
6. must have

B

2. must have gotten
3. must enjoy
4. must exercise
5. must have come
6. must have drunk

C

2. She must not like chicken
3. He must not have slept enough
4. They must have learned Italian there
5. She must not be married
6. He must have ridden it to school

D

2. must not
3. might
4. might not
5. must
6. must not

Lesson 26

A

2. must not touch
3. must wear
4. must show
5. must not drive
6. must take

B

2. She doesn't have to take
3. Do we have to work
4. Does the mayor have to give
5. You don't have to walk
6. He has to pass

C

2. don't have to bring
3. must not fish
4. don't have to carry
5. don't have to pay
6. must not feed

D

2. have to teach
3. didn't have to apologize
4. must tell *OR* have to tell
5. had to move
6. Did; have to revise
7. didn't have to sleep
8. must hire *OR* have to hire

Lesson 27

A

2. shouldn't worry
3. shouldn't give
4. should listen
5. should leave
6. shouldn't open

B

2. should I meet
3. should I hang
4. should I order
5. Should I throw
6. should I plan

C

2. Jack shouldn't have played
3. I should have asked you first
4. We should have helped her
5. She shouldn't have sold it
6. you shouldn't have scared your little sister
7. You should have come with us

D

2. shouldn't have eaten
3. shouldn't have ordered
4. should take
5. shouldn't have stopped
6. shouldn't be

Lesson 28

A

2. 'd better stay away *OR* had better stay away
3. 'd better slow down *OR* had better slow down
4. 'd better close the window *OR* had better close the window
5. 'd better keep quiet here *OR* had better keep quiet here
6. 'd better wash your hands *OR* had better wash your hands

B

2. 'd better sweep
3. 'd better not play
4. 'd better register
5. 'd better not arrive
6. 'd better not forget
7. 'd better turn
8. 'd better not quit

C

2. We'd better not go outside *OR* We had better not go outside
3. We'd better put the vase on the top shelf *OR* We had better put the vase on the top shelf
4. You'd better not miss the deadline *OR* You had better not miss the deadline
5. You'd better not spend a lot of money this month *OR* You had better not spend a lot of money this month

Lesson 29

A

2. When will you return home
3. Has Jenny sent the documents
4. Does your neighbor have
5. Are your friends graduating
6. Where have you traveled
7. Who did Sarah visit

B

2. Whose idea
3. What languages
4. How often
5. Whose car
6. how much

C

2. What is he apologizing for
3. What is she hiding from
4. What are they laughing at
5. What are you reaching for
6. What are they arguing about

D

2. What is your roommate like
3. What was your first date like
4. What was the cake for
5. What is this big bowl for

Lesson 30

A

2. Who did Craig tell the secret
3. Who beat the Bears
4. Who did the Owls beat

B

2. Who is going to visit Jane
3. What happened downtown
4. What will Tim order for lunch
5. What keeps dropping from the ceiling
6. Who have the police arrested
7. What did Erica print for the meeting
8. Who called this morning

C

2. Who invited you
3. How many people are coming
4. What should I give her
5. Which will she like

Lesson 31

A

2. why she looks worried
3. where I can buy that laptop
4. who that singer is

B

2. what was in Lucy's backpack
3. how the thief got into
4. who left this file
5. where you stayed in LA
6. which sandwich Laura wanted

C

2. if/whether these shoes are on sale
3. if/whether I told you about the art exhibit
4. if/whether someone is sitting here
5. if/whether the bus to Oak Park stops here

D

2. Do you know what it is called
3. I don't know if/whether I should believe her
4. Can you tell me when my suit will be ready
5. I don't remember if/whether it was a dog or a cat
6. I wonder who Christine called

Lesson 32

A

2. shouldn't we
3. can you
4. haven't you
5. do you

B

2. You can't take me to the concert, can you
3. Melissa rides her bike to work, doesn't she
4. Chad is going on a business trip, isn't he
5. We haven't gone hiking together, have we

C

2. Wasn't Lucas waiting for his sister at the airport
3. Don't I look good in blue jeans
4. Didn't Melanie leave for work yet
5. Won't we have fun at the beach
6. Hasn't Roger had a girlfriend before

D

2. No
3. No
4. Yes
5. No
6. Yes

Lesson 33

A

2. The juice was spilled
3. The onion was cut
4. The windows were washed
5. The letters were sent

B

2. joined
3. be canceled
4. carry
5. is known
6. be cooked
7. wears
8. were included

C

2. were being planted
3. aren't being used
4. wasn't being cleaned
5. are being developed
6. was being performed
7. isn't being helped
8. were being printed

D

2. North America hadn't been discovered
3. my purse had been taken
4. it has been updated
5. we've been introduced
6. The ring had been sold
7. It has been closed
8. All of the things have been packed

Lesson 34

A

2. is baked
3. was caused by a tornado
4. were delivered
5. are prepared by Antonio Bruno
6. was arrested

B

2. photographers → by photographers
3. was appeared → appeared
4. ✓
5. ✓
6. isn't belonged → doesn't belong
7. ✓
8. delayed → were delayed

C

2. is married *OR* got married
3. was lost
4. be done *OR* be finished
5. be born

D

2. got broken
3. Did; get caught
4. didn't get hurt
5. Did; get dressed
6. didn't get fired

Lesson 35

A
2. was given some medicine
3. were given cards
4. was given a good grade
5. were given some cookies
6. was given a package
7. were given balloons
8. was given a gold medal

B
2. I was paid $50 (by Bob)
3. Money is lent to foreign residents
4. Visitors will be shown the gardens (by Ms. Sanders)
5. The story was told to his grandchildren
6. We were offered a discount
7. Students are taught yoga
8. Some questions will be asked to the movie star (by the reporter)

C
2. will be paid to the driver
3. must be shown passports
4. are taught manners by their parents
5. was sent to the girl by Ned

Lesson 36

A
2. Sharing a room
3. Cooking a meal at home
4. Finding a job
5. Parking on this road
6. Seeing the singer on stage

B
2. Drinking coffee is
3. Sitting close to the TV leads
4. Eating fruits doesn't affect
5. Wearing a hat causes

C
2. Taking care of children; requires
3. Reviewing the article again; doesn't seem
4. Becoming a famous actress; is
5. Riding an elephant; doesn't sound
6. Speaking in front of people; doesn't make

D
2. It's comfortable to sleep on a sofa *OR* It's uncomfortable to sleep on a sofa
3. It's necessary to have a cell phone *OR* It's unnecessary to have a cell phone
4. It's convenient to take the bus *OR* It's inconvenient to take the bus
5. It's fun to watch movies alone *OR* It's boring to watch movies alone

Lesson 37

A
2. risk losing
3. deny meeting
4. keep walking
5. finish eating
6. suggest taking
7. give up skating

B
2. putting sugar in his coffee
3. not locking the door
4. studying Spanish
5. not going to Susie's party

C
2. living
3. being photographed
4. being taught
5. spending
6. being injured

D
2. read → reading
3. ✓
4. having rented → renting
5. ✓
6. carrying not → not carrying

Lesson 38

A
2. to catch
3. living
4. moving
5. to finish
6. shopping
7. to allow

B
2. expected to arrive
3. promised not to watch
4. offered to share
5. decided not to ride
6. agreed not to hide
7. intended to call

C
2. to be built
3. to provide
4. to use
5. to be recognized
6. to be amazed

D
2. to have fixed
3. to be growing
4. to have stopped
5. to have changed
6. to be listening

Lesson 39

A
2. to quit
3. working *OR* to work
4. making
5. to keep
6. rising *OR* to rise

B
2. remember going
3. Remember to pick
4. regret buying
5. forget visiting
6. regret to announce
7. forget to pack

C
2. tried to make an omelet
3. tried to call Sarah
4. try studying with a partner
5. Try following the recipe
6. try sending her a text message

D
2. stop to check
3. stop spending
4. need signing
5. Stop changing
6. need to take
7. need updating

Lesson 40

A

2. wants me to sell it to him
3. wants me to take him
4. want me to move back
5. wants me to meet her

B

2. told Cori to prepare for the presentation
3. invited Kevin to go out for drinks tonight
4. allowed Denise to go home early
5. advised Jane to call the customer soon
6. encouraged Steve to attend the seminar

C

2. him joining
3. it from spreading
4. her saying
5. them waiting
6. us from taking
7. me laughing

D

2. to live
3. them going
4. to study
5. her taking
6. him to apologize
7. playing
8. us to do

Lesson 41

A

2. He let her play outside
3. She had him sign the form
4. He made them wait in line
5. She let him use her scissors

B

2. made me fall
3. get them to read
4. get him to take
5. had your eyes tested
6. let Phil ride
7. get a tooth pulled

C

2. help us (to) solve
3. help you (to) feel
4. help me (to) bake

D

2. listened to him speak
3. saw her leave
4. heard them call
5. saw him finish
6. felt it shake

Lesson 42

A

2. went to the park to fly kites
3. went to the hall to listen to the speech
4. went to the restaurant to deliver groceries
5. went to the bank to get some cash

B

2. so that we won't get hungry later
3. so that I can look at the stars at night
4. so that I wouldn't forget
5. so that you don't injure yourself
6. so that an old lady could sit there

C

2. for a conference
3. to enter the National Museum
4. to wish her good luck
5. for a hammer
6. to help the environment
7. for my cousin's wedding
8. for a drink

D

2. letter to send
3. dress to wear
4. decision to make
5. chance to listen
6. movies to watch

Lesson 43

A

2. Maria was sorry to miss the phone call
3. I was relieved to find my credit card
4. I was surprised to get so many presents for my birthday
5. Don was glad to help his wife with the housework

B

2. are (*OR* aren't) difficult to learn
3. is (*OR* isn't) expensive to own
4. is (*OR* isn't) hard to get
5. are (*OR* aren't) easy to grow
7. It is (*OR* isn't) difficult to learn languages
8. It is (*OR* isn't) expensive to own a pet
9. It is (*OR* isn't) hard to get a good job
10. It is (*OR* isn't) easy to grow plants

C

2. cheap for me to get
3. impossible for us to carry
4. generous of him to lend
5. dangerous for beginners to try
6. selfish of Evan to eat

D

2. happy to be
3. difficult for you to get
4. hard for me to find
5. relieved to hear
6. nice of you to invite

Lesson 44

A

2. who to date
3. where to hang
4. when to meet
5. how to change

B

2. where to put
3. how to play
4. when to come
5. who to hire
6. whether to join

C

2. whose story to believe
3. which book to read
4. what color to paint the wall
5. which way to go
6. whose advice to follow

D
2. where to have
3. who to invite
4. whether to buy
5. how to cook
6. what to do

Lesson 45

A
2. for cleaning
3. without leaving
4. at cooking
5. by calling
6. on making

B
2. As a result of training
3. in favor of changing
4. In addition to offering
5. in spite of having
6. instead of celebrating

C
2. 's used to speaking
3. object to staying
4. when it comes to building
5. looking forward to taking

D
2. have → having
3. ✓
4. by ask → by asking
5. start → starting
6. ✓

Lesson 46

A
2. felt like having
3. Do you mind pushing
4. was busy cleaning
5. have difficulty understanding
6. was worth reading

B
2. spent a lot of money fixing my car
3. is busy preparing for her presentation
4. can't help worrying about their children all the time
5. has trouble/difficulty seeing without her glasses

C
2. It took her three weeks to make
3. It cost her $500 to buy
4. It took them two hours to watch
5. It cost them $68 to see
6. It cost him $25 to get

D
2. can't wait to leave
3. can't help feeling
4. can't help laughing
5. can afford to stay
6. can't wait to meet

Lesson 47

A
2. There's a bicycle
3. There are four birds
4. There are three books
5. There's an umbrella
6. There's a calendar

B
2. tourists
3. a table
4. air
5. athletes
6. rain
7. an apartment
8. novels

C
2. movies look
3. juice contains
4. museum displays
5. cookies have
6. delivery truck brings

D
2. Music aren't → Music isn't
3. baby → a baby
4. A people → People
5. ✓
6. rices → rice
7. ✓
8. game → games
9. This street have → This street has

Lesson 48

A
2. an engineer
3. ice
4. a tie
5. news
6. an envelope
7. politics
8. a picture
9. meat
10. information

B
2. three jars of jam
3. a bar of soap
4. A kilo of cheese
5. two bottles of beer

C
2. paper
3. times
4. time
5. lights
6. light
7. glass
8. glasses
9. a room
10. room
11. a hair
12. hair

Lesson 49

A
1. earrings; bracelets; jewelry
2. money; coins; pennies
3. table; chairs; furniture
4. mail; regular letters; postcards
5. luggage; brown suitcase; backpacks

B
2. words
3. a suggestion
4. Travel
5. news
6. a big meal

C
2. work
3. articles
4. job
5. trips
6. scenery

Lesson 50

A

1. two pairs of pants
2. a pair of sunglasses; two skirts
3. four shirts; a pair of pants
4. three caps; one skirt; three pairs of shorts

B

2. Binoculars help
3. My vocabulary improves
4. The surroundings are
5. Do these pants seem
6. A museum ticket costs
7. Pajamas feel
8. Time is
9. My son plays
10. These shoes make
11. Personal belongings need
12. Your steak smells

C

2. Congratulation → Congratulations
3. ✓
4. is → are
5. ✓
6. hasn't → haven't
7. a pair of glass → a pair of glasses
8. a shorts → a pair of shorts *OR* shorts
9. good → goods
10. ✓

Lesson 51

A

2. a newspaper
3. the dream
4. The bike
5. an umbrella
6. the vase
7. an old man
8. a store

B

1. the
2. a; the; the
3. an; the
4. a; the
5. the; the
6. a; the

C

2. a bathrooms → bathrooms
3. A mayor → The mayor
4. ✓
5. a sugar → sugar
6. ✓
7. the idea → an idea

D

2. a superhero
3. a city
4. a motorcycle
5. an enemy
6. the city
7. the enemy

Lesson 52

A

2. Muffins are great for breakfast or as a snack
3. Garages provide space to park cars
4. Cell phones help you keep in touch with friends
5. Nouns are words for people, places, or things
6. Sailors travel on ships

B

2. -
3. A
4. The
5. an
6. -
7. -
8. a
9. The
10. the

C

2. The blue whale *OR* Blue whales
3. the microscope *OR* microscopes
4. Bones
5. the tiles
6. judges

D

2. The tomato is a vegetable
3. Todd is an excellent singer
4. Judy is a lawyer in Florida
5. This is an old desk
6. The cactus is a tough plant

Lesson 53

A

2. **The** TV uses a lot of electricity.
3. In 2010, China had **the** largest population in **the** world.
4. **The** sky is beautiful. There are so many stars.
5. We go to **the** movies a lot. We enjoy it.
6. I use **the** Internet everyday for research.
7. Do you prefer listening to **the** radio or watching TV?
8. "I hope **the** rain stops soon." "I do too."
9. **The** government passed a new child protection law.
10. Ronald and I went fishing in **the** ocean yesterday.

B

2. the cinema
3. books
4. Flour
5. The wind
6. the universe
7. TV
8. songs

C

2. April is the fourth month
3. Who is the oldest child
4. Brad's Café serves the best coffee
5. I'm the only person in my class
6. Matthew has lived in the same house

D

2. It is very important to save **the** environment.
3. Plants and animals living on the land and in **the** ocean need a clean environment, too.
4. Recycling is **the** first thing we can do.
5. **The** second thing is reducing pollution.
6. There are many ways to help, but **the** best way is to do something right now before it's too late.

Lesson 54

A
2. the sea
3. home
4. the theater
5. bed
6. the universe
7. work
8. the earth
9. home
10. bed

B
2. Alex is at the school
3. Tony and Bob are in jail
4. Beth is at the church
5. Lynn and Ray are at church

C
2. Saturday
3. dinner
4. home
5. the winter *OR* winter
6. the best party
7. the Jacksons
8. Mrs. Carson

Lesson 55

A
1. it
2. I
3. you; them
4. you
5. us
6. they; me
7. He
8. her

B
2. Her
3. yours
4. their
5. our
6. mine

C
2. ✓
3. Their → Theirs *OR* Their hotel
4. is → are
5. mine briefcase → mine *OR* my briefcase
6. a your date → your date
7. were → was
8. The ours → Ours

D
2. We
3. her
4. us; your
5. they
6. Mine
7. yours
8. you

Lesson 56

A
2. the owner of this truck
3. the director of that movie
4. last night's concert
5. the ingredients of the food
6. A turtle's shell
7. next month's election
8. the roof of the building

B
2. Angela's
3. yesterday's picnic
4. Brazil's president
5. Ron's
6. the hairdresser's
7. rabbit's hair
8. my neighbor's

C
2. one of his coworkers
3. Some toys of my brother's *OR* Some of my brother's toys
4. one of my goals
5. some classmates of Rita's *OR* some of Rita's classmates
6. a tradition of ours
7. Some of their drinks
8. A hobby of Melinda's

D
2. the end of the show
3. the magician's name
4. A friend of mine
5. the manager of that theater

Lesson 57

A
2. her
3. yourself
4. us
5. themselves
6. me
7. himself
8. yourselves

B
2. Did; pack everything themselves
3. didn't bake this pie ourselves
4. made them myself
5. booked all of the tickets herself
6. Did; fix the sink yourself

C
2. see himself
3. make yourself
4. trust ourselves
5. Behave yourselves
6. help themselves
7. turn itself

D
2. by yourself
3. yourself
4. yourself
5. by yourself
6. yourself

Lesson 58

A
2. them
3. ones
4. They
5. it
6. one
7. ones

B
2. My blue one
3. some wild ones
4. a dry one
5. his best ones
6. the wrong ones

C
2. that expensive one
3. these
4. This brown one

D
2. the gold ones
3. the cozy one on the hill
4. the big ones
5. the spicy one with chicken

6. The ones near the entrance

Lesson 59

A

2. some forms
3. any wind
4. some pills
5. some time
6. any children

B

2. some apple juice
3. any drugstores
4. any candles
5. some salt
6. some suggestions

C

2. something
3. any
4. some
5. anyone *OR* anybody
6. someone *OR* somebody
7. some
8. anywhere
9. any
10. somewhere
11. anything
12. any

D

2. Any customer *OR* Any customers
3. any items
4. Some sofas
5. any trouble
6. any question *OR* any questions

Lesson 60

A

2. any problem
3. no mistakes
4. any advice
5. no snow
6. no secrets
7. no energy
8. any alcohol

B

2. This highway has no gas stations
3. I didn't plan anything for today
4. Aaron didn't do any homework all afternoon
5. There was nobody at the gym this morning
6. I went nowhere last night

C

2. ✓
3. Not any → No
4. isn't nothing → is nothing *OR* isn't anything
5. ✓
6. no → none *OR* no movies
7. don't know nobody → know nobody *OR* don't know anybody

D

1. any
2. some
3. none
4. no
5. some
6. any
7. no

Lesson 61

A

2. All luggage
3. every age group
4. All paintings
5. Every worker
6. all schools

B

2. Each chapter includes
3. Each piece of chocolate is
4. Each band member plays
5. Each can contains

C

2. all staff members get
3. Each guest receives
4. every dish looks
5. All bags need
6. each seat turns
7. Every neighborhood has
8. all perfume smells

D

2. No one *OR* Nobody
3. Not everyone *OR* Not everybody
4. everywhere
5. nothing
6. nowhere
7. Not everything

Lesson 62

A

2. much work
3. many clients
4. Many birds
5. much advice
6. many magazines

B

2. a lot of
3. A lot
4. much
5. much *OR* a lot of
6. a lot of
7. a lot

C

2. Few items
3. a few friends
4. a little salad
5. little noise
6. a few blocks
7. a little soup
8. few trains

D

2. so many
3. a lot of
4. much
5. little
6. a little

Lesson 63

A

2. None of the girls
3. Most of the players
4. Some of the main dishes
5. None of the appetizers
6. All of the desserts

B

2. some of us
3. a little of it
4. any of you
5. half of it
6. Most of them

C

2. All fish live in water
3. a little ice cream with my pie
4. Most of us don't know Jenny
5. Some people don't have a mobile phone
6. a few of them made mistakes
7. Half (of) the cup is filled

D

2. (of) the snow; melts
3. of the bedrooms; has
4. of my friends; own
5. of their earrings; cost
6. (of) his fridge; is

Lesson 64

A

2. either
3. both
4. Either
5. Neither
6. Both
7. neither
8. Either
9. both
10. neither

B

2. either test
3. Neither jacket
4. either drawing
5. Both cameras
6. Neither girl
7. either house
8. both toys

C

2. Neither of the subway lines; goes *OR* go
3. Both of us; look
4. Either of them; is *OR* are
5. Neither suit; fits
6. Both (of) these flashlights; need
7. Either event sounds
8. neither of us; plays *OR* play

Lesson 65

A

2. tastes sweet
3. Large families
4. wrong answer
5. got dirty
6. is true
7. long hair
8. sounds familiar
9. looks fresh
10. strong wind

B

2. I wasn't alone
3. Is this the only train
4. I feel sorry
5. *The Beatles* became famous
6. The hotel doesn't have an outdoor pool
7. The snake is alive
8. The company's main office moved
9. I'm glad to meet you
10. Tomorrow is an important day

C

2. beautiful pink roses
3. large white table
4. cute little puppies
5. nice new gray suit

Lesson 66

A

2. stolen
3. sleeping
4. barking
5. signed
6. renovated

B

2. The boy climbing the tree
3. All the songs performed by the band
4. the motorbike parked over there
5. The woman speaking right now
6. the flowers growing in your garden

C

2. used computer
3. woman staring
4. guided tour
5. cheering crowd
6. characters described

D

2. photo taken
3. crying baby
4. broken toy
5. girl laughing

Lesson 67

A

1. amazing
2. disappointing; disappointed
3. confusing; confused
4. frightened; frightening

B

2. tired; relaxing
3. embarrassed
4. boring
5. puzzling; puzzled
6. depressing
7. shocking
8. interesting; bored
9. depressed
10. excited; interested

C

2. exciting
3. surprising
4. shocked
5. disappointing
6. satisfied

Lesson 68

A

2. dramatically
3. lazily
4. kindly
5. carefully
6. responsibly

B

2. completely normal
3. church regularly
4. totally differently
5. really loud
6. the window tightly
7. the new mall surprisingly rapidly
8. amazingly cheap

C

2. closely the instructions → the instructions closely

3. absolute → absolutely
4. ✓
5. smoothly relatively→ relatively smoothly
6. angry → angrily
7. gently the furniture → the furniture gently
8. ✓

D
2. immediately
3. slightly
4. patiently
5. Hopefully

Lesson 69

A
2. surprisingly strong
3. getting hungry
4. famous speakers
5. extremely rapidly
6. normally busy
7. became popular
8. open automatically

B
2. acted bravely
3. smells sweet
4. look sharp
5. waited anxiously
6. looked closely

C
2. accurate
3. incorrect; immediately
4. glad
5. shortly
6. carefully

D
2. deliciously → delicious
3. proper → properly
4. easily → easy
5. angrily → angry
6. extreme → extremely
7. ✓

Lesson 70

A
2. long
3. comfortably
4. near
5. early
6. silent
7. hardly
8. high

B
1. lately
2. late
3. nearly
4. high
5. immediately
6. Surprisingly
7. happily

C
2. free
3. good
4. well
5. freely
6. well
7. free

D
2. ✓
3. high → highly
4. longly → long
5. good → well
6. ✓
7. lately → late
8. freely → free

Lesson 71

A
2. left it there yesterday
3. waiting for you downstairs
4. have a doctor's appointment tomorrow
5. can meet you then
6. move this sofa upstairs now
7. sit outside today

B
Sample answers:
2. I usually use public transportation *OR* I rarely use public transportation
3. I always brush my teeth after meals *OR* I often brush my teeth after meals
4. I sometimes go jogging in the morning *OR* I never go jogging in the morning
5. I rarely travel to foreign countries *OR* I sometimes travel to foreign countries
6. I always watch TV on weekends *OR* I never watch TV on weekends

C
2. just arrived
3. isn't usually friendly
4. has already gone to work
5. can sometimes help a cold
6. have hardly seen him lately
7. don't often go skiing in the winter
8. always had to study a lot in college

D
2. never used to go
3. doing anything outside
4. really hate
5. should often exercise
6. going to the mall tomorrow
7. meet there then

Lesson 72

A
2. too dirty
3. enough milk
4. high enough
5. too slowly
6. long enough
7. too small
8. enough beds

B
2. comfortable enough
3. too many mistakes
4. carefully enough
5. too much homework
6. enough cash
7. too suddenly
8. way too short
9. enough games
10. far too early

C
2. well enough for you
3. enough time for me to go
4. too dark to read
5. enough sunlight to survive
6. too loudly for us to have
7. safe enough for you to walk

8. too big for our living room

Lesson 73

A

2. so much pain
3. so different
4. so often
5. so many animals
6. so funny

B

2. such an old song
3. so excited
4. such polite children
5. such a strange dream
6. so well
7. such great news
8. so heavily

C

2. such a hobby
3. Such knowledge
4. such accidents
5. such an age

D

2. I was so sick that I couldn't go to work
3. The service was so slow that we left the café
4. It was such an impressive movie that people clapped at the end
5. Michelle left so quickly that I didn't have a chance to say goodbye
6. Rudy has such great style that people dress like him

Lesson 74

A

2. less difficult
3. quieter *OR* more quiet
4. hungrier
5. less regularly
6. more carefully
7. less painful
8. more surprised

B

2. faster than our previous models
3. fitter than ever before
4. cooler than any other air conditioners
5. more powerful than its competitors
6. more easily than in other beds

C

2. more customers than
3. less clothes than
4. more traffic than
5. more children than
6. less wine than

D

2. less busier → less busy
3. ✓
4. simple → simpler *OR* more simple
5. many mistakes → more mistakes
6. ✓

Lesson 75

A

1. much higher
2. a bit bigger; even lighter
3. far younger; much older
4. a little farther *OR* a little further; a lot longer

B

2. taller and taller
3. more and more afraid
4. closer and closer
5. more and more quickly

C

2. the more successful we will be
3. the more valuable it becomes
4. the faster they fall asleep
5. the more carefully people invest

D

2. The sweeter the better
3. The scarier the better
4. The more the better
5. The easier the better

Lesson 76

A

2. The most popular song
3. the warmest day
4. the most people
5. the highest score

B

2. more comfortably
3. the earliest
4. darker
5. older
6. most polluted
7. least
8. the saddest

C

2. the shortest
3. (the) closest
4. (the) most frequently
5. the politest *OR* the most polite
6. The least common
7. (the) least often
8. the least heavy

D

2. the most experience
3. the least interest
4. the least money
5. the most votes
6. the least damage

Lesson 77

A

2. the quietest street in town *OR* the most quiet street in town
3. the most relaxing holiday I've ever had
4. the hardest of all materials
5. the most honest person I know
6. the most famous composer of the 18th century
7. the healthiest student in our class
8. the slowest of all
9. the most ancient paintings in our museum
10. The most expensive gift I've ever received

B

2. by far the most loudly
3. easily the biggest

4. by far the funniest
5. easily the most dangerous

C
2. the largest
3. the second most expensive
4. The newest
5. the third oldest
6. the second most

D
2. one of the noisiest neighbors
3. one of the most boring meetings
4. one of the greatest artists
5. one of the most important jobs

Lesson 78

A
2. as often as Kevin
3. as heavy as they look
4. as famous as the others in the city
5. as calmly as I could
6. as badly as we had feared

B
2. The Golden Gate Bridge isn't as old as the Brooklyn Bridge
3. The Brooklyn Bridge isn't as wide as the Golden Gate Bridge
4. The Golden Gate Bridge is longer than the Brooklyn Bridge
5. The Brooklyn Bridge is older than the Golden Gate Bridge
6. The Golden Gate Bridge is wider than the Brooklyn Bridge

C
2. as many women as men
3. as much cash as Ted
4. as much light as my brother's room
5. as many seats as the new theater

D
2. the same school as you
3. the same time as her
4. the same height as you
5. the same day as yours
6. the same city as them

Lesson 79

A
2. just as important as
3. nearly as terribly as
4. almost as hungry as
5. nearly as well as
6. just as confused as

B
2. twice as big as
3. three times as expensive as
4. twice as long as
5. four times as fast as
6. three times as heavy as

C
2. as unique as possible
3. as truthfully as possible
4. as soon as you can
5. as loudly as I can
6. as often as he can

D
2. As far as I remember, Donna is coming back from her trip tomorrow
3. As far as I'm concerned, the red dress looks best
4. As far as I know, Mr. Brown is in his office

Lesson 80

A
2. at
3. at
4. on
5. in; in
6. in
7. on; on
8. at

B
2. in the tent
3. on the car
4. on the door
5. at the desk
6. on the desk
7. at the bus stop
8. in the car
9. at the crosswalk
10. at the door
11. on their faces
12. in their bags

C
1. at the door
2. on the carpet; on the sofa
3. at the mall
4. in the library; on the grass
5. on the floor; in the yard
6. in his office

Lesson 81

A
2. on
3. at
4. on
5. in
6. at
7. in
8. on

B
2. at the eye doctor's
3. in the car
4. on the menu
5. in rows
6. at Carrie's house
7. on the bus
8. in the ocean

C
2. in the middle of the table
3. at the bottom of the ladder
4. on the left side of the door
5. at the top of the poster

D
2. at the 15th floor → on the 15th floor
3. In the plane → On the plane
4. in the party → at the party
5. in her home → at her home
6. in a map → on a map
7. on the world → in the world

Lesson 82

A
1. at; at
2. on; at; on
3. in; On; at
4. in; in; on
5. on; at; in
6. at; in; at; at

B
2. in the 19th century
3. at lunch
4. (on) March 8
5. in the future
6. in the winter
7. at night

C
2. in
3. -
4. - *OR* on
5. at
6. - *OR* on
7. at; in

Lesson 83

A
2. in the meantime
3. at the moment
4. in years
5. at once
6. at the latest

B
2. At the same time
3. in advance
4. In the end
5. At first

C
2. on time
3. at the end of
4. In the end
5. on time
6. in time

D
2. in time
3. at that time
4. in years
5. in advance

Lesson 84

A
2. for
3. during
4. for
5. for
6. during
7. during

B
2. until 9 o'clock
3. by dinnertime
4. until next Saturday
5. until the beginning of July
6. by August
7. by the end of the week

C
2. won't be submitted until this Friday
3. doesn't pay the staff until the last day of every month
4. wasn't chosen until 5 o'clock
5. didn't receive the test results until yesterday

D
2. After
3. During
4. within
5. in
6. until

Lesson 85

A
2. in boots
3. by taxi
4. with glasses *OR* in glasses
5. with a tour guide
6. in capital letters
7. by phone
8. in shorts
9. in love
10. with chopsticks

B
2. for
3. in
4. by
5. with
6. on

C
2. with anger
3. in use
4. by fax
5. on (the) air

D
2. in a hurry
3. on sale
4. by check
5. by e-mail

Lesson 86

A
2. Because of her headache, Maria had to go home early
3. Because of their bad hearing, my grandparents rarely hear the phone ring
4. Thanks to her computer class, Betty knows computers better than I do
5. Thanks to their reservation, Helen and Ryan didn't have to wait
6. Thanks to the map, Jim was able to find his hotel without any problem

B
2. Instead of
3. instead
4. instead of
5. instead of
6. Instead

C
2. In spite of washing my shirt
3. in spite of her busy schedule
4. In spite of the darkness
5. in spite of being nervous
6. In spite of taking vitamins

D
2. because of
3. instead
4. instead of
5. Despite

Lesson 87

A
2. 're learning about geography
3. 's pointing at a sign
4. 's paying for the newspaper
5. 's thinking about chocolate cake
6. 're waving at the cameras

B
2. leads to many health problems
3. shouted at each other
4. apologized for losing

5. belong to Monica
6. forgets about appointments

C
2. look at
3. ask about
4. ask for
5. look after
6. look for

D
2. answer to → answer
3. ✓
4. married with → married
5. Look after → Look at
6. ✓
7. replied for → replied to
8. call to → call

Lesson 88

A
2. calm down
3. show up
4. hold on
5. work out

B
2. 's taking off
3. 're cleaning up
4. 's running away
5. 's turning down

C
2. run out of
3. get along with
4. break up with
5. got out of
6. signed up for

D
2. Why did you turn the TV on *OR* Why did you turn on the TV
3. she made it up
4. You have to try these shoes on *OR* You have to try on these shoes
5. I want to throw it away
6. You can't just take them away
7. Susan pointed out the mistake *OR* pointed the mistake out

Lesson 89

A
2. close to
3. related to
4. terrible at
5. suitable for
6. fond of
7. eager for
8. curious about

B
2. shocked at the news
3. responsible for sales
4. similar to limes
5. concerned about Sue's performance
6. scared of the noise
7. full of people

C
2. good for
3. familiar with
4. good to
5. familiar to

D
2. excellent at
3. capable of
4. kind to
5. late for

Lesson 90

A
2. in
3. of; to
4. to; to
5. between
6. of
7. in

B
2. cost of
3. key to
4. responsibility for
5. example of
6. difference between
7. change in

C
2. A good way of thanking people
3. Belief in Santa Claus
4. a desire for wealth
5. Mary's reply to your suggestion
6. the conversation between Chuck and Arnold
7. a request for a vegetarian meal

D
1. a great need for
2. an answer to
3. The search for; knowledge of
4. The demand for; an increase in
5. The lack of; the reason for

Lesson 91

A
2. While he brushed his teeth, he watched the news. *OR* He brushed his teeth while he watched the news
3. He fell while he was snowboarding
4. While she played the guitar, she sang *OR* She played the guitar while she sang
5. While they were walking in the forest, they saw a deer

B
2. By the time Frank called Julie back, she was already asleep
3. Max applied for jobs until he finally got one
4. Hans kept studying Russian until he became fluent
5. We were already back in the hotel by the time it began to rain
6. By the time our seminar ended, everyone was pleased with it

C
1. 'll let
2. won't order; arrive
3. hear; 'll be
4. Will; feed; am
5. meet
6. returns; will; tell

D
2. ✓
3. By → By the time
4. you are going to be → you are
5. during → while
6. ✓

Lesson 92

A

2. as she was looking through her bag
3. as he crossed the finish line
4. as she was pouring it
5. as they introduced themselves

B

2. as gas becomes more expensive
3. As Melissa drank more water
4. As the population grows
5. as we went up the mountain

C

2. As the sign says, you can't park your car
3. As I promised, I bought my wife
4. As I mentioned on the phone, Sandra is giving
5. As I explained in the e-mail, Mr. Jennings has

D

2. As this area has a warm climate
3. As the elevator was broken
4. As Claire didn't understand the instructions
5. As our products are high quality

Lesson 93

A

2. so that she won't gain any more weight
3. so that she can speak it fluently
4. so that he will get a promotion
5. so that she can have more space for her children
6. so that he won't be late for school again

B

2. to make some extra money
3. for running
4. so that your hands don't get cold
5. for drinks
6. to send Mom's birthday card
7. so that I won't forget

C

2. so loud that I couldn't concentrate
3. so that he can get
4. so bright that I need
5. so thin that we couldn't skate
6. so that we won't be

Lesson 94

A

2. Although my computer is old, it works perfectly
3. Although I washed my sneakers twice, the smell didn't disappear
4. Although I didn't put much salt on the food, Sam said it was too salty
5. Although Greg is just a beginner, he plays golf really well
6. Although my grandparents are over 70 years old, they're still very active

B

2. in spite of the flight's delayed departure
3. Although Terry practiced his speech many times
4. despite failing the test
5. even though she isn't famous
6. In spite of the fact that I've been on a diet for a month

C

2. though
3. In spite of
4. although *OR* though
5. though
6. in spite of

Lesson 95

A

2. putting pepper in her soup
3. Opening the window
4. Receiving the award
5. looking at himself in the mirror

B

2. Needing to borrow a blouse for an interview, Shelly asked her sister
3. Noticing the smoke from the building, we called 911
4. Eating his burger, Max dropped some ketchup on his pants
5. Being married to a pilot, I don't see my husband every day
6. Riding my bicycle around the neighborhood, I saw many of my friends

C

2. not owning my house
3. Feeling refreshed after our vacation
4. not wanting to argue anymore
5. Riding on the boat
6. being stuck
7. Not being old enough

Lesson 96

A

2. if he doesn't reply
3. If Emma gets a scholarship
4. if there's nothing interesting on TV
5. if I don't pay the electricity bill
6. If we hurry to the theater

B

2. If I become a doctor, I'll open a children's hospital
3. If I move to France, I'll learn to paint
4. If I learn to paint, I'll have an exhibit
5. If I graduate college, I'll work at the UN

C

1. won't take
2. Send; travel
3. open; 'll eat
4. lock; leave
5. mix; don't get
6. don't order; won't be
7. Take; hurt
8. pour; sinks

D

2. Unless Sarah has an important appointment, she doesn't wear

makeup
3. You can't borrow new DVDs unless you return the old ones first
4. Unless Rick calls his mom back, she will keep worrying
5. Unless you are interested, I'm not going to ask you again

Lesson 97

A
2. if you didn't live near me
3. if I weren't (*OR* wasn't) so shy
4. If I drew well
5. If he didn't own a garden
6. if she had glasses

B
2. Daniel would read many books; he didn't play so many video games
3. Eric weren't *OR* wasn't on a business trip; he would attend the wedding
4. our heater turned on; we wouldn't have to call the repairman
5. Cindy would go dancing tonight; she had a partner

C
1. would do
2. take; won't be
3. will; arrive; mail
4. wouldn't ask; weren't *OR* wasn't
5. would have; went
6. get; 'll give

D
1. would be
2. would love; tasted
3. 'll go; have
4. visit
5. weren't; would feel

Lesson 98

A
2. if he hadn't studied business in college
3. If we had worked hard
4. If Tom hadn't scored three goals
5. if I hadn't had a bad dream
6. If we had returned the book on time

B
2. If Lucy had practiced enough, she would have done well in her speech
3. If Greg hadn't drunk too much wine, he wouldn't have gotten a headache
4. If Mike and Jenny hadn't run on the icy sidewalk, they wouldn't have fallen
5. If we had known about Claire's birthday, we would have sent her a present
6. If my computer hadn't broken, I would have completed my report

C
1. would have given
2. had locked; wouldn't have gotten
3. knew; 'd tell
4. hadn't been; would've come
5. had; I'd buy
6. wouldn't use; were *OR* was

D
2. he had gone to the bank, he would have cash
3. he hadn't grown up in Spain, he couldn't cook Spanish food well
4. he hadn't had a big lunch, he would feel hungry
5. he hadn't forgotten his keys, he could get in his car

Lesson 99

A
2. I wish we had more space
3. I wish I could ski like him
4. I wish I were (*OR* was) stronger
5. I wish I weren't (*OR* wasn't) alone
6. I wish he weren't (*OR* wasn't) so busy

B
2. visited
3. had gone
4. lived
5. weren't *OR* wasn't
6. hadn't read

C
2. I hope
3. I wish
4. I wish
5. I hope
6. I wish

D
2. If only he had been nice to Judy
3. If only I hadn't left the cookies in the oven too long
4. If only he weren't (*OR* wasn't) so scared
5. If only we had visited her in the hospital
6. If only I didn't have a stomachache

Lesson 100

A
2. which cost $500
3. who was born in 1992
4. who doesn't like roller coasters
5. which might not get fixed

B
2. who don't want
3. who plays
4. which are
5. which goes
6. who doesn't lie
7. which don't have
8. who understands

C
2. have a leather bag that doesn't get dirty easily
3. is the music album that has sold over one million copies
4. brought Samantha a shirt that wasn't her size
6. that provides the best view is on the top floor
7. that won the big award has only been in two movies

8. that are chefs invited us to dinner on Friday

Lesson 101

A

2. that William can cook
3. that she hasn't met before
4. that you might wear
5. that we attended today
6. that I've ever seen

B

2. A person you can get medicine from
3. a plant you can make beer with
4. A place you can wash your clothes at
5. a tool you can open a wine bottle with

C

2. are photos which were taken last week
3. has two sisters she shares a bedroom with
4. who write to him are traveling abroad
5. is a VIP member of the gym he exercises at *OR* is a VIP member of the gym at which he exercises
6. Christina got on was crowded

D

2. ✓
3. in I am living → in which I am living *OR* which(*OR* that) I'm living in *OR* I'm living in
4. makes them → makes
5. ✓
6. with that → with whom
7. a park had → a park which(*OR* that) had

Lesson 102

A

2. the teacher; whose school trained all of the fighters
3. the pilot; whose parents Malachi killed
4. the warrior; whose leg was injured during battle
5. the princess; whose planet Malachi attacked

B

2. a garden whose flowers look
3. a vegetable whose seeds have
4. a country whose oil industry is
5. A company whose employees aren't
6. a store whose furniture doesn't cost

C

2. What attracts me to Jenny
3. What you wear
4. what she learned
5. what caused Kevin's illness
6. What scares Patrick

D

2. whose
3. that
4. What
5. what
6. that
7. whose
8. what

Lesson 103

A

2. My English professor, who I won't ever forget, is very intelligent and friendly
3. Tracey had already decorated a room for her twins, who weren't born yet
4. Everyone enjoyed Annie's chocolate cookies, which she baked yesterday
5. Matt owns that small car, which his friends always joke about
6. Kevin's parents, who have been working as lawyers, will retire soon

B

2. My neighbors painted their fence yellow, which made their garden look bright
3. Lisa didn't eat anything at the family dinner, which worried her whole family
4. Kevin showed up late for the meeting, which isn't normal for him
5. The final match was canceled due to rain, which wasn't good news for the fans
6. I took a vacation last week, which was very relaxing for me

C

2. , who
3. , who
4. , which
5. which *OR* that
6. , who
7. , which
8. , which
9. who *OR* that

Lesson 104

A

2. why Andy didn't take
3. where a lot of accidents happen
4. why she's so tired all the time
5. when my daughter was born
6. where I buy my groceries

B

2. the restaurant where you can get the city's best pizza
3. the day (when) summer vacation begins
4. the reason (why) the concert is canceled
5. the beach where swimming is not allowed
6. the time (when) some animals start to hunt

C

2. the day which → the day when(*OR* that)
3. ✓
4. the stadium → the stadium where
5. the way how → the way (that) *OR* how
6. ✓

D

2. when
3. who

4. which
5. where
6. why

Lesson 105

A

2. He said that he was trying to lose weight
3. He said that his parents hadn't been to Europe
4. He said that he didn't like the food at that restaurant
5. He said that his neighbor's dogs barked too much
6. He said that Cindy and Julie weren't paying their rent

B

2. She said she couldn't watch scary movies alone
3. He said he needed to buy a new wallet
4. She said she would call Derek later
5. He said the mall wouldn't be open this month
6. They said they had lived in Toronto for 10 years
7. He said Monica could sing beautifully
8. She said Max and Sue weren't dating anymore

C

2. Jane said Robert doesn't/didn't like jazz music
3. Dana said she studied English literature in college
4. Bill said he wouldn't be attending Joel's presentation
5. Sylvia said her office is/was too small
6. Ted said Roger can/could draw portraits well
7. Mr. Phillips said the clock wasn't broken when he left

Lesson 106

A

2. He told them they looked like twins
3. She told him he couldn't smoke in the building
4. They told her they hadn't cleaned the bathroom yet
5. She told me she was learning to cook Thai food

B

2. said goodbye to his brother
3. told Joey he should wait
4. said nothing to me
5. told Nate that it was snowing
6. said that the concert had been canceled

C

2. She told Harry not to turn on the radio
3. She asked Laura to take out the garbage
4. She told Beth to get some rest
5. She told Christine not to open the present yet
6. She asked Roy not to leave too early

D

2. wanted to know who my favorite actor was
3. asked if I had any hobbies
4. wanted to know where I was from
5. wondered if I was interested in sports

Lesson 107

A

2. it is believed that a broken dish brings good fortune
3. it is said that brides wearing pearls will have bad marriages
4. it is thought that whistling inside a building will cause you to lose money
5. it is believed that people with big ears live longer

B

2. Dogs are believed to feel emotions
3. Exercise is known to reduce stress levels
4. Carrots are thought to be good for eyesight
5. That house on the hill is said to belong to a famous singer
6. The rose is thought to be the flower of love

C

2. said that he likes
3. thought to be
4. believed that Mr. Crow will soon decide
5. expected that he will tell
6. said to have lived

Lesson 108

A

2. There haven't been
3. there isn't
4. Are there
5. there weren't
6. there has been
7. there were
8. Was there

B

2. There may not be enough copies
3. Will there be any live music
4. There used to be cheap clothes
5. There couldn't be much snow
6. There must be a fire
7. There used to be many fish

C

2. There seem to be some problems with the project
3. There appears to be a concert at city hall
4. There seem to be flowers on your desk
5. There appears to be no mail today

D

2. there were a lot of
3. there aren't any
4. there won't be any
5. There was no
6. There might be some

Lesson 109

A

2. Neither have we
3. So does my son
4. Neither are my kids
5. So has my husband
6. Neither did my family
7. So should I
8. Neither can I

B

2. I'm afraid so
3. I hope not
4. I believe not *OR* I don't believe so
5. I guess so
6. I'm afraid not
7. I suppose so

C

2. Neither
3. not
4. So
5. so
6. so
7. not

Lesson 110

A

2. He supposes (that) Jake will win the race
3. They feel (that) the restaurant is too crowded
4. She knows (that) the bookstore opens at 9 o'clock
5. He believes (that) what Jen said isn't true

B

2. She insisted (that) they invite Sam and Liz
3. She demanded (that) he not smoke in her car
4. He proposed (that) he cook dinner tonight
5. She suggested (that) we not go to the exhibit
6. He advised (that) I not leave my bag there

C

2. I'm disappointed that Lesley canceled our date
3. Pam is glad that the music festival isn't sold out
4. It's important that you drink enough water
5. It's vital that schools teach history
6. It's essential that people exercise regularly

D

2. not miss
3. not climb
4. learn
5. lower
6. not wait

Review Test Answers

TEST 1

2. I don't wear socks
3. Are they in the kitchen
4. Mike and Kim are preparing
5. Do you always eat breakfast
6. It isn't raining
8. are you learning
9. I don't go
10. He lives
11. Does she speak
12. I'm not working
14. She's visiting
15. Jamie and I don't see
16. we talk
17. I'm listening
18. Do you know
19. His voice sounds
21. c) 22. c)
23. b) 24. a)
25. a) 26. b)
27. c) (doesn't → isn't)
28. a) (isn't tasting → doesn't taste)
29. c) (plan → planning)
30. a) (Are → Do)
31. d) (has → is having)
32. b) (be → being)

TEST 2

1. She was dancing
2. You weren't working; was having
3. Did you get; I didn't check
4. did you turn off; Were you listening
5. I met; Was she shopping
6. Mark didn't visit; He wanted
8. prepares
9. didn't use to wear *OR* never used to wear
10. Does; play
11. don't drink
12. Did; use to spend
14. did → was doing
15. She's used to jogging → She used to jog
16. was making → made
17. ✓
18. was wanting → wanted
19. ✓
21. d) 22. a)
23. c) 24. d)
25. b) 26. d)
27. c) (traveled → was traveling)
28. d) (wasn't believing → didn't believe)
29. c) (walked → were walking)
30. c) (were → did)
31. a) (Did → Were)
32. d) (was buying → bought)

TEST 3

2. I've played
3. Did you read
4. It hasn't rained
5. Mr. Young hurt
6. She hasn't eaten *OR* She didn't eat
8. Jack has worked *OR* Jack has been working
9. have you stayed
10. I haven't studied *OR* I haven't been studying
11. have you lived *OR* have you been living
12. I haven't traveled
14. had arrived
15. met
16. had moved
17. took
18. did; had
19. returned; had left
21. a) 22. d)
23. d) 24. c)
25. a) 26. b)
27. b) (had → have)
28. a) (haven't → hadn't)
29. a) (didn't spend → hasn't been spending *OR* hasn't spent)
30. d) (have graduated → graduated)
31. c) (been → gone)
32. d) (I ever taste → I've ever tasted)

TEST 4

2. After we watch the fashion show
3. I won't take the children
4. until he loses 10 pounds
5. Will you tell me
6. If the restaurant doesn't sell red wine
8. I'll eat
9. I'll be driving
10. Will you be swimming
11. we won't know
12. Mr. Perez won't teach *OR* Mr. Perez won't be teaching
14. I'll graduate

15. I'll have studied
16. We'll get
17. We'll have dated
18. Eric and I will have left
19. I'll send
21. b) 22. c)
23. c) 24. a)
25. b) 26. d)
27. d) (do you watch → are you watching *OR* are you going to watch)
28. a) (wasn't → isn't)
29. b) (be believing → believe)
30. c) (will be → was)
31. b) (going to make → making)
32. c) (have joined → be joining)

TEST 5

2. Do I have to submit my résumé
3. I'll be able to ride a bike
4. should we meet
5. Has Tony been able to spend much time
6. We'd better not open the windows
8. was able to; was able to pass
9. should; should buy
10. could; couldn't be
11. must; must turn off
12. have to; doesn't have to get up
14. might have made
15. Should; ask
16. must not have read
17. shouldn't forget
18. might get
19. could have started
21. b) 22. a)
23. c) 24. c)
25. a) 26. d)
27. a) (could → couldn't *OR* wasn't able to)
28. c) (may → should)
29. b) (clean → have cleaned)
30. b) (must → have to)
31. b) (leave → have left)
32. a) (don't have to → must not)

TEST 6

2. What did you study
3. Do you come
4. When does the bank open
5. Did I call
6. Where do you go
8. Who should we give
9. Which computer is yours
10. What are you going to order
11. Who helped you
12. Which sport does Tom enjoy
14. whose class I should take
15. What kind of dance does she teach
16. if her class will be
17. when must I register
18. Are you open
20. b) 21. d)
22. a) 23. b)
24. a) 25. c)
26. b) (you did stay → did you stay)
27. b) (do you want → wants)
28. c) (does he → did he)
29. c) (Yes → No)
30. a) (To where → Where)
31. a) (How → How often)
32. d) (did he go → he went)

TEST 7

2. 's married
3. wasn't asked
4. cleans
5. were built
6. doesn't arrive
8. Is the package being shipped
9. The meeting had been arranged
10. The renovations won't be completed
11. Menus were being handed
12. Have all of today's games been postponed
14. Various classes are offered to
15. The students are taught
16. Some scholarships are given to
17. the school sends
18. The intern isn't paid
19. Mr. Miller hopes
21. a) 22. b)
23. a) 24. c)
25. b) 26. c)
27. d) (of → by)
28. c) (didn't write → wasn't written)
29. d) (are belonged → belong)
30. a) (be → get)
31. a) (didn't know → wasn't known)
32. c) (did → 'm done)

TEST 8

2. it's difficult for her to get up
3. Did you decide not to study

4. They're busy preparing
5. in order not to miss the last train
6. Would you mind not making
8. singing
9. washing *OR* to be washed
10. to quit
11. being caught
12. to be chosen
14. invite you to attend
15. recommend taking
16. consider signing
17. decide to join
18. remember to register
19. to learn
21. d) 22. b)
23. d) 24. c)
25. a) 26. b)
27. b) (hanging → to hang)
28. d) (cut → cutting)
29. b) (paint → painted)
30. d) (not to oversleep → in order not to oversleep)
31. b) (to notice → noticing)
32. b) (to having → to have)

TEST 9

2. A few hairs are
3. The news helps
4. Two pieces of cake cost
5. Wood is
6. Some juice contains
7. pictures
8. furniture
9. an article; flowers
10. a glass; ice
11. team
12. an e-mail; assignments
14. staffs → staff
15. jewelries → jewelry
16. ✓
17. polices → police
18. was → were
20. b) 21. d)
22. d) 23. a)
24. c) 25. a)
26. b) (baggages → baggage)
27. a) (vocabularies → vocabulary)
28. d) (pant → pants)
29. b) (times → time)
30. b) (surrounding → surroundings)
31. a) (audiences → audience)
32. a) (belonging → belongings)

TEST 10

2. the radio
3. A pharmacist
4. the manager
5. an essay
6. a table
8. watch TV
9. The rooms at that hotel
10. some cereal for breakfast
11. The Smiths were my neighbors
12. attend church
14. a same → the same
15. the engineer → an engineer
16. movies → the movies
17. ✓
18. the present → a present
20. a) 21. c)
22. d) 23. a)
24. b) 25. c)
26. a) (the work → work)
27. c) (nearest bank → the nearest bank)
28. a) (A health → Health)
29. c) (a summer → summer *OR* the summer)
30. a) (an army → the army)
31. a) (Cello → A cello *OR* The cello)
32. b) (the bed → bed)

TEST 11

2. ones
3. hers
4. one
5. yourselves
6. him
8. this month's magazine
9. A classmate of mine
10. The roof of our house
11. Katie's husband
12. my sister's necklace
14. look after herself; cared for her
15. paid for school (himself)
16. helped him
17. gave him an award (himself)
18. believe in yourself *OR* believe in yourselves
20. a) 21. c)
22. b) 23. d)
24. a) 25. b)
26. d) (we → us)
27. d) (them → themselves)
28. a) (A your car → Your car)
29. c) (Bolivia → Bolivia's)
30. c) (theirs → their)

31. d) (his black one → his black ones)
32. c) (Mr. Roberts → Mr. Roberts')

TEST 12

2. no room
3. any milk
4. No movies
5. any plans
6. some advice
8. Either of the parks seems *OR* Either of the parks seem
9. All paper comes
10. half of them are
11. Both (of) my children go
12. Each of these boxes costs
14. Neither
15. either
16. some
17. any
18. few
20. a) 21. b)
22. d) 23. c)
24. a) 25. a)
26. d) (different something → something different)
27. c) (are → is)
28. b) (didn't tell → told)
29. a) (some → any)
30. c) (neither → either)
31. d) (none → no)
32. a) (few → little)

TEST 13

2. surprised
3. perfectly
4. outdoor
5. melting
6. suddenly
8. too heavily for us to go
9. such a beautiful garden
10. so deeply that I didn't want
11. too long for Katie to wear
12. Ellie always talks so politely
14. so → such
15. satisfied → satisfying
16. ✓
17. suitably → suitable
18. I usually am → I'm usually
20. a) 21. d)
22. c) 23. b)
24. a) 25. c)
26. b) (good → well)
27. b) (signing → signed)
28. c) (free → freely)
29. b) (happily → happy)
30. d) (fastly → fast)
31. a) (time enough → enough time)
32. d) (recent → recently)

TEST 14

2. more smoothly
3. less
4. as soon as
5. the coldest
6. as exciting as
8. one of the smartest animals
9. as many calls as
10. the most amazing experience
11. twice as crowded as the other days
12. The more you practice, the better you'll sing
14. smaller
15. more expensive
16. much
17. (the) largest
18. heavy
20. b) 21. c)
22. d) 23. a)
24. d) 25. c)
26. b) (very → much *OR* even *OR* a lot)
27. a) (as just → just as)
28. c) (the less → the least)
29. d) (in → of)
30. b) (warm and warm → warmer and warmer)
31. b) (than → as)
32. c) (lowest → lower)

TEST 15

2. anything at dinner
3. the baseball game on Friday
4. something on my face
5. her at the hairdresser's
6. my hometown in years
8. replied to
9. concerned about
10. look after
11. search for
12. excellent at
14. within
15. Thanks to
16. instead
17. by

18. till
19. by
21. d) 22. c)
23. d) 24. b)
25. a) 26. a)
27. b) (on → in)
28. b) (on every → every)
29. c) (despite of → despite *OR* in spite of)
30. a) (for → at)
31. b) (to the church → the church)
32. b) (away them → them away)

TEST 16

2. so that I can sit down
3. Even though Lisa was on a diet
4. until the sun set
5. By the time I buy Christmas presents
6. As Tim was talking on the phone
8. Traveling in Europe
9. not wanting to gain any more weight
10. Being scared
11. watching the animal show
12. Not knowing how to cook curry
14. Despite → Despite the fact that *OR* In spite of the fact that *OR* Though *OR* Although *OR* Even though
15. By → By the time
16. ✓
17. busy so that → so busy that
18. when design → when designing
19. will end → ends
21. c) 22. b)
23. b) 24. d)
25. c) 26. a)
27. b) (while → during)
28. a) (By → By the time)
29. d) (will check → check)
30. a) (dirty so → so dirty)
31. d) (although → though)
32. b) (so that → for)

TEST 17

2. 'll have; book
3. catches; drinks
4. asks; won't accept
5. 'll make; is
6. Don't go; don't feel
8. it weren't (*OR* wasn't) snowing; I would go jogging
9. Brian wouldn't have forgotten about the meeting; I had reminded him
10. We could send Sam a wedding gift; we knew his address
11. Angela hadn't broken her leg; she wouldn't be at the hospital
12. Timothy had studied hard; he could have passed the English test
13. wouldn't have woken
14. hadn't called; would have missed
15. doesn't rain; 'll visit
16. 'll buy; go
17. had come; would have liked
18. were
20. c) 21. a)
22. b) 23. a)
24. b) 25. d)
26. a) (you'll → you)
27. b) (isn't → is)
28. d) (had → had had)
29. b) (visited → had visited)
30. b) (attended → had attended)
31. d) (listens → listened)
32. d) (have joined → join)

TEST 18

2. a restaurant where we can have
3. the novelist whose stories I like
4. What makes me angry
5. The library from which I borrowed
6. the way I cook
8. what caused the fire
9. who stole your bag
10. , which was very fun
11. , who still live in my hometown
12. that I went to Paris
14. ✓
15. the river → the river where
16. which name → whose name
17. came → who(*OR* that) came
18. cooked it → cooked
20. a) 21. b)
22. d) 23. a)
24. b) 25. c)
26. c) (that → which)
27. d) (work → works)
28. c) (who → whom)
29. a) (The thing what → What)
30. c) (which it has → which has)
31. a) (The way how → The way (that) *OR* How)
32. d) (stop → stops)

TEST 19

2. Dr. Turner told Nancy (that) she would feel much better
3. Richard asked if the bathroom was on the first floor
4. Jake told Annie (that) he was writing a letter to John
5. Helen asked if she could use the computer
6. Jeff said (that) he hadn't tried bungee jumping
8. She asked Lisa to make some toast for her
9. She told Mike to stop playing video games
10. She asked Sam not to talk loudly
11. She told Janice not to be late for class
12. She asked Kim to lend her some money
14. cows are believed to face
15. it is known that some penguins dance
16. cats are thought to like
17. it is said that eating stones helps
18. it is believed that dolphins don't sleep
20. a) 21. c)
22. b) 23. d)
24. a) 25. c)
26. a) (said → told)
27. b) (lives → lived *OR* had lived)
28. a) (He → It)
29. c) (calls → called)
30. b) (said to that → said that)
31. c) (They → They're)
32. a) (to Jessie → Jessie to)

TEST 20

2. I'm afraid not
3. So can Jake
4. I think not
5. Neither did mine
6. I hope so
8. I don't think so
9. Are there enough eggs
10. There haven't been any new employees
11. We were surprised that Aaron asked
12. There wasn't much traffic
14. not miss
15. talk
16. join
17. read
18. not go
19. are
21. d) 22. c)
23. c) 24. a)
25. d) 26. b)
27. c) (don't → not)
28. b) (be should → should be)
29. d) (don't hope so → hope not)
30. c) (get → got)
31. b) (went → go)
32. c) (was I → have I)

GRAMMAR
GATEWAY
INTERMEDIATE

Index

Index

The numbers in the index are lesson and section numbers.

August 22, 2019

Hackers Language Research Institute
23, Gangnam-daero 61-gil, Seocho-gu, Seoul, Korea
Inquiries publishing@hackers.com

ISBN 978-89-6542-319-5 (13740)

Printed in South Korea

4 5 6 7 8 9 10 26 25 24 23 22

Strengthen your English skills!
HackersIngang (HackersIngang.com)

- MP3 files for use with this book
- Video lectures on basic-level grammar
- Free English content and online forums